Colonialism and Its Legacies

Colonialism and Its Legacies

Edited by Jacob T. Levy

with Iris Marion Young

LEXINGTON BOOKS
Lanham • Boulder • New York • Toronto • Plymouth, UK

Published by Lexington Books
A wholly owned subsidiary of The Rowman & Littlefield Publishing Group, Inc.
4501 Forbes Boulevard, Suite 200, Lanham, Maryland 20706
www.lexingtonbooks.com

Estover Road, Plymouth PL6 7PY, United Kingdom

Copyright © 2011 by Lexington Books

All rights reserved. No part of this book may be reproduced in any form or by any electronic or mechanical means, including information storage and retrieval systems, without written permission from the publisher, except by a reviewer who may quote passages in a review.

British Library Cataloguing in Publication Information Available

Library of Congress Cataloging-in-Publication Data

Colonialism and its legacies / edited by Jacob T. Levy.
 p. cm.
 Includes bibliographical references and index.
 ISBN 978-0-7391-4292-9 (cloth : alk. paper) — ISBN 978-0-7391-4294-3 (electronic)
 1. Colonies. 2. Europe—Colonies. 3. Imperialism. I. Levy, Jacob T., 1971–
JV185.C62 2011
325'.3094—dc22   2011007093

The paper used in this publication meets the minimum requirements of American National Standard for Information Sciences—Permanence of Paper for Printed Library Materials, ANSI/NISO Z39.48-1992.

Printed in the United States of America

Contents

Preface *Jacob T. Levy*	vii
Acknowledgments	ix
Introduction *Iris Marion Young and Jacob T. Levy*	xi
1 Diderot's Theory of Global (and Imperial) Commerce: An Enlightenment Account of "Globalization" *Sankar Muthu*	1
2 Empire, Progress, and the "Savage Mind" *Jennifer Pitts*	21
3 Under Negotiation: Empowering Treaty Constitutionalism *Vicki Hsueh*	53
4 *Wasáse*: Indigenous Resurgences *Taiaiake Alfred*	79
5 The "World-System": Europe As "Center" and Its "Periphery" beyond Eurocentrism *Enrique Dussel*	97
6 The Singularity of Peripheral Social Inequality *Jessé Souza*	121
7 After Colonialism: The Impossibility of Self-Determination *Pratap Bhanu Mehta*	147
8 Indian Conceptualization of Colonial Rule *Bhikhu Parekh*	171

9 Resistance to Colonialism: The Latin American Legacy of José Martí *Ofelia Schutte*	181
10 Subaltern History as Political Thought *Dipesh Chakrabarty*	205
11 Double Consciousness and the Democratic Ideal *Emmanuel C. Eze*	219
12 Colonialism and the State of Exception *Margaret Kohn*	243
Index	267
About the Contributors	275

Preface

Jacob T. Levy

This book began as an editorial collaboration between Iris Marion Young and me. Unsurprisingly, she brought to the project a much broader and deeper knowledge of the various subjects and literatures under discussion here. She had hopes of beginning serious research of her own in postcolonial theory and had begun her project (now published as her final monograph, *Responsibility for Justice*) about economic connections between the wealthy West and developing countries, a project that also led her to think about colonialism's ongoing political and economic legacies. I had the opportunity and good fortune to be able to learn from her during this project's development, but even now I know that I am well behind where she was when we started. Her death in 2006 has meant that the final editorial work has been mostly mine. But measured by intellectual contribution and editorial vision, this has been far more her work.

Since he wrote his contribution to this volume, Emmanuel Eze has also passed away. This volume is dedicated to their memories.

Acknowledgments

This book contains many essays that were delivered at a conference of the Conference for the Study of Political Thought in Chicago in 2004. That conference was supported by a collaborative research grant from the National Endowment for the Humanities and by the Norman Wait Harris Fund of the Center for International Studies at the University of Chicago. We thank all the participants in that conference, and in particular the discussants: Steven Pincus, Maria Torres, Kirstie McClure, Thomas McCarthy, Richard Boyd, Patricia Nordeen, Charles Mills, and Fred Dallmayr.

The conference, and associated research group prior to it, and work on the present book were also supported by a grant from the Social Sciences Division of the University of Chicago. Fione Dukes, in her capacity as administrator of these grants, made an indispensable contribution. John Comaroff, Steven Pincus, and Patchen Markell took part in the research group and helped to form the agenda for the conference. Markell's participation then and his intellectual, moral, and logistical support since were especially important to the conference and this book and are deeply appreciated.

Additional thanks are due to the students in Young's graduate seminar on postcolonial theory, and those in Levy's seminar on European studies, and to Levy's co-instructor Mark Antaki.

Neil Roberts, Victor Muñiz-Fraticelli, Emily Nacol, Teisha Ruggerio, Douglas Hanes, Sarah Wellen, Mylène Freeman, Stephanie Ovens, and Ju-Hea Jang contributed valuable research and editorial assistance at various stages of the project.

Introduction

Iris Marion Young and Jacob T. Levy[1]

Modernity—the centuries since 1500—has been at once the era of the European state and the era of the European empires. Over the same centuries that medieval polities were coalescing and crystallizing into Weberian states, waves of European settlement and conquest spread over the world—first Latin America and coastal regions of Africa and the "East Indies"; then the remainder of the Americas, Australasia, and all of south Asia; all of Africa, parts of China, and the Middle East. From 1500 through 1950, very nearly all of the inhabited world came under the power of one or another European state, or a European-derived settler state.

Extra-local empires were nothing new in human history; indeed, the sixteenth century saw both the Mughal and the Ottoman Empires near or reach their own high-water marks. Although Columbus' first voyage followed by mere months the completion of the so-called reconquest of Spain, the millennium-long expansion of Islamic empires had not yet ended. In the sixteenth century Tartar states still threatened Russia and central Europe, and kept alive the memory of the Mongol Empire out of which they had emerged—the largest empire in human history before Spain conquered much of the western hemisphere.

Still, the half millennium of European colonialism and imperialism ultimately reached a global scale that dwarfed what had come before. Even if the age of European empires is broken into many discrete events, there are *many* such events—the conquest and settlement of Latin America, that of English and French North America, that of Australia, the subjection of India, the scramble for Africa—that would rank among the largest-scale conquests in human history. And these events include a substantial share of the greatest political evils ever committed.

Yet all of this seemed, for many years, tangential to the story of modernity familiar to political theorists and philosophers. That account centered on the replacement of religious authority by civil; the wars of religion and their aftermath; the Enlightenment; and the Scientific, Glorious, American, French, Industrial, and Russian revolutions. Canonical political theorists are remembered as linked to each, whether forward or backward—Hobbes to civil authority, the Wars of Religion, and the Scientific Revolution; Rousseau to the Enlightenment and the French Revolution; and so on. It was, in brief, a history of the modern European state, and of moral questions about and within that state: who should govern it, and what actions it should take.

It was not only a history basically internal to Europe (and to European settler states). It was also a history of theorists and theories analyzing and contributing to that intra-European history. Hannah Arendt treated the nineteenth-century scramble for Africa as a part of her account of twentieth-century totalitarianism, but this was something of an oddity. Even when, after the world wars, it became impossible for western political and social theory to assume a history of unidirectional moral and political progress, the failures of interest were intra-European failures.

By the time of the revitalization of Anglophone political philosophy with the publication of John Rawls' *A Theory of Justice* in 1971, decolonization had reshaped the political map. The world was, juridically, almost completely a world of sovereign and formally equal states. And the great debates projected back through modern intellectual history were fundamentally debates about the internal governance of such states: what rights individuals had against states, what duties states must fulfill toward their citizens, how states ought to be governed, whether they must be obeyed, whether they could treat their citizens unequally, how they ought to manage their domestic economies, and so on. Even interstate questions were tangential at best.[2] Colonial and imperial relations—relations between metropolitan states and their conquered colonies and territories—figured approximately not at all.

Rawls revitalized, in particular, social contract theory. Contractarianism treats life outside the state—the kind of state we can recognize as the modern European Weberian state—as prepolitical and extrapolitical, outside the core concerns of political philosophy. Social contract theory moreover envisions a kind of natural teleology—every rational human society will, eventually, come to create a state to rule over itself. While relations of colonialism and imperialism were of great importance in Grotius and Pufendorf, the enduring power of Hobbes, Locke, and Rousseau's images of the state of nature and the social contract left only a marginal place for normative argument about the relations between civil societies governed by contractual states and the vast parts of the world still understood as "natural."[3]

The odd case of the American Revolution pushed the problem of imperialism further to the margins of social contract theory. In the beginning, said

Locke, all the world was America, understood as the state of nature; then America created its governments in contractarian fashion and cast off its status as colony at the same time. But the Anglo-America that seemingly entered into social contracts in 1775–1789 was not at all the America that had been Locke's state of nature. Anglo-America had made a century of progress in conquering state-of-nature America.

In any case, social contract theory came more and more to be understood as relevant to the politics of one, self-contained and well-defined, state. If the first great work of social contract theory was Grotius' *Rights of War and Peace* and the last was *Theory of Justice,* the contrast could hardly be more stark. The earlier work is nearly *all about* interpolity relations including imperial relations; the later takes as the point of departure for political philosophy a self-governing society closed off from the rest of the world, unaffected by it and not affecting it. And Rawlsian questions (or the questions of his libertarian or communitarian critics) were projected backward through time, a tradition was highlighted, emphasized, or constructed (depending on one's tastes) that had *always* been centrally about intrastate questions of justice, the relationship of the ideal or the legitimate state to its own citizens.

We take it that these blinders are now substantially gone, and among the purposes of the present volume are to mark and to help consolidate this change in the intellectual landscape since, roughly, the beginning of the 1990s.

The change includes a number of different developments. One has been the recovery of the colonialism and imperialism themselves as topics within the history of political thought. There has been a tremendous proliferation of studies of how the political philosophers and social theorists of European modernity thought about European colonial projects, of how their thought on those questions affected the development of other features of their thought, and of how their more familiar arguments were implicated in either their own or later colonialist ideas.[4] Sometimes these have involved examining letters, speeches, political and professional activities, or minor writings of European theorists better known for their canonical works on intrastate political philosophy. But often they have involved clear-eyed reexamination of those canonical works themselves, and the realization that the colonial and imperial projects were of central concern to the familiar political philosophers. Of course, some theorists critiqued these projects, others justified and legitimated them, and many did some of both, or critiqued some kinds of imperialism while justifying others.

Besides new scholarship on the history of Western thought about colonialism—work that takes full part of the methodological diversity of studies of the history of political thought in general, involved in disputes about how to think about categories such as "Enlightenment" and "liberalism"—we have seen new work that treats colonialism as *shaping* the history of European political thought. Ideologies of support for and opposition to colonialism did not develop in isolation from the mainstream of political thought, and ideas and doctrines that have not typically been associated with colonialism may nevertheless have been influenced by the colonial context of European and American theory and philosophy. This new work has asked whether, and how, modern political ideas have been formed under the shadow or in the service of projects of colonialism and imperialism. And so scholars have increasingly pressed us to allow the recovered history of thought about colonialism affect our understanding of the central ideas of modern European and American political thought—liberty, equality, property, individual worth, human rights, agency, history—as articulated in the tradition of Western political philosophy. That is, rather than focusing only on what given theorists had to say about colonialism and imperialism, this line of research studies what their arguments about colonialism illuminate about their theories as a whole, or what the general intellectual climate surrounding colonialism teaches us about western political thought in general. This research supposes, or argues, that colonialism and imperialism have to be understood as central rather than marginal in studying the history of European political ideas.

The first two chapters in this book offer historical scholarship, both studying European ideas about colonialism and the way in which colonial projects and mind-sets shaped European political thought. Sankar Muthu's contribution examines Diderot, not only as a critic of colonialism, but as a theorist whose criticisms of colonialism informed and shaped his understanding of the spread of commerce among peoples, a major theme in eighteenth-century political thought. Jennifer Pitts's "Empire, Progress, and 'the Savage Mind'" studies different ways in which eighteenth- and nineteenth-century Scottish and English theorists understood ideas of development and progress, distinguishing between a racializing and imperialist understanding of non-European peoples as *cognitively* backward or immature and more careful analyses of *social* change over time.

A second strand of scholarship has been the theoretical reexamination of colonialism and imperialism as phenomena and events. While normative political philosophy is not much concerned with understanding social phenomena, other kinds of political and social theory traditionally have been. Industrialization, capitalism, the modern state, nationalism, democracy as a social condition, revolutions, secularization, the Holocaust, and totalitarianism have all been studied by political theorists seeking not (primarily) to justify or criticize but (mainly) to explain and understand them as part of our moral, political, and social condition or history. Often, these studies have been concerned with *modernity* as an era or condition, and with these dimensions of political life as aspects of some broader understanding of modernity. Pre–twentieth century theorists had analyzed colonialism and imperialism, not only criticized or justified them; and in the early twentieth century,

Marxist theorists did as well. But postwar European and Anglo-American political theory was slow to do the same. Once European colonialism was accepted as having been a defining feature of the modern era, and not an aberrant archaic holdover, much important work could be done. Here Tzevtan Todorov's 1982 book *The Conquest of America* stands out as a singularly important contribution, but, again, the real proliferation of work did not begin (at least in English) for another decade or so.[5] Enrique Dussel's chapter in this volume offers a powerful reinterpretation of the political economy of modernity, and of the idea and periodization of modernity, through an analysis of the place of imperialism in the building of the modern worldsystem.

Work along these lines has gradually become difficult to sharply distinguish from the third strand of scholarship: postcolonialism. In the last two decades work in the literary and cultural humanities has led the way in rereading European and North American texts in the context of movements of colonialism and imperialism. Much of the work of literary scholars has been groundbreaking, both in reviving specific texts, asking important new questions, and developing new methods of literary and social critique. A good deal of this work in postcolonial studies uses methods of deconstruction, psychoanalytic interpretation, and genealogy. At the same time, historians and anthropologists have questioned old stories of progress, development and the civilizing mission of European interaction with peoples of precolonial America, Asia, and Africa, and revealed more influence of the values and ideas of these peoples on European thought and society, as well as the ingenuity, adaptability, and resistance of these peoples.

Unlike either the study of European political thought about colonialism, or the study of imperialism as a phenomenon and event within Europeandemarcated modernity in the tradition of European social theory, postcolonialism emphasizes the need to study non-European and non-Western thought and action, including thought about the phenomenon of colonialism itself. This often intellectually requires destabilizing received European thought about the rest of the world, which in turn requires treating that thought as itself something to be explained and analyzed rather than being taken for granted. Edward Said's 1978 *Orientalism* is probably the most influential book on the latter kind of work; Gayatri Spivak's 1988 article "Can the Subaltern Speak?" energized the former.[6]

Relatively little of this kind of work has been done in political theory or political philosophy, and this volume aims in part to highlight the relevance and importance of postcolonialism for those fields, to introduce some of the ideas of postcolonial and subaltern studies to a broader political theory audience than is so far familiar with them. We think that political theorists and philosophers have much to learn from this work, and can benefit from the incorporation of these methods into our own field. Moreover, we also think that political theorists and philosophers can bring another distinctive set of question and methods to the study of colonialism and its contemporary legacies, including conceptual analysis and the identification and evaluation of normative assumptions and arguments in political, legal, philosophical and literary discourse. Dipesh Chakrabarty's contribution explicitly offers a bridge over this disciplinary gap, treating "Subaltern History as Political Thought."

Until recently, philosophers and political theorists in Europe and North America have read texts primarily from Europe and North America, and theorized problems generated by the tradition of European thought. Important political theorists such as Mohandas Gandhi, Leopold Senghor, Franz Fanon, C. L. R. James, Leopoldo Zea, Jose Carlos Mariategui, or Sayyid Qutb have not been treated as part of the political theory canon of the twentieth century. These, as well as many other leaders and writers from Asia, Latin American, and Africa, engaged in projects of rethinking such fundamental human values as freedom, community membership, and the responsible use of power from within distinctive contexts of resistance and social transformation. What difference do these contexts make to the way they conceptualize political issues? How do they both utilize and transform the European traditions they read? What does the thought of these and other non-Western writers offer to a twenty-first-century project of transnational understanding and evaluation of global inequality?

"Postcolonial" is used as a description, not only of theory that seeks a postcolonial epistemic and moral vantage point, but also of work that theorizes about the long-term and ongoing effects of the European colonial projects. In this volume, Jessé Souza's "The Singularity of Peripheral Social Inequality" aims to show how colonial "modernization" has created and maintained entrenched social inequality in formerly colonized societies. Pratap Bhanu Mehta's "After Colonialism: The Impossibility of Self-Determination" examines paradoxes of postcolonial and anti-imperial politics, and the conceptual difficulties involved in transcending legacies, the rejection of which is treated as foundational. And Taiake Alfred's "Wasáse" powerfully denies that colonialism can be thought of as being in the past at all, in the case of the conquered indigenous peoples in colonial settler states, while arguing for forms of political organization and resistance that reject the forms into which the settler states force indigenous politics.

We have said that the purposes of this volume included marking and consolidating the progress that has been made in all of these areas of research, and introducing postcolonial work in particular to a political theory audience. The final, and in some ways overarching, purpose, is to bring these lines of research into engagement with one another, and to highlight the intellectual gains that can be made from such engagement. Postcolonial approaches often expand and enrich the first two kinds of scholarship mentioned above, and a majority of the essays in this volume cross the categories we have laid out. Ofelia Schutte treats José Martí as a political thinker, and studies the political thought of this *resister* against colonialism. Margaret Kohn's chapter studies the political thought of Achille Mbembe, and uses his postcolonial analyses of the law and lawlessness of colonialism to shed light on the idea of states of emergency and exception that has become important in recent political theory, and on the practice of colonialism itself. Bhikhu Parekh, whose studies of Gandhi were among the first works in Anglo-American political theory studying a major non-Western philosophical critic of colonialism, aims in "Indian Conceptualization of Colonial Rule" to show how Indian ideas and categories of thought shaped the British colonial fact in the subcontinent. Vicki Hseuh's study of treaty constitutionalism in colonial Pennsylvania offers both a history of the practice of settler colonialism and a history of the normative legal and political ideas in play—but centered on moments of negotiation and cross-cultural adjudication, however unequal. Emmanuel Eze's "Double Consciousness and the Democratic Ideal" turns the history of imperialism and the colonial formation of racial categories back onto the development of European political ideas.

NOTES

1. Editor's note: Unavoidably, the text that follows was completed by me and never seen by Iris Marion Young. It is a coauthored essay; many passages in it were written by her, and we discussed its shape and content at length. I prefer to bring our collaboration to completion as a collaboration, even at the risk of putting some words under her name which she lacked the opportunity to read or revise. —Jacob T. Levy

2. This began to change with the publication of Michael Walzer's *Just and Unjust Wars* (New York: Basic Books, 1977) and Charles Beitz's, *Political Theory and International Relations* (Princeton: Princeton University Press, 1979). But the beginning was slow to turn into anything more than that. Impressionistically, only by the mid-1990s did international and global questions become especially prominent in the discipline.

3. On this feature of social contract theory, see Dipesh Chakrabarty's contribution to this volume, as well as Sankar Muthu, *Enlightenment Against Empire* (Princeton: Princeton University Press, 2003).

4. The chapters in this book discuss and engage with many of these works. A sample of some of the most important and influential includes Anthony Pagden, "Dispossessing the Barbarian: The Language of Spanish Thomism and the Debate over the Property Rights of the American Indians," in Pagden, ed., *The Languages of Political Theory in Early-Modern Europe* (Cambridge: Cambridge University Press, 1987); Robert A. Williams, *The American Indian in the Western Legal Thought: The Discourses of Conquest* (New York: Oxford University Press, 1990); James Tully, "Rediscovering America: The Two Treatises and Aboriginal Rights," in *An Approach to Political Philosophy: Locke in Contexts* (Cambridge: Cambridge University Press, 1994); Lynn Zastoupil, *John Stuart Mill and India* (Palo Alto, CA: Stanford University Press, 1994); Bhikhu Parekh, "Liberalism and Colonialism: A Critique of Locke and Mill," in J. P. Neverdeen Pieterse and Bhikhu Parekh, eds., *The Decolonization of Imagination: Culture, Knowledge, and Power* (London: Zed Books, 1995); Tully, *Strange Multiplicity: Constitutionalism in an Age of Diversity* (Cambridge: Cambridge University Press, 1996); Frederick G. Whelan, *Edmund Burke and India: Political Morality and Empire* (Pittsburgh,

PA: University of Pittsburgh Press, 1996); Barbara Arneil, *John Locke and America: The Defense of English Colonialism* (Oxford: Oxford University Press, 1996); Anthony Pagden, *Lords of All the World: Ideologies of Empires in Spain, Britain and France c. 1500–c. 1800* (New Haven, CT: Yale University Press, 1995); Uday Singh Mehta, *Liberalism and Empire: A Study in Nineteenth-Century British Liberal Thought* (Chicago: University of Chicago Press, 1999); Richard Tuck, *The Rights of War and Peace* (Oxford: Oxford University Press, 2000); Sankar Muthu, *Enlightenment Against Empire* (Princeton: Princeton University Press, 2003); Jennifer Pitts, *A Turn to Empire: The Rise of Imperial Liberalism in Britain and France* (Princeton: Princeton University Press, 2005).

5. Tzvetan Todorov, *The Conquest of America* (New York: Harper, 1984).

6. Edward Said, *Orientalism* (New York: Pantheon Books, 1978); Gayatri Chakravorty Spivak, "Can the Subaltern Speak?" in Cary Nelson and Lawrence Grossberg, eds., *Marxism and the Interpretation of Culture* (Urbana: University of Illinois Press, 1988).

Chapter One

Diderot's Theory of Global (and Imperial) Commerce: An Enlightenment Account of "Globalization"[1]

Sankar Muthu

Political thinkers of the long eighteenth century often sought to understand the rapidly evolving practices and institutions of their time (the development of "polite" civil societies, the proliferation of sites of printed and oral communication, and the emergence of distinctively modern [though preindustrial] profit-oriented material enterprises) in the context of debates over "commerce" and "commercial society." The spirited defense of these social transformations and the idea that they produced peace, political stability, and the lessening of religious and ideological antagonisms characterized many modern political writings. Such texts usually aimed to defang clerical power, to reduce the influence of mystical and other-worldly spiritual modes of knowledge upon the distribution and use of social power, to temper the traditional prerogatives of royal absolutists in their ambitions for trans-European supremacy, and to supplant what were often seen to be increasingly anachronistic ideals of martial, republican citizenship. "Polite," "civil," "commercial" societies, it was hoped, would be less violent and fanatical and more peaceful, humane, and just. Such strands of political thought just before and following the Peace of Westphalia and then in light of the settlements of the Treaty of Utrecht aimed, in distinct ways, to justify the emergence of a European state system that would regulate its activities in accordance both with an appropriate *ius gentium* (a law of nations, or international law) born of the cruelties of the wars of religion and as a result of the moderation arguably fostered by the development of transnational social, commercial, and material interests.

This array of social and political developments as well as the thinkers who aimed to understand, categorize, historicize, and variously justify them—though it is best at the outset to emphasize the often deep conflicts within this broad and only partly self-conscious intellectual enterprise—have been understood to constitute "Enlightenment" itself.[2] Enlightenment theorizations of global commerce are particularly fraught with tensions. Within a European context, those who engaged in defenses of commerce (and the associated languages that so often informed it: communication, intercourse, sociability, exchange, publicity, luxury) could plausibly trumpet the actual or potential gains of such developments, despite the deep concerns (and at times the outright antagonism) that some republican or quasi-republican advocates of ancient political economy and defenders of royalist and/or clerical institutional power expressed. Nevertheless, the tolerant and peaceful humanism that was theorized as the ultimate result of commerce stood in tension with what had also become increasingly obvious to many Enlightenment-era thinkers: the brutal violence, destructiveness, and corruption that transnational commerce, in particular, produced outside of and within Europe as a result of the activities of European sovereigns directly in their imperial enterprises abroad, of their commercial proxies (most usually the Indies trading companies), and of a wide variety of other corporate entities and individuals who routinely crossed borders far outside of Europe.

I. ON THE RIGHTS—AND DUTIES—OF COMMERCE IN A GLOBAL AGE

Much scholarly attention has been focused upon the European contexts of the intellectual debates surrounding commerce, but the transcontinental dimension of such debates, those writings that attend largely to the genuinely global aspects of commerce, demand far more treatment than they have received. Such writings constitute one of the early chapters of the history of globalization debates. Strikingly, there is an increasing awareness of the *global* reach of social, commercial, and political developments in eighteenth-century political thought and a concern that traditional moral categories might have to be significantly transformed for the purposes of attending to such global concerns. Kant suggested precisely along these lines in 1795 that "since the community of nations of the earth has now gone so far that a violation of right on one place of the earth is felt in all, the idea of a cosmopolitan right is no fantastic and exaggerated way of representing justice [*Recht*]" (8: 360).

Among the most complex responses to the globalizing ventures of European governments and imperial trading companies are the texts by Enlightenment-era thinkers who both sought to defend global commerce and to subject it to critical scrutiny. This effort was informed in part by the early modern discourse about the right to travel, communicate, and engage in partnership and commerce with others, perhaps the most notable example of which is Francisco de Vitoria's 1539 relectio on the activities of the Church and the Castilian crown in the Americas.[3] As Vitoria himself implied: the language of hospitality that pertained to those who crossed borders and found themselves on foreign soil had a long history, in light of which those who aimed to restrict the movements of those seeking contact, communication, or trade with others were often criticized.[4] Before the long eighteenth century, the right to commerce, communication, and its variants—such as Hugo Grotius's defence of the *mare liberum* (the free or open seas) and accordingly of the aggressive activities of the (Dutch) United East India Company—were most often used to legitimate European imperial exploits.[5] In this essay, I examine how Denis Diderot transformed the ancient language of hospitality into a global ethic of transnational exchange, while also subverting the traditionally imperialist political implications of most early modern defenses of a right to commerce. For a variety of political thinkers of the long eighteenth century, the dilemma posed by their understanding of global commerce concerned how it might be possible to formulate a moral framework that could generate both a commitment to the flow of goods, ideas, and communication across borders and an account of the deep injustices and oppression that such global practices often engendered.

The right of commerce in a global, and rapidly globalizing, context—which Kant believed were the conditions that made a theory of cosmopolitan justice (*ius cosmopoliticum, Weltbürgerrecht*) a necessity—pertained not simply to the sovereign representatives of a country or to any particular corporate entity, but to humanity as a whole. On this view, the right of commerce was thought to consist of the right to cross borders, seek contact with others, exchange ideas and goods, and foster partnerships. In part, this rested upon the view that those crossing borders were not simply diplomats, sovereign representatives, and soldiers (who could thus be understood under the traditional categories of *ius gentium* that regulated state-to-state interactions), but also imperial trading companies that were often chartered by governments (but were not formally sovereign entities themselves), missionaries, natural historians and other scientists, navigators, private groups of merchants, and other individuals. Thus, a number of eighteenth-century thinkers aimed to legitimize the emergence of international civil societies that, on a global scale, might in the future achieve some of the work globally that newspapers, journals, independent academies, collaborative scientific projects, coffeehouses, salons, and other forums of commerce and communication appeared to perform within European civil societies. Yet many of these thinkers were also concerned about the ways in which a right to commerce could be used to justify the maintenance and the spread of violent, unjust institutions and practices abroad.

The language of commerce in the eighteenth century itself denoted a wide array of practices from communication or interaction to market-oriented trade and industry. Thus, the Latin "commercium" and the English and French "commerce" mask the multifaceted meanings historically associated with such terms. In German, such shades of meaning can be made explicit, as with *Verkehr* and *Wechselwirkung*, which are both generally translated into English as commerce. Kant, for example, goes back and forth between these terms, employing *Verkehr* often to refer to trade or market-based exchanges and the more wide-ranging *Wechselwirkung* to describe the communicative and interactive functions of commerce. Politically, such nuances allowed Kant both to attack the injustices of imperialism as the horrid practices of "the commercial states of our part of the world," while also celebrating the future potential of the "spirit of commerce" in fostering peace among nations—a spirit also more narrowly described by Kant at one point as "the power of money."[6] Kant's use of the Latin *commercium* itself as well as its German offshoots is foreshadowed by Diderot's varied understanding of the concept of commerce in the *Histoire des deux Indes*. The contemporary tendency either to celebrate or to attack "the Enlightenment" and its supposed overarching project, which is said fundamentally to include a justification for modern market-oriented commerce, hides from view the subtle range of meanings of the concept of commerce that many eighteenth-century thinkers deployed in the course of analyzing and assessing the rise of global commerce in its multiple forms.

In what follows, I focus upon one of the most important and influential Enlightenment treatises on global commerce: Abbé Raynal's multivolume project on the history of global ties in the modern world. The *Histoire philosophique et politique des établissements et du commerce des Européens dans les deux Indes* [*Philosophical and Political History of European Settlements and Commerce in the Two Indies*] was published under the name of the Abbé Guillaume-Thomas Raynal, a Jesuit who was a friend of the *philosophes* and presided over the production of this ten-volume work.[7] The *Histoire* catalogued the history of Europe's relations with the non-European world from 1492 onward.[8] In addition to a narration of discoveries, conquests, colonization, battles, and trade, the *Histoire* also offered moral analyses of both European and non-European societies, institutions, and practices. Many writers contributed anonymously to the *Histoire*. We now know that Diderot contributed most of the radical anti-imperial and anti-slavery passages and sections, all of which can be found from the third edition (1780) onward.[9] Although the *Histoire* was banned in France and placed on the Vatican's Index, it was one of the most popular "forbidden" publications of the period, as Robert Darnton has shown.[10] Outside of France, its admiring readers included Edmund Burke, Adam Smith, most likely Johann Gottfried Herder and Immanuel Kant, and, perhaps most famously, the Haitian revolutionary leader Toussaint L'Ouverture.

Diderot's many contributions to Raynal's *Histoire* call into question the standard depiction of the "Enlightenment" as a philosophical epoch that sought, among other things, simply to defend modern commercial interests and their (arguably) peaceful and stabilizing effects. (II) While Diderot's positive commentary upon commerce is not insubstantial and while at times it portrays commerce according to what conventional interpreters expect of a *philosophe*, even his favorable assessments of commerce tend to be framed by deep concerns about political injustice. I then turn toward Diderot's more directly critical commentary upon global commerce by analyzing his (III) concerns about commercial ambition, greed, and materialism and the psychological and material effects that globalizing forms of commerce—whether carried out by private merchants, chartered trading companies, or directly by states—have had both within Europe and abroad. I conclude my interpretation of the *Histoire* by (IV) explaining why Diderot believed that global commerce might play a crucial role in alleviating social and political injustices that were, in his view, largely the result of global commerce. For Diderot and Raynal, the paradox of what we might now call globalization offers unprecedented, if underdeveloped, resources and opportunities to counter the injustices that themselves often arise from emerging global institutions and processes. Finally, (V) I conclude by noting how such perspectives can offer the beginnings of an illuminating genealogy of globalization debates.

II. COMMERCE AND COMMUNICATION: THE PROMISE OF GLOBAL INTERACTIONS IN THE *HISTOIRE*

In a passage from the opening chapter of the *Histoire* that comes closest to what is so often taken to be "the Enlightenment view" on commerce, Diderot surveys the developments of the modern age:

> I have asked myself: who dug these canals? Who drained these plains? Who founded these towns? Who assembled, clothed, and civilized these peoples? And then all the voices of enlightened men [*des hommes éclairés*] among them have responded: it is commerce; it is commerce. (I, introduction)

Diderot describes commerce as the primary catalyst behind the flourishing of the arts, sciences, and indeed modern civilization in general, all of which have helped Europe to lift itself, we are told, from the "barbarism" under which it had lived for so long. This familiar narrative is linked to another, more disturbing image at the outset of the *Histoire*, which sets the ambivalent tone for the rest of the work. After expressing the hope that future readers might be unaware of the author's native country, government, profession and religion ("I want them to consider me as their fellow-citizen [*concitoyen*] and their friend")—and so by attempting to consider the welfare of all humans and the effect that newly emerging global relationships have had on societies throughout the world (rather than writing a history of global relations from the perspective of Christianity, Europe, or France)—Diderot asserts that we might then be able to view sovereigns from a less partisan, more humane disposition. From this perspective, sovereigns no longer resemble the beneficent icons they portray themselves to be, but rather are exposed as manipulative, cruel figures. A critical account of transnational relations can allow us to castigate the politically powerful, to "pour insult and shame on those who oppress" human beings throughout the world. Thus, images of injustice and political oppression as well as of the productive enterprises made possible by commerce open the *Histoire*. Far from presuming that the development of transnational commerce and communication will promote the cause of political justice, and thereby weaken the most tyrannical regimes, Diderot presumes throughout the *Histoire* that commerce is a set of practices and institutions that are most often shaped by despotic political powers who aim to benefit a small elite at the expense of the mass of humanity. By the end of the *Histoire*, commerce emerges as a multifaceted concept that operates differently according to the social and political circumstances that shape it.

Usually, then, Diderot portrays commerce as a *political* set of institutions and practices, rather than as an apolitical enterprise that should be allowed to develop in its own peaceful and relatively autonomous sphere and whose social and political effects are generally beneficial. The consequences of this for his understanding of the relationship between European and non-European peoples are significant, since eighteenth-century commerce was driven by imperial politics. Indeed, the overlap between state power and commerce was inescapable when the most sensational fortunes (and some of the most sensational commercial failures) were made from, among other activities, the Caribbean plantations and the various Indies Companies, which were chartered by governments. Diderot argues that the ultimately destructive passion for profit-making that leads individuals to participate in imperial ventures is fostered by political forces, rather than by individuals in civil society who are driven by some set of "natural" passions such as economic self-interest, ambition, or desire for fame. Accordingly, he argues that "[g]old only becomes the idol of a people, and virtue only falls into contempt, if a badly constituted government provokes such corruption" (XIX, 14). His particular concern is that European governments, which serve a small class of individuals and institutions and rule arbitrarily, without impunity, will usually produce and encourage selfish and destructive passions. For this reason, Diderot finds it distressing, rather than hopeful, to realize that "[m]en are what government makes them" (XIX, 14). In the *Histoire*, when commerce "works" in corrupt and absolutist environments, when it manages to be conducive to human welfare, it is often despite pernicious forms of state power; ultimately, reforming unjust commercial practices and institutions will first require state power itself to be transformed.

Still, the range of Diderot's positive commentary about commerce is noteworthy, for it helps us to understand under what conditions he believed commerce might serve to weaken social and political injustices. One suggestive argument along these lines takes place in an analysis of India's "pariahs." In a discussion about what might have originally occasioned such an extreme practice of social dislocation, Diderot speculates that, paradoxically, Indians' relatively benign system of punishment, which he contrasts with Europe's "half barbarous governments," might have allowed the most odious criminals to live, but only as outcasts from civil society (I, 8). Over time, he contends, this punishment unjustly transferred to the descendants of such criminals. This sociological conjecture about the possible origins of modern, inhumane institutions concerns us here because it leads to his analysis of what the ethnography about India portrayed as the striking differences in the experiences of the pariahs of India: their social status and economic well-being appeared to be better on the coasts than inland. Diderot speculates that the coasts necessitate the intermingling of tribes and castes for the purposes of commercial trade, such that traditional prejudices become dissipated "little by little"; the coasts are "where commerce and mutual needs unite men with each other, and necessarily introduce more just notions of human nature." In contrast, the "lack of communication" among peoples in areas with less commercial activity "nourishes those rooted prejudices" that oppress the lowest Indian castes (I, 8).

In a related argument that emerges in a discussion of the ancient Britons, Diderot asserts that since the inhabitants of island nations cannot spread over vast lands or withdraw to the interior of a continent, one might expect that they would begin to plant crops and develop a sedentary, "civilized" (i.e., settled, agriculturally based) lifestyle faster than peoples on continents. Yet Diderot argues that the opposite appears to be the case; in addition, inhabitants of islands often engage in behavior that strikes outsiders as ferocious and despotic. He suggests that vestigial traces of such behavior may even be found in the Great Britain of his day. Island life is isolated and the lack of communication among a variety of peoples, each with its distinctive forms of life and outlooks, can foster the ferocity that some travelers and chroniclers of ancient history discuss; in this respect, "it is commerce among peoples that diminishes their ferocity. It is their separation that makes it endure" (III, 1). Diderot later contends that the Europeans who settled in Surinam came from a large number of European countries, yet, despite their many national and religious differences, they appear to live together amicably:

> Such is the progress of the spirit of commerce that it stifles all the prejudices of nationality or religion before the general interest that should be the bond among humans. What are these vain denominations of Jews and Christians, French or Dutch? Miserable inhabitants of an earth so painful to cultivate, are you not brothers? (XII, 24)

The very work of surviving as a human, Diderot goes on to assert, is an onerous burden that demands collective enterprises and active communication, but to the miseries constitutive of life itself, humans add self-imposed burdens by so often failing to forge bonds of solidarity with others. Thus, he offers a viewpoint here that comes close to the conventional view of what Enlightenment theories of commerce are supposed to represent, for commerce might in certain conditions yield peaceful social ties by bringing disparate peoples together in the pursuit of collective survival and prosperity. It is crucial to note, however, that the term "commerce" in such passages, "the bond among humans" as Diderot describes it above, refers primarily to the combination of market trade and mutual interaction—especially in the service of some socially valuable goal—rather than to profiteering as such. Indeed, the whole range of Diderot's positive commentary upon commerce in the *Histoire* makes clear that the beneficial aspects of commerce usually refer to "commerce" understood broadly as communication and exchange of both goods and ideas.

III. THE THIRST FOR GOLD: COMMERCE AND ITS LONG TRAIN OF DESTRUCTION

What is likely to be missed by monolithic accounts of "the Enlightenment project" is the subtlety of Diderot's critique of commerce, which focuses on both the psychological characteristics that foster a zeal for global commercial activity, and the concrete social and political effects that result from it. For Diderot, the quest for profit fuels the destructive passions that promote transnational subjugation and empire-building, through trading companies and outright colonization; nearly every western European country, in his view, is fixated upon what he calls the "thirst" or the "passion" for gold. Diderot contends that "[o]f all the passions that are kindled in the human heart, there is none that is so violent in its intoxication as the passion for gold" (XVI, 5). The intense passions brought about by seeking fortunes is not a universal passion that stirs all humans, but rather a politically stoked set of dispositions that arises because of the work of political leaders and in general state power. "The rage of conquest is the malady of a single man who draws the multitude after him" (XVI, 5). Those who undertake what is often a life of hardship abroad do not act out of a deep-seated desire to maximize their economic gain and material interests; rather, they are frequently naïve dupes who are lured *en masse* into global commercial enterprises. "It is the oppression of government that enables these chimerical ideas of fortune to be adopted by the credulity of the people" (XVIII, 32). Diderot argues that each European government fails to provide for all within the metropole, while it also restricts many forms of emigration and works with other governments to return deserters to their land of origin; in such desperate straits, individuals are driven to accept the promises of state-supported charlatans from trading companies and other imperial enterprises who offer fortunes abroad.

Diderot goes further than simply articulating the political conditions under which commerce becomes violent and destructive by shrewdly interpreting the psychological sources and consequences of global trade. He argues that the fundamental motivating impulses behind commerce, regardless of the political circumstances, tend to stifle our most basic feelings of compassion and other social, productive instincts. To begin with, in his view, humans do not, as a rule, conform to the principles of strict probity. Accordingly, the increasing importance and expansion of commerce lends itself to dishonesty, corruption, and a wide array of social injustices that often lead to tragic consequences both within Europe and abroad. "Personal interest and general habit conceal the criminal nature and the meanness of such [commercial] proceedings. I do no more than what others do, it is said, and therefore we accustom ourselves to commit actions for which our conscience soon ceases to reproach us." In light of his argument that commercial practices can numb our moral faculties, Diderot's call to become more critically minded about the deep-rooted injustices of our commercial behavior and institutions appears to him to have little chance of persuading those already seized by the most zealous commercial desires. For not only those who occupy positions of enormous power, but all individuals who let commercial desires guide them become corrupted as a result: "The influence of gold is as fatal to individuals as to nations. If you do not take care, you will be intoxicated with it. You will desire piling wealth upon wealth. . . . If you become avaricious, you will become rigid, and the sentiment of commiseration and benevolence will be extinguished within you" (XIX, 6).

Throughout the *Histoire*, Diderot ponders what could counter prejudices that were rooted in national, religious, ethnic, and other particular identities. As we have seen, he sometimes asserts that commercial interactions can foster the bonds of humanity. But commerce can also be a pernicious force, in his view, that can stoke such prejudices or that can disrupt social and political peace even in the absence of such prejudices. This argument emerges, for instance, in Diderot's discussion about marriages between Spaniards and Amerindians in the New World. After noting that intermarriage is nothing new in the Spanish experience given Spain's multiethnic national history (and hence the presence of much "Moorish blood" among the Spanish), Diderot muses about whether the mixture of races could improve the lot of humanity by minimizing conflicts that are based at least partly upon the notion of human difference. If the "various races of mankind were lost in one," would wars and other examples of transnational violence and oppression come to an end? Diderot's response is skeptical (intermarriage as such, it should be noted, is not problematic for him, as some of his other contributions to the *Histoire* make clear). His concern is that even if the mixture of diverse peoples were to occur routinely throughout the globe, the true sources of transnational injustice would by no means be eliminated. As he argues, "discord seems to arise between brothers; could it be expected therefore that if mankind became one family . . . then they should no longer thirst after each other's blood? For is not this fatal thirst excited and maintained by that of gold?" (XIII, 7). The intensity of the most zealous commercial passions can engender destruction, violence, and the multiple forms of oppression that Diderot surveys at length in the *Histoire*, especially when such passions are fused with the tacit or active support of state power. To be sure, in Diderot's view, prejudice based upon a sense of difference, of whatever kind, can serve at least partly as a catalyst for the most horrific injustices. From the initial contacts between the Spanish and Amerindians to the interactions of every other European country with non-Europeans, he asserts that the perceived experience of difference itself lay at the heart of unequal treatment. Even in such passages, however, commerce is never far from his mind. Thus, Diderot argues that

> hardly had domestic liberty been reborn in Europe than it was buried in America. The Spaniard, the first to be thrown up by the waves onto the shores of the New World, thought he had no duty to people who did not share his colour, customs, or religion. He saw in them only tools for his greed[.]

The "Portuguese, Dutch, English, French, Danes, all the [European] nations" continued precisely in this spirit, he adds, and "without remorse sought to increase their fortune in the sweat, blood and despair of these unfortunate humans. What a horrible system!" (XI, 24). After having noted the experience of difference in such cross-cultural encounters, Diderot thus goes on to imply that it was not simply a prejudiced view of difference, but the combination of this with commercial desires that yielded the most propitious conditions for mass cruelty.

The cohesion of Diderot's writings on commerce becomes clear once we begin to reflect further on the relationship between commerce and arguments against its sometimes imperial character in the *Histoire*. To be sure, commerce provides only one key to Diderot's varied anti-imperialist arguments—the others range from arguments that attack the role of the Church and missionaries, arguments based upon the damage done to European societies and the impossibility of fairly and efficiently governing far-flung imperial realms, and claims that Europe's half-barbarous societies are hardly the model for any other country to adopt, to arguments about the horrific devastation visited upon non-European peoples, and the error of judging foreign practices and institutions, such as those of hunting and pastoral peoples, simply by the standards of one's own society.[11] Diderot's ambivalent judgment of commerce in the *Histoire* both shapes his discussion of, and in turn is shaped by, the relationships that he theorizes among travel, trade, profit, and empire.

It is within this broader context of commerce, hospitality, and empire that Diderot denigrates monopolistic commerce, the basis upon which the Indies trading companies and much imperial trade was conducted. Imperial monopolies erode ancient norms of hospitality, in his view, since they lead companies and states to secure exclusive commercial relationships by occupying fortified trading posts or directly establishing colonies. Such economic monopolies have produced nothing but devastation, he argues, adding that the political monopoly of sovereign power within European states has been similarly pernicious. Taken together, then, "[e]xclusive privileges have ruined the Old and the New World" (XIX, 6). The profiteers who enjoy monopolistic privileges, care only for their short-term gain and profit precisely because of the corrupting guarantees afforded by monopolies. Such are the social and political conditions under which the otherwise positive tendency of commerce to soften narrow prejudices (as we saw earlier) instead weakens the ties of solidarity and humanity. Thus, referring to the figure of the monopolist who participates in global commerce, Diderot contends that "the interest of the nation [at home or abroad] is nothing to him, since for a small and momentary advantage, but a certain one, he has no scruples about doing a great and permanent mischief . . . he will starve at once a whole country, or leave it quite bare" (XIX, 6).

Yet, regardless of whether monopolies are the basis of an international trade that exploits many areas of the non-European world, Diderot argues at length in the *Histoire* that the general character of modern commerce takes a heavy toll more specifically upon the political health of European countries. As Britain increases its national revenues and as it becomes the most commercial country in Europe, in his view, it becomes seized ever more forcefully by the desire for wealth, which is now the "universal and ruling passion" there. As a result, Diderot portrays the British Parliament, "the senate of the empire," as utterly venal; the nearly open bribing for votes is a direct result, he contends, of its commercial wealth. Moving from the domestic to the international realm of British power, he argues that even the imperial administration on which England prides itself is sure to be weakened as a result. "If the mercantile spirit [*l'esprit mercantille*] has been able to diffuse in the mother-country the contagion of personal interest," Diderot asks, "how is it possible that it should not have infected the colonies of which it is the foundation and support?" (XIV, 45). Financially, European states' own economic basis is weakened by this commercial mania, for, as he explains, governments have been tempted to accumulate enormous debts as a result of the influx of gold and silver from the New World into their reserves. This profligacy was the source of the great paradox, on Diderot's view, that "the most opulent nations" of Europe in his day—England, Holland, and France—were also the greatest in debt (XIX, 11). Their wealth itself engenders a brash confidence that leads them to undertake activities far beyond what could be justified based upon the actual productivity of their societies. Diderot asserts that such irresponsibility, itself generated in part by the vast wealth from global enterprises, will continue to oppress further generations and eventually all nations, given the interconnectedness of the global economy. Just as with the escalation of debt, the false confidence engendered by global commerce also induces political instability and violence, as European states become increasingly hostile and arrogant toward one another.

IV. REFORMING GLOBAL COMMERCE THROUGH COMMERCIAL INTERACTION?

Given that curtailing commerce was nearly impossible, and might even prove counterproductive in the long run, could commerce itself somehow be a source of social and political reform? As we have seen, Diderot believes that the tyrannical ambitions that accompany global trading practices show that commerce can often be a source of enormous injustices. Thus, it might seem that commerce as such would be incapable of bringing about more salutary conditions. As J. G. A. Pocock has noted, "All the great Enlightened histories, the *Decline and Fall* included, celebrate the establishment of modern Europe; the *Histoire des deux Indes* is perhaps the first to present it as self-endangered."[12] Given Diderot's view that politics fundamentally shapes commerce, perhaps only a vast change in the political will of nations to conduct their commercial enterprises differently could yield real results. This would suggest that commerce is an evil that needs to be reformed before it could ever become socially productive; yet, Diderot, as we have also seen, often describes the benefits of commerce, not simply as an ideal, but in practice. In the end, for Diderot, commerce is both a source and a target of reform. Commerce itself must play a role in challenging injustice, in his view, for it helps to foster small pockets of liberty, and it leads to the interactions of diverse individuals and peoples and the communication of ideas and practices. The improvements made as a result of commerce in one sphere have the potential of furthering human welfare elsewhere, given the interconnections that are fundamental to commerce itself. As Diderot writes:

> [t]he connections of commerce are all very close [*très-intimes*]. One of its branches cannot experience any opposition without the others being sensible of it. Commerce intertwines peoples, fortunes, exchanges. It is one entire whole, the diverse parts of which attract, support, and balance each other. It resembles the human body, all the parts of which are affected when one of them does not fulfill its proper function. (XIX, 6)

While many of these parts fail to function, in his view, others manage to produce and to sustain social reforms that promote human welfare, break down prejudices, and encourage even broader developments.

Diderot's call to restore the "happy fraternity that constituted the delight of the first ages" presents some sense of his ideal of commerce: "Let all peoples, in whatever country fate has placed them, under whatever government they live, whatever religion they practise, communicate as freely with each other as the inhabitants of one hamlet with those of a neighbouring one . . . that is to say, without duties, without formalities, without predilections." This vision of an open commerce, broadly understood to signify the free trade not only of goods, but of ideas and sentiments, already exists, in his opinion, in small and fragmented ways throughout the globe. Diderot's hope appears to be that commerce might, in part, create and sustain the crucibles for future reform, and perhaps even revolution. The islands of liberty sustained by commercial interactions, as ideas and goods exchange and circulate, could ideally be used over many generations to resist, to battle against, and ultimately to reform other aspects of commerce that are oppressive, that enervate political energies, and that deny liberty both to those in European nations and to those abroad.

Ultimately, in this view, global commerce is a double-edged sword. For Diderot, political reform depends crucially upon individuals becoming sensible of their own freedom, in order to break free from the psychological "chains" that limit their ability to assess critically their own conditions. He suggests hopefully that "[w]e may even venture to assert that men are never so truly sensible of their freedom as they are in commercial interaction" (V, 33). Rather than the material gains and luxuries that commerce yields, and the productivity behind them, the genuine improvement to human welfare enabled by commerce and communication lies instead in their potential to change individuals' sense of their own condition, a condition that in part is corrupted and oppressed by commerce, but that could nevertheless be reformed in part by the communicative and material interactions that global commerce itself makes possible. These interrelated understandings of commerce should seem familiar if we recall that the term "globalization" today refers to a similarly broad set of practices and institutions. Diderot's disposition toward commerce—one that led him to draw out the diverse strands of commercial practices and their varying social, economic, and political consequences—makes possible the view that some such strands could be set in opposition to others.

V. TOWARD A GENEALOGY OF "GLOBALIZATION" DEBATES

Diderot and Raynal morally condemn (and justify resistance against) the unjust practitioners of global commerce. Still, as we have seen, they also seek to promote global *commercium*—crossing borders, seeking contact, fostering interaction and communication, exchanging goods and ideas—which, in their view, can yield the conditions that might mitigate the evils wrought by pernicious forms of transcontinental commerce. As nonexploitative interactions across borders multiply, Diderot's ultimate hope is that the "general will of humanity" will finally become a realizable political goal toward which future generations of increasingly interconnected peoples can struggle.

It is worth considering how such Enlightenment perspectives highlight, and at times call into question, the ways in which global commerce and its history are often portrayed today. Among the many peculiarities of the current debate among citizens, policymakers, and scholars about "globalization," three features are especially curious. First, the debate remains highly polarized, with the salutary effects of global capitalism and liberal political regimes offered on one side and the pernicious consequences of the free flow of international capital (investments, technology, and labor, in addition to information) arrayed on the other. Thus, the topic of globalization elicits not only heated discussions, but often particularly dogmatic and two-dimensional debates. Second, commentators tend to portray this stark divide as a choice that only very recent political, economic, and technological developments have made possible. On this conventional view, the world of nation-states has broken down and is being replaced by an increasingly (if still incompletely) unified international order; this has been brought about by a rapid proliferation of transnational communication, travel, and commerce, which is now, with the end of the Cold War (and supposedly for the first time) a truly *global* phenomenon. Third, participants in such debates often refer to two sets of ideas that are seen as integral to (or antithetical to) the supposed processes, institutions, and political effects of globalization: (1) Enlightenment ideals or values and (2) imperial power. Some thinkers assert that globalization is a universalizing antidote to local prejudices and attachments that otherwise could develop into Balkanizing passions and hatreds; on this view, globalization is a process that carries forward what are taken to be the humane and tolerant values of "the Enlightenment."[13] In contrast, others portray the process of globalization as an unjust attack, led by international regimes such as the World Trade Organization and the International Monetary Fund, upon local forms of cultural, associational, and democratic life. On this view, the "Enlightenment project" not only failed to liberate humanity from its chains, but its celebration of modern commerce instead helped to form international regimes and an alliance of powerful (usually "Western") governments that constitute the latest version of "civilizing" imperial rule[14]; although the old colonial regimes were largely dismantled from the late 1940s through the 1960s, some form of imperial rule has returned with a vengeance, we are told, in the guise of global capital, transnational corporations, and the international, regional, and domestic regimes that support them.[15]

Political debates about globalization have a long and neglected history—neglected in part because the development of global communications, institutions, and commercial ventures; the attendant ethical questions over eroding sovereignty; and the potential or actual impact on the environment and human welfare are sometimes mistakenly seen today as unprecedented developments.[16] Moreover, despite the numerous references to Enlightenment values and "modernity" in the contemporary globalization literature, there is little discussion about the fact that debates concerning global commerce, communication, and their social and political effects were launched by a number of Enlightenment thinkers—most notably (but not only) as a way of theorizing the commercial ventures of imperial trading companies and the globalizing institutions and practices of expanding European empires. As I have argued, among the many incisive eighteenth-century attempts to theorize the rise of such global economic and political relations are Denis Diderot's contributions about commerce in Abbé Raynal's *Histoire des deux Indes*.

Diderot's contributions (in addition, it should be noted, to Raynal's own observations about commerce in the *Histoire* that I have not surveyed in this chapter) allow us, first, to examine a thinker who is profoundly ambivalent about global commerce; this itself offers a sharp and useful philosophical contrast to the historically shortsighted perspective that informs many contemporary contributions to debates about globalization. Second, a study of some of the Enlightenment origins of globalization debates provides us with a much needed intellectual genealogy of how different thinkers in other social and political contexts have wrestled with the perceived trend toward global institutions and processes. Diderot's reflections about commerce and global relations represent a productive intellectual disposition precisely because he seeks both to understand the ways in which global commerce and communication afford possibilities for social and political reform and to identify (as well as analyze) the severe injustices that they have generated. Third, by examining these writings, I aim to challenge the still common view that "the Enlightenment," as such, celebrated the rise of modern commerce and the social and political effects that were thought to follow from it.[17] Among other problems, this view overlooks the fact that a number of prominent eighteenth-century thinkers viewed European empires as (among other things) global commercial enterprises that were manifestly unjust and politically disastrous.

Diderot's and Raynal's writings on global commerce have not been given the attention they deserve by scholars in part because they do not easily fit within the standard expectations that are usually derived from "the Enlightenment" on the topic of commerce. A frequent claim about the core value of Enlightenment political thought or "modernity" is that it laid the ethical groundwork for what became modern capitalism by providing vigorous defenses of the idea of commerce.[18] As I have indicated, contemporary debates over globalization have offered yet another venue for these well-worn arguments, with scholars either attacking or supporting the commercial virtues and *le doux commerce* (gentle or peaceful commerce) that "the Enlightenment" is said to have defended and celebrated. There are, indeed, eighteenth-century writings that can be described plausibly as solely defending the rise of modern commerce and the virtues that were sometimes associated with it, as well as less emphasized writings of the same period that hold it responsible for many of the injustices of modern life.[19] Nevertheless, as with other elements of the standard depictions of "the Enlightenment" or "the Enlightenment project," the assumption that eighteenth-century thinkers widely and un-ambivalently supported the rise of modern commerce masks the rich complexity of many Enlightenment-era political writings—including those by prominent and influential thinkers such as Diderot and Raynal.

Moreover, such characterizations often fail to come to terms with the fact that modern political thought about commerce was indelibly stamped by the imperial experience. Albert Hirschman remarks that "the persistent use of the term *le doux commerce* strikes us as a strange aberration for an age when the slave trade was at its peak and when trade in general was still a hazardous, adventurous, and often violent business."[20] Yet this was not a peculiarity that went unnoticed among the many eighteenth-century thinkers who reflected deeply upon the formation of a global economy, for they understood this development to be intimately linked to the practices and institutions of imperial commerce, such as slavery. Diderot and Raynal are two such thinkers, and their arguments about commerce reveal how much is lost when a single Enlightenment narrative crowds out the nuances and flattens the paradoxes of a remarkably diverse intellectual age. The combination of Diderot's celebrations of commerce and his fierce criticisms of it appear odd only if we work on the assumption that well-known eighteenth-century thinkers must fit a preconceived standard of what fundamentally constitutes "the Enlightenment." When such views are set aside, when we pluralize the very idea of "Enlightenment" and view it as a number of strands that at times reinforce and that other times stand in tension with one another, a significant number of eighteenth-century writings emerge as profoundly ambivalent reflections upon what is sometimes described today as globalization.

NOTES

1. Many thanks to Jacob Levy, Kirstie McClure, and to the late Iris Marion Young for helpful comments and suggestions.
2. For instance, see J. G. A. Pocock, *Barbarism and Religion*, vol. 1 (Cambridge: Cambridge University Press, 1999), 106–14. It should be noted that such political developments and intellectual projects do not amount, in Pocock's view, to a description of "the" Enlightenment (or of "the Enlightenment project"), a singular, nonpluralistic characterization of the political thought of the long eighteenth century that he vehemently rejects. Cf. Jonathan I. Israel, *Enlightenment Contested: Philosophy, Modernity, and the Emancipation of Man* (Oxford: Oxford University Press, 2006), 863–71.
3. Francisco de Vitoria, "De Indis," in *Political Writings*, ed. Jeremy Lawrance and Anthony Pagden (Cambridge: Cambridge University Press, 1991). See also Georg Cavallar, *The Rights of Strangers* (Aldershot, UK: Ashgate, 2002), 107–12.
4. Francisco de Vitoria cites Virgil's *Aeneid* accordingly: "What men, what monsters, what inhuman race, / What laws, what barbarous customs of the place, / Shut up a desert shore to drowning men, / And drive us to the cruel seas again!" (Aeneid, I. 539–40; Dryden's translation as quoted in Vitoria, 278).
5. On Grotius's *De Indis* (later known *De iure praedae*, of which the "Mare Liberum" was one chapter), see Richard Tuck, *The Rights of War and Peace* (Oxford: Oxford University Press, 1999), 79–94; and David Armitage, "Introduction" to Hugo Grotius, *The Free Sea* (Indianapolis, IN: Liberty Fund, 2004), xi–xx.
6. Immanuel Kant, *Kants gesammelte Schriften, herausgegeben von der Preussischen Akademie der Wissenschaften zu Berlin* (Berlin: Walter de Gruyter, 1902—), vol. 8, p. 358; vol. 8, p. 368; ibid; Immanuel Kant, *Practical Philosophy* (Cambridge: Cambridge University Press, 1996), 329, 336–37.
7. The *Histoire* was first published in 1772 (with an imprint of 1770). It was published in extensively revised and enlarged forms in 1774 and 1780. Numerous editions followed with further alterations. All of Diderot's contributions can be found from the 1780 edition onward. Anthony Strugnell and a team of scholars that he commissioned are now at work on a modern critical edition of the *Histoire* which will be published by the Voltaire Foundation. Since this edition has not yet been published, there is no standard edition that is used to cite the *Histoire*; moreover, volume and page numbers differ from edition to edition. Thus, I have cited Raynal's *Histoire* by book and chapter (the *Histoire* is divided into nineteen books, a division that is consistent across many editions). I have used the following editions: [Abbé] Guillaume-Thomas Raynal, *Histoire philosophique et politique des établissements et du commerce des Européens dans les deux Indes* (Genève: Jean-Leonard Pellet, 1780), ten volumes; and [Abbé] Guillaume-Thomas Raynal, *A Philosophical and Political History of the Settlements and Trade of the Europeans in the East and West Indies*, trans. J. O. Justamond (London: W. Strahan and T. Cadell, 1783), eight volumes. A small selection of Diderot's contributions to the *Histoire* is available in a contemporary English translation. See Denis Diderot, *Political Writings*, ed. John Hope Mason and Robert Wokler (Cambridge: Cambridge University Press, 1992), 169–214. The passages from the *Histoire* that I quote in this essay have all been checked against the 1780 Pellet edition.
8. The most important and substantial recent interpretation of Raynal's *Histoire* is J. G. A. Pocock, *Barbarism and Religion* (Cambridge: Cambridge University Press, 2005), vol. 4, chapters 13–17. Two insightful recent studies—both dissertations—about Raynal's *Histoire* are Anoush Terjanian, *"Doux commerce" and its Discontents: Slavery, Piracy, and Monopoly in Eighteenth-Century France* (dissertation, Johns Hopkins University, 2006) and Sunil Agnani,

Enlightenment Universalism and Colonial Knowledge: Denis Diderot and Edmund Burke, 1770–1800 (dissertation, Columbia University, 2004). For fairly recent collections of scholarly essays on the *Histoire* that investigate both the substance of the ideas in the text and the complicated historiography and textual attributions for the various editions of the *Histoire*, see *Lectures de Raynal: l'Histoire des deux Indes en Europe et en Amérique au XVIIIe siècle, Studies on Voltaire and the Eighteenth Century*, ed. Hans-Jürgen Lüsebrink and Manfred Tietz (Oxford: Voltaire Foundation, 1991), vol. 286; and *L'Histoire des deux Indes: réécriture et polygraphie, Studies on Voltaire and the Eighteenth Century*, ed. Hans-Jürgen Lüsebrink and Anthony Strugnell (Oxford: Voltaire Foundation, 1995), vol. 333. See also William R. Womack, "Eighteenth-century Themes," in *Histoire philosophique et politique des deux Indes of Guillaume Raynal, Studies on Voltaire and the Eighteenth Century*, vol. 96, 129–265.

9. For a comprehensive analysis of Diderot's manuscripts that links them to sections of Raynal's *Histoire*, see Michèle Duchet, *Diderot et l'Histoire des deux Indes ou l'Écriture Fragmentaire* (Paris: Libraire A.-G. Nizet, 1978). I have used this study as my guide to locate all of Diderot's contributions to the *Histoire*.

10. Robert Darnton, *The Forbidden Best-Sellers of Pre-Revolutionary France* (New York: W. W. Norton, 1996), 22–82.

11. I have analyzed the range of Diderot's anti-imperialist arguments, in the *Histoire* and elsewhere, in *Enlightenment against Empire* (Princeton: Princeton University Press, 2003), chapter 3. Cf. Srinivas Aravamudan, *Tropicopolitans* (Durham, NC: Duke University Press, 1999), 289–300. See also Laurent Dubois, "An Enslaved Enlightenment: Rethinking the Intellectual History of the French Atlantic," *Social History*, vol. 31, no. 1 (February 2006), pp. 1–14.

12. J. G. A. Pocock, *Barbarism and Religion*, vol. 4, p. 325. I should note that Adam Smith's *Wealth of Nations*—which in this respect was clearly influenced by Raynal and Diderot—may well also count as such as a grim, yet still "enlightened," historical narrative.

13. For an influential analysis of these arguments, see Benjamin Barber, *Jihad vs. McWorld* (New York: Times Books, 1995).

14. John Gray, *False Dawn: The Delusions of Global Capitalism* (New York: New Press, 1998).

15. For a complex account along these lines—one that, it should be noted, simultaneously attempts to complicate this view—see Michael Hardt and Antonio Negri, *Empire* (Cambridge: Harvard University Press, 2000).

16. An emerging scholarly literature is beginning to address the problems with such a view. See Emma Rothschild, "Globalization and the Return of History," *Foreign Policy*, no. 115 (Summer 1999), 106–16; David Armitage, "Is There a Prehistory of Globalization?" in *Comparison and History: Europe in Cross-National Perspective*, ed. Deborah Cohen and Maura O'Connor (London: Routledge, 2004); Duncan S. A. Bell, "History and Globalization: Reflections on Temporality," *International Affairs* (2003), vol. 79, no. 4, pp. 801–14. Also, see the essays in *Globalization and Global History*, ed. Barry K. Gills and William Thompson (London: Routledge, 2006).

17. For a recent discussion of this view and its shortcomings, see the introductory essay in Istvan Hont, *Jealousy of Trade: International Competition and the Nation-State in Historical Perspective* (Cambridge: Harvard University Press, 2005).

18. The classic study of intellectual history along these lines remains Albert Hirschman, *The Passions and the Interests: Political Arguments for Capitalism before Its Triumph* (Princeton: Princeton University Press, 1977). Cf. Ellen Meiksins Wood, who differentiates the English and French contexts into "capitalist" and "bourgeois" societies that shaped differing Enlightenment ideologies of commerce. E. M. Wood, "Capitalism or Enlightenment?" *History of Political Thought*, vol. 21, no. 3 (Autumn 2000), pp. 405–26. Cf. Ellen Meiksins Wood, *Empire of Capital* (London: Verso, 2003), chapters 5–6.

19. Among the most notable examples of the former is Bernard Mandeville's *The Fable of the Bees*; for an example of the latter, see Andrew Fletcher's *Discourse Surrounding the Affairs of Scotland*. Mandeville famously provides a vigorous defense of modern commerce and its "publick benefits," while Fletcher describes at length the disastrous effects of modern commerce in European societies and calls for the establishment of a reformed set of ancient

institutions of political economy (most notoriously, that of slavery). For a recent collection of eighteenth-century writings on such topics, see *Commerce, Culture & Liberty,* ed. Henry C. Clark (Indianapolis, IN: Liberty Fund, 2003). Also, see Jerry Z. Muller, *The Mind and the Market: Capitalism in Modern European Thought* (New York: Alfred A. Knopf, 2002), chapters 1–5; and Donald Winch, *Riches and Poverty: An Intellectual History of Political Economy in Britain, 1750–1834* (Cambridge: Cambridge University Press, 1996).

20. Hirschman, *The Passions and the Interests* (Princeton: Princeton University Press, 1977), 62.

Chapter Two

Empire, Progress, and the "Savage Mind"

Jennifer Pitts[1]

I. INTRODUCTION

This chapter is an effort to explore the implications of what might be called a cognitive-development conception of progress for views of Europe's relation to non-European societies among British thinkers in the eighteenth and nineteenth centuries. Such a conception emerged in the thought of some Scottish Enlightenment thinkers, including William Robertson and Henry Home, Lord Kames and was adopted and intensified by later thinkers such as James and J. S. Mill. It suggested that societal development was, at root, the result of the improved cognitive capacities of individual members of a society; most importantly, an improvement of individuals' capacity for abstract thought. Some of the key tropes of this approach, such as the image of the savage as having the mind or willpower of a child, recur repeatedly in nineteenth-century British thought. But this model of cognitive development was not the only available conception of societal progress. Adam Smith, for instance, offered a highly sophisticated alternative narrative of societal development, in which interactions among similarly rational and reasonable individual human beings alter in response to changing modes of subsistence and the new experiences and requirements imposed by those new circumstances. Other contemporaries including the moral philosopher James Dunbar took up key features of this alternative approach.[2] I want to suggest that whether thinkers regarded progress as individual cognitive development or as an irreducibly social phenomenon had important implications for the ways they judged—and conceived European relations with—ostensibly "backward" societies: most important, what sorts of obligations Europeans had to various non-European peoples, and what European imperial rule could be expected to achieve in the imposition of progress on such societies.

The cognitive-development conception regarded societal progress as the result of an improvement of *individuals'* understanding and, as a result, emphasized the mind, capacities, and beliefs of "the savage" in the singular.[3] Thinkers employing this mode of analysis maintained that the development of institutions and practices such as property, contracts, and treaties, did not exist in early stages of society because the members of such societies could not conceive of such abstract ideas, but rather were cognitively limited to the concrete, the immediate, the particular. Related claims were that "the savage" has no conception of the future and is capable of thinking only about his immediate needs and desires, and that the savage is incapable of "exerting himself" in ways crucial for participation in progress or civilized life. This conception of progress tended to literalize the image of the "infancy of society," to suggest that individual members of such societies should themselves be seen as childlike in their capacities, and morally and politically immature; the cognitive-development approach thus had a tendency to infantilize and, indeed to some degree, to dehumanize members of "primitive" societies. In addition, the view that progress is a matter of individual cognitive development underpinned the belief that all forms of progress occur together; so that advancement or backwardness in one realm, such as technological development or aesthetic refinement, was regarded as an index of a society's condition in all other regards as well, including its moral development and capacity for political independence. Finally, a claim closely associated with the cognitive-development model, especially as it was articulated by many nineteenth-century thinkers, was that certain societies are stagnant—whether because their members lack the inclination to exert themselves in pursuit of improvement, or because their minds are held captive by custom—while only a few societies (ancient Greece, Rome, and their European successors) have, as J. S. Mill put it, "any spring of unborrowed progress" within them.[4] This claim served to justify imperial rule in that it suggested that without outside (European) intervention, stationary societies would never succeed in progressing to higher stages of development.

Common to the prominent Scottish Enlightenment theories of development is the claim that peoples in the earliest stage of society, the "savage" hunting stage, recognize immediate possession as the only form of property; and that as societies progress through the pastoral and agricultural stages, they develop systems that recognize more attenuated and abstract forms of property.[5] Smith was one of the first Scottish thinkers to develop such an account, probably first in the public lectures he gave in Edinburgh in 1748–1750 on rhetoric and the history of philosophy, and then in the lectures on jurisprudence that he gave at Glasgow between 1752 and 1763.[6] But understandings of what caused this evolution of more abstract forms of property varied subtly but significantly. Many theorists of this period, such as Kames and Robertson, whose theories of development were probably very much influenced by Smith's argument, asserted that it is cognitive changes in *individuals* in early-stage societies that make possible new modes of property.[7] Thus Kames, for instance, argued that, "in the progress of nations toward maturity of understanding, abstract ideas become familiar: property is abstracted from possession; and in our conceptions it is now firmly established that the want of possession deprives not a man of his property."[8] For Smith, in contrast, individuals living at different "stages" of society possess equivalent capacities of reason and employ similar processes of moral reasoning. Moreover, while he believed that systematic variation could be observed from one societal stage to the next in the content of moral views, legal structures, and political institution, Smith did not take this variation to imply that human beings develop new capacities for moral judgment or abstract thought as their societies progress. Of all the Scottish historians, Smith was the most consistently respectful of precommercial societies as well as the most consistently skeptical about European claims to superiority and the expansion of European political power around the globe; I suggest that Smith's nuanced and noncognitivist understanding of progress lay behind this respectful posture.

Smith's account of development shows how manners, laws, and moral beliefs evolve as modes of subsistence change, and he stressed that most societies' customs and values are appropriate and reasonable given their circumstances. Despite occasional phrases that suggest the evolution of conceptual abilities from hunting to commercial societies, Smith's lectures on jurisprudence, as I argue further below, develop an explanation of the evolution of property as a series of *social* responses to the different demands of new modes of subsistence. He describes, from the earliest stage of society, individuals whose rationality and capacity for moral reasoning are the same as those of individuals at later stages.

Another Scottish Enlightenment historian who offered a strikingly thorough-going critique of many of the assumptions and conclusions of the cognitive-development approach to progress was James Dunbar. Although Dunbar's philosophical anthropology was by no means as original or as sophisticated as Smith's, and although Dunbar occasionally reverted to claims about members of "rude" societies as ignorant or immature, his effort to analyze societal development, without succumbing to the simplistic and denigrating portrait of early-stage societies implied by the cognitive-development approach, enabled him to offer compelling and perceptive criticisms of many of the presumptions of European notions of progress in his day.

Some of the central features of Smith's theory of societal development were shared by others among his contemporaries (particularly Adam Ferguson, whom I do not discuss here), and many, including Robertson and

Kames, interlaced cognitive-development arguments with more complex social arguments. The cognitive-development strand in Scottish historical thought was, however, taken up and made even starker and less ambivalent by later British thinkers, including James and J. S. Mill. I begin with a discussion of some of the recurrent elements of the cognitive-development approach to progress, with reference primarily to Robertson. In the following section, I treat more briefly the account of societal development offered by Smith, which I argue relies very little on the idea of the improvement of individual capacities; I then turn to Dunbar's rather less well known account. I close with a brief consideration of James and J. S. Mill's account of backwardness and progress in order to examine the cognitive-development perspective as it developed in the nineteenth century in an especially clearly articulated form. In the stark form that this cognitivist view took in the writings of the Mills, the cognitive incapacities of "rude" nations are attributed to all non-European societies, including, most prominently, India; claims that such "barbarians" are incapable of certain abstract ideas become the basis for legal and political arguments justifying the imposition of European despotism over such societies. I suggest that such arguments are not an extension of Scottish developmental theories as such, but rather are of one strand in a family of thought that included far more respectful, and morally and politically inclusive, approaches to non-European societies.

II. WILLIAM ROBERTSON'S "HISTORY OF THE HUMAN MIND"

Cognitive development has been recognized as an important element in Scottish Enlightenment theories of progress.[9] Christopher Berry, for instance, has placed the notion at the center of Scottish stadial theories: "The history of property as portrayed in the four stages rests on a model of 'natural' development. What develops are the human cognitive and emotional capacities."[10] Some of the important concomitants of the idea of cognitive development have been noted by Berry and others, including the analogy between savages and children and the claims that savages have no capacity for abstract thought and no conception of futurity. But there are important differences among the Scottish historians and later thinkers' accounts of how cognitive capacities develop: differences with implications for the political evaluation of various societies and for judgments about European relations with non-European societies.

William Robertson's account of the "rude nations" of America in his *History of America* presents the cognitive-development approach with particular clarity, and so stands in especially striking contrast with Smith's approach, notwithstanding the probable influence of Smith's lectures on Robertson's theory.[11] Robertson maintained that abstract reasoning is largely unavailable to human beings in the savage state, and he viewed individuals' cognitive limitations as the primary cause of these societies' simplicity. He insisted on the limitations, not simply of cognitive capacity, but also of individuals' initiative and energy; indeed, their lack of initiative served as an explanation for their failure to progress to later stages of development. By explaining savage society primarily in terms of the characteristics of individuals, Robertson conveyed the thought that the explanation of practices in "primitive" societies is to be sought at the level of individual cognition or emotion, rather than in the complex interactions among members of a society, and between them and their surroundings.[12] Robertson took the idea that the hunting stage is the "infancy of society" to suggest that *individual* adults in "early ages of society" are similar to children in their faculties and motivations; the result was that his characterization of Amerindians was dismissive and even dehumanizing.[13] Indeed, he also compared "the savage's" inability to think beyond immediate stimuli to that of "a mere animal."[14]

In making such arguments, Robertson relied on the Lockean sensationalist psychology that held that all our ideas can be traced back to sensory impressions.[15] Locke held that children's first ideas are always particular and immediate, and that "Ideots, Savages and the grosly Illiterate," like children, are incapable of forming abstract ideas and general maxims, which require more mature minds.[16] Robertson, too, argued that just as individuals first perceive concrete objects and then generalize about them, so members of savage societies can think only about present objects and immediate sensations and do not have fully developed powers of reason.

> As the individual advances from the ignorance and imbecility of the infant state to vigour and maturity of understanding, something similar to this may be observed in the progress of the species. With respect to it, too, there is a period of infancy, during which several powers of the mind are not unfolded, and all are feeble and defective in their operation. In the early ages of society, while the condition of man is simple and rude, his reason is but little exercised, and his desires move within a very narrow sphere. Hence arise two remarkable characteristics of the human mind in this state. Its intellectual powers are extremely limited; its emotions and efforts are few and languid. Both these distinctions are conspicuous among the rudest and most unimproved of the American tribes.[17]

Robertson's theory of development thus presumes not just that Amerindians are metaphorically in the "infancy" of human development, but also that they also actually share many childish qualities, such as improvidence and the preference for useless ornaments over necessities.

Robertson argues that savage improvidence results from indolence and unruly appetites, as well as from the specifically cognitive inability to conceive the future.[18] Despite his own counsel about the need to remain suspicious of the tales Europeans have reported from America,[19] Robertson uncritically presents the tale from Labat's *Voyages* as evidence for this argument: the "Caribbee" would not for anything part with his "hammoc" in the evening, when his need for it presses itself upon his mind; but, as Robertson puts it, "in the morning, when he is sallying out to the business or pastime of the day, he will part with it for the slightest toy that catches his fancy" (the trope of the toy is in keeping with the infantilization of savage peoples).[20] Citing Adair, Robertson adds that Amerindians have no permanent houses because they only think to build them at the close of winter, when the immediate memory of cold makes housing occur to them; as summer comes on, savages lose interest in the work, remembering again only when winter strikes, and it is too late to build solid housing.[21]

Robertson rather casually mingles two very different claims. The first is that, given their constant struggle for subsistence, members of societies in early stages lack the means, the leisure, and the physical security to engage in speculations that are not of clear and direct utility for survival.[22] The second is that individuals in such societies lack some of the basic elements of mature rationality, such as the ability to distinguish basic needs from frivolous desires, the ability to set aside immediate desires for longer-term interests, the ability to foresee future needs based on past experience, and imagination and curiosity.[23] When analyzing social phenomena, Robertson resorted in the first instance to explanations at the level of individual cognition. He was explicit in according theoretical priority to the individual and argued that in the case of "rude nations" in particular, it was necessary to regard actions and practices as the result of the "sentiments or feelings" of individuals: the "natural order of inquiry," he maintained, should lead one to study first the "bodily constitution of the Americans" and then the "powers of their minds" before "consider[ing] them as united together in society."[24] "The character of a savage," he argued, "results almost entirely from his sentiments or feelings as an individual."[25] Where Smith analyzed institutions of societies at early stages by asking what social practices would result from the judgments of a group of rational individuals under a certain set of environmental constraints, Robertson began his explanations with the individual temperament he considered peculiar to savages.[26] Savages "waste their life in listless indolence" because of an "aversion to labor." They fail to make provision for future needs because "they either want sagacity to proportion this provision to their consumption, or are . . . incapable of any command over their appetites"; they regard others with a "careless indifference."[27] Robertson's account of the simplicity of governmental arrangements in savage society, accordingly, proceeds from a claim about the immature faculties of the individual members: "Where individuals are so thoughtless and improvident as seldom to take effectual precautions for self-preservation, it is vain to expect that public measures and deliberations will be regulated by the contemplation of remote events. They have neither foresight nor temper to form complicated arrangements with respect to their future conduct."[28]

Robertson's treatment of other non-European peoples was characterized by greater respect and subtlety, and he seems to have restricted his reliance on cognitivist explanation to his treatment of "savages": in the *History of America*, his discussions of the Mexican and Peruvian "empires"—which he regarded as considerably advanced—do not rely on individual-level or cognitive explanations. In his analysis of societal development, Robertson seems to have presumed, as Smith did not, a stark division between savage society and all later stages. This is apparent as well in the account of India in his *Historical disquisition concerning the knowledge which the Ancients had of India* (1791), where Robertson displays some of the subtlety of Smith's cross-cultural comparisons, as well as a similarly critical posture toward European pretensions of moral and cultural superiority over other societies.[29] Robertson dedicates the long appendix to the *Disquisition* to arguing that the "genius, manners, and institutions" of India show it to have been a highly advanced society from the time of the earliest European (ancient Greek and Roman) accounts of it.[30] He argues that certain Indian institutions, which Europeans might imagine would thwart societal improvement or the development of the mind, are in fact reasonable social arrangements. The caste system, for instance, was intended by early legislators to provide for the "subsistence, the security, and the happiness of all the members of the community," and though it may be "repugnant" to Europeans, it "will be found, upon attentive inspection, better adapted to attain the end in view, than a careless observer is, on a first view, apt to imagine."[31] Robertson's interpretive generosity toward the caste system—his effort to overcome the dismissal of the unfamiliar as irrational (which he regards as lamentably typical of European judgments)—is characteristic of his account of India.[32] Notably, in his analysis of India, while he certainly addresses the *consequences* of institutions for the ideas and habits of individuals, Robertson never resorts to individuals' cognitive capacities to *explain* practices and institutions, as he does consistently for savage society in the *History of America*.[33] In contrast, as I discuss below, James and J. S. Mill were to adopt the cognitivist model, and at the same time collapsed all non-European societies into a single category of "rudeness." Their explanations of the laws and institutions of India, consequently, rely regularly on claims about individual cognition and the barbarian "mind."[34]

The eloquent conclusion to the *Disquisition* makes clear Robertson's own understanding that accounts of progress were fundamental to the politics of empire. Here Robertson contends that the European conquest of India has been particularly cruel because the conquerors fail to understand that Indian society is a highly developed one. He expresses the hope that better historical analysis might stem the depredations, by engendering respect among Europeans for a sophisticated and complex society.

> I own . . . that I have all along kept in view an object more interesting, as well as of greater importance [than mere description of Indian society and institutions], and entertain hopes, that if the account which I have given of the early and high civilization of India, and of the wonderful progress of its inhabitants in elegant arts and useful science, shall be received as just and well-established, it may have some influence upon the behaviour of Europeans towards that people.[35]

Even in the *History of America*, despite his often uncritical reliance on his European sources, Robertson indicated the pitfalls of using travelers' and missionaries' reports as evidence, observing that those who wrote such reports, especially among the Spanish, were led by either economic interest or religious zeal to exaggerate the characteristics of foreign peoples that best served their own agenda to enslave or convert the people they encountered.[36] Like Smith and Ferguson, Robertson noted that partiality in favor of one's own social practices is a general human vice, one that often leads writers to describe as degenerate or irrational what are merely unfamiliar practices, and one against which he believed the historian must constantly struggle.

> It is extremely difficult to procure satisfying and authentic information concerning nations while they remain uncivilized. To discover their true character under this rude form, and to select the features by which they are distinguished, requires an observer possessed of no less impartiality than discernment. For, in every stage of society, the faculties, the sentiments and desires of men are so accommodated to their own state, that they become standards of excellence to themselves, they affix the idea of perfection and happiness to those attainments which resemble their own, and wherever the objects and enjoyments to which they have been accustomed are wanting, confidently pronounce a people to be barbarous and miserable. Hence the mutual contempt with which the members of communities, unequal in their degrees of improvement, regard each other.[37]

And yet Robertson himself appears curiously blind to his own counsel throughout much of his account of Amerindians. Bruce Lenman has answered the question "what lies behind the sustained prejudice which Robertson displayed in dealing with Amerindian and creole?" with the observation that "Robertson was not trying to invent modern historical anthropology and failing." Rather, he writes, the *History of America* "can only be understood in the light of the concept of the historian as moral legislator."[38] But even if Lenman is right to assert that Robertson's *own* conception of the "historian as moral legislator" led him to support Spanish governance in South America as the likeliest avenue for Amerindian progress, alternative understandings were available in Robertson's day, both of what constituted responsible anthropology, and of the moral and political contributions historians could make in the context of European expansion. Adam Smith and James Dunbar offer two such alternatives.[39]

III. SMITH'S ALTERNATIVE TO THE COGNITIVE-DEVELOPMENT APPROACH

Contrary to what a number of scholars have argued or assumed, I want to suggest that Smith's account of societal development did not center, as Robertson's did, on the development of individuals' capacities. Rather, Smith's was a narrative of the evolution of social interactions among human beings he assumed to be fully rational, mature, capable of abstract thought, and equipped with capacities for moral reasoning much like those in more complex societies.[40] He presumed that the *process* of moral reasoning (though not the content of moral beliefs) is similar in all human societies. Smith's argument about development, consequently, takes place not at the level of individuals, but at the level of social interactions: he asks how rational individuals would respond to the conditions and incentives typical of a given mode of subsistence, and he argues that as the mode of subsistence alters under the pressures of population growth, societies respond by developing structures of organization and authority, norms to govern property and punishment, and values and manners to accommodate their new conditions.

Two prominent elements of the cognitive-development approach are notably absent in Smith's theory of development: the notion that "savages" are childlike or immature in their mental capacities, and the claim that they are incapable of envisioning or planning for the future. Smith's avoidance in his major works of the savage-child analogy is particularly striking, for in the early and fragmentary essay on the "History of Astronomy," he had described the "impotence of mind" displayed by people in "savage ages," and written that a "child caresses the fruit that is agreeable, as it beats the stone that hurts it. The notions of a savage are not very different."[41] Yet, when Smith returned in the *Theory of Moral Sentiments* to the same example of a child beating a stone, he compared him to a dog and a choleric man, but, significantly, abandoned the reference to the savage.[42] To my knowledge, Smith never repeated the suggestion that the individual members of early-stage societies are themselves mentally immature or childlike. Also absent from the *Lectures on Jurisprudence* and the *Theory of Moral Sentiments* are claims that such individuals cannot conceive of futurity.

Similarly, Smith did not regard savages as incapable of forming the abstract ideas necessary to the institution of property; he argued rather that they had not yet experienced the needs that would lead them to institute extended property rights. In discussing the development of property as an institution,

Smith does assert that people "at first ... conceived" of property as immediate possession only.[43] Yet in Smith's account this is not because of their limited imagination. His analysis of the evolution of property and government in the *Lectures on Jurisprudence* suggests, rather, that members of societies of all stages of development make moral judgments by the same process: by an implicit appeal to the judgment of an impartial spectator. When the spectator method is used in the context of a hunting society to determine rightful possession (to ask what actions would provoke appropriate resentment), Smith argues, it produces the view that only direct possession constitutes legitimate possession.[44] Smith's narrative of the "progress" by which this notion of property, natural to hunting societies, gradually gives way to one that recognizes ownership even when an owner is absent relies not on changes in the capacities of the people involved, but rather on the emergence of new kinds of valuable possessions thanks to the natural development of a new mode of subsistence. Smith's theory of the history of property is thus one of structural societal change in response to the evolution in mode of subsistence, not individual cognitive advancement.

Smith's account of a property dispute in an indigenous Canadian society, drawn from the Jesuit missionary Charlevoix, exemplifies his approach to hunting societies and his ideas about how they might conceive property rights and moral obligations, and make moral judgments. He describes a case in which members of a hunting society recognize direct possession alone as legally authoritative, but are also able to imagine and acknowledge more extended forms of property. He tells of a woman of a Canadian hunting society who left a string of wampum, which was clearly precious to her, in the field of another woman, who then took it. When the first woman appealed to one of the chief men of the village, he told her that "in strict law" she no longer had a right to the wampum. The chief added, however, that the second woman ought to give back the beads, or she would risk a scandalous reputation for avarice; recognizing the force of his argument, it seems, she returned the beads. The anecdote, as Smith has told it, neatly suggests that although a certain institution of property, even the simplest form of direct possession, may be appropriate to a given stage of society, there is no reason to assume that the society's members are therefore incapable of imagining more abstract forms of property.[45] The story also suggests a possible mechanism for the evolution of abstract property rights in people's natural moral reactions to new situations, and in the exercise of an equity that, it seems, is accessible to members of any society.[46]

Smith discusses the evolution of contracts in similar terms, showing that oral and then written contracts emerge only in later stages of society, not because individuals in earlier stages are incapable of understanding contractual obligations, but rather because the material and social conditions for securing obligation do not obtain.[47] For Smith, what makes a contract binding lies not in the intention of the promiser in making a promise, but rather in the relation between the promiser and the person promised to: the obligation to fulfill a promise stems from "the reasonable expectation produced by a promise."[48] If an impartial spectator—as always, someone taking account of the social circumstances—judged the nonperformance of a promise or contract worthy of resentment, then it would constitute a breach of obligation. The objects of greatest value in a hunting society, for instance, are not worth the trouble of enforcing contracts.[49] Another reason contracts emerge only in later stages is the "difficulty and inconvenience of obtaining a trial" in early, typically egalitarian societies, which convene the whole body of the people for trials. Such societies, Smith proposes, would naturally reserve judicial proceedings for cases that severely disrupt the social order, such as murder and robbery.[50]

Societal adjudication of *nonviolent* breaches of contract must await the development of a more extensive judicial system, which itself requires an expansion of government that occurs only in wealthy pastoral or agricultural societies. Smith notes that societies in early stages, if they do not recognize contracts, certainly acknowledge related values such as a "sense of honor or veracity," and they often have analogous means of providing the clarity necessary to make promises binding.[51] Smith thus sought to show that all human beings employ the same faculties in responding to certain persistent dilemmas of social interaction, and that the complexity of the solutions they develop will depend not on individual capacities but on a range of material and social factors. This complex social explanation differs starkly from the view that the absence of formal contracts in early stages of society indicates an incapacity on the part of "savages," as individuals, to conceive of obligation in sufficiently abstract terms, as in J. S. Mill's claim, discussed below, that "barbarians will not reciprocate. They cannot be depended on for observing any rules. Their minds are not capable of so great an effort."[52]

A wide range of values and customs may be shown to be reasonable or understandable given the situation of the agents, according to Smith. Diverse customs and practices have developed as appropriate responses to circumstances—including climate, geography, and mode of subsistence. It makes little sense, then, to rank virtues on any universal scale, for many virtues are appropriate to some but not all social stages.[53] Both firmness and gentleness are virtues; each is suited to certain circumstances, and yet under others proves less praiseworthy—that is, less deserving of approbation by an appropriately situated impartial spectator. "In general," Smith argued, "the style of manners which takes place in any nation, may commonly upon the whole be said to be that which is most suitable to its situation. Hardiness is the character most suitable to the circumstances of a savage; sensibility to those of one who lives in a very civilized society. Even here, therefore, we cannot complain that the moral sentiments of men are very grossly perverted."[54] By no means will every custom or quality lauded by a society be truly praiseworthy, even in context, but Smith approaches unfamiliar practices with the presumption that they are appropriate to their circumstances, and he attempts to understand why they might have come to be valued before criticizing some practices as infringements of such universal values as equity or humanity.

Smith's discussion of infanticide in the *Theory of Moral Sentiments* illustrates such an approach to the judgment of social practices. Here he seeks to understand a seemingly appalling practice in its social context while also using a notion of equity to make moral judgments across cultural and historical boundaries. Even infanticide may be excused in some societies, Smith maintains, for the "extreme indigence of a savage" makes it reasonable for such a parent to abandon a child rather than to condemn him- or herself to die with it. "That in this state of society, therefore, a parent should be allowed to judge whether he can bring up his child, ought not to surprise us so greatly." The impartial spectator, whose moral sentiments might normally be expected to find such a practice outrageous, can in this case enter imaginatively into the situation of the burdened parent and concur with a judgment that abandoning the child is preferable to dying with it.[55]

Finally, while Smith undoubtedly believed that commercial society made possible legal and moral refinements, he was at the same time conscious that such a view could be an all too easy self-deception.[56] He noted that all societies from the rudest to the most polished are biased in favor of their own way of life. While judgments of value and virtues vary with the "different situations of different ages and countries," each flatters itself a universal standard and believes that each quality or ideal habitual among themselves represents the "golden mean of that particular talent or virtue."[57]

Drawing on a theory of development that emphasized the role of accident in history, Smith, in the *Wealth of Nations*, suggested both the precariousness of Europe's superior force and its irrelevance from a moral point of view. Europe's strength was not the result even of any durable, not to mention innate, superiority. Whatever advances in moral refinement Europe could boast, these neither justified international preeminence, nor ensured that Europeans would treat more vulnerable others with the justice and humanity to which they were entitled. Smith argued that all peoples' rights should be respected, but that this only happens when countries are forced to respect each other by a more equal balance of power than then existed. "To the natives ... both of the East and West Indies," he wrote,

> these misfortunes ... seem to have arisen rather from accident than from any thing in the nature of these events themselves. At the particular time when these discoveries were made, the superiority of force happened to be so great on the side of the Europeans, that they were enabled to commit with impunity every sort of injustice in those remote countries. Hereafter, perhaps, the natives of those countries may grow

stronger, or those of Europe may grow weaker, and the inhabitants of all the quarters of the world may arrive at that equality of courage and force which, by inspiring mutual fear, can alone overawe the injustice of independent nations into some sort of respect for the rights of one another.[58]

The language of abstract rights is rare in Smith's work, and he does not specify what rights nations should be understood to have: whether rights not to be interfered with, or perhaps simply not to be robbed and destroyed. It would seem that the particular content of the rights of nations can only be worked out in practice, like systems of morality more generally, and that something close to parity of power is necessary for such rights to be fairly specified and respected.

IV. JAMES DUNBAR: THE "TOO GENERAL TERMS OF BARBAROUS AND CIVILIZED"

Smith's theory of social development was, to be sure, uniquely subtle among Scottish Enlightenment theories. But Smith was not alone in articulating a theory of progress that was at the same time an indictment of European triumphalism, as is perhaps best indicated by a work of essays first published in 1780 by the Aberdeen moral philosopher James Dunbar.[59] Dunbar's account of development is less detailed and sophisticated than Smith's, and it does not draw on such a powerful or well-developed theory of moral judgment. But Dunbar's essays are striking and original in their perceptive criticism of the self-congratulatory strain within European theories of progress. Indeed, though his contribution has gone largely unrecognized, Dunbar explicitly and eloquently drew connections between theories of progress, the dangers of European presumptuousness, and the injustices of European commercial and imperial expansion.[60] Dunbar's *Essays* are further indication that stadial theories of development did not lead ineluctably to the sort of European self-confidence that underwrote empire, but that, on the contrary, such theories could furnish trenchant criticism of European assumptions about progress and their connection to empire.

Dunbar's account of societal development and his approach to cross-cultural judgment share many of the features that render Smith's account relatively respectful of precommercial societies and critical of European presumptuousness. First, he maintains that human societies are far more similar to one another than European observers have been inclined to imagine.[61] Second, he insists that the various elements generally thought of as composing "civilization" do not necessarily occur together historically. The categories *barbarous* and *civilized*, he argues, are both empirically unhelpful and normatively problematic in their suggestion that some peoples unite all advantages and virtues, and others all the miseries and vices to which human life is subject. Third, Dunbar emphasizes that the development of human societies toward "civilization" is a process at once natural and universal, and fraught with accident and contingency, so that the apparent backwardness of a society cannot be assumed to reflect the talents or capacities of its members. Fourth, he notes the human tendency to regard one's own culture as the height of intellectual and moral attainment, and he warns Europeans against this trap of bias and the injustices it licenses.

His arguments are often derivative of Smith as well as of other sources, including Rousseau and Raynal; his account of the earliest stage of human development is particularly indebted to Rousseau's *Discourse on Inequality* in its identification of a moment at which humanity, by supplementing instinct with imagination, breaks decisively from the animal world.[62] It should be emphasized, however, that Dunbar's critique of European triumphalism did not rest on a primitivist fantasy of the noble savage. Ever the moderate, Dunbar positioned himself between two schools of thought on progress: the majority of philosophers, who agreed with popular opinion that progress in the arts and sciences was morally beneficial; and a few recent observers, led by Rousseau, who decried it as "the fertile source of corruption, debasement, and infelicity."[63] Despite his evident admiration for Rousseau, whom he followed, for instance, in positing a "serene and joyous" golden age between mere animal existence and fully developed society, Dunbar was also committed to the idea that a gradual improvement of arts and manners, though not inevitable, is natural to and desirable for human beings.[64] What makes Dunbar's account distinctive and compelling, however, is not this rather inconclusive effort at compromise between primitivism and perfectibilism, but rather his perceptive analysis of the methods, and common pitfalls, of cross-cultural judgment.

The very analytic categories upon which theories of progress such as Robertson's are based are, here, called into question: the undifferentiated classifications *rude* and *cultivated* are, Dunbar suggests, empirically useless and normatively pernicious. He is unusually self-conscious about the use of such terms as at once ostensibly descriptive and also evaluative, and he proposes that these "names implying almost unlimited censure or applause" should be discarded in favor of more precise and limited terms.[65]

> Were it not then better to set aside from correct reasoning the too general terms of barbarous and civilized, substituting in their room expressions of more definite censure and approbation? Indeed the common acceptation of these words is founded upon a very general, but very false and partial opinion of the state of mankind. It supposes that the difference between one nation and another may be prodigiously great; and some happy and distinguished tribes of men are, in all respects, generous, liberal, refined, and humane; while others, from their hard fate, or their perverseness, remain in all respects illiberal, mischievous, and rude.[66]

Dunbar himself does propose a tentative enumeration of "civilized" qualities, including steady private affections, fidelity to engagements, order of internal laws, equity and humanity in conduct toward foreigners, sciences and fine arts, and commerce (though he qualifies the last three in a Rousseauian vein). And yet no nation, he argues, has possessed all of them fully, nor has any people survived, except during brief periods of "convulsion and anarchy," without the most important of them. Dunbar thus denies that all aspects of progress occur in lockstep. He observes that technological, economic, and scientific progress do not necessarily entail moral progress, and that even apparently "rude" nations possess attributes reserved by most theories for commercial nations.[67] Given the "mixed and complicated nature" of what is called civilization, Dunbar argues, historical arguments ought to be made about the development of particular institutions and practices, not about an imagined whole called "civilization." The historiographic error is also a moral one, since the label of backwardness is not simply a descriptive category but a moral judgment about whole peoples.

Dunbar rebukes those who assume that "savage" societies are either uniform in their characteristics or altogether vicious. In an extended denunciation of Josiah Tucker's judgments of Amerindians, Dunbar quotes Tucker as claiming, "without one exception, that the savages, in general, are very cruel, and vindictive, full of spite and malice."[68] Dunbar insists that there is cultural diversity even among "rude" societies; and the reason he gives is not Robertson's—the diversity of climates in the Americas—but rather the operation of imagination, "caprice," and "fashion" that he maintains occurs in all human societies.[69] Dunbar is not simply offering a more favorable redescription of savage customs; indeed, he too notes the cruelty of many "savage" practices. The force of his argument lies rather in his suggestion that standard European judgments of such societies have been distorted by certain assumptions and tendencies, such as superficial and parochial criteria of refinement, or the belief that societies are monoliths in which a single practice is an index of the entire society's condition.

Dunbar closely follows Smith's arguments about custom in *Theory of Moral Sentiments*, and he draws similar conclusions about the variability of standards of beauty, the reasonableness of many unfamiliar customs, and also the need to turn criticism on many European practices.[70] In his discussion of customs of adornment in savage societies, Dunbar argues that the practice of body painting, nearly universal in early societies, originated for practical reasons such as protection from sun, cold, or insects, but soon evolved into a form of cultural expression and "became subject to the caprice and vicissitude of fashion."[71] In some societies, he argues, fashion led from painting to scarring: "Thus a practice, at first innocent or salutary, became, by degrees, pernicious; and while it aimed at farther decoration, or at emblematical expression, tended in reality to deform the species."[72] While Dunbar asserts that it is the "progress of society" that has made such practices obsolete in Europe, he notes (like Smith) that custom has introduced new and perhaps equally destructive and unquestioned practices in Europe: "the swathing of infants, the confinement of dress, and other absurd practices in our economy, unprecedented among Barbarians, might be mentioned as counterparts of the same violence among polished nations."[73] He argues, further, that if "untutored" tribes have been led, by evolutions of fashion, to deform the bodies of their children, they do not do so with the "avowed purpose of deranging the intellectuals of man," which Dunbar describes as "a conduct so flagitious and enormous as has never stained the manners of savage and untutored tribes." Yet this is precisely the turn that practices of disfigurement took in Europe: "not many ages ago, even this enormity existed in the manners of Europe, where, in various instances, the forming of fools for the entertainment of the great, was the ultimate end proposed in mutilating the human figure."[74] Dunbar maintains that all such practices are unnatural and that they "degrade the dignity of our species"; but his argument, consistently, is that all human societies have proven themselves capable of such degradation; advances in politeness and civility are no proof against inhumane custom.[75] Conversely, just as all societies, at any stage of advancement, are capable of making inhumanity customary, all codes of law evince a combination of wisdom and credulity. Codes of law and religion "which afford, in one view, so striking examples of credulity and fanaticism, may be regarded, in another, as monuments of human sagacity."

Finally, Dunbar not only perceived the inadequacy of standard methods of cross-cultural judgment; he also aptly diagnosed Europeans' increasing tendency to set themselves apart from their fellow human beings, and their growing readiness to dehumanize those for whom they had cultural contempt.

> Hence the rank which Europe, at this day, usurps over all the communities of mankind.
> She affects to move in another orbit from the rest of the species. She is even offended with the idea of a common descent; and, rather than acknowledge her ancestors to have been co-ordinate only to other races of Barbarians, and in parallel circumstances, she breaks the unity of the system, and, by imagining specific differences among men, precludes or abrogates their common claims. According to this theory, the oppression or extermination of a meaner race, will no longer be so shocking to humanity. Their distresses will not call upon us so loudly for relief. And public morality, and the laws of nations, will be confined to a few regions peopled with this more exalted species of mankind.[76]

Dunbar's predictions proved apt, not least regarding the increasing narrowness of the international legal community.[77]

Like Smith, Dunbar looked to the further course of progress, and to the long-term operations of global commerce, as possible remedies for the global imbalance of power and the specious European self-understanding that had resulted. He followed Smith, too, in suggesting that Europeans' recent military advantage, which had made possible the astonishingly rapid conquests of vast territories by a "few adventurers," would be temporary and that the natural and moral equality of all people would eventually come to be respected, when the natural course of progress had better balanced nations' relative strength.[78] Dunbar shared with Smith, and with Raynal, a sense of the paradoxical nature of global commerce.[79] Commerce, argued Dunbar, in bringing together distant peoples, offers the possibility of enlarging their understandings and increasing their commitment to the idea of human equality. But its effect has too often been the reverse: to encourage the presumptuousness of the more opulent and powerful.

> Commerce, the boast of modern policy, by enlarging the sphere of observation and experience, promised to undeceive the world, and to diffuse more liberal and equal sentiments through the several parts of an extended system. But commerce, it is to be feared, has, in some instances, been productive of the very contrary effects; and by exposing, if I may say so, the nakedness of society, and uniting, in one prospect, its most distant extremes, has heightened the insolence of nations, and rendered their original and natural equality, to a superficial observer, more incredible.[80]

Dunbar offered his essays as a corrective to the false and pernicious belief in their own moral superiority that Europeans had drawn from their fortuitous commercial and political power.[81]

V. JAMES AND J. S. MILL: THE COGNITIVE-DEVELOPMENT MODEL EXTENDED

While Europeans in the late eighteenth century undoubtedly were becoming increasingly secure in their sense of superiority—intellectual, moral, political, economic, and technological—over the rest of the world, we nonetheless find among a number of eighteenth-century thinkers, as Smith and Dunbar attest, a continued sense of the fragility of their own civilization's achievements, persistent doubts about the justice of European political and social orders, and respect for the achievements and reasonableness of other societies. By the early nineteenth century, however, liberals had come to share with the broader political and intellectual climate, especially in Britain, a civilizational self-confidence not yet presumed by their predecessors, and an increasing sense that profound differences in individual mentality and character distinguished Europeans from the rest of the world.[82]

Robertson, as I have noted, restricted to the earliest stages of societies his claim that certain peoples lack intellectual maturity: hunting societies without developed agriculture, cities, or money. One of the striking aspects of James Mill's adoption of some of the language and premises of Scottish historical theories is his collapsing of the series of stages into a dichotomy of barbarous and civilized.[83] Claims that thinkers such as Kames and Robertson had (however falsely) made of hunting societies were applied by James Mill to Asian civilizations that the earlier thinkers had regarded as highly advanced.[84] The elder Mill's *History of British India* (1817), contemptuous of Indian society as barbaric and the Indian population as incapable of participation in their own governance, guided not only his own views about what was desirable and possible for the British to do in India, but also those of a generation of policymakers, including J. S. Mill—though the intolerance and inadequacy of his portrait of Indian society were also criticized by Orientalist scholars.[85] Though deeply influenced by Scottish theories of societal development, in drawing on the language of cognitive development, James Mill, and through him, his son, adopted and extended one of that tradition's most politically and morally exclusive strands.[86] And while James Mill's account of India was unusually disparaging, his premise that the minds of Asians in backward and stagnant societies differed significantly from those of Europeans was more widely shared in the nineteenth century.

For the elder Mill, barbarous reason is obscured by caprice, a flaw to be found in Indian rulers and nomadic hunters as much as in children.[87] Thus he maintained that the practices of rude peoples, including Indians and the Chinese (the societies he wrote about in greatest detail) illustrated the debility of their minds, their inability to recognize their interests, and the enslavement of their reason to whim or passion.[88]

> A civilized government, when it is strongly its interest to be at peace with you, will, you may calculate with considerable certainty, remain at peace. On a barbarous, or semicivilized government, its view of its true interests is so feeble and indistinct, and its caprices and passions are so numerous and violent, that you can never count for a day. From its hatred of all restraint, and its love of depredation, it is naturally and essentially at war with all around it. The government of India, therefore, is not to be preserved with less than a perpetual war expenditure.[89]

While Mill's language in the foregoing passage might suggest that he attributed irrationality to the structures of barbarous governments, elsewhere he asserts that individual *members* of semicivilized societies suffer from inferior mental capacities. He criticizes William Jones for entrusting to Indians the complex task of writing the code of Indian law: "as if one of the most difficult tasks to which the human mind can be applied, a work to which the highest measure of European intelligence is not more than equal, could be expected to be tolerably performed by the unenlightened and perverted intellects of a few Indian pundits."[90]

James Mill saw himself as at once a utilitarian and an heir to the philosophical history of the Scottish Enlightenment. What emerged was a problematic fusion: an index of progress in which utility is the sole standard against which any nation can be measured. As Mill wrote in the *History*, "exactly in proportion as Utility is the object of every pursuit may we regard a nation as civilized. Exactly in proportion as its ingenuity is wasted on contemptible or mischievous objects . . . the nation may safely be denominated barbarous."[91] Such a conclusion did justice to neither tradition. James Mill's conviction that utilitarian theory and its own legal distinctions and categories offered the only benchmark of rationality "in every pursuit" illustrates a limited imagination about the possible diversity of human institutions and customs that bears little resemblance either to the sociological sensitivity of the Scottish historians, or to Bentham.

To be sure, Bentham was notoriously confident in the universal applicability of his principles and methods; as he wrote in his essay on the "Influence of Time and Place in Matters of Legislation," "Legislators who, having freed themselves from the shackles of authority, have learnt to soar above the mists of prejudice, know as well how to make laws for one country as for another: all they need is to be possessed fully of the facts."[92] But while he deplored the follies, confusions, and corruptions of traditional bodies of law, and sought a solution in legal codification on utilitarian principles (his *pannomion*, meant to be usable by "All Nations Professing Liberal Opinions"), Bentham, far from appealing to his principles to prove the superiority of Britain and other European countries, insisted that British laws, policies, and institutions were a signal failure by utilitarian standards. And in contrast to James Mill's frequent recourse to examples from the arts to illustrate the backwardness of societies like India and China, Bentham was ecumenical on aesthetic questions; indeed, J. S. Mill was to criticize this quality as a lack of proper discrimination.[93]

J. S. Mill, who called his father "the last survivor of th[e] great school" of Scottish moral philosophy, and who largely adopted his father's view of Indian society, also took up the notion that societal development is a matter of the improvement of individuals' cognitive capacity.[94] The younger Mill directly linked such claims to a justification for despotic colonial rule over backward peoples by more advanced nations. His conceptions of "civilization" and barbarism seem to have altered little from his fullest statement of his conception of progress, in the early essay "Civilization," through late works such as *On Liberty*, *Considerations on Representative Government*, and "A Few Thoughts on Non-Intervention," in which he elaborates the political implications of that view of progress.

"Civilization," published in 1836, proposes a simple and unified developmental scale, one in which the "ingredients of civilization . . . begin together, always co-exist, and accompany each other in their growth."[95] Almost any institution, practice, or art will bear the mark of a society's place in the scale of civilization, high or low, and Mill often writes as though these were the only two relevant categories. He thus, like James Mill, flattens the relatively complex series of stages employed by Scottish historians to a simple dichotomy of civilized and barbarous. Mill repeatedly describes the differences between civilized and savage or barbarous societies as differences between the characters, psychological attributes, and mental capacities of their members. One does not find collective action in savage societies, he argues in "Civilization," because "[i]t is only civilized beings who can combine. All combination is compromise: it is the sacrifice of some portion of individual will, for a common purpose. The savage cannot bear to sacrifice, for any purpose, the satisfaction of his individual will. His social cannot even temporarily prevail over his selfish feelings, nor his impulses bend to his calculations."[96] Mill suggests that what is lacking is not necessarily cognitive ability, for the savage "is often not without intelligence," but willpower, or the control of reason over the appetites. The failing, still, is one of individual capacities.

The slave, whom Mill here treats as an extreme variant of the savage, cannot subject his will to "a superior purpose of his own. He is wanting in intelligence to form such a purpose; above all, he cannot frame to himself to conception of a fixed rule: nor if he could, has he the capacity to adhere to it."[97] After characterizing the failings of savages and slaves in their extreme forms, Mill extends the argument to peoples who "approach to the conditions of savages or of slaves" to explain, for instance, why civilized belligerents usually defeat their less civilized foes. Because "discipline . . . is an attribute of civilization," "none but civilized states have ever been capable of forming an alliance. The native states of India have been conquered by the English one by one."[98] Mill argues that the reason for such patterns is that cooperation, like other attributes of civilization, "can be learnt only by practice," and he describes this learning process as one undergone by individuals.[99]

Mill's primary concern in "Civilization" is the political and moral effects of civilization in its most developed form in Britain, and here he deploys the "savage" primarily to foreground the key characteristics of civilized society: "the diffusion of property and intelligence, and the power of cooperation" (124). If Mill's category of savage society appeared only in "Civilization," it might be thought to be a literary device, a rough but effective means of highlighting what was most significant about British society and assisting the case, made at the end of the essay, for a Millian reform of British universities.[100] But far from serving simply as a foil for civilization, such an account of the barbarous and semicivilized as deficient in powers of mind and will recurs throughout Mill's career to justify imperial rule and a suspension of international norms in European relations with non-European societies.

In "A Few Words on Non-Intervention" of 1859, for instance, Mill uses the category to argue for a strict distinction between the legal and political standards applied within Europe and those reserved for the treatment of barbarian societies. Reciprocity, mutual respect for sovereignty, and the law of nations, he argues, should govern relations among civilized nations. Relations between civilized nations and "barbarians" cannot, properly speaking, be considered political relations at all. One of the reasons he offers, in a passage that recalls the account in "Civilization" of Indians' failure to ally against the British, is the incapacity of barbarians to abide by treaties and agreements: "barbarians will not reciprocate. They cannot be depended on for observing any rules. Their minds are not capable of so great an effort."[101] "Non-Intervention" is striking in its use of a philosophical anthropology, at best speculative, to justify the exercise of vast coercive political and military power:

> To characterize any conduct whatever towards a barbarous people as a violation of the law of nations, only shows that he who so speaks has never considered the subject. A violation of great principles of morality it may easily be; but barbarians have no rights as a *nation*, except a right to such treatment as may, at the earliest possible period, fit them for becoming one. The only moral laws for the relation between a civilized and a barbarous government, are the universal rules of morality between man and man.[102]

Mill's argument for the political and legal exclusion rested on the assumption by European states of the authority to judge what was in the best interests of backward peoples, an authority stemming from just the sort of sure knowledge about how to bring about progress that Smith's more chastened approach to societal development denied was possible.

Mill's adherence to an implicit cognitive-development approach to progress also underlies his famous qualification of his argument in *On Liberty* with the proviso that the case for minimal interference in individuals' lives by the state or by other people did not apply to children or young persons, but

> only to human beings in the maturity of their faculties.... Those who are still in a state to require being taken care of by others, must be protected against their own actions as well as against external injury. For the same reason, we may leave out of consideration those backward states of society in which the race itself may be considered as in its nonage. The early difficulties in the way of spontaneous progress are so great, that there is seldom any choice of means for overcoming them; and a ruler full of the spirit of improvement is warranted in the use of any expedients that will attain an end, perhaps otherwise unattainable.[103]

It should be emphasized that J. S. Mill justified civilizing despotism not simply on the grounds that such rule was necessary to undermine the power of entrenched and oppressive political structures and social hierarchies. Rather, his claim was that the rational capacities of *individuals* in such societies were so immature that they were incapable of being "guided to their improvement by conviction or persuasion."[104] Here, as in "Non-intervention," Mill grounds—on weakly theorized anthropological assertions and on the tendentious metaphor of the infancy of society—a claim for Europeans' moral authority to exercise despotic power over societies they deem backward and stagnant.

VI. CONCLUSION

It may be tempting to regard the very idea of societal development or progress as imperialist in character, given the central justificatory role that theories of progress have played in European imperial expansion, particularly in the nineteenth century. A dominant form that such theories took in the nineteenth century depicted progress as a matter of increasing rationality and cognitive capacity, so that members of societies regarded as being at "earlier" stages of development are described not simply as rational human beings acting within different contexts of social organization but rather as themselves cognitively limited: mired in error or enslaved to superstition, incapable of the abstract thought necessary for abiding by contracts or treaties, "untrustworthy" and lacking in "character," and incapable of participating in their own governance not simply because of illiteracy or lack of education but because of civilizational deficiencies deeply rooted in individuals' minds and characters.[105] And yet within the family of eighteenth-century understandings of historical progress were accounts that could be developmental while resisting the implication that non-Europeans ought to be excluded from ordinary standards of political respect, inclusion, or reciprocity, as the work of Adam Smith and James Dunbar, among others, demonstrates.[106] Later thinkers such as James and J. S. Mill who adopted a cognitive-development approach to the study of human history, and extended to all non-Europeans the diagnosis of individual immaturity, abandoned this more complex view of societal development and the more chastened approach to cross-cultural judgment that it generated. Such nineteenth-century liberals bore out, with disastrous consequences, Dunbar's apprehension that Europeans were as yet incapable of responding with "liberal and equal sentiments" to radical cultural diversity and global inequalities.

NOTES

1. This chapter was presented at the 2004 international meeting of the Conference for the Study of Political Thought: "Colonialism and its Legacies." I am grateful to conference participants and especially to the late Iris Marion Young and Jacob Levy for helpful feedback.

2. I have treated Smith's thought at greater length in *A Turn to Empire* (Princeton: Princeton University Press, 2005), chapter 2.

3. I have not used quotation marks around each use of terms characteristic of eighteenth- and nineteenth-century theories of progress, such as "backward," "savage," and "barbarous," but it should be emphasized that they are implied throughout. It should be noted that Scottish stadial, or four-stage, theorists used the terms "savage" and "barbarian" not only as evaluative terms but also in a more purely taxonomic sense (*savage* indicating hunting societies and *barbarian* pastoral societies).

4. "Review of Grote's *History of Greece*," *Collected Works of John Stuart Mill* [hereafter CW] (Toronto: University of Toronto Press, 1963—), vol. 11: 313. Henry Maine, similarly, asserted the uniquely progressive nature of European societies and their ancient progenitors and suggested an explanation at the level of individual capacity and motivation (though his analysis in the rest of the work operates more at the level of social interactions): "It is indisputable that much the greatest part of mankind has never shown a particle of desire that its civil institution should be improved" from their first moment of codification; and "progress seems to have been there arrested [in China], because the civil laws are coextensive with all the ideas of which the race is capable" in *Ancient Law* (Washington, DC: Beard Books, 2000 [1861]), 14. Walter Bagehot, in his self-consciously Darwinian account of progress, attributed Europe's advance to the "contest of races," the "conflict of nations," the "competitive examination of constant war" and argued that "[t]his principle explains at once why the 'protected' regions of the world—the interior of continents like Africa, outlying islands like Australia or New Zealand—are of necessity backward" in *Physics and Politics* (London: Kegan Paul, 1881 [1872]), 82–83.

5. See Ronald Meek, *Social Science and the Ignoble Savage* (Cambridge: Cambridge University Press, 1976), chapter 4; Alan Swingewood, "Origins of Sociology: The Case of the Scottish Enlightenment," *British Journal of Sociology* 21.2, 1970; Spadafora notes that Hume, Ferguson, and Dunbar outlined similar stages but did not envision progress in primarily economic terms: *The Idea of Progress in Eighteenth-Century Britain* (New Haven, CT: Yale University Press, 1990), 271–72.

6. Ronald Meek has proposed that Smith was the first in Scotland to develop a four-stages theory and that his account greatly influenced the other Scottish historians. While Dalrymple (in 1757) and Kames (in 1758) *published* versions of such a theory earlier than Smith (who first used stadial arguments in print in *Wealth of Nations* in 1776), Meek argues that they very likely based their own accounts on Smith's lectures (Meek, *Ignoble Savage*, 99–114). Meek emphasizes the similarities and chains of influence between Smith's theory and the others, rather than the differences I address here.

7. One of Smith's students later reported that Smith believed (and others agreed) that Robertson had "borrow'd the first vol. of his hist[or]y of Cha[rles] 5"—that is, his "View of the Progress of Society in Europe," his most theoretical account of historical development. Ross notes that Robertson "could have heard Smith lecture on law at Edinburgh" but was unlikely to have heard the Glasgow lectures. On Smith's apparent worries about the plagiarism of his ideas and his concern to establish the originality of his theory of development, see Ross, *The Life of Adam Smith* (Oxford: Clarendon Press, 1995), 105–6, and Meek, "Smith, Turgot, and the 'Four Stages' Theory," *History of Political Economy* 3, no. 1 (1971), reprinted in *Adam Smith: Critical Assessments IV*, ed. John Cunningham Wood (London: Croom Helm, 1983), 142–55, see specifically 147–49.

8. Henry Home, Lord Kames, *Elucidations Respecting the Common and Statute Law of Scotland* (Edinburgh: William Creech, 1777), 229; see Christopher J. Berry, *Social Theory of the Scottish Enlightenment* (Edinburgh: Edinburgh University Press, 1997), 98. In the *Sketches of the History of Man* (1774), Kames proposed a "sense of property" as an inherent human sense (along with congruity, symmetry, dignity, and grace) and argued that just as these senses

develop in individuals, the sense of property progresses "from its infancy among savages to its maturity among polished nations" (Edinburgh: William Creech, 1788) 116–17. As a polygenist who held that Amerindians probably constituted a separate species, Kames had a radically different view of human difference from those of most Scottish Enlightenment thinkers; belief in inherent biological differences among human groups was far rarer among British thinkers in this period than it was to become in the nineteenth century; see Nancy Stepan, *The Idea of Race in Science: Great Britain 1800–1960* (London: Macmillan, 1982), 29–35 and Roxann Wheeler, *The Complexion of Race: Categories of Difference in Eighteenth-Century British Culture* (Philadelphia: University of Pennsylvania Press, 2000).

9. For the phrase "history of the human mind," see Robertson: "In order to complete the history of the human mind, and attain to a perfect knowledge of its nature and operations, we must contemplate man in all those various situations wherein he has been placed"; *The History of America* (London: A. Strahan, 1803), vol. 2: 50.

10. Berry, *Social Theory*, 94. Gladys Bryson wrote that the "historical method [of the eighteenth century] is vitiated by a fundamental assumption . . . that the starting point for all humanistic study, including history, is man's nature, his psychology"; *Man and Society: The Scottish Inquiry of the Eighteenth Century* (Princeton: Princeton University Press, 1945), 109; also 142–44.

11. Robertson first published the *History of America* in 1777, eight years after publishing his *History of the Reign of the Emperor Charles V* (1769). For discussions of Robertson's views on empire and non-European societies see Jeffrey Smitten, "Impartiality in Robertson's *History of America*," *Eighteenth-Century Studies* 19, no. 1 (Autumn 1985), 56–77; Mark Duckworth, "An Eighteenth-Century Questionnaire: William Robertson on the Indians," *Eighteenth-Century Life* 11 (1987), 36–49; Karen O'Brien's excellent chapters on Robertson in *Narratives of Enlightenment: Cosmopolitan History from Voltaire to Gibbon* (Cambridge: Cambridge University Press, 1997); and the essays in Stewart J. Brown, ed., *William Robertson and the Expansion of Empire* (Cambridge: Cambridge University Press, 1997). Bruce Lenman's essay in that volume is particularly critical of Robertson's account of Amerindians and his "ferociously Eurocentric cosmopolitanism"; "From Savage to Scot," 201.

12. The 1759 review attributed to Robertson of Kames's *Historical Law-Tracts* (also 1759), which offers a brief account of the four stages of society, bears little trace of the cognitive-development model but sounds, instead, much more like Smith's approach in that it suggests development is a complex social phenomenon; and while Robertson remarks (as Smith does) that "wants, the desires, and the passions of men accustomed to such various forms of society" will differ greatly, he maintains that the laws of different stages are reasonable and appropriate to the mode of subsistence, not (as he argues in the *History of America*) that they result from cognitive limitations. See Robertson, *Miscellaneous Works and Commentaries*, ed. Jeffrey Smitten (London: Routledge, 1996), 96. The review was published anonymously in the *Critical Review*, vol. 7, April 1759; the editorial introduction to *Miscellaneous Works* argues for the attribution to Robertson.

13. *History of America* 2: 88–89. Ferguson, in contrast, applied the phrase "infant state" to societies and argued that the human species "has a progress as well as the individual," but he did not suggest that members of "rude" societies were themselves childlike or immature; *An Essay on the History of Civil Society* (Cambridge: Cambridge University Press, 1995 [1767]), 10, 74.

14. *History of America* 2: 85.

15. For a discussion of the influence of Locke's epistemology on Robertson and others, see Berry, *Social Theory*, 91–92.

16. *Essay Concerning Human Understanding*, ed. Peter H. Nidditch (Oxford: Clarendon Press, 1975 [1689]), I.ii.27. He added that "[t]heir Notions are few and narrow, borrowed only from those Objects, they have had most to do with, and which have made upon their Senses the frequentest and strongest Impressions."

17. Robertson, *History of America*, 2:88, also see Berry, *Social Theory*, 92.

18. "There are several people in America whose limited understandings seem not to be capable of forming an arrangement for futurity; neither their solicitude nor their foresight extend so far. They follow blindly the impulse of the appetite they feel, but are entirely

regardless of distant consequences, and even of those removed in the least degree from immediate apprehension"; *History of America*, 2: 90.

19. He writes, for instance, that information regarding religious rites is flawed and presented with "so little fidelity" because priests and missionaries have been best equipped to carry out this inquiry but are also apt to "accommodate [whatever they contemplate] to their own system"; *History of America*, 2: 189. Also see 2: 53–54.

20. *History of America*, 2: 90–91. He adds: "If in concerns the most interesting, and seemingly the most simple, the reason of man, while rude and destitute of culture, differs so little from the thoughtless levity of children, or the improvident instinct of animals, its exertions in other directions cannot be very considerable." Robertson cites the *Voyages* of Jean-Baptiste Labat (1663–1738) and James Adair's (ca. 1709–1783) *History of the American Indians*. Rousseau (though without attribution to Labat) had written similarly in his *Discourse on Inequality* of the Carib who "sells his cotton bed in the morning and comes weeping to buy it back in the evening" as evidence that the savage has "no idea of the future"; *The Discourses and Other Early Political Writings*, ed. Peter Gourevitch (Cambridge: Cambridge University Press, 1997), 143.

21. *History of America*, 2: 90.

22. "What, among polished nations, is called speculative reasoning or research, is altogether unknown in the rude state of society, and never becomes the occupation or amusement of the human faculties, until man be so far improved as to have secured, with certainty, the means of subsistence, as well as the possession of leisure and tranquillity"; *History of America*, 2: 89; also see 94. Smith had made a similar claim in his *History of Astronomy* (see *Essays on Philosophical Subjects*, ed. W. P. D. Wightman and J. C. Bryce [Indianapolis: Liberty Fund, 1982], 48–49), an early essay that Smith himself later characterized as a "fragment of an intended juvenile work" (in a 1773 letter to Hume); Ross, *Adam Smith*, 101.

23. The savage has "as little inclination as capacity for useless speculation" (*History of America*, 2: 94). Also see Robertson's treatment of religion in early societies: "when the faculties of the mind are so limited, as not to have formed abstract or general ideas . . . it is preposterous to expect that man should be capable of tracing with accuracy the relation between cause and effect, or to suppose that he should rise from the contemplation of the one to the knowledge of the other, and form just conceptions of a Deity, as the Creator and Governor of the universe" (*History of America*, 2: 192–93).

24. *History of America*, 2: 100.

25. *History of America*, 2: 56; also see 59–60. Robertson's order of inquiry follows the approach Kames had taken in the *Sketches of the History of Man* (1774), which began with the "Progress of men independent of society" (book I) before addressing the "Progress of men in society" (Book II) and then the "Progress of sciences" (book III). Compare Ferguson's insistence that "[m]ankind are to be taken in groups, as they have always subsisted. The history of the individual is but a detail of the sentiments and thoughts he has entertained in the view of his species: and every experiment relative to this subject should be made with entire societies, not with single men"; *Essay on the History of Civil Society*, 10.

26. *History of America*, 2: 97, 100.

27. *History of America*, 2: 226; The savage "pursues his own career, and indulges his own fancy, without inquiring or regarding whether what he does be agreeable or offensive to others."

28. *History of America*, 2: 224. Compare Smith's account of the adjudication of disputes in a "nation of hunters" as a social phenomenon: "The society consists of a few independent families, who live in the same village and speak the same language, and have agreed among themselves to keep together for mutual safety. But they have no authority over one another. The whole society interests itself in any offence. If possible they make it up between the parties, if not they banish from their society, kill, or deliver up to the resentment of the injured, him who has committed the crime"; LJ(B) 19; also see 27–28.

29. Stewart Brown suggests that Robertson "was growing in cultural sensitivity and toleration"; the India work, his last, was published in 1791, two years before his death; "Introduction" to *Robertson and the Expansion of Empire*, 6.

30. Geoffrey Carnall proposes based on manuscript evidence that "the appendix may have been written first, with the narrative as an afterthought"; Carnall, "Robertson and Contemporary Images of India," in Brown, ed., 211.

31. *An Historical Disquisition Concerning the Knowledge the Ancients Had of India* (London: 1804 [1792]), 201. Robertson credits the caste system with promoting both the abundance and high quality of India's manufactures and the "immutability in the manners of its inhabitants" (202).

32. Robertson remarks upon the complexity and sophistication of Indian jurisprudence (217), the magnificence and relative elegance of Indian architecture (220–21), "their genius in fine arts" including poetry and drama, which demonstrate their "polished manners and delicate sentiments" (231ff), and their achievements in science, logic and metaphysics, ethics, and astronomy and mathematics (240ff). As O'Brien writes, the account "does not escape the Eurocentrism of Robertson's earlier works," since he measures each of these achievements against a European standard; O'Brien, *Narratives of Enlightenment*, 165. While Robertson, a clergyman, is critical of Hindu religion, he presents it as characteristic of the theology of any "enlightened nation," in its mixture of ignorance and error: for "the limited powers of the human mind [are unable] to form an adequate idea of the perfections and operations of the Supreme Being." He warns that Christians are "extremely apt to err" in the judgment of religious opinions that "differ widely from our own"; *Disquisition*, 279, 269.

33. He argues, for instance, that because of the caste system, every Indian knows from birth "the station allotted to him" and so accommodates himself "with ease and pleasure" to his destined function.

34. James Mill's *History of British India* is, as Geoffrey Carnall has aptly noted, "a remorselessly detailed demolition of everything that Robertson claimed in the *Disquisition*," and Mill at several moments cites Robertson's arguments about rude nations in the *History of America* against his claims for Indian civilization in the *Disquisition*—"Robertson sober, as it were, contrasted with Robertson drunk"; Carnall, "Robertson and Contemporary Images of India," 221. Martti Koskenniemi's survey of international lawyers' views of non-European societies makes clear how widespread the stark dichotomy of barbarous versus civilized became in the nineteenth century; Koskenniemi, *Gentle Civilizer of Nations: The Rise and Fall of International Law 1870–1960* (Cambridge: Cambridge University Press, 2001), 103 ff.

35. Robertson, *Disquisition*, 285.

36. *History of America*, 2: 54–56. Bruce Lenman notes that Robertson was one of the few Scottish historians to be well acquainted with the Spanish sources, most of them relying heavily on French sources, especially Lafitau and Charlevoix; Lenman, "From Savage to Scot," 198.

37. *History of America*, 2: 53–54. Jeffrey Smitten maintains that despite Robertson's often denigrating portrait of Amerindians, even Book IV of the *History of America*, like Book VII comparing the Mexican and Peruvian empires and Robertson's treatment of the Spanish, lived up to Robertson's "long-standing commitment to impartiality," in that Robertson alludes to some (few) virtues of savage life and resists "closure of final judgment"; Smitten, "Impartiality in Robertson," 57–59. But Robertson's use of sources on Amerindians is perhaps more tendentious than Smitten's article suggests; Robertson draws on evidence from Charlevoix, for instance, to support a far more dismissive portrait than Charlevoix's own (and compare Smith's use of Charlevoix in the *Lectures on Jurisprudence*, ed. R. L. Meek, D. D. Raphael, and P. G. Stein (Indianapolis: Liberty Fund, 1982), LJ(A) i.47 and ii.96.

38. Lenman, "From Savage to Scot," 205–7. Lenman adds: "there was only one way forward for North American Indians. It was a path of unconditional assimilation conceived as stadial progression, and if they did not take it the fault was theirs" (209).

39. Adam Ferguson, though far more admiring of the virtues and values of earlier stages of society, and more critical of "civilized" mores, than others such as Robertson or Kames, also shared aspects of the cognitive-development approach. We thus find a distinctive sort of ambivalence in Ferguson: more than Smith or Dunbar he regarded social development as linked to developments at the level of the individual mind, so that he argued, for instance, that native Americans, though "able masters in the detail of their own affairs . . . study no science, and go in pursuit of no general principles. They even seem incapable of attending to any distant consequences" beyond those they have directly experienced (*Essay*, 88). But he also praised the

"savage" for having "a penetration, a force of imagination and elocution, an ardour of mind, an affection and courage, which the arts, the discipline, and the policy of few nations would be able to improve" (76). Also, in contrast to so many of those working with cognitive-development assumptions, Ferguson was attentive to the pitfalls of cross-cultural observation and judgment, and he warned against the tendency to suppose ourselves the standard of "politeness and civilization" and to assume that our very partial information about other societies (or our own past) can enable us to fill out a reliable portrait of them.

40. For the view that Smith's theory was, like others, a theory of cognitive development, see Berry, *Social Theory*, 96–98; Nicholas Phillipson, similarly, claims that Smith's "was a theory which showed that people who lived in civilisations different from our own not only possessed different manners and opinions but different minds and different selves"; Phillipson, "Providence and Progress," in Brown, ed., 59. J. G. A. Pocock has argued that Smith's "narrative shows the mind as itself developing"; *Barbarism and Religion*, II.315.

41. III.2, in *Essays on Philosophical Subjects*, 49. Rousseau argued in the *Second Discourse* that savages "did not even dream of vengeance except perhaps mechanically and on the spot like the dog that bites the stone thrown at him"; *Discourses*, ed. Gourevitch, 154.

42. *Theory of Moral Sentiments*, ed. D. D. Raphael and A. L. Macfie (Indianapolis: Liberty Fund, 1984), II.iii.1.1.

43. Note, however, that particular word choices in the *Lectures on Jurisprudence* do not have the definitive character they might in published works.

44. LJ(A) i.36–44; after "applying" the method of the impartial spectator "to the case of hunters," Smith concludes: "In this age of society therefore property would extend no farther than possession" (44).

45. LJ(A) i.47. Smith argues that the nomadism of hunting societies naturally leads them to recognize property in only the things one has "about one's person."

46. LJ(A) i.47. The much briefer treatment at LJ(B) 150 sounds more like cognitive-development accounts: "Among savages property begins and ends with possession, and they seem scarce to have any idea of any thing as their own which is not about their bodies." It is impossible to know how close the language here came to Smith's lecture, but the differences between this and the LJ(A) passage suggest that to read it as a description of savages' cognitive limitations may be misleading. It is worth noting that in the LJ(B) passage, too, Smith suggests that members of hunting societies use a spectator method to arrive at their notion of legitimate possession.

47. Among those conditions are that "the intention of the promiser [must] be expressed so clearly that no impartial spectator can be in doubt about the content of the agreement" and that "the things that are the subject of the agreement must also be considered of significant value" LJ(A) ii.62.

48. LJ(B) 175; also see LJ(A) ii.56 ff., Peter Stein, *Legal Evolution: The Story of an Idea* (Cambridge: Cambridge University Press, 1980), 39–40. Knud Haakonssen notes that this understanding of promises "brings out very clearly a basic feature of Smith's moral philosophy, namely, that it is about the *relations* between persons"; *The Science of a Legislator: The Natural Jurisprudence of David Hume and Adam Smith* (Cambridge: Cambridge University Press, 1981), 112–14.

49. Smith notes as well that language in its early stages (indeed until very late in the development of society) is too imprecise to engender such certainty on the part of the recipient of a promise that a breach would be actionable. Smith's point about language is not that savages cannot think abstractly, but rather that they have not yet developed the terms in which to express commitment beyond a reasonable doubt.

50. LJ(A) ii.62.

51. He offers as an example rituals of "stipulation" or "solemnities" such as the Armenian custom, reported by Tacitus, in which parties to an agreement suck a bit of blood from one another's thumbs; Smith suggests that even such "horrid ceremonies," rather than illustrating the "fear and terror" or superstition of the people, make sense as a means of establishing certainty and thus obligation at a time when language alone cannot do so (LJ[A] ii.70).

52. Mill, "A Few Words on Non-Intervention," CW 21:118.

53. We should note that Smith uses the term "humanity" in two distinct ways: sometimes it seems to serve as a category of general morality, as when he calls infanticide "so dreadful a violation of humanity"; more often, however, the term has the less universal connotation of gentleness or "sensibility"; see TMS V.2.15 and V.2.13.

54. TMS V.2.13. Smith's faith in the uniformity and basic rectitude of human nature led him to believe that however misguided particular practices might be, people of all societies were able and generally likely to make decent moral decisions. He contrasts systems of natural philosophy, which ordinary people may be unequipped to judge and which therefore may persist without "any sort of resemblance to the truth," with systems of moral philosophy, which must soon perish if too far from the truth; see TMS VII.ii.4.14.

55. Compare Robertson's more judgmental and character-based assessment of the supposed tendency of savage societies to kill elderly members: "incapable of attending to the wants or weaknesses of others, their impatience under an additional burden prompts them to extinguish that life which they find it difficult to sustain"; *History of America*, 2: 220.

56. In producing opulence and leisure, commercial society allows greater concern for the welfare of others than is possible in poorer and rougher societies; it promotes the establishment and continual refinement of rules of social engagement; and it is most hospitable to the development of what Smith called natural justice; see TMS V.2.9 and II.ii.1.5.

57. TMS V.2.7.

58. WN IV.vii.c.80.

59. Dunbar (1742–1798) was a regent at King's College, Aberdeen from 1765 to 1794; *Essays on the history of mankind in rude and cultivated ages* was published in a very slightly revised edition of 1781, the edition cited here (in reprint: Christopher J. Berry, ed. [Bristol: Thoemmes, 1995]). For a brief biography see Berry, "James Dunbar and the American War of Independence," *Aberdeen University Review* 45 (1974), 255–66.

60. Both Bryson and Meek dismiss Dunbar's *Essays* in just a few sentences; Bryson, *Man and Society*, 80–81; Meek, *Ignoble Savage*, 190–91. Christopher Berry, the foremost expert on Dunbar's thought, mentions in passing Dunbar's critique of Europeans' treatment of New World peoples in his introduction to the *Essays*; his unpublished dissertation emphasizes the distinctiveness of Dunbar's account of social stages, rooted in the development of language rather than of property.

61. Dunbar, partly because of his interest in the origin of language and his positing of a pre-linguistic stage of human history, tended to emphasize the similarities among all currently known human societies and their shared state of great advancement beyond the earliest stage. Thinkers who posited hunting societies such as native Americans as the earliest stage tended, by contrast, to emphasize the distance between hunting and commercial societies rather than their shared features of imagination and culture. On Dunbar's views about language, see Berry, "Dunbar and the Enlightenment Debate on Language," in *Aberdeen and the Enlightenment* (Aberdeen: Aberdeen University Press, 1987), 241–50.

62. "The springs of ingenuity are put into motion. . . . The acquisitions of industry, or invention, confer a right which suggests the idea of property; and the distinctions of natural talents lay a foundation for corresponding distinctions in society"; *Essays*, 31.

63. *Essays*, 154–55. Christopher Berry has criticized older readings of Dunbar as a primitivist: see his "Introduction" to Dunbar's *Essays*, page xiv. Berry himself notes the "primitivist tenor" of moments in the *Essays* and emphasizes Dunbar's "wistfulness" about a purity in both language and morals that preceded the age of refinement but insists that Dunbar saw cultivated society as "in the last analysis superior"; *James Dunbar: A Study of His Thought and of His Contribution to and Place in the Scottish Enlightenment*, (PhD diss., London School of Economics, 1971), 199–203.

64. The question whether progress in arts and sciences entails moral progress is not central to his enterprise as it is to Rousseau's, but in a Rousseauian vein he writes, for instance, that while the "inventions and improvements" thus introduced do "honour to our nature," "it may be questioned, whether the enlargement of our faculties, and all the advantages from arts, counterbalance the feuds and animosities which they soon introduced into the world" (*Essays*, 32).

65. Dunbar was similarly alert to linguistic distortions when, arguing that the relation of metropole to colony should be one of "perfect equality," he wrote that "the terms which denote

parental and filial relation . . . are metaphors extremely liable to abuse. The one country is no more the mother than the daughter"; see Berry, "American War," 261, quoting Dunbar's *De Primordiis Civitatus oratio in qua agitur de Bello Civili inter M. Britannium et Colonias nunc flagrante* (London, Strahan: 1779).

66. *Essays*, 151–52.

67. Thus "the truest politeness of mind may be found among nations to whom these [vulgar and commercial] arts are almost totally unknown"; Smith, for whom commercial society underpins polite manners, would not go so far.

68. Dunbar and Tucker engaged in mutual recriminations over these claims. Dunbar added in a later edition: "When the benevolence of this writer is exalted into charity, when the spirit of his religion corrects the rancour of his philosophy, he will learn a little more reverence for the system to which he belongs, and acknowledge, in the most untutored tribes, some glimmerings of humanity, and some decisive indications of a moral nature" (see the Dublin edition of 1782: Essay V, note H, 135).

69. Dunbar, like Smith, did not regard individuals in early-stage societies as themselves mentally immature; in a rare instance of such a comparison he wrote that the Tahitian Omiah was as "circumscribed as a child in the number of his ideas," noting that Omiah combined his limited ideas to approximate unfamiliar concepts, calling a butler "king of the bottles." But Dunbar also insisted that Omiah was "in understanding and in years a man"; Essay II, note E, 110.

70. Dunbar seems to follow Smith in his discussion of the variability of standards and practices of human beauty, treating, like Smith, ideas among different races, and bodily deformation including Chinese foot-binding and European corsets. Though Dunbar does not mention Smith in this section, elsewhere he praises *Theory of Moral Sentiments* and cites it at length; see, for instance, Essay II, notes A and G (the latter citing Smith's "Considerations concerning the first formation of language," which was first published as an appendix to the third edition (1767) of TMS; see Berry, "Smith's *Considerations*."

71. *Essays*, 380.

72. Dunbar does remark that in Africa, "the art of disfiguring the human person, is almost the only art which has made such progress among the rude inhabitants, as to mark their departure from a state of nature" (384).

73. Dunbar, 390–91.

74. *Essays*, 384.

75. Dunbar suggests that moral comparisons of different stages of society—"running the parallel of public manners in different periods of civil progress"—are pointless (391).

76. *Essays*, 161–62. Dunbar later observes that "cultivated and polished" nations often behave exactly like aristocrats toward their "supposed inferiors": "Both carry themselves with equal insolence, and seem alike to forget or to deny the inherent and unalienable rights of the species" (439).

77. For an argument that the scope of the law of nations was too narrow from the eighteenth to the nineteenth century, see C. H. Alexandrowicz, *Introduction to the History of the Law of Nations in the East Indies* (Oxford: Clarendon Press, 1967); also see Pitts, "Boundaries of Victorian International Law," in Duncan Bell, ed. *Victorian Visions of Global Order* (Cambridge: Cambridge University Press, 2007), 67–88.

78. "[T]he diffusion of knowledge gradually tends to reduce mankind more nearly to a level in the enterprizes of peace and war" (317). He adds that the "fall of Europe will mark, perhaps, at some future aera, the enterprize of the species at large," or, perhaps, that Europe will only lose its relative political advantage while both Europe and the rest of the world gain in well-being in absolute terms.

79. On Raynal's and Diderot's ambivalence about global commerce, see Sankar Muthu's essay in this volume. Dunbar cites Raynal elsewhere in his essays.

80. *Essays*, 176.

81. Dunbar declines to "decide on [the] comparative perfections" of nations at different stages of development: "The manners, the crimes of illiterate savage tribes, are apt enough to appear to us in their full dimension and deformity; but the violations of natural law among

civilized nations have a solemn varnish of policy, which disguises the enormity of guilt"; Dunbar, 453.

82. I have discussed this broader shift in *A Turn to Empire*, where I treat the thought of James and J. S. Mill at greater length.

83. Duncan Forbes too closely associated James Mill's argument with that of all Scottish philosophical history of earlier generations, arguing that Mill was "wholly in the tradition of the philosophical history of the eighteenth century," and that "Mill's approach to India was unsympathetic not simply because he was a disciple of Bentham, but because he brought with him from Scotland a conception of progress which was lacking in Bentham's thought"; Forbes, "James Mill and India," 23–24. In contrast, Knud Haakonssen has rightly distinguished Mill from the pluralist approaches of Smith and Millar and observed that a key difference is Mill's recourse to the action of individuals to explain historical change, and his lack of any "theoretical conception of social and institutional change"; "James Mill and Scottish Moral Philosophy."

84. For Mill, all non-Europeans, from South Sea islanders to the peoples of the Chinese empire, were essentially "rude" or "barbarous," whatever might be said about their particular means of subsistence, forms of government, or arts and practices. He wrote as if every aspect of these cultures that might show them to be inferior to European civilization was telling (such as the supposed lack of taste in the shapes of Chinese vases), whereas anything that might suggest refinement was either trivial or misleading. To claims for the beauty of Chinese porcelain, he responded that their lack of refinement in glass-making, so similar to porcelain, only proved their incapacity to innovate; to the idea that they had invented the printing press, he replied, "what an abuse of terms! Because the Chinese cut out words on blocks of wood, and sometimes, for particular purposes, stamp them on paper." "Review of De Guignes. *Voyages à Peking, Manille, et l'Ile de France, faits dans l'intervalle des années 1784 à 1804.*" *Edinburgh Review* 14 (July 1809): 407–29 at 425, 427.

85. H. H. Wilson, editor of several editions (with harshly critical footnotes) of the *History*, attributed the "harsh and illiberal spirit" of civil servants in India to the influence of Mill's work; see Majeed, *Ungoverned Imaginings*, 129. Also see Makdisi, *Romantic Imperialism*; and Thomas, *Philosophic Radicals*, 98–119, which astutely points out the "puritanism" of Mill's interpretation of India, as well as his reliance on missionary sources for "detailed accounts the grosser customs of a people he had placed so low in his scale of civilization" (108). Uday Mehta has aptly noted that "Mill's views regarding India, its past and its present" were "pathetically foolish in their lack of nuance"; *Liberalism and Empire*, 90. J. H. Burns offers a concise and often searing critique of James Mill's method and judgments; he concludes that "the almost blood-curdling arrogance of Mill's cultural chauvinism" is unredeemed by either felicity of language or "any clearly articulated method"; Burns, "The Light of Reason," 18.

86. James Mill's unusual and extreme animus against everything Indian cannot, indeed, be attributed to any single sociological commitment, but his adherence to the idea of cognitive development plays an important role in his articulation of the causes and symptoms of Indian backwardness.

87. "Among children, and among rude people, little accustomed to take their decisions upon full and mature consideration, nothing is more common than to repent of their bargains, and wish to revoke them" (*History* I.161).

88. In his 1809 article about China, Mill allied himself with the work of Millar, and yet, characteristically, he transformed a theory of multiple stages of historical development into a dichotomous and judgmental gauge of progress. Mill writes, "Since the philosophical inquiry into the condition of the weaker sex, in the different stages of society, published by Millar, it has been universally considered as an infallible criterion of barbarous society, to find the women in a state of great degradation"; he goes on to claim that the Chinese treatment of women demonstrates that China is on a par with "savages." "Review of de Guignes," 428.

89. "Affairs of India," 147–48. Similar examples abound in the *History of British India*, where Mill describes the "suspicious tempers and narrow views of a rude period" (I.145) and "the ignorant and depraved people, of whose depravity we have so many proofs" (V. 449). "The Hindus have, through all the ages, remained in a state of society too near the simplicity

and rudeness of the most ancient times, to have stretched their ideas of property so far" (I.173). Also see I. 192–93, I. 232, II. 147.

90. "With no sanction of reason could anything better be expected than that which was in reality produced; a disorderly compilation of loose, vague, stupid, or unintelligible quotations and maxims, selected arbitrarily . . . attended with a commentary, which only adds to the mass of absurdity and darkness: a farrago, by which nothing is defined, nothing established." *History* V. 426.

91. *History*, II.105. Javed Majeed has aptly noted that Mill's tone of definitiveness—his "pseudo-deductive style of argument which stresses the certainty of conclusions derived from unassailable premises" owed as much to Mill's puritanical spirit as to his utilitarianism (Majeed, *Ungoverned Imaginings*, 186–87).

92. *Works of Jeremy Bentham*, John Bowring, ed., Edinburgh and London, 1843, I, 180–81. I have discussed some of James and J. S. Mill's differences from Bentham on the subjects of empire and development, and the latter's rather tendentious characterization of Bentham's thought, in *A Turn to Empire* (Princeton: Princeton University Press, 2005).

93. The younger Mill wrote that Bentham "thought it an insolent piece of dogmatism in one person to praise or condemn another in a matter of taste: as if men's likings and dislikings, on things in themselves indifferent, were not full of the most important inferences as to every point of their character"; "Bentham," CW X.113.

94. See Ball, "Introduction" to James Mill, *Political Writings*, xiv.

95. "Civilization" (1836), CW XVIII.120.

96. "Civilization," CW CVIII.122.

97. "Civilization," CW XVIII.122. The "ignorant labourer" in a "rude state of society" cooperates with no one outside his family; such people learn the "practical lesson of submitting themselves to guidance" in order to acquire "habits of discipline" (123–24).

98. "Civilization," CW XVIII.122–23.

99. "Civilization," CW XVIII.123.

100. Alexander Brady, for instance, remarks in his introduction to the volume of Mill's essays on politics and society that "whatever its deficiency" as anthropology, Mill's definitions of civilized and savage life "in no way hampered Mill in discussing that in which he was principally interested—certain aspects of contemporary Britain on which he had strong opinions" (CW XVIII.xxv).

101. CW XXI.118. In "Civilization," Mill argued similarly that the answers to the "great questions in government . . . vary indefinitely, according to the degree and kind of civilization and cultivation already attained by a people, and their peculiar aptitudes for receiving more" (CW X.106).

102. "Non-intervention," CW XXI.119. Mill adds, "Nations which are still barbarous have not got beyond the period during which it is likely to be for their benefit that they should be conquered and held in subjection by foreigners."

103. *On Liberty*, CW XVIII.224.

104. *On Liberty*, CW XVIII.224. Also see *Considerations on Representative Government*; CW XIX. 567. Uday Mehta has argued that liberal universalism, notably in Locke and Mill, distinguishes "between anthropological capacities and the necessary conditions for their actualization": while the capacities are acknowledged to be universal, various peoples are politically disenfranchised as not being in a position to realize those capacities; Mehta, *Liberalism and Empire*, 47.

105. Martti Koskenniemi's discussion of international lawyers' views on empire shows how commonly claims about backward peoples' immaturity or lack of certain legal concepts were used in the nineteenth century to justify their exclusion from the ordinary standards of international law. John Westlake, for instance, argued in 1891 that sovereignty could not be attributed to African chiefs, nor could they transfer sovereignty, because they lacked the concept; in 1894, he wrote that "[I]nternational law has to treat natives as uncivilised." Joseph Hornung wrote of "barbarians": "They are children, of course, but then, let us treat them as one treats children, through gentleness and persuasion." Westlake, "Le conflit Anglo-Portugais" (1891) and *Chapters on the principles of international law* (1894); Joseph Hornung, "Civilisés et barbares" (Part 4, 1886), cited by Koskenniemi, *Gentle Civilizer*, 127 and 130; see also chapter 2 throughout.

106. A similar case could be made for Adam Ferguson's writings.

Chapter Three

Under Negotiation: Empowering Treaty Constitutionalism

Vicki Hsueh[1]

A treaty is more than just a transient agreement to exchange a few furs for European trade goods . . . through dialogic interaction, the sharing of sufferings, the clearing of barriers to communication, the reciprocal exchanges of gifts and goodwill, and the mutualization of interests and resources, different peoples could attain one mind, and link arms together.

—Robert Williams, *Linking Arms Together*

Negotiation is impure.

—Jacques Derrida, *Negotiations*

I. INTRODUCTION

The history of treaty-making between English colonies and indigenous tribes and nations in the Americas during the seventeenth and eighteenth centuries has spurred new and important thinking in political theory about the modes by which cultural difference can be adjudicated in the wake of colonialism. Among the most notable of recent interventions are the works of James Tully, Iris Marion Young, and Robert Williams.[2] Tully, for example, looks to the treaties established between agents of the Crown and Aboriginal nations from the 1630s up until 1832, drawing out three conventions of constitutionalism—mutual recognition, continuity, and consent—that arose out of treaty practices of "dialogue and mediation."[3] Williams likewise emphasizes, as in the opening epigraph, the spirit of reciprocity, sharing, and connection set in motion by Iroquois treaty rituals of condolence and gift-giving.[4] And, in one of the most expansive conceptions, Young takes inspiration from the seventeenth- and eighteenth-century treaty relations between mid-Atlantic indigenous tribes and English settlers, where "each regarded the other as distinct political formations," to propose a decentered, diverse, democratic federalism guided by principles of relationality and dialogue.[5]

Taken collectively, these works bring much-needed attention to dimensions of colonialism and constitutionalism that have been long overlooked. Although many have emphasized the forms of political conquest and territorial domination established by the English settlement of the Americas, few theorists have attended to the cross-cultural modes of interaction and adjudication that also developed in the period. In particular, although each looks at slightly different moments in the seventeenth- and eighteenth-century history of colonial-indigenous treaties (i.e., both Williams and Tully focus on the treaties established by the Iroquois confederacy, or Haudenosaunee, during and after the Encounter Era, while Young primarily focuses on late seventeenth- and early eighteenth-century treaties established in the mid-Atlantic region), all three emphasize that treaties are conducted through distinctive cross-cultural forms of adjudication, such as dialogue, accommodation, and consent. These conventions, as Tully explains, represent options that have been hidden, indeed at times suppressed, by the language of an imperial "modern constitutionalism," which justified European conquest of the Americas in either assimilating or excluding cultural difference.[6] While not always free from domination and violence, the history of treaty practices built upon dialogue and negotiation can generate new models of cultural adjudication that, as Young further clarifies, are capable of "affirming colonial North America as a terrain of interaction, constructing American subjectivity as ambiguous, and fashioning a relational understanding of government jurisdictions."[7]

This essay looks to further extend and develop contemporary understandings of treaty constitutionalism, and it does so by taking as its point of departure the treaties negotiated between the proprietor of the colony of Pennsylvania, William Penn, and various Lenni Lenape and Susquehannocks tribes in and around the Delaware territories during the 1680s and 1690s. In part, my focus on these treaties is intended as a historical addition to contemporary accounts (Tully and Williams primarily focus on the treaties conducted by the Iroquois confederacy; Young cites Penn's colony as an exemplary case through which to reconsider how negotiation and dialogue shaped multicultural relations). The treaties that I examine here look to bridge contemporary works by offering examples that address and also go beyond the covenant chain.

Pertinently, the treaties negotiated between Penn and the Lenape and Susquehannocks provide suggestive historical material for a conceptual expansion of treaty constitutionalism—one in which power plays both a more prominent and a more dynamic role than depicted in contemporary accounts. While Tully, Williams, and Young have been highly attuned to the ways in which treaties negotiate political diversity and cultural difference, they have also tended to insulate treaty constitutionalism from certain elements of power, most especially inequality on the ground and aspects of aggression and conflict. To a degree, this happens for heuristic reasons. Tully sets aside the "vast inequalities of wealth and power" between colonists and native peoples in order to better isolate the conceptual features of treaty constitutionalism, while Young depicts treaty negotiations as a process of "widespread cooperation" which can be contrasted to the eruptions of "conflict between Indians and colonists."[8] Indeed, as Young aptly states, "I do not wish to romanticise the relations among native peoples of this period, or between the native peoples and the European-descended settlers. . . . The point is only to find in the past grounds for bracketing ossified assumptions about jurisdiction, governance and the relation of self-determining people."[9]

But for Tully, Young, and Williams, there is also an essential political investment in depicting treaty constitutionalism as a contrast to inequality and conflict. That is, although each pursues slightly different conceptual projects, they share the view that treaty constitutionalism is a means to combat the forms of domination and exploitation that arise in the colonial context: treaty constitutionalism comes to be a viable model of adjudication precisely because it does not create a chronic relation of oppression between colonizer and colonized. As Williams indicates in the opening epigraph, "[A] continuing bond of trust and solidarity" is established by the agreement "to link arms" in a multicultural treaty relationship.[10]

Yet, as I will argue in this chapter, while contemporary accounts have focused on both the extreme forms of oppression that treaty constitutionalism opposes and the features of trust and solidarity fostered by treaty relations, they have not directly tackled what might be seen as the *middle register* of treaty constitutionalism—where treaty negotiations allow for the expression, circulation, and production of various forms of power. As I will illustrate, through a reading of the treaties conducted between Penn and the Lenape and Susquehannocks, this middle register enables diverse groups to negotiate various cross-cultural interests and relations, but it also may be shaded by various risks and elements of exclusion, opportunism, and indeterminacy.

A closer examination of power may allow us to more fully address the context of cultural and political diversity in which treaty constitutionalism comes to be relevant. For example, treaty participants—such as Penn, English settlers in Pennsylvania, non-Iroquois tribes such as the Lenape, and Iroquois-speaking Susquehannocks—were situated in a context of overlapping jurisdictions and authorities, and they possessed different and continually changing resources, opportunities, and interests. As a result of these conditions on the ground, treaty constitutionalism enabled *multiple* forms of power not only to be facilitated but to be extended and even, at times, reproduced.[11]

Most notably, Penn, who faced challenges by the Crown, Pennsylvania colonists, and other English proprietary governments over territory and trade in the Delaware territory, turned to treaties to supplement a curtailed proprietary authority. Both expansionary and protective, the treaties, from Penn's perspective, facilitated a *monopolistic power* that increased his control over the means to make peace, extended his relations with local Lenape and Susquehannock tribes, and produced deeds to land that reserved possession, not to the Pennsylvania colony or to England, but to Penn alone. By contrast, treaty practices, when viewed from the vantage point of the Lenape and Susquehannock tribes, help to illustrate two versions of a *decentralized power*. As the historians Francis Jennings, Thomas Sugrue, James Merrell, and Daniel Richter have noted, the Lenape and the Susquehannocks treaties were a way not simply to pacify relations with Europeans, but also to create zones of protection independent of Iroquois authority.[12] Meanwhile, Penn and the Lenape and Susquehannocks all relied upon the *relational power* of treaty interpreters and "go-betweens," who possessed cross-cultural knowledge of colonial and indigenous languages, protocols, and customs. This information was certainly necessary to facilitate communication and exchange between colonists and indigenes but they also were, at least in practice, often not sufficient to ensure on-going concord and trust. To be clear, my account here is a historicized one and thus is quite particular in its detail and focus. I would not argue that the treaties negotiated between Penn and the Lenape and Susquehannocks could or should stand as representative for all forms of treaty constitutionalism. But my account does provide a detailed portrait of a moment in a wayward genealogy of treaty practice, offering features and aspects that might usefully either be paralleled or contrasted with contemporary enactments.[13]

As I will argue by way of conclusion, the late seventeenth-century treaties between English colonists and indigenous tribes in the Delaware territories, illuminate elements of power—especially features of protectionism, influence, and exclusion—that help deepen our understanding of both the possibilities and limitations of treaty constitutionalism.[14]

II. TREATY NEGOTIATION AS MONOPOLISTIC POWER

The treaties negotiated between the seventeenth-century proprietor of the colony of Pennsylvania, William Penn, and various Lenape and Susquehannock tribes have long stood as iconic images of cultural accommodation. Memorialized in Benjamin West's famous nineteenth-century portrait of the treaties at Shackamaxon, Penn, in particular, has been depicted in myth-historical terms as amicable: "Onas" ("Brother") to indigenous peoples, "shaking hands with some Indian or, seated beneath a tree on a sunny day, passing the native a peace pipe across a cheerful fire."[15] "Penn's 'Holy Experiment,'" the historian Thomas Sugrue notes, "has been continually depicted as a representation of the possibility, however fleeting, of harmony between the European colonists and the North American Indians."[16] However, recent studies by Sugrue, James Merrell, Daniel Richter, and others have challenged and substantially adjusted the romantic image of William Penn as selfless partner to the Delaware tribes. Once treated as a noble exception in the history of English conquest and acquisition, Penn has recently come to appear as a much more complex figure with, at times, contrary moral, religious, economic, and political attachments.

Penn's interest in treaty negotiation exemplifies this complexity: treaties served as a supplement to Penn's curtailed proprietary power and were used by him to consolidate territorial, economic, and moral authority. Penn's early advertisements described Pennsylvania as the "seed of a nation" blessed by both God and Charles II—a nation, as one of the colony's most popular advertisements claimed, "begun and nourished by the care of wise and populous countries, as conceiving them best for the increase of human stock and beneficial for commerce."[17] At founding, however, this "increase of human stock" was far from harmonious. Penn had, even before the colony's charter had been officially granted in 1681, promised thousands of acres of land to prospective colonists and "First Purchasers." Furthermore, Penn advertised in his 1681 promotional account of the colony that such parcels were to be "free from any Indian incumbrance."[18]

Yet, in the early years of the colony, Penn struggled to offer the land he had promised so freely. While many of the members of Penn's private business association, the Free Society of Traders, were granted the desirable lots near Philadelphia, settlers who had given Penn payment for lots on the Schuykill River or near Philadelphia found themselves saddled with smaller plots far off the river or in the dense woods of the Delaware Valley with Swedes, Dutch, and Finnish settlers.[19] Unsurprisingly, many of the first settlers were upset about the plots of land they received. As surveyor, Thomas Holme, wrote to Penn in November of 1683, "I finde it may be requisite for thy affaire in the concernes of this City (where many people may (probably) come, more then formerly expected) to reduce the breadth of the high street lotts . . . & yet leave sufficient room, to make way for new purchasers amongst them to some content, to prevent being placed backward, of which many are unwilling."[20]

Compounding his promise to deliver land lots discharged of native title, Penn needed to negotiate the myriad interests of a new colony whose size and population vastly exceeded those of previous English settlements, and this enlarged founding population posed new theoretical and practical problems of governance. Between the years 1681–1682, more than twenty-three ships sailed to Pennsylvania, and even in the first year of the colony's founding, nearly 2,000 colonists of English, Welsh, Scottish, Irish, German, and French Huguenot origin were settled in the territory—with more than four times as many to move to the colony within the first five years. Penn needed not only to harmonize relations among the new colonists but to *insert* these diverse newcomers within a territory already inhabited by various local tribes, such as the Lenape and Susquehannocks, and also by Swedish and Finnish settlers, who had remained in the territory following the decline of the New Sweden settlement.[21]

Above all, the task of governance was affected by a significant political shift (namely, that Charles II and the Committee of Trade and Plantations had severely curtailed the proprietary privileges granted to Penn). Rather than a grant that referenced the expansive privileges of the "Palatin of Durham" as he initially favored, Penn ultimately was granted the status of a proprietor, "as of our Castle of Windsor, in our County of Berks, in free and common socage, by fealty only, for all services, and not *in capite*, or by knights service."[22] What this meant, more simply, was that although Penn was granted the privilege to settle and sell lands in the area between Maryland and New York and also the power to draft a constitution for the colony, he did not possess the power to issue hereditary titles, pardon treason or murder, establish churches, or engage in unrestricted war or trade.[23] Penn thus faced the challenge of managing a diverse religious, ethnic, and economic population without the resources to definitively settle arguments relating to trade, faith, or crime.

The restriction on Penn's proprietary privileges marks a critical turning point in English colonialism and in the forms of governance used by English settlements. For much of the early and middle seventeenth century, the proprietary model of English settlement in the Americas was widespread. Partly commercial and partly private, the proprietary model was especially useful, as the historian Christopher Tomlins notes, in allowing the Crown to expand colonial reaches with relatively limited outlay of funds and military support. For much of the early modern period, the most influential examples of proprietary settlement, such as Maryland and Carolina, were styled as palatinates—frontier marshlands facing unforeseen challenges and equipped in kind with a wide range of political, military, economic, and religious privileges. Although these colonies often lacked the arms and funds to execute outright conquest and assimilation, they settled territories by using alternative strategies of negotiation with neighboring European settlements, indigenous tribes and nations in order to gain a foothold in trade and settlement within occupied ground. Yet, by the end of the century, the "proprietorial design for English colonization was fast being eclipsed by the expanding

English state," as Tomlins has argued, and Penn's restricted powers as proprietor represented the Crown's greater interest in consolidating and nationalizing colonial enterprise.[24]

Treaties offered Penn a pivotal way to pursue an informal, yet monopolistic power that could service both expansionary and defensive interests, even though his proprietary capabilities had been restricted. Contrary to conventional understanding, Penn's practice of treaty-making was not unique or particularly enlightened, but rather a policy long practiced by other British and European settlements, who sought to extinguish Indian land claims by purchase. Yet in a curious twist, Penn's turn to treaty practices of "correspondence," "dialogue," and "negotiation" were as much attempts to circumvent the restrictions of the Crown as they were attempts to consolidate power and influence in contested indigenous ground. Set within rivalries over land and borders, Penn's treaty negotiations with the Lenni Lenape and Iroquois-speaking Susquehannocks served as a means, unrestricted by the charter, to establish better control of land that remained ambiguous in the terms of the charter, particularly to the south on the Maryland border and to the north and west along the Delaware.[25]

In the south, Penn sought to secure his claim to land, which was threatened by agents of Maryland, who alternately intimidated or bribed Pennsylvania settlers to abandon their loyalty to Penn.[26] Meanwhile, to the north and west, Penn needed to challenge previous alliances and agreement made by the Lenape and Susquehannocks with European settlers. Since the 1620s, Swedish and Finnish settlers had established extensive trade and exchange relationships with Susquehannocks and Lenape, according to ethnographers Terry Jordan and Matti Kaups, "and produced a mixed backwoods culture that later pioneers carried to large areas of America."[27] Lenape tribes such as the Siconese (also known as the Sickoneysincks and Ciconicins), had established agreements with representatives of the New Netherlands for territories on Delaware Bay and Swanendale in 1629 and 1630.[28] From the 1640s until the collapse of New Sweden, Swedish and Finnish settlers purchased land and established trade relationship with Susquehannocks and Lenape tribes. "New Sweden's masterstroke," notes historian Karen Kupperman, "was to take up an intermediary role in the vital trade between Europeans and Indians."[29] By learning indigenous languages, practices, and customs, Swedish setters facilitated trade between Indians and other Europeans, such as the Dutch and English to the north. As Kupperman reflects, "[s]haring one major advantage—location—the Swedes and Indians made up for their drawbacks: lack of support from Sweden and the Susquehannocks' fear of interference by the powerful Iroquois League to the north."[30] Even after the official seizure of New Sweden by the Dutch, Swedish and Finnish settlers continued to reside in settlements on the Delaware River and Bay, maintaining their fur and crop trade with various Delaware tribes.[31]

Treaties thus allowed Penn to claim, in public and against the counter-claims of Maryland and the previous Delawarean settlers, his legitimate authority over the ambiguous borders.[32] In the early years of the colony's settlement, Penn had been detained in England negotiating territorial claims with the Duke of York and he sent his agents and administrators to negotiate treaties with a variety of local tribes: first, with the Lenni Lenape, located near the Delaware valley, and subsequently with the Iroquois-speaking Susquehannocks, who had settled farther north. As the express words of the deeds and memorandum indicated, Penn did not speak directly with tribal chiefs and kings—although he often intimated that he had in his promotional materials, such as the popular *Letter to the Free Society of Traders*.[33] Rather, Penn's agents conducted most of the treaties, which brokered exclusive, proprietary, and final transfers of lands in Penn's name, as expressed in his *Memorandum of Additional Instructions to Wm Markham & Wm Crispin & Jno Bezer* on 28 October 1681:

> First, To Act *all in my Name as* Proprietary & Govrnr
> Secondly, To buy Land of the true Owners wch I thinke is the Susquehanna People
> Thirdly, *To treat Speedily wth the Indians for Land before they are Furnisht by others wth things that Please them* take advice in this.[34]

As evidenced above, the treaties were conducted explicitly for Penn as proprietor; they were not directly representative of crown interest, nor were they necessarily in the interests of Pennsylvania colonists, who at times directly opposed the deeds.[35] Furthermore, the *Memorandum* indicates the instrumental features of treaty-making for Penn: while identifying the "true Owners" of the land was important, it seemed essential largely because Penn sought to challenge competing claims "by others." Most of all, as Penn's third instruction indicates, the "Indians" needed to be treated "speedily" because their preferences were perceived as fluid and changeable. Thus, Penn's representatives were strongly encouraged to offer provisions and gifts to solicit tribes. For example, the account book for the *Deed at Passyunk*, August 1682, recorded the provisions and gifts that the noted Indian interpreter Captain Lasse Cocke supplied to the members of the Lenape tribe. Namely, funds were laid out "to Maintaining the Indians in Meat & Drink when Govr Markham & others that came with him to make first Purchase of Land" and for "Presents given to the Indians," which included shot and alcohol: "8lb Powder at 2/8 per & 20lb of Led at 5d per & 6 Gallns Rum 5 per."[36]

Broken down into detail, treaties helped to consolidate Penn's proprietorial power in three critical ways: control over the practices needed to conduct trade (cultural and linguistic knowledge through translators and representatives); management of the resources used to decide peace (guns, alcohol, and other provisions); and possession of exclusive title with native tribes. Notably, in his public proclamations and letters, Penn suggested that his treaties were more moral and less corrupting than the agreements that local tribes had made previously with Swedish and Finnish settlers. Penn, for instance, decried gifts of alcohol, suggesting in his *Letter to the Free Society of Traders (1683)*, one of the most popular accounts of the new colony, that: "Since the Europeans came into these parts, they [the indigenes] are grown great lovers of strong liquors, rum especially, and for it exchange the richest of their skins and furs . . . but when Drunk, [they are] one of the most wretched spectacles in the world."[37] However, in practice, his representatives and interpreters were to rely on quite familiar forms of gift, trade, and solicitation: "Led," "rum," and "shot" were all frequent and customary presents given to the Lenni Lenape and Susquehannocks, according to deed records.[38] Just as importantly, Penn was careful to make sure that the rum and ammunition regularly offered to the Lenape and Susquehannocks as incentives and signs of good faith were not available to the broad population of Pennsylvania colonists. Penn passed a law in the First Legislative Assembly of Pennsylvania, December 5, 1682, that explicitly prevented any

> person within this Province doe from hence forth presume to Sell or exchange any Rhum or brandy or any Strong Liquors at any time to any Indian within this Province & if any one shall offend therein ye persons convicted Shall for every Such offence pay five pounds.

Penn further noted in the law that "divers Persons as English Dutch Swedes &c: have been wont to sell to ye Indians Rhum & brandy and Such like distill'd Spiritts." Alcohol, Penn concluded, had a deleterious effect on both the "Indians" and the "colonists": the "Indians are not able to govern themselves in ye use thereof but doe commonly drink of it to such excess as makes them sometimes to destroy one another & greiviously anoy and disquiet ye People of this Province & Peradventures those of Neighbouring Governmts."[39]

In the guise of providing a resource—unencumbered title to land—to the colonists, Penn thus strengthened both his *internal* and *external* power in the colony. Internally, Penn's restrictions on the resources used in treaty negotiation—alcohol, guns, and even language, in the form of access to translators and negotiators—dissuaded Pennsylvania colonists from engaging in their own negotiations with local indigenes. Externally, Penn used his ability to conduct treaties to service a variety of ends. First, treaties allowed Penn to circumvent the new restrictions placed upon his proprietorial authority by the Crown: they did not need to be reviewed by the Privy Council for they did not have the status of colonial law. Second, treaties were styled by Penn to pose both a moral and commercial challenge to other colonial settlements, both English and European, who were described in print as corrupting and greedy. Lastly, the peace Penn offered to the Lenape and Susquehannocks was also in many ways peace in the form of protectionism, where Lenape and Susquehannock alliances with Penn served as a buffer against Iroquois tribes and other European settlers. Accordingly, treaty negotiation, from the perspective of Penn and his representatives, both intersected and attempted to change a number of other relations that were deeply contested at the time: the authority of the British metropole over the colonial peripheries; the regulation of commercial entities by Crown institutions; the competitive relations between English settlements and other European empires, such as the French, Dutch, and Spanish settlements; the interactions between colonists and indigenes.[40] Treaties thus helped to supplement and consolidate the limited—and often ambiguous—power that Penn held as the proprietor of a colony that was itself mixed in multiple ways.

In this way, Penn's interests in monopolization and protectionism recall Charles Tilly's assessment of state-making as "organized crime," in which "the makers of state" look to "monopolize the means of violence within a delimited territory."[41] By offering pacification to local tribes, Penn was able—without excessive arms or financial investment—to open up various trading and diplomatic opportunities.[42] Indeed, while to an extent, Penn's power can be seen as conventionally realist in its preoccupation with territorial control and relative diplomatic power, his pacific outlook also added additional dimensions of moral and ethical complexity to familiar realist interests. Entrepreneurial and diplomatic aims intermingled with—indeed even amplified—moralizing messages, allow a proprietor with limited political and economic resources to forestall conflict, create alliances, and pursue territorial ambitions.

At the same time, Penn's ability to monopolize was not absolute: he may have attempted to use formal agreements between indigene and colonial elites to order uncertainty, but the on-going tension on the ground reflected that any treatied easement was often relative and limited. Contestation continued in part because of the practical difficulty of including all parties affected by negotiation—whether directly or indirectly. In a notable example, as the *Remonstrance for the Inhabitants of Philadelphia*, 1684, demonstrated, Pennsylvania colonists were, despite Penn's treaties, still unhappy over the lands they held.[43] While Penn may have sought to "pacifye" relations and to claim privilege in contestations over disputed sections of land, treaties did not fully resolve the thicket of conflicts on the ground. In addition, as I will illustrate next, the course of treaty agreements were affected as much by the different interests of negotiating groups as by the volatile environments in which those groups sought to create security, alliance, and protection.

III. TREATY NEGOTIATION AS DE-CENTERED POWER

In this section, I draw on a variety of contemporary ethnohistorical studies to provide a provisional assessment of the interests and forms of power that can be attributed to the Lenapes and Susquehannocks, who engaged in treaty negotiations with Penn and his representatives. Historians and ethnographers have long confronted the difficult task of characterizing indigenous perspectives from the period of English colonization in the Americas. The bulk of extant sources on the mid-Atlantic region in the seventeenth and eighteenth centuries are European (i.e., mercantile, missionary, and travel accounts from English, Dutch, French, German, and Swedish sources). Such materials call for cautious interpretation because they were written by or rely on information from individuals with various colonial, economic, military, and/or religious interests. In addition, extant accounts were often imprecise and at times deliberately misleading in their attribution of various Iroquois, Lenape, Susquehannock, and Conoy tribal interests and relations. Nonetheless, as the historian Joyce Chaplin has argued, it would be problematic to argue, therefore, that no indigenous account could or should be made from these kinds of materials: that is, positing an absolute Otherness to an indigenous voice is not a sufficient response to the difficulty of producing an indigenous account from English sources. Instead, as she suggests, our interpretative goal may have to be shifted from the identification of individual intent to the detection of patterns of belief and understanding through "triangulation" of sources.[44] The works that I reference here rely upon extant English and Swedish sources and are thus not without gaps and inaccuracies. But taken collectively, they help to build an account that traces tendencies and patterns in indigenous governance, while also remaining open to variations in and among various native tribes.

For the Lenape and Susquehannocks, treaty negotiation with Penn offered, albeit differently, a way to respond both to changes in Iroquois power and to waves of European colonialism. Three tribes dominated in the Pennsylvania region: the Lenni Lenape, who occupied the lower Delaware Valley and were close allies to the Minisinks to the north; the Susquehannocks, who lived in the Susquehanna Valley above Chesapeake Bay; and to the north, the Iroquois confederacy of the Oneidas, Onondagas, Cayugas, and Senecas.[45] Within the "artificial bounds" of the territory claimed by Penn, indigenous interests never revolved exclusively around the English, as Daniel Richter and James Merrell have argued.[46] Instead, in the period between 1650 and 1700, indigenous relations were complex and varied, shaped by conflicts and alliances within native America and also by incursions from English, Dutch, Swedish, Finnish, and French settlers in and around the territories associated with Pennsylvania, New York, and Maryland.

In particular, the growing centralization of Iroquois governance over the course of the seventeenth century deeply affected Lenape and Susquehannocks. While over the last twenty years scholars have contested and redefined the precise nature of the "empire" attributed to the Iroquois, there remains a rough consensus that the Iroquois—even though more divided among themselves and less domineering than previously portrayed—were nonetheless heavy influences on indigenous nations in the east and mid-Atlantic. After the 1660s, the Five Nations struggled with a series of substantive internal and external challenges. After major population losses resulting from European disease and settlements, the "people of the Five Nations," as Daniel Richter explains, "drew upon their traditional patterns of warfare to shore up both their economy and their population. When warfare itself threatened Iroquois existence, headmen modified old rituals of peacemaking to evolve a system of intercultural diplomacy."[47]

By the mid-seventeenth century with the escalation of English and French imperial rivalry, the Iroquois faced increasing pressure to overcome factionalism at home and to consolidate military and diplomatic ties. Prior to 1660, Iroquois treaties emphasized reciprocity and exchange. As Robert Williams notes, the Iroquois utilized words of peace, rituals of condolence, and giving of gifts to conduct the 1645 treaty negotiations at Trois-Rivieres between Mohawk headmen and Frenchmen, Hurons, and Algonquins. But by the mid-1660s, the Five Nations struggled to maintain internal stability as they faced new conflicts with the Mahicans, New England Algonquians, and Susquehannocks, all of whom had developed military and diplomatic strength in alliances and on their own. In response, the Iroquois adapted old traditions to meet new circumstances, reorganizing the covenant chain to emphasize hierarchy and centralization.[48] "[T]he capacity to innovate," as Richter maintains, "within a framework of tradition provides a key to Iroquois survival."[49] Iroquois treaty negotiations subsequently placed a greater emphasis on establishing a hierarchy of power and status and were reinforced by geographic centers of authority and payment of tribute. To the Iroquois, this outcome embodied, among other things, a step toward the ideal of peace and cooperation among peoples. However, to those either excluded from or subordinated by the processes of treaty negotiation, such as the Susquehannocks and Algonquians, the post-1660s changes in the Iroquois covenant chain represented a significant loss of political autonomy. Lenapes and Susquehannocks were key groups that sought to respond to these shifts in Iroquois power, and in treaty negotiations they did so in markedly different ways.

For the Lenape, treaty negotiations reflected the interests of small bands and communities that were not linked by an overarching political structure of representation. Prior to European settlement in the Americas, the Lenapes were defined by kinship and organized in small communities where neither men nor women held position of exclusive authority.[50] Bands were decentralized and scattered where contact between Lenape bands was based, according to Sugrue, on reciprocal exchanges with "little evidence of political structures that transcended kin groups."[51] Although at various points they had been semi-agricultural and horticultural, the mid-seventeenth-century Lenape increasingly relied on fishing, hunting, and gathering, along with growing participation in the fur trade—a consequence of massive population losses due to epidemics in the wake of the 1620s settlements of the Dutch, Swedes, and Finns. By the end of the century, various Lenape, located in and around the Delaware River and near European trading posts, relied even more heavily on European goods, and due to their limited involvement in the harvesting of beaver, served as mediators between markets and more far-flung tribes.[52] As mediators, they had historically sought to avoid conflict and overt aggression; they looked to treaties as a way to create limited, local regions of protection and isolation from Iroquois authority. "Indeed," as Francis Jennings has argued, "the Iroquois found considerable difficulty speaking even for themselves in Pennsylvania because of intercolonial jealousies: New Yorkers wanted to keep the Iroquois from falling under Pennsylvania's sway, and Pennsylvania wanted to preserve 'their' Indians from outside influence, as New York's via the Iroquois. During William Penn's lifetime, Pennsylvania stayed out of the Covenant Chain confederation."[53]

By contrast, the Susquehannocks were organized on markedly different political, social, and economic lines. Susquehannocks, along with the Five Nations of the Iroquois League, and the five Huron nations, were descendents of the Late Woodland Owasco culture, which was structured around large horticultural communities, which ranged in size from several hundred to one thousand members. "Owasco communities," Richter notes, "seem to have been extremely independent, isolated, and hostile toward outsiders. Warfare was prevalent, and reciprocal retaliation produced an ongoing cycle of feuding not easily stopped."[54] While the Lenape had taken on a mediating role in the seventeenth century, the Susquehannocks possessed a more aggressive outlook and were frequently embroiled in a number of European and Native conflicts. For a time, Richter comments, the Susquehannocks prospered materially and "turned their village into a fortress bristling with European firearms."[55] They had access to traders on both the Maryland Chesapeake and the Swedish, Dutch, and English Delaware. They also apparently had firm control of hunting territories throughout the Susquehanna watersheds and points west. But the Susquehannocks also were drawn into intense conflict with the Dutch in New York and English settlers in Maryland and Virginia.[56] Ultimately, over the course of the century, peoples of both the Delaware and Susquehanna watersheds had become increasingly dependent on European trade for clothing, tools, and weapons.[57] By the 1680s, as waves of new English settlers arrived, trading conditions worsened for local tribes and pressure to sell native land increased substantially. Due to increasing competition, Lenape were excluded from the fur trade by their Susquehannock and Iroquois neighbors to the north and west. Meanwhile, Susquehannock conflicts with the Iroquois splintered and weakened the nation; as some Susquehannoks returned north to the protection of the Iroquois, others fled to the New York and Virginia settlements.

Given the numerous conflicts that divided tribes along the Delaware, when Lenape or Susquehannock tribes negotiated treaties with Penn's administrators, they did so to draw defenses against Iroquois confederacy to the north or to secure more local support in regional conflicts. In addition, the treaties with Penn and his administrators allowed both Lenape and Susquehannocks to be sheltered from taking sides in the wars against France or in neighboring conflicts. Treaties thus enabled Lenape and Susquehannocks to pursue various forms of *decentralized* power that differed in structural terms from Penn's. Treaties allowed Penn to reserve a type of monopolistic power to himself as proprietor and head of the Society of Traders, while restricting Pennsylvania colonists, Finns and Swedes, and nearby Marylanders from developing their own relations with the Lenape and Susquehannocks. But for the Lenape, treaties were a way to establish realms of mediation and pacification. The decisions made by Lenape bands were not connected to a wider indigenous infrastructure or political hierarchy. Rather, power in intimate Lenape bands was fluid and diffuse, not hierarchical: agreements reflected communal decisions and were based on discussion and persuasion. In contrast, the larger band of Susquehannocks was organized along more aggressive lines, and they used treaty negotiations more defensively to construct an alternative to the covenant chain.

This period of treaty negotiation between Penn and the Lenape and Susquehannocks is theoretically pertinent because it illustrates the variable forms of power that shape and can be shaped by treaty constitutionalism. For Penn, proprietorial insecurities motivated his interest in treaties as an instrument that could supplement and consolidate monopolistic power. By contrast, for the more hierarchical Susquehannocks, treaties were viewed as defensive measures that could create and help to fortify an alternative system of alliances and agreements that would serve as a zone of protection in the face of increasing threats by the Iroquois and other regional neighbors such as the Dutch in New York. And, in yet another way, Lenape communal life was facilitated by treaties which were to provide limited protection and mediation. Recalling Michel Foucault's characterization, here power is "employed and exercised through a net-like organization," where "individuals circulate between its threads" and are "always in the position of simultaneously undergoing and exercising this power. They are not only its inert or consenting target; they are always also the elements of its articulation."[58]

In this sense, these historical examples remind us that power could circulate in potent and dynamic ways in treaty constitutionalism. Treaties, that is, could facilitate power in multiple and subjective arrays. If, on the one hand, these treaties did not impose wholesale domination or exploitation, they neither—in their relationality and flexibility—eliminated the influence of personal and group interest. To that end, my account extends current accounts of treaty constitutionalism by expanding on the role of power, and in fact this expansion is a complement to the accounts of power described in both Young and Tully's greater *oeuvre* of work.

Like Young's work on inclusion and democracy, the treaty negotiations under examination here remind us that it is not simply that groups can possess different conceptions of power in processes of negotiation but also that those conceptions of power are often further affected by differences within groups and by unequal positioning on the ground, where access to resources, opportunity, and information can vary widely. We might then productively re-work our conception of treaty constitutionalism so that the various pursuits of interest and instrumentalities are not necessarily flaws or indictments of treaty constitutionalism, but rather elements that warrant a heightened degree of acknowledgement and consideration. We might need, for example, to focus greater attention on the redistribution of resources and opportunities. In addition, resource equity alone might not resolve the exclusions and instrumentalities that can be present in treaty constitutionalism. As Young has suggested, "[s]ocial justice . . . requires not the melting away of differences, but institutions that promote reproduction of and respect for group differences without oppression."[59] For, as we have seen in the examples above, elements of exclusion, elitism, and opportunism were created not solely because of inequalities in resource and opportunity, but also because of the interactions between diverse conceptions of power generated by culturally and socially different groups.

In that respect, treaty constitutionalism may be particularly prone to a type of *indeterminacy of outcome,* not only because groups are fluid and their conditions on the ground are subject to change, but also because the institution of the treaty negotiation is itself open-ended, where multiple voices come together and agreements are subject to on-going review. Treaties evoke Tully's discussion of agonic democracy, where "no agreement will be closed at a frontier; it will always be open to question, to an element of nonconsensus, and so to reciprocal question and answer, demand and response, and negotiation."[60] Treaties operated in spaces in which multiple understandings of power and influence overlapped in animated and mobile ways, as if in densely woven webs. At times, consensus may have been produced, but given differences among groups and the changeability of conditions on the ground, there was always the potential that participant understandings could shift. As I will discuss in the next section, some aspects of this indeterminacy can be observed in the relational power of the cultural knowledge employed in treaty constitutionalism, where speaking another's language or practicing another's customs served as powerful tools that allowed different groups to relate to one another, yet cultural knowledge itself was not necessarily a reliable guarantee of enduring respect or responsibility.

IV. TREATY NEGOTIATION AS RELATIONAL POWER

Many have argued that treaties between English and indigenous nations were fatally flawed from the start because treaty participants possessed such different—and, arguably, mutually exclusive—conceptions of land possession and use.[61] The English tended to view land as a commodity to be bought and sold: deeds were accordingly treated as conveying absolute right to land, where gifts of rum, wampum, and goods were seen as payment for land title. By contrast, indigenous conceptions of land emphasized land usufruct: deeds were largely viewed as provisional agreements that needed to be revisited and renewed over time, and any gifts were seen as part of on-going protocols and customs of greeting and negotiation. "The Lenape notion of the transfer of partial or usufruct rights in a land transaction," Sugrue indicates, "had no impact on the wording of deeds, all of which stipulated the permanent and absolute renunciation of Indian rights to the land conveyed."[62] At least on first appraisal, the treatied deeds between Penn and the Lenape and Susquehannocks seem to illustrate a clash of cultural and political understanding, where indigenous conceptions of land and culture were, at best, misunderstood or, at worst, deliberately manipulated to service Penn's interests. As I discuss in this section, certain forms of cross-cultural understanding did seem to take place in treaty negotiation, but they were often variable and indeterminate as guarantees of enduring respect or harmony. Penn and his interpreters and go-betweens did seem to possess a fairly thorough knowledge of Lenape and Susquehannock protocols and values, but these understandings did not appear to compel any necessary commitment or sense of responsibility to treaty participants over the long term.

As I argued earlier, Penn made frequent and public indication of his knowledge and validation of Lenape and Susquehannock cultures in promotional materials, such as *The Letter to the Free Society of Traders*. In addition, Penn and his administrators recognized that Lenape and Susquehannocks viewed treaty agreements as open-ended and subject to on-going review and renewal. Even though the deed agreements themselves referred to the permanent transfer of land to the English, Penn and his representatives nonetheless revisited and renewed "confirmatory" treaties with Lenape and Susquehannocks from the 1680s until as late as 1718: Penn was, for example, willing to make multiple payments to tribes until 1700 when financial difficulties beset the colony.[63] What these "confirmatory" treaties suggest is that the open-ended nature of treaty negotiations could be turned to multiple ends. Penn and his administrators were not wholly ignorant of Lenape protocols and practices; instead, they used Lenape customs, such as the renewal of treaties, when it was useful for diplomatic reasons. However, these decisions could be changed and revisited, at times causing conflict with, and even betrayal of, earlier agreements.

This element of indeterminacy can be seen in greater detail in the dialogic aspects of treaty constitutionalism. Although treaty negotiations were affairs of arbitration between elites, they were also reliant on interpreters and "go-betweens" whose interests, knowledge, and capabilities reveal a core ambiguity in intercultural dialogue and accommodation.[64] For example, the Swedish colonist, Lars Parsson (Lasse) Cocke, fur trader and magistrate, negotiated many of the early treaties (1682–1699) with the Lenape, Susquehannocks, and members of the Iroquois confederacy; while James Logan, an early secretary to Penn, negotiated treaties with the Lenape for land and trade access.[65] Negotiation practices extended beyond simply translating speeches and trading wampum: in arranging meetings, interpreting manners and gestures, and providing incentives, negotiators needed to possess a cross-cultural understanding of language, custom, and culture.

Yet, as James Merrell has noted, the cross-cultural work of translation, reciprocity, and diplomacy was deeply imbued with power *and* contingency. Negotiators, although fluent in cross-cultural practices, were often partisans to one side or another. For instance, Penn's secretary, James Logan, was conversant in Iroquois protocols of condolence and Algonquian practices of orientation, owned a copy of the Bible in Algonquian, and housed Lenape representatives during treaty negotiations. Still, Logan, who had at times referred to local tribes and nations as "children," famously exhibited little commitment to intercultural understanding beyond matters relating to trade and land. Meanwhile, Cocke, who had been raised in the Delaware lower counties prior to the Pennsylvania settlement, eagerly naturalized to Penn's colony and expanded his fur trade. Cocke and Logan were not unique in their power-laden practices of cultural negotiation. As Merrell comments,

> [t]he very preoccupation that gave the trader valuable negotiating tools—the traffic in peltry—might also hinder him when called to serve. Intent on satisfying the demands of his Indian and Philadelphia customer, with an eye always on "the sweet profits" to be made in trade, the fur peddler, "can with eagerness go thro the greatest hardships and Difficaltyes for sake of Gaine."[66]

Negotiators, despite—or indeed even perhaps because of—their cross-cultural facility, could use their skills to service instrumental, even coercive, interests. "However skilled he was, chicanery was also part of the go-between's repertoire. Moreover," Merrell notes, for all the talk about these figures standing squarely between native and newcomer, mediators themselves saw, and set, limits to their acquaintance with another world. A good ear and a glib tongue could achieve a meeting of the minds . . . a meeting of the hearts proved another matter.[67]

What Cocke and Logan do is not, strictly speaking, a negotiation of cultural identity in our more modern sense—where practices, customs, and sensibilities delineate specific group, ethnic, or even civilizational membership. Rather, here, cross-cultural knowledge is a *relational* type of power, which allows individuals to gain access to the modalities of living and survival in a place and a time. In a sense, this form of power is rooted in a conception of locale, where knowledge is developing the skills and relationships needed to survive in a specific time and place. Treaty parties were dependent upon one another (at least to some degree), and each sought to rely on others—whether through discussion, exchange, or alliance—in order to forward various respective interests. Here, engagement with another's culture seems to be a practical acknowledgement of dependence—where independence from context and circumstance, a kind of sovereign agency, is not only regarded as impossible but impractical.

These cases depict a form of treaty constitutionalism in which power cannot be conceived in terms of a zero-sum game. Rather, the treaty is a multilateral struggle where various forms of power and interest are both expressed and reproduced, calling to mind the epigraph by Jacques Derrida which opened this chapter.[68] For Derrida, the "shuttle" of negotiation is not "noble."[69] As Derrida submits, "there is always something about negotiation that is a little dirty, that gets one's hands dirty . . . something is being trafficked, something in the order of a traffic, or the relations of force."[70] Derrida reminds us, that is, that negotiations are exchanges which may not always be freed from coercion and unexpected outcomes. Negotiations, after all, are motivated by unruly forces—desires, ambitions, interests. And while the ends of a negotiation may have been concrete initially, the processes of negotiation—in which positions are offered, adjusted, and changed—carries with it, what Derrida describes as, "absolute uncertainty," as resources change, desires shift, and alliances shuffle.[71] Derrida, in that respect, offers a characterization of negotiation that poses both a challenge and opportunity: while treaty constitutionalism allows for the inclusion and the expression of overlapping jurisdictions and multiple authorities, those agreements can be haunted by the risk of indeterminacy. Such features are not necessarily cause for pessimism but rather reminders of the energies and mobilizations that may be needed accompaniments to our pursuits of multicultural adjudications.

V. CONCLUSION

My focus in this chapter has been primarily local and historical: through a close reading of a specific period, I have looked to extend the accounts of treaty constitutionalism offered by Tully, Young, and Williams, while adding yet another case example to further expand the field of consideration. Our understanding of treaty constitutionalism, I have suggested, can be deepened by viewing it as set of practices that were shaped by, and duly shaped, differential forms of power. In the cases that I have examined, no one group possessed an authoritative conception of treaty negotiation and no single participant or legislator wholly determined a treaty's direction. At the same time, while treaty negotiations created cross-cultural adjudication and agreement, they did so in ways that, at times, created moments of exclusion, fostered opportunism, and risked conflict and contention.

There are both historical and contemporary implications that might be productively drawn from this analysis. From a historical perspective, the treaties negotiated between Penn and the Lenape and Susquehannocks help to challenge broad-brush accounts which tend to view English empire as a monolith erected only by territorial conquest and cultural assimilation. Such accounts, I would argue, can overlook the degree to which English colonial order was also at times supported and supplemented by cross-cultural agreements, understandings, and knowledges: far from imposing a "civilized" order upon "primitive" inhabitants, the treaties examined here revealed Penn's reliance, for example, on Lenape and Susquehannocks to provide land and alliances. Equally pertinent, historical examples of treaty negotiations help to illuminate the wide variety of indigenous diplomatic, territorial, and social interests and agendas in the past and allow us a degree of insight into the many agreements and conflicts that historically shaped indigenous communities. When viewed as practices of power, such understandings are crucial to deepening our understanding of a complex and equivocal past.

On a conceptual level, the features of power that I have discussed here can be used to extend normative accounts of treaty constitutionalism. In particular, we might reconfigure our assessment to include not only the possibilities for potent cross-cultural connection, but also the risks of inequality, exclusion, and indeterminacy. Such elements, especially with respect to contemporary cases, suggest the need for greater attentiveness to the contexts and forms of power that characterize treaty negotiations, and our efforts may need to be both wide-ranging and persistent.

More specifically, the historical contexts of treaty constitutionalism suggest the need for awareness of and sensitivity to the possible unexpected and conflicted outcomes of treaty negotiations. We might, as a consequence, look to strengthen treaty constitutionalism by energizing our efforts to attend to contemporary examples where group interests may not be fully expressed by treaty negotiators or when, alternatively, treaty participants are radically divergent not just in their respective interests but in their conceptions of power.

Indeed, the differences between contemporary and past forms of treaty constitutionalism warrant especially heightened consideration. Particularly now, when the Crown/nation-state and indigenous nations are more often than not situated in radical inequity with respect to power and privilege, what may superficially appear as a balanced setting can be belied by institutional, economic, and political forces of the Crown/nation-state.[72] As the theorist Taiaiake Alfred has argued, indigenous interests can be co-opted by the mechanisms of treaty making, where even tribal leaders find their interests and ambitions acquiescent "to the state's agenda."[73] For example, in a 2002 case in British Columbia, Canada, native leaders sought to bar native treaties from being brought to a public referendum that allowed more than 4 million B.C. residents to mail in their votes on native issues that ranged from whether hunting and fishing on Crown land should be maintained for all B.C. residents to whether aboriginal self-government should have the characteristics of municipal government. Local chiefs of bands such as the Hupacasath in Port Alberni protested that the referendum would diminish aboriginal rights: while public input was in principle desirable, the practical effect of the public's influence made it impossible for native leaders to fully discuss and deliberate highly contentious issues.[74] Moreover, the challenges to treaty negotiation can reside within indigenous tribes as well: internal struggles and external challenges can undermine indigenous leadership and representation. In fact, at times, as Alfred argues, in such situations, a stance of "contention" may be more appropriate for indigenous nations—"a non-cooperative, non-participatory position vis-à-vis the state, its actors, and its policies."[75]

Deepening our understanding of treaty constitutionalism's relationship to power allows us to acknowledge the vulnerabilities as well as strengths that can be opened in the acts of speaking, engaging, and negotiating across cultural difference, providing hopefully yet more resources for responding to the challenges of adjudication.

NOTES

1. My thanks and appreciation to Craig Borowiak, Michaele Ferguson, Jacob Levy, Steven Pincus, Sarah Song, James Tully, and Iris Marion Young for their suggestions and comments on previous versions of this essay. A version of this essay was originally published in Vicki Hsueh's *Hybrid Constitutions*, pp. 83–112, published in 2010 by Duke University Press. All Rights Reserved. Used by permission of the publisher.

2. Recent works include: James Tully, *Strange Multiplicity: Constitutionalism in an Age of Diversity* (Cambridge: Cambridge University Press, 1995); Iris Marion Young, "Hybrid Democracy: Iroquois Federalism and the Postcolonial Project," from *Political Theory and the*

Rights of Indigenous Peoples, eds. Duncan Ivison et al. (Cambridge: Cambridge University Press, 2000), 237–58; also Young, *Inclusion and Democracy* (Oxford: Oxford University Press, 2001), especially chapter 7, "Self-Determination and Global Democracy," 236–75; Robert A. Williams Jr., *Linking Arms Together: American Indian Treaty Visions of Law and Peace, 1600–1800* (New York: Oxford University Press, 1997); also Williams, "Linking Arms Together: Multicultural Constitutionalism in a North American Indigenous Vision of Law and Peace," *California Law Review* 82, no. 4 (1994), 981–1052.

3. Tully, *Strange Multiplicity: Constitutionalism in an Age of Diversity* (Cambridge: Cambridge University Press, 1995), 116–19.

4. Williams, "Linking Arms Together: Multicultural Constitutionalism in a North American Indigenous Vision of Law and Peace," *California Law Review* 82, no. 4 (1994), 1048–49.

5. Iris Marion Young, "Hybrid Democracy: Iroquois Federalism and the Postcolonial Project," in *Political Theory and the Rights of Indigenous Peoples,* ed. Duncan Ivison et al. (Cambridge: Cambridge University Press, 2000), 246.

6. Tully, *Strange Multiplicity,* 119.

7. Young, "Hybrid Democracy: Iroquois Federalism and the Postcolonial Project," 239–40.

8. Tully, *Strange Multiplicity,* 83; Young, "Hybrid Democracy: Iroquois Federalism and the Postcolonial Project," 240, 246–47.

9. Young, "Hybrid Democracy: Iroquois Federalism and the Postcolonial Project," 246.

10. Williams, "Linking Arms Together: Multicultural Constitutionalism in a North American Indigenous Vision of Law and Peace," 1048.

11. In this account, my conception of power draws upon the formulations offered by Michel Foucault, Jacques Derrida, Tully, and Young. See citations below.

12. See Bruce G. Trigger, ed., *Handbook of North American Indians* (Washington, DC: Smithsonian Institution, 1978), vol. 15; Francis Jennings, "'Pennsylvania Indians' and the Iroquois," in *Beyond the Covenant Chain,* ed. D. Richter and J. Merrell (Syracuse, NY: Syracuse University Press, 1987), 80–84; Daniel K. Richter, "A Framework for Pennsylvania Indian History," *Pennsylvania History* 57 (1990): 236–61; Thomas J. Sugrue, "The Peopling and Depeopling of Early Pennsylvania: Indians and Colonists, 1680–1720," *PMHB,* CXVI:1 (1992), 3–30.

13. I adopt a Skinnerian approach to clarify the different meanings of treaty constitutionalism and to understand the specific contexts and conditions in which those forms were raised as relevant, while bringing in the interpretative insights of contemporary historical and literary studies that regard English-American colonial settlement in its diversity and differences. On the issue of historical interpretation, see *Meaning and Context: Quentin Skinner and His Critics,* ed. James Tully (Princeton, NJ: Princeton University Press, 1988), 29–67, 231–88. See also Quentin Skinner, *Liberty Before Liberalism* (Cambridge and New York: Cambridge University Press, 1998), especially 101–20; Ludwig Wittgenstein, *Philosophical Investigations,* 3rd ed., trans. G. E. M. Anscombe (New York: Macmillan, 1958), especially 122, 198–201, 203.

14. Young, "Hybrid Democracy: Iroquois Federalism and the Postcolonial Project," 239–40, 246.

15. James Merrell, *Into the American Woods: Negotiators on the Pennsylvania Frontier* (New York: W. W. Norton, 1999), 28.

16. Sugrue, "The Peopling and Depeopling of Early Pennsylvania: Indians and Colonists, 1680–1720," *PMHB,* CXVI:1 (1992), 3. In addition, my account draws particularly on recent work which emphasizes trans-Atlantic and cross-colonial dynamics. See Sally Schwartz, *"A Mixed Multitude": The Struggle for Toleration in Colonial Pennsylvania* (New York: New York University Press, 1987); Daniel K. Richter, "A Framework for Pennsylvania Indian History," *Pennsylvania History* 57 (1990): 236–61; Andrew R. Murphy, *Conscience and Community: Revisiting Toleration and Religious Dissent in Early Modern England and America* (University Park: Pennsylvania State University Press, 2001), 247–94; Mary K. Geiter, "The Restoration Crisis and the Launching of Pennsylvania, 1679–81," *English Historical Review,* CXII (1997), 313–14.

17. *Some Account of the Province of Pennsylvania* (London: printed and sold by Benjamin Clark, 1681), reprinted in *The World of William Penn*, edited by Richard S. Dunn and Mary Maples Dunn (Philadelphia: University of Pennsylvania Press, 1986), 59.

18. Ibid.

19. Gary B. Nash, "City Planning and Political Tension in the Seventeenth-Century: The Case of Philadelphia," *Proceedings of the American Philosophical Society* 112 (1968), 54–73; Hannah Roach, "Planting of Philadelphia: A Seventeenth Century Real Estate Development," *PMHB*, 92 (1968), 185–89.

20. Letter from Thomas Holme to William Penn, 9 November 1683, *The Papers of William Penn*, ed. Mary Maples Dunn, Richard S. Dunn, Richard Ryerson, and Scott M. Wilds; asst. ed. Jean R. Soderlund (Philadelphia: University of Pennsylvania Press, 1981–6), II, 501. Hereafter cited as *PWP*.

21. For primary source reference on the early population, see *Early Census of Philadelphia County Inhabitants*, 14 April 1683, *William Penn and the Founding of Pennsylvania, 1680–1684: A Documentary History* (hereafter cited as *WPFP*), ed. Jean Soderlund (Philadelphia: University of Pennsylvania Press, 1983), 212–16. The editors of *The Papers of William Penn* have also compiled a particularly helpful list of first purchasers in Pennsylvania during 1681–1685, which includes biographical information. See *First Purchasers of Pennsylvania, 1681–1685* in *PWP*, II, 630–64. Also, while I do not discuss the issue of slavery here, the colony's history of slavery adds yet another layer of complication to its intercultural relations. See Gary B. Nash, "Slaves and Slaveholders in Colonial Philadelphia," *William and Mary Quarterly*, 3rd service, 30:2 (1973): 223–56; Herbert Aptheker, "The Quakers and Negro Slavery," *Journal of Negro History* 25:3 (July 1940): 331–62.

22. See *Charter to Pennsylvania*, 4 March 1681, *WPFP*, 42. For historical accounts of the Charter in the period's colonial policy, see Philip S. Haffenden, "The Crown and the Colonial Charters, 1675–1688," *WMQ* 15 (1958): 297–311.

23. *Charter to Pennsylvania*, 4 March 1681, *WPFP*, 42. See Soderlund's introduction to *WPFP*, 7. As historian Jean R. Soderlund flatly points out, Penn ultimately failed to achieve the powers of the palatinate charter, and "therefore ended up with a patent that gave the proprietor considerably less power than he desired."

24. Christopher Tomlins, "Law's Empire: Chartering English Colonies on the American mainland in the seventeenth century," in *The Reach of Empire: Law, History, Colonialism*, ed., Diane Kirkby and Catherine Colebourne (New York and Manchester, UK: Manchester University Press, 2001), 36. See also, C. L. Tomlins, "The Legal Cartography of Colonization, the Legal Polyphony of Settlement: English Intrusions on the American Mainland in the Seventeenth Century," *Law and Social Inquiry* 26 (2001), 315–72, especially 328–47; Kenneth MacMillan, "Common and Civil Law? Taking Possession of the English Empire in America, 1575–1630," *Canadian Journal of History* 38 (2003), 409–24; John Juricek, "English Territorial Claims in North America under Elizabeth and the Early Stuarts," *Terrae Incognitae* 7 (1975): 7–22.

25. As Penn wrote to the Committee of Trade, 14, in August, 1683, "I have exactly followed the Bishop of London's council by buying & not taking away the natives land, with whom I have Settled a very Kind Correspondence." *PWP*, 435. On the various indigenous tribes and nations in Pennsylvania, see Bruce G. Trigger, ed., *Handbook of North American Indians* (Washington, DC: Smithsonian Institution, 1978), vol. 15, 366–67; Randall Miller, "Amerindian (Native American) Cultures in Pre- and Early European Settlement Periods in Pennsylvania," *Pennsylvania Ethnic Studies Newsletter* (1989), 1–4; Regula Trenkwalder Schönenberger, *Lenape Women, Matriliny, and the Colonial Encounter: Resistance and Erosion of Power* (Bern and New York: P. Lang, 1991); Lorraine E. Williams, "Indians and Europeans in the Delaware Valley, 1620–1655," in *New Sweden in America*, ed. Carol E. Hoffecker et al. (Newark: University of Delaware Press, 1995), 112–20.

26. Letter from William Clarke, Commissioner, Dover River, 21 June 1683, *PWP*, 400–401. For example, as Commissioner William Clarke wrote to Penn, on 21 June 1683:

> Lord Baltimore did the Last thurd day Cause A proclaimacon to be read publiquely in sumersett County Court; that all persons that would seat Land in Either the whor Kill or

Jones Countys; That he would procure them Rights at one hundred pounds of Tobacco per Right, and that they should pay but one shilling for every hundred Acres of Land yearly rent, And if the Inhabitents of both these Countys would *Revolt from william Penn and owne him to be theire proprietary and Governr that they should have the same termes*; Reports ware also given out that the Lord Baltimor did *Intend shortly to Com with A Troop of horse to take possession of these Two Lower Countys; which Caused greate fear to a Rise in the peoples mindes.* (My emphasis)

27. Terry G. Jordan and Matti Kaups, *The American Backwoods Frontier: An Ethnic and Ecological Interpretation* (Baltimore: Johns Hopkins University, 1989), 5. For primary accounts, see "Report of Governor John Printz [New Sweden]," 1647, *Narratives of Early Pennsylvania, West New Jersey, and Delaware, 1603–1707*, ed. Albert Cook Myers (New York: Charles Scribner's Sons, 1912), 117–29; also, "Report of Governor Johan Rising [New Sweden]," 1655, ibid., 153–65.

28. See, for example, "Deed: Sickoneysincks to the Dutch for Swanendale," 1 June 1629, in *Early American Indian Documents, Treaties, and Laws, 1607–1789: Pennsylvania and Delaware Treaties, 1629–1737*, ed. Alden T. Vaughn and Donald H. Kent (Washington, DC: University Publications of America, c. 1979), 5; Stellan Dahlgren and Hans Norman, *The Rise and Fall of New Sweden* (Stockholm: Almquist & Wiksell, 1988), 92–116.

29. Karen Ordahl Kupperman, "Scandinavian Colonists Confront the New World," in *New Sweden in America*, ed. Carol E. Hoffecker et al. (Newark, DE: University of Delaware Press, 1995), 89–111.

30. Ibid.

31. Marshall Becker, "Lenape Maize Sales to the Swedish Colonists: Cultural Stability during the Early Colonial Period," in *New Sweden in America*, ed. Carol E. Hoffecker et al. (Newark: University of Delaware Press, 1995), 120–35; also Lorraine E. Williams, "Indians and Europeans in the Delaware Valley, 1620–1655" in the same volume, 112–20.

32. Penn was granted Pennsylvania by Charles II in March 1681. Later, the three lower counties (now referred to as Delaware) were added, with controversy, in August 1682. See, for example, Penn's letter to Robert Turner, Anthony Sharp, and Roger Roberts, *PWP*, 88. Even before arriving in Pennsylvania, Penn's administrators negotiated for land in the southeast of Bucks Country in 1682. Penn continued to acquire deeds, first, along the Delaware River, then extending westward, by the fall of 1683, along the Schuykill and Susquehanna rivers.

33. *Letter to the Free Society of Traders*, 1683, *WPFP*, 314.

34. *Memoranda of Additional Instructions to William Markham and William Crispin and Jno Bezer*, 28 October 1681, *PWP*, II, 129. My emphasis.

35. *Remonstrance from the Inhabitants of Philadelphia*, July 1684, *PWP*, II, 573.

36. Quotes in paragraph from Bill for Lasse Cock's Services, 1682, ibid., II, 242–43.

37. *Letter to the Free Society of Traders*, 1683, *WPFP*, 314.

38. Quotes in paragraph from Bill for Lasse Cock's Services, 1682, ibid., II, 242–43. For background, see also Marshall Becker, "Lenape Land Sales, Treaties, and Wampum Belts," *PMHB*, CVIII (1984); James H. Merrell, *Into the American Woods: Negotiators on the Pennsylvania Frontier* (New York: W. W. Norton, 1999), 1–10.

39. Paragraph quotes from William Penn's Great Law Passed by his First Legislative Assembly of Pennsylvania, December 5, 1682. MS, Division of Public Records, Harrisburg, PA.

40. Elizabeth Mancke, "Negotiating an Empire: Britain and its Overseas Population, c. 1550–1780," in *Negotiated Empires: Centers and Peripheries in the Americas, 1500–1820*, ed. Christine Daniels and Michael V. Kennedy (New York and London: Routledge, 2002), 248–49. "Relations among states," Mancke explains, "between the metropole and colonial peripheries, and among rival commercial interests were all negotiated over the seventeenth and eighteenth centuries, repeatedly and often simultaneously . . . Authority in the colonies, therefore, did not trickle down from the center to the peripheries *but was negotiated between the regions*." My emphasis.

41. Charles Tilly, "War-Making and State-Making as Organized Crime," in Peter B. Evans, Dietrich Rueschemeyer, Theda Skocpol, eds., *Bringing the State Back In* (Cambridge and New York: Cambridge University Press, 1985), 172.

42. Ibid., 170–72.

43. *Remonstrance from the Inhabitants of Philadelphia*, July 1684, *PWP*, II, 573.

44. Joyce Chaplin, *Subject Matter: Technology, the Body, and Science on the Anglo-American Frontier, 1500–1676* (Cambridge, MA: Harvard University Press, 2001), 24–26. For a wider view of the work relating to the recovery of native experience, see James Axtell, "The Ethnohistory of Early America: A Review Essay," *WMQ* 35 (1978), 110–14; also, Axtell, *The Invasion Within: The Contest of Cultures in Colonial North America* (New York: Oxford University Press, 1985); Edward G. Gray, *New World Babel: Languages and Nations in Early America* (Princeton: Princeton University Press, 1999); David Murray, *Forked Tongues: Speech, Writing, and Representation in North American Native Texts* (Bloomington: University of Indiana Press, 1991); Jane T. Merritt, *At the Crossroads: Indians and Empires on a Mid-Atlantic Frontier* (Chapel Hill: University of North Carolina Press, 2003); Karen Ordahl Kupperman, *Indians and English: Facing Off in Early America* (Ithaca, NY: Cornell University Press, 2000); Colin Calloway, *New Worlds for All: Indians, Europeans, and the Remaking of Early America* (Baltimore: Johns Hopkins University Press, 1997); Richard White, *The Middle Ground* (New York and Cambridge: Cambridge University Press, 1991).

45. Francis Jennings, "'Pennsylvania Indians' and the Iroquois" in *Beyond the Covenant Chain: The Iroquois and Their Neighbors in Indian North America, 1600–1800*, ed. Daniel K. Richter and James H. Merrell (University Park: Pennsylvania State University Press, [1987] 2003), 75–92.

46. Richter, *Beyond the Covenant Chain: The Iroquois and Their Neighbors in Indian North America, 1600–1800*, ed. Daniel K. Richter and James H. Merrell (University Park: Pennsylvania State University Press, [1987] 2003), 6. Also, as Daniel Richter argues, despite the increase in ethnohistorical and "middle ground" historical accounts of indigene-colonial relationships, Penn's treaties with the Lenni Lenape, Susquehannocks, and Iroquois continue to be susceptible to idealized, even sentimental, interpretations. Daniel K. Richter, "A Framework for Pennsylvania Indian History," *Pennsylvania History* 57 (1990): 236–61. Francis Jennings also addresses both Penn's enthusiasm, economic concerns, and his interest in managing the welter of competing claims to land title in the area. See Francis Jennings, "Brother Miquon: Good Lord!" in *The World of William Penn*, 195–210.

47. Richter, *Beyond the Covenant Chain*, 21.

48. Neal Salisbury, "Toward the Covenant Chain: Iroquois and Southern New England Algonquians, 1637–1684," in *Beyond the Covenant Chain: The Iroquois and Their Neighbors in Indian North America, 1600–1800*, ed. Daniel K. Richter and James H. Merrell (University Park: Pennsylvania State University Press, [1987] 2003), 61–74.

49. Richter, *Beyond the Covenant Chain*, 21.

50. Sugrue, "The Peopling and Depeopling of Early Pennsylvania: Indians and Colonists, 1680–1720," *PMHB*, CXVI:1 (1992): 9–11.

51. Ibid.

52. Randall Miller, "Amerindian (Native American) Cultures in Pre- and Early European Settlement Periods in Pennsylvania," *Pennsylvania Ethnic Studies Newsletter* (1989), 1–4; Regula Trenkwalder Schönenberger, *Lenape Women, Matriliny, and the Colonial Encounter: Resistance and Erosion of Power* (Bern and New York: P. Lang, 1991); Lorraine E. Williams, "Indians and Europeans in the Delaware Valley, 1620–1655," in *New Sweden in America*, ed. Carol E. Hoffecker et al. (Newark: University of Delaware Press, 1995), 112–20.

53. Jennings, "'Pennsylvania Indians' and the Iroquois," 81.

54. Richter, "A Framework for Pennsylvania Indian History," 239.

55. Ibid., 245.

56. Jennings, "'Pennsylvania Indians' and the Iroquois," 80–84.

57. Richter, "A Framework for Pennsylvania Indian History."

58. Michel Foucault, *Power/Knowledge: Selected Interviews and Other Writings, 1972–1977*, ed. and trans. Colin Gordon (New York: Pantheon Books, 1980), 88.

59. Iris Marion Young, *Justice and the Politics of Difference* (Princeton, NJ: Princeton University Press, 1990), 47. Also see especially chapter 2, "The Five Faces of Oppression," 39–65.

60. James Tully, "The Agonic Freedom of Citizens," *Economy and Society* 28 (1999): 167–68.

61. See, for example, William Cronon, *Changes in the Land: Indians, Colonists, and the Ecology of New England* (New York: Hill and Wang, 1983).

62. Sugrue, "The Peopling and Depeopling of Early Pennsylvania: Indians and Colonists, 1680–1720," 22.

63. Jennings, "'Pennsylvania Indians' and the Iroquois," in *Beyond the Covenant Chain*, ed. D. Richter and J. Merrell (Syracuse, NY: Syracuse University Press, 1987), 75–92, and Sugrue, "The Peopling and Depeopling of Early Pennsylvania: Indians and Colonists, 1680–1720," 3–30.

64. To be sure, treaty elites represented their constituents to varying degrees. For example, Penn, as I have noted, often sought to exclude his colonists from intervening, while Lenape decisions were typically communal. The Susquehannocks were organized along more hierarchical lines, but elites were supposed to represent the band's interests.

65. Marshall Becker, "Lenape Land Sales, Treaties, and Wampum Belts," *PMHB*, CVIII (1984); James H. Merrell, *Into the American Woods: Negotiators on the Pennsylvania Frontier* (New York: W. W. Norton, 1999).

66. Merrell, *Into the American Woods*, 80.

67. Ibid., 56.

68. Ibid., 12.

69. Ibid., 13.

70. Ibid.

71. Ibid., 31.

72. Ibid., 70–80.

73. Taiaiake Alfred, *Peace, Power, Righteousness: An Indigenous Manifesto* (Don Mills, Ont.: Oxford University Press, 1999), 76. Also, see Alfred, "Deconstructing the British Columbia Treaty Process," in *Dispatches from the Cold Seas: Indigenous Views on Self-Government, Ecology, and Identity*, ed. C. Rattay and T. Mustonen (Tempere Polytechnic, 2001).

74. Jim Beatty, "Natives lose court bid to block B.C. referendum on treaties: Ballots will begin arriving in the mail next week," *The Vancouver Sun*, March 28, 2002, A3.

75. Alfred, *Peace, Power, Righteousness*, 76.

Chapter Four

Wasáse: Indigenous Resurgences

Taiaiake Alfred

It is time for our people to live again. This chapter begins a journey on the path made for us by those who have found a way to live as *Onkwehonwe*, original people. The journey is a living commitment to meaningful change in our lives and to transforming society by re-creating our existences, regenerating our cultures, and surging against the forces that keep us bound to our colonial past. It is the path of struggle laid out by those who have come before us; and now it is our turn, we who choose to turn away from the legacies of colonialism and take on the challenge of creating a new reality for ourselves and for our people.

    The journey and this warrior's path is a kind of *Wasáse*, a ceremony of unity and strength and commitment to action. Wasáse is an ancient Rotinoshonni war ritual, the Thunder Dance. The new warrior's path, the spirit of Wasáse, this Onkwehonwe attitude, this courageous way of being in the world, all come together to form a new politics in which many identities and strategies for making change are fused together in a movement to challenge white society's control over Onkwehonwe and our lands. Wasáse, as I am speaking of it here, is symbolic of the social and cultural force alive among Onkwehonwe dedicated to altering the balance of political and economic power to re-create some social and physical space for freedom to reemerge. Wasáse is an ethical and political vision and the real demonstration of our resolve to survive as Onkwehonwe and to do what we must to force the Settlers to acknowledge our existence and the integrity of our connection to the land.

    There are many differences among the peoples that are indigenous to this land. Yet the challenge facing all Onkwehonwe is the same, and centers on regaining freedom and becoming self-sufficient by confronting the disconnection and fear at the core of our existences under colonial dominion. We are separated from the sources of our goodness and power: each other, our cultures, and our lands. These connections must be restored. Governmental power is founded on fear. Fear is used to control and manipulate us in many ways; so, the strategy must be to confront fear and display the courage to act against and defeat the state's power.

The first question that arises when this idea is applied in a practical way to the situations facing Onkwehonwe in real life is this: How can we regenerate ourselves culturally and achieve freedom and political independence when the legacies of disconnection, dependency, and dispossession have such a strong hold on us? Undeniably, we face a difficult situation. The political and social institutions that govern us have been shaped and organized to serve white power and they conform to the interests of the states founded on that objective. These state-serving institutions are useless to the cause of our survival, and if we are to free ourselves from the grip of colonialism we must reconfigure our politics and replace all of the strategies, institutions, and leaders in place today. The transformation will begin inside each one of us as personal change, but decolonization will become a reality only when we collectively commit to a movement based on an *ethical* and *political* vision, and a conscious rejection of the colonial postures of weak submission, victimry, and raging violence. It is a political vision and solution that will be capable of altering power relations and rearranging the forces that shape our lives. Politics is the force that channels social, cultural, economic powers and makes them imminent in our lives. Abstaining from politics is like turning your back on an animal when the beast is angry and intent on ripping your guts out.

It is the kind of politics we practice that is the crucial distinction between the possibility of a regenerative struggle and what we are doing now. Conventional and acceptable approaches to making change are leading us nowhere. Submission and cooperation, which define politics as practiced by the current generation of Onkwehonwe politicians, are, I contend, morally, culturally, and politically indefensible and should be dismissed scornfully by any right-thinking person and certainly by any Onkwehonwe who still has dignity. I pay little attention to the conventional aspects of the politics of pity, such as self-government processes, land claims agreements, and aboriginal-rights court cases, because building on what we have achieved up until now in our efforts to decolonize society is insufficient and truly unacceptable as the end-state of a challenge to colonialism. The job is far from finished. It is impossible to predict what constraints and opportunities will emerge, but it is clear that we have not pushed hard enough yet to sit satisfied with the state's enticements. Fundamentally different relationships between Onkwehonwe and Settlers will emerge not from negotiations in state-sponsored and government-regulated processes, but after successful Onkwehonwe resurgences against white society's entrenched privileges and the unreformed structure of the colonial state.

As Onkwehonwe committed to the reclamation of our dignity and strength, there are, theoretically, two viable approaches to engaging the colonial power that is thoroughly embedded in the state and in societal structures: armed resistance and nonviolent contention. Each has a heritage among our peoples and is a potential formula for making change, for engaging with the adversary without deference to emotional attachments to colonial symbols or to the compromised logic of colonial approaches. They are both philosophically defensible; but are they both equally valid approaches to making change, given the realities of our situations and our goals? We need a confident position on the question as to what is the right strategy. Both armed resistance and nonviolent contention are unique disciplines that require commitments that rule out overlapping allegiances between the two approaches. They are diverging and distinctive ways of making change, and the choice between the two paths is the most important decision the next generation of Onkwehonwe will collectively make.

This is the political formula of the strategy of armed resistance: facing a situation of untenable politics, Onkwehonwe could conceivably move toward practicing a punishing kind of aggression, a raging resistance invoking hostile and irredentist negative political visions seeking to engender and escalate the conflict so as to eventually demoralize the Settler society and defeat the colonial state. Contrast this with the strategic vision of nonviolent contention: Onkwehonwe face the untenable politics and unacceptable conditions in their communities and confront the situation with determination yet restrained action, coherent and creative contention supplemented with a positive political vision based on reestablishing respect for the original covenants and ancient treaties that reflect the founding principles of the Onkwehonwe-Settler relationship. This would be a movement sure to engender conflict, but it would be conflict for a positive purpose and with the hope of re-creating the conditions of coexistence. Rather than enter the arena of armed resistance, we would choose to perform rites of resurgence.

These forms of resurgence have already begun. There are people in all communities who understand that a true decolonization movement can emerge only when we shift our politics from articulating grievances to pursuing an organized and political battle for the cause of our freedom. These new warriors understand the need to refuse any further disconnection from their heritage, and the need to reconnect with the spiritual bases of their existences as Onkwehonwe. Following their example and building on the foundation of their struggles, the potential exists to initiate a more coordinated and widespread action, and to reorganize communities to take advantage of gains and opportunities as they occur in political, economic, social, and cultural spheres and spaces created by the movement. There is a solid theory of change in this concept of an Indigenous peoples' movement. The theory of change is the lived experience of the people we will encounter in this work. Their lives are a dynamic of power generated by creative energy flowing from their heritage through their courageous and unwavering determination to re-create themselves and act together to meet the challenges of their day.

A common and immediate concern for anyone defending the truth of their heritage is the imperative to repel the thrust of the modern state's assault against our peoples. The Settlers continue to erase our existences from the cultural, social, and political landscape of our homelands. Onkwehonwe are awakening to the need to move from the materialist orientation of our politics and social reality toward a restored spiritual foundation, channeling that spiritual strength and the unity it creates into a power that can affect political and economic relations. A true revolution is spiritual at its core; every single of the world's materialist revolutions have failed to produce conditions of life that are markedly different from those which it opposed. Whatever the specific means or rationale, violent, legalist, and economic revolutions have never been successful in producing peaceful coexistence between peoples; in fact, they always reproduce the exact set of power relations they seek to change, and rearrange only the outward face of power.

Another problem of Indigenous politics is that there is no consistency of means and ends in the way we are struggling to empower ourselves. Approaches to making change that advocate reforming the colonial legal system or state policy, and those that seek empowerment through the accumulation of financial resources, may seem to hold promise, but they are opposed to basic and shared Onkwehonwe values in either the means they would use to advance the struggle or in the ends they would achieve. Legalist, economic, and for that matter violent insurgent approaches, are all simply mimicking foreign logics, each in a different way. How you fight determines who you will become when the battle is over, and there is always means-ends consistency at the end of the game. For Onkwehonwe, the implication of a legalist approach is entrenchment in the state system as citizens with rights defined by the constitution of the colonial state, which is the defeat of the idea of an independent Onkwehonwe existence. The implication of the economic development approach is integration into the consumer culture of mainstream capitalist society, which is the defeat of the possibility of ways of life associated with Onkwehonwe cultures. And, of course, violence begets violence. The implication of an approach to making change using armed force to attack institutions and the structure of power is an ensuing culture of violence that is in its very existence the negation of the ideal of peaceful coexistence at the heart of Onkwehonwe philosophies.

Despite the visible and public victories in court cases and casino profits, neither of these strategies generates the transformative experience that re-creates people like the spiritual-cultural resurgences. The truly revolutionary goal is to transform disconnection and fear into connection and to transcend the colonial culture and institutions. Onkwehonwe have been successful on personal and collective levels by rejecting extremism on both ends of the spectrum between the reformist urgings of tame legalists and unfocused rage or armed insurgents.

Consider the futility of our present politics, and the perversity of what I will call "aboriginalism," the ideology and identity of assimilation, where Onkwehonwe are manipulated by colonial myths into a submissive position and are told that by emulating white people they can gain acceptance and possibly even fulfillment within the mainstream society. Many Onkwehonwe today embrace the label of "aboriginal," but this identity is a legal and social construction of the state, and it is disciplined by racialized violence and economic oppression to serve an agenda of silent surrender. The acceptance of being aboriginal is as powerful an assault on Onkwehonwe existences as any force of arms brought upon us by the Settler society. The integrationist and unchallenging aboriginal vision is designed to lead us to oblivion, as individual successes in assimilating to the mainstream are celebrated, and our survival is redefined strictly in the terms of capitalist dogma and practical-minded individualist consumerism and complacency.

Within the frame of politics and social life, Onkwehonwe who accept the label and identity of an aboriginal are bound up in a logic that is becoming increasingly evident even to them as one of outright assimilation—the abandonment of any meaningful notion of being Indigenous.

Outright assaults and insidious undermining have brought us to the situation we face today, where the destruction of our peoples is nearly complete. Yet resurgence and regeneration constitute a way to power-surge against the empire with integrity. The new warriors who are working to ensure the survival of their people are not distracted by the effort to pass off as "action" analyses of the self-evident fact of the defeat of our nations. They don't imagine that our cause needs further justification, in law or the public mind. They know that assertion and action are the urgencies; all the rest is a smokescreen clouding this clear vision.

The experience of resurgence and regeneration in Onkwehonwe communities thus far proves that change cannot be made from within the colonial structure. Institutions and ideas that are the creation of the colonial relationship are not capable of ensuring our survival—this has been amply proven as well by the absolute failure of institutional and legalist strategies to protect our lands and our rights, as well as in their failure to motivate younger generations of Onkwehonwe to action. In the face of the strong, renewed push by the state for the legal and political assimilation of our peoples, and a rising tide of consumerist materialism making its way into our communities, the last remaining remnants of distinctive Onkwehonwe values and culture are being wiped out. The situation is urgent and calls for even more intensive and profound resurgences on even more levels, certainly not moderation. Many people are paralyzed by fear or idled by complacency and will sit passively and watch the destruction consume our people. But my words are for those of us who prefer a dangerous dignity to safe self-preservation.

People have always faced these challenges. None of what I am saying is new, either to people's experience in the world or to political philosophy. What is reemerging in our communities is a renewed respect for Indigenous knowledge and Onkwehonwe ways of thinking. I hope to document and glorify this renewal, in which Onkwehonwe are linked in spirit and strategy with other Indigenous peoples confronting empire throughout the world. When we look into the heart of our own communities, we can relate to the struggles of peoples in Africa, or Asia, and appreciate the North African scholar Albert Memmi's thoughts on how, in the language of his day, colonized peoples respond to oppression:

> One can be reconciled to every situation, and the colonized can wait a long time to live. But, regardless of how soon or how violently the colonized rejects his situation, he will one day begin to overthrow his unliveable existence with the whole force of his oppressed personality.[1]

The question facing us is this one: For us today, here in this land, how will the overthrow of our unlivable existence come about?

Memmi was prescient in his observations on the reaction of people laboring under colonial oppression. Eventually, our people too will move to revolt against being defined by the Settlers as "aboriginal" and against the dispossession of our lands and heritage, and we will track our oppression to its source, which is the basic structure of the colonial state and society. Memmi also wrote, "revolt is the only way out of the colonial situation, and the colonized realizes it sooner or later. His condition is absolute and cries for an absolute solution; a break and not a compromise." Settlers and tamed aboriginals in purportedly stable and peaceful countries like Canada, Australia, the United States, and New Zealand may reject those words, but only because the imperial evil is so well disguised and deeply denied in these countries; the burden of persistent colonialism has become mundane and internalized to Onkwehonwe life only, and its effects subsumed within our cultures and psychologies. Especially in the smug placidity of middle- and upper-class North America, the implications of Memmi's utterance are surely frightening. What and why do we have to break? Break up, break apart, break me . . . ? It is all a question of one's experience and mentality, of course. All of the world's big problems are in reality very small and local problems. They are brought into force as realities only in the choices made every day and in many ways by people who are enticed by certain incentives and disciplined by their fears. So, confronting huge forces like colonialism is a personal and, in some ways, a mundane process. This is not to say it is easy, but looking at it this way does give proper focus to the effort of decolonizing.

The colonizers stand on guard for their ill-gotten privileges using highly advanced techniques, mainly cooptation, division, and when required, physical repression. The weak people in the power equation help the colonizers too, with their self-doubts, laziness, and unfortunate insistence on their own disorganization!

Challenging all of this means even redefining the terminology of our existence. Take the word, "colonization," which is actually a way of seeing and explaining what has happened to us. We cannot allow that word to be the story of our lives, because it is a narrative that in its use privileges the colonizer's power and inherently limits our freedom, logically and mentally imposing a perpetual colonized-victim way of life and view on the world. Onkwehonwe are not faced with the same adversary their ancestors confronted, but with a colonization that has recently morphed into a kind of postmodern imperialism that is more difficult to target than the previous and more obvious impositions of force and control over the structures of government within their communities. Memmi's "break" must itself be redefined.

The challenge is to reframe revolt. Classically, the phases of revolt are thought of along a continuum moving from the self-assertion of an independent identity, to seeking moderate reforms of the system, to protesting and openly rejecting authority, and then to revolutionary action to destroy the state and replace it with another order of power. Thinking along these lines, it is ironic that our own politicians find themselves being unwitting conservatives. Twenty years ago they were positioned at the cutting edge of change— Red Power, political and cultural revivalism, court challenges for rights, land claims, etc. But now those same people are in positions of leadership, and on the whole they are resisting attempts to move the challenge to the next stage. Our politicians find themselves cooperating with their (former) enemies and adversaries to preserve the nonthreatening, very limited resolutions they have worked with the colonial powers to create and define as end objectives. They have accommodated themselves to colonialism, not defeated it. And they have forgotten that the ancestral movement always sought total freedom from domination and a complete revolt against empire, not halfway compromises and weak surrenders to watered-down injustices.

I have heard it said, prophetically, in my own community that "the people will rise up again when the chiefs' heads are rolling on the ground." While it is clear that guerrilla and terrorist strategies are futile—certainly so from within the center of industrial capitalist countries—the spirit of the ancestors who went to war against the invaders is compelling and honorable. I refuse to pass moral judgment against those oppressed people who act against imperial power using arms to advance their cause; their acts of resistance are only the moral equivalents to the heinous and legalized capitalist crimes that are destroying people's lives and the land. And where people meet state violence with arms to defend themselves and their lands in necessary acts of self-preservation, they are of course justified in doing so. But, because I hold a strong commitment to struggles for freedom, I do not believe that armed struggle is the right path for our people to take. Violent revolt is simply not an intelligent and realistic approach to confronting the injustice we face, and will not allow us to succeed in transforming the society from what it is to a state of peaceful coexistence. Anyway, I sense that even if my own strategic disagreement with, or some other people's moral judgments against, armed action did not solidify against a group's advocacy and use of violence, rejection and approbation by communities would surely come in the wake of the indirect effects of armed revolt on the mass of Onkwehonwe, who would without a doubt be further abused and violated by repressive counterviolence the state would use in retaliation.

Using violence to advance our objectives would lead to frustration and failure for political and military reasons, but it would also falter for deeper spiritual and cultural reasons. I find it very difficult to see any value in asking our future generations to form their identities on and live lives of aggression; would this not validate and maintain the enemy colonizer as an omnipresent and superior reality of our existence for generations to come? This is not the legacy we want to leave for our children. To remain true to a struggle conceived within Onkwehonwe values, our Wasáse—our warrior's dance—the end goal must be formulated as a spiritual revolution, a culturally rooted *social* movement that transforms the whole of society, and as *political* action that seeks to remake the entire landscape of power and relationship to reflect truly a liberated post-imperial vision.

Wasáse is spiritual revolution and contention. It is not a path of violence. And yet, this commitment to nonviolence is not pacifism, either. This is an important point to make clear: I believe there is a need for morally grounded defiance and nonviolent agitation combined with the development of a collective capacity for self-defense, so as to generate within the Settler society a reason and incentive to negotiate constructively in the interest of achieving a respectful coexistence. The rest of this book will try to explain this concept (an effort the more academically inclined reader may be permitted to read as my theorizing the liberation of Indigenous peoples).

My goal is to discover a real and deep notion of peace in the hope of moving us away from valuing simplistic notions of peace such as certainty and stability; for these are conceptions that point only to the value of order. Some readers may find themselves confused by the seeming contradictions in my logic and question "peace" as the orienting goal of this warrior-spirited work, and wonder if perhaps a concept like "justice" may be more to the point and truer to the spirit of a book that takes a war dance as its emblem. But justice as a liberatory concept and as a would-be goal is limited by its necessary gaze to the politics, economics, and social relations of the past. However noble and necessary justice is to our struggles, its gaze will always be backward. By itself, the concept of justice is not capable of encompassing the broader transformations needed to ensure coexistence. Justice is one element of a good relationship; justice is concerned with fairness and right and calculating moral balances, but it cannot be the end goal of a struggle, which must be conceived as a movement from injustice and conflict through and beyond the achievement of justice to the completion of the relationship and the achievement of peace.

The old slogan, "No justice, no peace," is a truism. We must move from injustice, through struggle, to a mutual respect founded on the achievement of justice, and then onward toward peace. Step by step. Lacking struggle, omitting respect and justice, there can and will be no peace. Or happiness. Or freedom. These are the real goals of a truly human and fully realized philosophy of change.

Peace is hopeful, visionary, and forward-looking. It is not just the lack of violent conflict or rioting in the streets. That simple stability is what we call order, and order serves the powerful in an imperial situation. If peace continues to be strictly defined as the maintenance of order and the rule of law, we will be defeated in our struggle to survive as Onkwehonwe. Reconceptualized for our struggle, peace is being Onkwehonwe, breaking with the disfiguring and meaningless norms of our present reality, and re-creating ourselves in a holistic sense. This conception of peace requires a rejection of the state's multifaceted oppression of our peoples simultaneously with and through the assertion of regenerated Onkwehonwe identities. Personal and collective transformation is not instrumental to the surging against state power, it is the very means of our struggle.

Memmi, who was so powerful in his exposure of colonial mentalities at play during the Algerian resistance against French colonialism, spoke of the fundamental need to cure white people, through revolution, of the "disease of the European" they have collectively inherited from their colonial forefathers. I believe his prescription of spiritual transformation channeled into a political action and social movement is the right medicine.

Following an awakening among the people and cultural redefinition, after social agitation, after engaging in a politics of contention, after creative confrontation, we will be free to determine our own existences. Wasáse, struggle in all of its forms, truly defines an authentic existence. This is the clearest statement on what I seek to cause with the ideas I am putting forward in this book. This is why I speak of warriors. To be Onkwehonwe, to be fully human, is to be living the ethic of courage and to be involved in a struggle for personal transformation and freedom from the dominance of imperial ideas and powers—especially facing the challenges in our lives today. Any other path or posture is surrender or complicity. And though I am speaking nonviolently of a creative reinterpretation of what it is to be a warrior, I am doing so in full reverence and honor of the essence of the ancient warrior spirit, because a warrior makes a stand facing danger, with courage and integrity. The warrior spirit is the strong medicine we need to cure the European disease. But, drawing on the old spirit, we need to create something new for ourselves and think through the reality of the present to design an appropriate strategy, use fresh tactics, and acquire new skills.

The new warriors make their own way in the world: they move forward heeding the teachings of the ancestors and carrying a creed that has been taken from the past and re-made into a powerful way of being in their new world. In our actions, we show our respect for the heritage of our people by regenerating the spirit of our ancestors. We glorify the continuing existence of our peoples, and we act on the knowledge that our survival as Onkwehonwe depends on living the rites of resurgence. Fighting these battles in this kind of war, our nations will be re-created. The new warriors are committed in the first instance to self-transformation and self-defense against the insidious forms of control that the state and capitalism uses to shape lives according to their needs—to fear, to obey, to consume.

When lies rule, warriors create new truths for the people to believe. Warriors battle against the political manipulation of their innate fears and repel the state's attempts to embed complacency inside of them. They counterattack with a lived ethic of courage, and seek to cause the reawakening of a culture of freedom.

Survival is bending and swaying but not breaking, adapting and accommodating without compromising what is core to one's being. Those who are emboldened by challenges and who sacrifice for the truth achieve freedom. Those who fail to find balance, who reject change, or who abandon their heritage altogether abandon themselves. They perish. The people who live on are those who have learned the lesson of survival: cherish your unique identity, protect your freedom, and defend your homeland.

Even from within a conservative viewpoint on politics, if self-government or self-determination are the goals, and if communities are seeking to restore a limited degree of autonomy for their people in relation to the state, it must be recognized that the cultural basis of our existence as Onkwehonwe has been nearly destroyed, and that the cultural foundation of our nations must be restored or re-imagined if there is going to be a successful assertion of political or economic rights. In other words, there certainly exists the moral right and the legal right for governance outside of assimilative or co-optive forms, but there is no capacity in our communities and there is no cultural basis on which to generate an effective movement against the further erosion of Onkwehonwe political authority. This has placed our continuing existence as *peoples*, or as nations and distinct cultures, in imminent danger of extinction.

I am not overstating the danger to make a point, or, as it may be suspected, for rhetorical purposes. Think of the pattern of societal decline described by Hannah Arendt: political authority falls after the loss of tradition and the weakening of religious beliefs. Spirituality breaks, there is a loss of traditional cultures and languages, and this is followed by political subjugation.[2] This pattern reduces the story of the 500-year conquest of *Anówarakowa Kawennote*, Great Turtle Island, to its essence. Imperialism has not been a totalizing, unknowable and irresistible force of destruction, but a fluid dynamic made of politics, economics, psychology, and culture. It remains so.

What is the path to meaningful change in our lives? The most common answers to that question come in the form of big political or economic solutions to problems conceived of as *historical*, or past, injustices: self-government, land claims, economic development, and the legal recognition of our rights as nations. I recognize, of course, that these are crucial goals. In the long-term, it will be absolutely necessary to redefine and reconstruct the governmental and economic relationship between Onkwehonwe and Settlers. Yet to the extent that self-government, land claims, and economic development agreements have been successfully negotiated and implemented, there is no evidence that they have done anything to make but a very small minority of our people happier and healthier.

In most cases, these agreements create new bureaucracies and put in place new levels and forms of government based on the colonial model, or new capitalist relationships with nonindigenous business partners. These new arrangements benefit a few people, mainly elected officials, entrepreneurs, lawyers, consultants, and, to a much lesser extent, the people who staff the various structures. Self-government, land claims, and economic development are abundantly positive for this fortunate minority. This is not to begrudge the fact that some of us have gained the education and skills needed to secure jobs or create businesses—these are the rewards of honest people who have worked hard to create strength for themselves. But in the midst of all of the apparent progress, there is a nagging sense among so many people that something is wrong even with these supposed solutions. There is a dawning awareness among those of us who think outside of ourselves, those who care about the not-so-fortunate and all-too-easily-ignored 90 percent of our people, those who get no benefit at all from the new political and economic orders being created by the collusion of interests that govern our communities today. It is the sinking feeling that political power and money, the things we've worked so hard to achieve, are still not going to be enough to liberate us from our present reality.

I am saying that the real reason most Onkwehonwe endure unhappy and unhealthy lives has nothing to do with governmental powers or money. The lack of these things only contributes to making a bad situation worse. The root of the problem is that we are living through a spiritual crisis, a time of darkness that descended on our people when we became disconnected from our lands and from our traditional ways of life. We are divided among ourselves and confused in our own minds about who we are and what kind of life we should be living. We depend on others to feed us and to teach us how to look, feel, live. We still turn to white men for the answers to our problems; worse yet, we have started to trust them. There are no more leaders and hardly a place left to go where you can just be *native*. We are the prophetic Seventh Generation: if we do not find a way out of the crises, we will be consumed by the darkness and whether it is through self-destruction or assimilation, we will not survive for another generation.

Large-scale statist solutions like self-government and land claims are not so much lies as they are irrelevant to the root problem. For a long time now, we have been on a quest for governmental power and money; somewhere along the journey from the past to the future, we forgot that our goal was to reconnect with our lands and to preserve our harmonious cultures and respectful ways of life. It is these things that are the true guarantee of peace, health, strength, and happiness, of survival. Before we can ever start rebuilding ourselves and achieve meaningful change in the areas of law and government, of economies and development, we must start to remember one important thing: our communities are made up of people. Our concern about legal rights and empowering models of national self-government has led to the neglect of the fundamental building blocks of our peoples: the women and men, the youth and the elders.

Some people believe in the promise of what they call "traditional government" as the ultimate solution to our problems, as if just getting rid of the imposed corrupt band or tribal governments and resurrecting old laws and structures would solve everything. I used to believe that myself. But there is a problem with this way of thinking too. The traditional governments and laws we hold out as the pure good alternatives to the imposed colonial systems were developed at a time when people were different than we are now; they were people who were confidently rooted in their culture, bodily and spiritually strong, and capable of surviving independently in their natural environments. We should ask ourselves if it makes any sense to try to bring back these forms of government and social organization without first regenerating our people so that we can support traditional government models. Regretfully, the levels of participation in social and political life, physical fitness, and cultural skills these models require are far beyond our weakened and dispirited people right now.

We will begin to make meaningful change in the lives of our communities when we start to focus on making real change in the lives of our people as individuals. It may sound clichéd, but it is still true that the first part of self-determination is the *self*. In our minds and in our souls, we need to reject the colonists' control and authority; their definition of who we are and what our rights are; their definition of what is worthwhile and how one should live; their hypocritical and pacifying moralities. We need to rebel against what they want us to become and start remembering the qualities of our ancestors, and acting on those remembrances. This is the kind of spiritual revolution that will ensure our survival.

What are the first steps in this revolution of the spirit?

For a start, let's think about the most basic question: what does it mean to be Onkwehonwe? Many times, I have listened to one of the wisest people I know, Leroy Little Bear, speak on one of the real differences between Onkwehonwe and European languages. European languages, he explains, center on nouns and are concerned with naming things, ascribing traits, and making judgments. Onkwehonwe languages are structured on verbs; they communicate through descriptions of movement and activity. Take my own name, for example. Taiaiake, in English, is a proper noun that labels me for identification. In Kanienkeha, it literally means, "he is crossing over from the other side." Struggling against and negotiating with the descendants of Europeans occupying our homelands for all these years, we have become very skilled, in the European way, at judging and naming everything, even ourselves: beliefs, rights, authorities, jurisdictions, land use areas, categories of membership in our communities, and so on, as if it were enough to speak these things to make them into a reality. In fighting for our future, we have been misled into thinking that "Indigenous," or "First Nations," "Carrier," "Cree" or "Mohawk" (even if we use *Kanien'kehaka*, or *Innu*, or *Wet'suwet'en*), is something that is attached to us inherently, and not a description of what we actually do with our lives.

The European way is to see the world organized in a system of names and titles that formalize their being. Onkwehonwe recall relationships and responsibilities through languages that symbolize doing. Apply this linguistic insight to our recent efforts to gain recognition and respect, and you start to get a sense of why we have fallen off the good path. We have mistaken the mere renaming of our situation for an actual reconnection with our lands and cultures. Living as Onkwehonwe means much more than applying a label to ourselves and saying that we are indigenous to the land. It means looking at the personal and political choices we make every day and applying an Indigenous logic to those daily acts of creation. It means knowing and respecting Kanien'kehaka, Innu, and Wet'suwet'en teachings; thinking and behaving in a way that is consistent with the values passed down to us by our ancestors. My people speak of the coming generations as "faces who are yet to emerge from the Earth." We have a sacred responsibility to rise up and fight so that our people may live again as Onkwehonwe.

What is the way to restore meaning and dignity to our lives? This is another way of framing the question that guides us as we trace the path of truth and struggle from where we stand today. Too many of our peoples are disoriented, dissatisfied, fearful, and disconnected from each other and from the natural world. Onkwehonwe deserve a different state of being where there are real opportunities for us to finally realize justice and peace in our lives, and where there is hope of creating a society in which it is possible to live a life of integrity and happiness.

The thoughts and vision I am offering through these words are rooted in the cultural heritage of Anówarakowa. And proudly so! They are not compromises between Indigenous and nonindigenous perspectives; nor are they attempts to negotiate a reconciliation of Onkwehonwe and European cultures and values. These words are an attempt to bring forward an indigenously rooted voice of contention, unconstrained and uncompromised by colonial mentalities. A total commitment to the challenge of regenerating our indigeneity, to rootedness in Indigenous cultures, to a fundamental commitment to the centrality of our truths—this work is an effort to work through the philosophical, spiritual, and practical implications of holding such commitments.

These commitments require the reader to challenge critically all of his or her artificial and emotional attachments to the oppressive colonial myths and symbols that we have come to know as our culture. I know that this is asking people to wander into dangerous territory; disentangling from these attachments can also feel like being banished, in a way. But stepping into our fear is crucial, because leaving the comfort zone of accepted truth is vital to creating the emotional and mental state that allows one to really learn. It is a new approach to decolonization. Less intense, or less threatening, ideas about how to make change have proven ineffective from our perspective. I believe it is because they are bound up in and unable to break free from the limiting logic of the colonial myths that they claim to oppose. The myths' symbols and embedded beliefs force aboriginal thinking to remain in colonial mental, political, and legal frameworks, rendering these forms of writing and thinking less radical and powerless against imperialism. The reflections, meditations, teachings, and dialogues that form the core of this book are indigenous and organic: they emerge from inside Onkwehonwe experiences and reflect the ideas, concepts and languages that have developed over millennia in the spaces we live, among our peoples. I want to bring the heritage and truth of Anówarakowa to a new generation and to engage passionately with Indigenous truths to generate powerful dynamics of thought, and action, and change. I did not write this book *about* change, I wrote it from *within* change. I wrote it with the plain intent of instigating further contention. My hope is that people who read these words will take from them a different way of defining the problem at the core of our present existence, one that brings a radically principled and challenging set of ideas to bear on how to remake the relationship between Onkwehonwe and Settler.

A big part of the social and political resurgence will be the regeneration of Onkwehonwe existences free from colonial attitudes and behaviors. Regeneration means we will reference ourselves differently, both from the ways we did traditionally and under colonial dominion. We will self-consciously re-create our cultural practices and reform our political identities by drawing on tradition in a thoughtful process of reconstruction and a committed reorganization of our lives in a personal and collective sense. This will result in a new conception of what it is to live as Onkwehonwe. This book is my contribution to the larger effort to catalyze and galvanize the movements that have already begun among so many of our people. Restoring these connections is the force that will confront and defeat the defiant evil of imperialism in this land. We need to work together to cleanse our minds, our hearts, and our bodies of the colonial stain and reconnect our lives to the sources of our strength as Onkwehonwe. We need to find new and creative ways to express that heritage. I wrote this work as an Onkwehonwe believing in the fundamental commonalty of Indigenous values; yet I wrote it from within my own experience. I aim to speak most directly to other Onkwehonwe who share my commitments and who are traveling the same pathway. These words are offered in the spirit of the ancient Wasáse, which was so eloquently captured by my friend Kahente when I asked her to tell me how she understood the meaning of the ritual:

> There is a spiritual base that connects us all, and it is stimulated through ceremony. The songs and dances that we perform are like medicine, *Ononkwa*, invoking the power of the original instructions that lie within. In it, we dance, sing, and share our words of pain, joy, strength and commitment. The essence of the ancestors' message reveals itself not only in these songs, speeches, and dances but also in the faces and bodies of all who are assembled. This visual manifestation shows us that we are not alone and that our survival depends on being part of the larger group and in this group working together. We are reminded to stay on the path laid out before us. This way it strengthens our resolve to keep going and to help each other along the way. It is a time to show each other how to step along that winding route in unison and harmony with one another. To know who your friends and allies are in such struggle is what is most important and is what keeps you going.

If nonindigenous readers are capable of listening, they will learn from these shared words, and they will discover that while we are envisioning a new relationship between Onkwehonwe and the land, we are at the same time offering a decolonized alternative to the Settler society by inviting them to share our vision of respect and peaceful coexistence.

The nonindigenous will be shown a new path and offered the chance to join in a renewed relationship between the peoples and places of this land, which we occupy together. I want to provoke. To cause reflection. To motivate people to creatively confront the social and spiritual forces that are preventing us from overcoming the divisive and painful legacies of our shared history as imperial subjects. The guiding question I asked earlier can be stated in another way: What is the meaning of self-determination? We have just now started on the journey together to find the full meaning of the answer to this question, but even so, I believe we all know that achieving freedom means overcoming the delusions, greeds, and hatreds that lie at the center of colonial culture. This work is an expression of that common yearning for freedom, drawing on the inarticulate and unsettled energy that still resides inside each of us.

Onkwehonwe have always fought for survival against imperialism and its drive to annihilate our existence. Our fight is no different from previous generations'—it is a struggle to defend the lands, the communities, and the languages that are our heritage and our future. But the new imperialism that we experience has a special character. The close danger of a technological empire and co-optation is the insidious effort of the Settler society to erase us from the cultural and political landscape of the countries they have invaded and now claim as their own. Survival demands that we act on the love we have for this land and our people. This is the counter-imperative to empire. Our power is a courageous love. Our fight is to recognize, to expose, and to ultimately overcome the corrupt, colonized identities and irrational fears that have been bred into us. It is worth repeating that survival will require not only political or cultural resurgence against state power, but positive movement to overcome the defining features of imperialism on a personal and collective level. These resurgences, multiplicities of thought and action, must be founded on Onkwehonwe philosophies and lead us to reconnect with respectful and natural ways of being in the world.

I understand that not everyone realizes or accepts that Onkwehonwe are on the verge of extinction. There are many people, the majority in fact in any community, who still refuse to acknowledge and accept the fact of our perilous condition. The Aboriginal Self-Termination movement is much stronger than any coordinated Onkwehonwe movement against imperialism and white dominion today. Most of our people are assimilated into the racist propagandas designed to rob them of their dignity and their lands, and have normalized the destruction of their nations. That conclusion may seem harsh, but it is truth. The edge of extinction does not afford the luxury of mincing words.

You may be wondering how it is that I fail to appreciate the efforts to reform and reconcile social relations that are currently under way in the more progressive colonial countries. But I do appreciate the nature of these reforms and reconciliations with colonialism too well. Fifteen years of working in Onkwehonwe communities and organizations has taught me that continued cooperation with state power structures is morally unacceptable. Everyone involved in the Indian Industry knows that we are negotiating with our oppressor from a position of weakness. Organizations purport to speak for people who turn around and vehemently deny the legitimacy and authority of those very organizations and their so-called leaders. And the communities are disintegrating socially and culturally at a terrifying speed as alienation, social ills, and disease outpace efforts to stabilize our societies. In this environment, negotiation is futile. It is counter-productive to our survival. It is senseless to advocate for an accord with imperialism while there is a steady and intense ongoing attack by the Settler society on everything meaningful to us: our cultures, our communities, and our deep attachments to land. The framework of current reformist or reconciling negotiations are about handing us the scraps of history: self-government and jurisdictional authorities for state-created Indian governments within the larger colonial system, and subjection of Onkwehonwe to the blunt force of capitalism by integrating them as wage slaves into the mainstream resource-exploitation economy. These surface reforms are being offered because they are useless to our survival as Onkwehonwe. This is not a coincidence, nor is it a result of our goals being obsolete. Self-government and economic development are being offered precisely *because* they are useless to us in the struggle to survive as peoples, and they are therefore no threat to the Settlers and, specifically, the interests of the people who control the Settler state. This is assimilation's end-game. Today, self-government and economic development signify the defeat of our peoples' struggles just as surely as, to our grandparents, residential schools, land dispossession, and police beatings signified the supposed supremacy of white power and the subjugation and humiliation of the first and real peoples of this land.

What it comes down to in confronting our imperial reality is that some of us want to reform colonial law and policy, to dull that monster's teeth so that we can't be ripped apart so easily. Some of us believe in reconciliation, forgetting that the monster has a genocidal appetite, a taste for our blood, and would sooner tear us apart than lick our hand. I think that the only thing that has changed since our ancestors first declared war on the invaders is that some of us have lost our heart. Against history and against those who would submit to it, I am with the warriors who want to beat the beast into bloody submission, and teach it to behave.

The time to change direction is now. Signs of defeat have been showing on the faces of our people for too long. Young people, those who have not yet learned to accommodate the fact that they are expected to quietly accept their lesser status, are especially hard hit by defeatism and alienation. Youth in our communities and in urban centers are suffering. Suicide, alcohol and drug abuse, cultural confusion, sexual violence, obesity: they suffer these scourges worse than anyone else. It is not because they lack money or jobs in the mainstream society (we shouldn't forget that our people have always been "poor" as consumers in comparison to white people). It is because their identities, their cultures, and their rights are under attack by a racist government. The wounds suffered by young Onkwehonwe people in battle are given little succor by their own elders, and they find only scorn or condescension in the larger world. These young people are fighting raging battles for their own survival every day, and when they become convinced that to fight is futile and the battle likely to be lost, they retreat. Yet they have pride and rather than submit to the enemy, they sacrifice themselves, sometimes using mercifully quick and sometimes using painfully slow methods.

Some people may find it shocking or absurd for me to suggest that an Onkwehonwe community is a kind of war zone. But anyone who has actually lived on a reserve will agree with this tragic analogy on some level. Make no mistake about it, Brothers and Sisters: the war is on. There is no postcolonial situation; the invaders our ancestors fought against are still here, for they have not yet rooted themselves and been transformed into real people of this homeland. Onkwehonwe must find a way to triumph over notions of history that relegate our existence to the past by preserving ourselves in this hostile and disintegrating environment. To do so, we must regenerate ourselves through action because living the white man's vision of an Indian or an aboriginal will just not do for us.

We are each facing modernity's attempt to conquer our souls. The conquest is happening as weak, cowardly, stupid, petty, and greedy ways worm themselves into our lives and take the place of the beauty and sharing and harmony that defined life in our communities for previous generations. Territorial losses and political disempowerment are secondary conquests compared to that first, spiritual, cause of discontent. The challenge is to find a way to regenerate ourselves and take back our dignity. Then, meaningful change will be possible, and it will be a new existence, one of possibility, where Onkwehonwe will have the ability to make the kinds of choices we need to make concerning the quality of our lives, and begin to recover a truly human way of life.

NOTES

*A version of this essay was first published as "First Words," pp. 19–38, in Taiaiake Alfred's *Wasáse: Indigenous Pathways of Action and Freedom*, published in 2010 by University of Toronto Press–Higher Education. Reprinted with permission of the publisher.

1. Albert Memmi, *The Colonizer and the Colonized*, trans. Howard Greenfeld (Boston: Beacon Press, 1991).
2. Hannah Arendt, *On Revolution* (New York: Viking Press, 1963).

Chapter Five

The "World-System": Europe As "Center" and Its "Periphery" beyond Eurocentrism

Enrique Dussel

In this chapter, we will study the question of Modernity, which comprises two paradigms. In the following passages, we will characterize both of them.

The first paradigm is from a Eurocentric horizon, and it formulates that the phenomenon of Modernity is *exclusively* European; that is, it develops from out of the Middle Ages and later diffuses itself throughout the entire world.[1] Max Weber situates the "problem of universal history" with the questions that is thus formulated:

> to what combination of circumstances should the fact be attributed that in *Western civilization*, and in Western civilization only,[2] cultural phenomena have appeared which (as *we*[3] like to think) lie in a line of development having *universal* significance and value.[4]

Europe had, according to this paradigm, exceptional *internal* characteristics that allowed it to supersede, through its rationality, all other cultures. Philosophically, no one else better than Hegel expresses this thesis of Modernity:

> The German Spirit is the Spirit of the new World. Its aim is the realization of absolute Truth as the unlimited self-determination (*Selbstbestimmung*) of *Freedom*—that Freedom which has its own absolute form itself as its purport.[5]

What calls attention here is that the Spirit of Europe (the German spirit) is the absolute Truth that determines or realizes itself through itself without owing anything to anyone. This thesis, which I will call the "Eurocentric paradigm" (in opposition to the "*world* paradigm"), is the one that has imposed itself not only in Europe and the United States, but also in the entire intellectual world of the world periphery. As we have said, the "pseudo-scientific" division of history into Antiquity (as antecedent), the Medieval Age (preparatory epoch), and the Modern Age (Europe) is an ideological and deforming organization of history. Philosophy and ethics need to break with this reductive horizon in order to open themselves to the "world," the "planetary" sphere. This problem is already an ethical one with respect to other cultures.

Chronology has its geopolitics. Modern subjectivity develops spatially, according to the "Eurocentric paradigm" from the Italy of the Renaissance to the Germany of the Reformation and the Enlightenment, toward the France of the French Revolution.[6] This paradigm concerns central Europe.

The second paradigm is from a planetary horizon, and it conceptualizes Modernity as the culture of the *center* of the "world-system,"[7] of the first "world-system"—through the incorporation of Amerindia[8] and as a result of the *management* of said "centrality." In other words, European Modernity is not an *independent*, autopoietic, self-referential system, but, instead, it is "part" of a "world-system": its *center*. Modernity, then, is planetary. It begins with the *simultaneous* constitution of Spain with reference to its "periphery" (the first of all, properly speaking, Amerindia: the Caribbean, Mexico, and Peru). *Simultaneously*, Europe, as a diachrony that has its premodern antecedents (the Renaissance Italian cities and Portugal), will go on to *constitute* itself as "center," as superhegemonic power that passes itself from Spain to Holland, to England, to France, and so on—over a growing "periphery": Amerindia, Brazil, and slave-supplying coasts of Africa; Poland in the sixteenth century[9]; consolidation of Latin Amerindia, North America, the Caribbean, Eastern Europe in the seventeenth century[10]; the Ottoman Empire, Russia, some Indian regions, sub-Asia, and the first penetration to continental Africa until the first half of the nineteenth century.[11] Modernity, then, would be for this planetary paradigm a phenomenon proper to the "system" or "center-periphery." Modernity is not a phenomenon of Europe as an *independent* system, but of Europe as "center." This simple hypothesis absolutely changes the concept of Modernity, its origin, development, and contemporary crisis; thus, it also changes the concept of the belated Modernity or post-Modernity.

Furthermore, we sustain a thesis that qualifies the prior: the centrality of Europe in the "world-system" is not the sole fruit of an internal superiority accumulated during the European Middle Age over and against other cultures.

Instead, it is also the effect of the simple fact of the *discovery*, conquest, colonization, and integration (subsumption) of Amerindia (fundamentally). This simple fact will *give* Europe the determining *comparative advantage over* the Ottoman-Muslim world, India, or China. Modernity is a fruit of this happening, not its cause. Subsequently, the *management* of the centrality of the "world-system" will allow Europe to transform itself in something like the "reflexive consciousness" (Modern Philosophy) of world history, and the many values, discoveries, inventions, technology, political institutions, and so on that are attributed to itself as its exclusive production are in reality the effect of the *displacement* of the ancient center of the third stage of the interregional system toward Europe—that is, following the diachronic way of the Renaissance to Portugal as antecedent, toward Spain, and later toward Flanders, England, and so on. Even capitalism is fruit, and not cause, of this juncture of European planetarization and centralization within the "world-system." The human experience of forty-five-hundred years of political, economic, technological, cultural relations of the "interregional system," will now be hegemonized by Europe, which had *never* been "center," and that during its best times only got to be a "periphery." The slipping takes place from central Asia toward the Eastern and Italian Mediterranean, more precisely toward Genoa and toward the Atlantic. With Portugal as an antecedent, it begins properly in Spain and in the face of the impossibility of China's even attempting to arrive through the Orient (the Pacific) to Europe and thus to integrate Amerindia as its periphery. Let us look at the premises of the argument.

I. DEPLOYMENT OF THE "WORLD-SYSTEM"

Let us consider the deployment of world history's departing from the rupture, due to the Ottoman-Muslim presence, of the third stage of the interregional system, which in its classic epoch had Baghdad as its center (from AD 762 to 1258), and the transformation of the "interregional system" into the first *"world-system,"* whose "center" would situate itself up to today in the North of the Atlantic. This change of "center" of the system will have its prehistory from the eighth through the fifteenth century AD, but before the collapse of the third stage of the interregional system, with the new fourth stage of the "world-system" *originating* properly with 1492. This change of "center" of the system will have its prehistory from the eighth through the fifteenth century AD, before the collapse of the third stage of the interregional system, but with the new fourth stage of the "world-system," it *originates* properly with 1492. Everything that had taken place in Europe was still a moment of *another* stage of the interregional system, yet the question remains: Which state originated the deployment of the "world-system"? Our answer is that it could annex Amerindia, from which it will go on to accumulate a prior nonexisting superiority toward the end of the fifteenth century as a springboard, or "comparative advantage."

But, why not China? The reason is very simple, and we would like to define it from the outset. For China,[12] it was impossible to discover Amerindia (a nontechnological impossibility, that is to say, empirically factual, but historical or geopolitical in origin), for it had no interest in attempting to arrive at Europe because the "center" of the interregional system (in its third stage) was in the East, either in Central Asia or in India. To go toward completely "peripheral" Europe could not be an objective of Chinese foreign commerce.

In fact, Cheng Ho, between 1405 and 1433, was able to make seven successful voyages to the "center" of the system; in fact, he arrived at Sri Lanka, India, and even Eastern Africa.[13] In 1479, Wang Chin attempted the same, but the archives of his predecessor were denied to him. China closed upon itself and did not attempt to do what precisely at that very same moment Portugal was undertaking. Its internal politics—perhaps the rivalry of the mandarins against the new power of the merchant eunuchs[14]—prevented its entry into foreign commerce. Had China undertaken it, however, it would have had to depart *toward the West* in order to reach the "center" of the system. The Chinese went toward the East, and they arrived at Alaska.

It appears that they even arrived as far as California and even still more to the South. But when they did not find anything that would be of interest to its merchants, and as they went farther away from the "center" of the "interregional system," they most probably abandoned the enterprise altogether. China was not Spain for geopolitical reasons.

However, to refute the old "evidence," which has been reinforced since Weber, we still need to ask ourselves: Was China culturally *inferior* to Europe in the fifteenth century? According to those who have studied the question,[15] China was not inferior, whether technologically,[16] politically,[17] or commercially, not even because of its humanism.[18] There is a certain mirage in this question. The histories of Western science and technology do not take strictly into account that the European "jump" (the technological *boom*) begins to take place in the sixteenth century, but that it is only in the seventeenth century that it shows its multiplying effects. The *formulation* of the modern technological paradigm (eighteenth century) is confused with the origin of Modernity, without leaving time for the crisis of the Medieval model. No notice is taken that the scientific revolution—in Kuhn's phrase—departs from a Modernity that has already begun, antecedently, as fruit of a "modern paradigm."[19] It is for that reason that in the fifteenth century (if we do not consider the posterior European inventions) Europe did not have any superiority over China. Needham even allows himself to be bewitched by this mirage, when he writes: "The fact is that the spontaneous autochthonous development of Chinese society did not produce any drastic change paralleling the Renaissance and the scientific revolution of the West."[20]

To place the Renaissance and the scientific revolution[21] as being *one and the same event* (one from the fourteenth century and the other from the seventeenth century) demonstrates the distortion of which we have spoken. The Renaissance is still a European event of a peripheral culture of the third stage of the interregional system. The "scientific revolution" is a fruit of the formulation of the modern paradigm, which needed more than a century of Modernity to attain its maturity. Pierre Chaunu writes: "Towards the end of the XVth century, to the extent to which historical literature allows us to understand it, the far East as an entity comparable to the Mediterranean . . . does not result under any inferior aspect, at least superficially, to the far West of the Euro-Asiatic continent."[22]

Let us repeat: Why not China? Because China found itself in the farthest East of the "interregional system," and because it looked to the "center": to India in the West.

So why not Portugal? For the same reason. That is, because it found itself in the farthest point of the West of the same "interregional system," and because *it also looked, and always did so, toward the "center"*: toward the India of the East. Colón's proposal (i.e., the attempt to reach the "center" through the West) to the king of Portugal was as insane as it was for Colón to pretend to discover a new continent, since he *only and always* attempted, yet could not conceive another hypothesis, to reach the "center" of the third stage of the interregional system.[23]

As we have seen, the Italian Renaissance cities are the farthest points of the West (peripheral) of the interregional system that articulated a new continental Europe with the Mediterranean after the Crusades failed in 1291. The Crusades ought to be considered as a frustrated attempt to connect with the "center" of the system, a link that the Turks ruptured. The Italian cities, especially Genoa (which rivaled Venice, which had a presence in the Eastern Mediterranean), attempted to open the Western Mediterranean to the Atlantic to reach once again the "center" of the system through the south of Africa. The Genoese placed all their experience in navigation and the economic power of their wealth at the service of opening for themselves this path. It was the Genoese who occupied the Canaries in 1312,[24] and it was they who invested in Portugal to help them develop their navigational power.

Once the Crusades had failed, they could not counter the expansion of Russia through the steppes, which advanced through the frozen woods of the North to reach the Pacific and Alaska in the seventeenth century[25]; therefore, the Atlantic would be the only European door to the "center" of the system. Portugal, the first European nation already unified in the eleventh century, transformed the re-conquest[26] against the Muslims into the beginning of a process of Atlantic mercantile expansion. In 1419, the Portuguese discovered the Madeiras Islands; in 1431, the Azores; in 1482, Zaire; and in 1498, Vasco de Gama reached India, the "center" of the interregional system. In 1415,

Portugal occupied the African-Muslim Ceuta; in 1448, El-Ksar-es-Seghir; in 1471, Arzila. But all of this is the *continuation* of the interregional system whose connection was the Italian cities:

> In the twelfth century when the Genoese and the Pisans first appeared in Catalonia, in the thirteenth century when they first reach Portugal, this is part of the efforts of the Italians to draw the Iberian peoples into the international trade of the time.... As of 1317, according to Virginia Raus, "the city and the part of Lisbon would be the great centre of Genoese trade."[27]

Portugal—with contacts in the Islamic world, with numerous sailors (farmers expelled from an intensive agriculture), with a money economy, in "connection" with Italy—opened once again peripheral Europe to the interregional system. But because of this, it did not stop being a "periphery." Not even the Portuguese could pretend to have abandoned this situation, since Portugal could have attempted to dominate the commercial exchange in the sea of the Arabs (the Indian Ocean),[28] but could *never* pretend to produce the commodities of the East (e.g., silk fabrics, tropical products, sub-Saharan gold). In other words, it was an intermediary and *always* peripheral power of India, China, or the Muslim world. With Portugal we are in the anteroom, but we are still neither in Modernity, nor are we in the "world-system," that is, the fourth stage of the system, which originated, at least, between Egypt and Mesopotamia.

So why does Spain begin the "world-system," and with it, Modernity? For the same reason that prevented China and Portugal from beginning the "world-system." Since Spain could not reach the "center" of the "interregional system" that was in Central Asia or India, it could not go toward the East since the Portuguese had already anticipated them and thus had exclusivity rights. Neither could Spain go through the south of the Atlantic, around the coasts of western Africa, until the cape of Buena Esperanza was discovered in 1487. Spain *only* had one opportunity left: to reach the "center," India, through *the Occident,* through the West, by crossing the Atlantic Ocean.[29] Because of this, Spain "bumps" into, "finds without looking," Amerindia. With that, the entire European "medieval paradigm" enters into a crisis. Thus, it inaugurates slowly but irreversibly the first *world* hegemony. This "world-system" is the only one that has existed in planetary history, and it is the modern system, European in its "center" and capitalist in its economy. This *Ethics of Liberation* pretends to situate itself explicitly within the horizon of this modern "world-system." (Is it perhaps the first practical philosophy that attempts to do so "explicitly"?) It takes into consideration not only the "center"—as has been done *exclusively* by Modern philosophy from Descartes to Habermas, thus resulting in a *partial,* provincial, regional view of the historical ethical *event*—but also its "periphery," and with this one, obtains a *planetary* vision of the human experience. This historical question is not informative or anecdotal. It has a philosophical sense that is *strictu sensu*! I have already treated the theme in another work.[30] In that work, I showed the existential impossibility of Colón, as a Renaissance Genoese, convincing himself that what he had discovered was *not* India. He navigated, according to his own imagination, close to the coasts of the fourth Asiatic peninsula (which Heinrich Hammer had already drawn cartographically in Rome in 1489),[31] always close to the "Sinus Magnus" (the great gulf of the Greeks, territorial sea of the Chinese), when in fact he traversed the Caribbean. Colón died in 1506 without having superseded the horizon of the third stage of the "interregional system."[32] He was not able to subjectively supersede the "interregional system"—with a history of forty-five hundred years of transformations, beginning with Egypt and Mesopotamia—and thus open himself to the new stage of the "world-system." The first one who suspected a *new* (the *last* new) continent was Americo Vespucci, in 1503, and therefore, he was existentially and subjectively the first "modern," the first to unfold the horizon of the "Asian Afro-Mediterranean system" as the "world-system," which incorporated for the first time Amerindia.[33] This revolution in the *Weltanschauung,* of the cultural, scientific, religious, technological, political, ecological, and economic horizon, is the *origin* of Modernity, seen from the perspective of a "world paradigm" and not solely from a Eurocentric perspective. In the "world system," the accumulation in the "center" is for the first time accumulation on a world scale.[34] Within the new system, everything changes qualitatively or radically. The very Medieval European "peripheral subsystem" changes internally as well. The founding event was the discovery of Amerindia in 1492.[35] Spain is ready to become the first modern state[36]; through the discovery, it begins to become the "center" of its first "periphery" (Amerindia), thus organizing the beginning of the slow shifting of the "center" of the older third stage of the "interregional system" (Baghdad of the thirteenth century), which had from peripheral Genoa (but from the western part of the "system") begun a process of reconnection—first with Portugal and now with Spain, with Seville to be precise. Genoese, Italian wealth suddenly flows into Seville. The "experience" of the Eastern Renaissance Mediterranean (and through it, of the Muslim world, of India and even China) are thus articulated by the imperial Spain of Carlos V—which reaches to the central Europe of the bankers of Augsburg; the Flanders of Amberes; and later, Amsterdam, along with Bohemia, Hungary, Austria and Milan, and especially the kingdom of the Two Sicilies[37] of the south of Italy, namely, Sicily, Cerdeña, the Balareares, and the numerous islands of the Mediterranean. But because of the economic failure of the political project of the "world empire," Emperor Carlos V abdicates in 1557: the path is thus left open for the "world system" of mercantile, industrial, and, today, transnational capitalism.

As an example, let us take a level of analysis among the many that may be analyzed—we would not want to be criticized as being a reductive economist because of the example that we have adopted. It is not coincidence that twenty-five years after the discovery of the silver mines of Potosí in the high Peru and the mines in Zacateca in Mexico (1546)—from which a total of eighteen thousand tones of silver arrived to Spain between the years of 1503 and 1660[38] —and thanks to the first shipments of this precious metal, Spain was able to pay, among the many campaigns of the Empire, the great armada that defeated the Turks in 1571 in Lepanto. This led to the dominion of the Mediterranean as a connection with the "center" of the older stage of the system. However, the Mediterranean had died as the road of the "center" toward the "periphery" on the West because now the Atlantic was structuring itself as the "center" of the new "world-system"![39]

Wallerstein writes: "Bullion was desired as a preciosity, for consumption in Europe and even more for trade with Asia, but it was also a necessity for the expansion of the European economy."[40]

I have read, among the many unpublished letters of the General Indian Archive of Seville, the following text of July 1, 1550, signed in Bolivia by Domingo de Santo Tomas:

> It was four years ago, to conclude the perdition of this land, that a mouth of hell[41] was discovered through which every year a great many people are immolated, which the greed of the Spaniards sacrifice to their god that is gold,[42] and it is a mine of silver which is named Potosí.[43]

The rest is well known. The Spanish colony in Flanders was to replace Spain as a hegemonic power in the "center" of the recently established "world-system"—that is, it liberates itself from Spain in 1610. Seville, the first modern port (in relations with Amberes), after more than a century of splendor, will cede its place to Amsterdam[44] (the city where Descartes would later write *Le Discors de la Methode* in 1636 and where Spinoza would live)[45]; it will cede naval, fishing, and crafts power, where the agricultural export flows; it will cede the great expertise in all the branches of production; it will cede to a city that will, among many aspects, bankrupt Venice.[46] After more than a century, Modernity already showed in this city a metropolis with its definitive physiognomy: its port; the channels, which as commercial ways reached to the houses of the bourgeoisie; the merchants who used their fourth and fifth floors as cellars, from which boats were directly loaded with cranes; and another thousand details of a capitalist metropolis.[47] From 1689 on, England would challenge and eventually end up imposing itself over Holland's hegemony, which England would always have to share with France, at least until 1763.[48]

Amerindia, meanwhile, constitutes the fundamental structure of the first modernity. From 1492 to 1500, about fifty thousand square kilometers are colonized in the Caribbean and on *terra firma*: from Venezuela to Panama.[49] In 1515, this number would reach three hundred thousand square kilometers with about three million dominated Amerindians. By 1550, more than two million square kilometers, which is an area greater than the whole of the European "center," and up to more than twenty-five million (a low figure) indigenous people[50] are also colonized, many of whom were integrated to a system of work that produced value (in Marx's strict sense) for the Europe of the "center"—that is, in the "encomienda," "mita," haciendas, and so on. We would have to add, from 1520 onward, the plantation slaves of African provenance, about fourteen million until the final stage of slavery in the nineteenth century, in places including Brazil, Cuba, and the United States. This enormous space and population will give to Europe, "center" of the "world-system," the *definitive comparative advantage* with respect to the Muslim, Indian, and Chinese worlds. It is for this reason that in the sixteenth century: "The periphery (eastern Europe and Hispanic America) used forced labor (slavery and coerced cash-crop labor [of the Amerindian]). The core, as we shall see, increasingly used free labor."[51]

For the goals of this philosophical work, it is of interest to indicate solely that with the birth of the "world-system," the "*peripheral* social formations"[52] were also born: "The form of *peripheral* formation will depend, finally, at the same time on the nature of the accumulated pre-capitalist formations and the forms of external aggression."[53] These will be, at the end of the twentieth century, the Latin American peripheral formations,[54] those of the African bantu, the Muslim world, India, the Asian Southeast,[55] and China, to which one must also add part of Eastern Europe before the fall of existing socialism.

II. MODERNITY AS "MANAGEMENT" OF PLANETARY "CENTRALITY" AND ITS CONTEMPORARY CRISIS

We have thus arrived at the central thesis of this chapter. If Modernity were, and this is our hypothesis, fruit of the "management" of the "centrality" of the first "world-system," we would now have to reflect on what this scenario implies.

First, one must be conscious that there are at least, in its origin, two Modernities. In the first place, Hispanic, humanist, Renaissance Modernity is still linked to the old interregional system of Mediterranean and Muslim Christianity.[56] In this, the "management" of the new system will be conceived out of the older paradigm of the old interregional system. That is,

Spain "managed" "centrality" as domination through the hegemony of an integral culture, a language, a religion (and thus, the evangelization process that Amerindia would suffer); it also dominated via military occupation, bureaucratic-political organization, economic expropriation, demographic presence (with hundreds of thousands of Spaniards or Portuguese who would forevermore inhabit Amerindia), ecological transformation (through the modification of the fauna and flora), and so on. This is the matter of the "Empire-World" project, which, as Wallerstein notes, failed with Carlos V.[57]

In the second place, the Modernity of Anglo-Germanic Europe began with the Amsterdam of Flanders, and it frequently passes as the *only* Modernity—that is, according to the interpretation of Sombart, Weber, Habermas, or even the postmoderns, who will produce a "reductionist fallacy" that occludes the meaning of Modernity and, thus, the sense of its contemporary crisis. To be able to "manage" the immense "world-system"—which suddenly opens itself to small Holland[58] which, from being a Spanish colony, now places itself as the "center" of the "world-system"—this second Modernity must accomplish or increase its efficacy through *simplification*. It is necessary to carry out an abstraction that favors the *quantum* to the detriment of *qualitas*; that *leaves out* many valid variables, such as cultural, anthropological, ethical, political, and religious (aspects that are valuable even for the European of the sixteenth century); and that will not allow an adequate "factual,"[59] or technologically possible, "management" of the "world-system."[60] This *simplification* of complexity[61] encompasses the totality of the "lifeworld" (*Lebenswelt*); of the relationship with nature, the new technological and ecological position that is no longer teleological; of subjectivity itself, the new self-understanding of subjectivity; of community, the new intersubjective and political relation; thus, as synthesis, a new economic attitude would establish itself (practico-productive).

The first Hispanic Renaissance and humanist Modernity produced a theoretical, or philosophical, reflection of the highest importance, and it has gone unnoticed in the so-called modern philosophy, which is only the philosophy of the "second Modernity." The theoretical-philosophical thought of the sixteenth century has contemporary relevance because it is the first, and only, that lived and expressed the original experience during the period of the constitution of the first "world-system." Thus, out of the theoretical "resources" that were available (i.e., the scholastic-Muslim-Christian and Renaissance philosophy), the central philosophical and ethical question that obtained was the following: "What right has the European to occupy, dominate, and 'manage' the recently discovered, militarily conquered, and currently being-colonized cultures?" From the seventeenth century on, the "second Modernity" did not have to question the conscience (*Gewissen*) with these questions that had already been answered, in fact: From Amsterdam, London, or Paris, in the seventeenth century and through the eighteenth century and onward, "Eurocentrism" (a superideology that would establish the valid legitimacy, without falsification, of the domination of the "world-system") would *no longer* be questioned until the end of the twentieth century. At that time, it will be then questioned by liberation philosophy as well as other movements.

In another work we have touched on the question.[62] Today we will only remind ourselves of the theme in general. Bartolome de las Casas demonstrates in his numerous works, using an extraordinary bibliographical apparatus, grounding rationally and carefully his arguments that the constitution of the "world-system" as European expansion in Amerindia (anticipation of the expansion in Africa and Asia) does not have any right; that it is an unjust violence, and it cannot have any ethical validity:

> The common ways mainly employed by the Spaniards who call themselves Christian and who have gone there to extirpate those pitiful nations and wipe them off the earth is by unjustly waging cruel and bloody wars. Then, when they have slain all those who fought for their lives or to escape the tortures they would have to endure, that is to say, when they have slain all the native rulers and young men (since the Spaniards usually spare only the women and children, who are subjected to the hardest and bitterest servitude ever suffered by man or beast), they enslave any survivors. . . . Their reason for killing and destroying such an infinite number of souls is that the Christians have an ultimate aim, which is to acquire gold, and to swell themselves with riches in a very brief time and thus rise to a high estate disproportionate to their merits. It should be kept in mind that their insatiable greed and ambition, the greatest ever seen in the world, is the cause of their villainies.[63]

Afterward, philosophy will no longer formulate this problematic, which showed itself unavoidable at the origin of the establishment of the "world-system." For the ethics of liberation, this question is today still fundamental.

In the sixteenth century, then, the "world-system" in Seville is established, as are philosophy questions from out of the old philosophical paradigm, including the praxis of domination; but it does not reach the formulation of the *new paradigm*. However, the origin of the new paradigm ought not to be confused with the origin of Modernity. Modernity begins more than a century before (1492) in the moment in which the paradigm, adequate to its very own new experience, is formalized—again using Kuhn's language. If we note the dates of the formulation of the new modern paradigm, we can conclude that it takes place in the first half of the seventeenth century.[64] This new paradigm corresponds to the exigencies of *efficacy*, technological "factibility," or governmentality of the "management" of an enormous "world-system" in expansion; it is the expression of a necessary process of *simplification* through "rationalization" of the life-world, of the subsystems (economic, political, cultural, religious, etc.). "Rationalization," as indicated by Werner Sombart,[65] Ernst Troeltsch,[66] or Max Weber,[67] is *effect* and not cause. On the other hand, to *manage* the "world-system," the effects of that *simplifying rationalization* are perhaps more profound and negative than Habermas or the postmoderns imagine.[68]

The corporeal Muslim-Medieval subjectivity is *simplified*: subjectivity is postulated as an *ego*, an I, about which Descartes writes:

> Accordingly this "I"—that is, the soul by which I am what I am—is *entirely* distinct from the body, and indeed is easier to know than the body, and would not fail to be whatever it is, even if the body did not exit.[69]

The body is a mere machine; *res extensa,* entirely foreign to the soul.[70] Kant himself writes:

> The human soul should be seen as being linked in the present life to two worlds at the same time: of these worlds, inasmuch as it forms with the body a personal unity, it feels but only the material world; on the contrary, as a member of world of the spirit [mind] (*als ein Glied der Geisterwelt*) [without body] it receives and propagates the pure influences of immaterial natures.[71]

This dualism—which Kant will apply to his ethics, inasmuch as the "maxims" ought not to have any empirical or "pathological" motives—is afterward articulated through the negation of practical intelligence, which is replaced by instrumental reason, the one that will deal with technical, technological "management" (i.e., ethics disappears before a *more geometric* intelligence) in the *Critique of Judgment.* It is here that the conservative tradition (such as that of Heidegger) continues to perceive the *simplifying* suppression of the organic complexity of life, which is now replaced by a technique of the "will to power" (via critiques elaborated by Nietzsche and Foucault). Galileo, with all the naive enthusiasm of a great discovery, writes:

> Philosophy is written in this grand book, the true universe, which stands continually open to our gaze. But the book cannot be understood unless one first learns to comprehend the language and read the letters in which it is composed. It is written in the *language of mathematics,* and its characters are triangles, circles and other geometric figures, without which it is humanly impossible to understand a single word of it; without these, one wanders about in a dark labyrinth."[72]

Heidegger already said that the "*mathematical* position"[73] before entities is to have them already know "ready-to-hand" (e.g., in the axioms of science) and to approach them only in order to use them. One does not "learn" a weapon, for instance; instead, one learns to make "use" of it, because one already knows what it is:

The *mathemata* are the things insofar as we take cognizance of them as what we already know them to be in advance, the body as the bodily, the plant-like of the plant, the animal-like of the animal, the thingness of the thing, and so on.[74]

Examples of the diverse moments that are negated by the indicated *simplification* include the "rationalization" of political life (bureaucratization), the capitalist enterprise (administration), the daily life (Calvinist asceticism or Puritanism), the decorporalization of subjectivity (with its alienating effects on living labor, as criticized by Marx, as well as on its drives, as analyzed by Freud), the nonethicalness of every economic or political gestation (understood only as, e.g., technical engineering), the suppression of practical-communicative reason (which is now replaced by instrumental reason), and the solipsistic individuality that negates the community. They are all apparently necessary for the "management" of the "centrality" of a "world-system" that Europe found itself in need of perpetually carrying out. Capitalism, liberalism, dualism (without valorizing corporeality), and so on are *effects* of the management of this function that corresponded to Europe as "center" of the "world-system." They are effects constituted through mediations in systems that end up totalizing themselves. Capitalism, mediation of exploitation and accumulation (effect of the "world-system"), is later on transformed into an *independent system* that, from out of its own self-referential and autopoietic logic, can destroy Europe and its periphery, and even the entire planet. And this is what Weber observes, but he does so reductively. That is to say, Weber notes part of the phenomenon but not the horizon of the "world-system." In fact, the formal procedure of *simplification* (that makes the "world-system" *manageable*) produces formal rationalized subsystems that later on do not have internal standards of self-regulation within the limits of Modernity and that could only be redirected at the service of humanity. It is in this moment that there emerge critiques from within the "center" (and from out of the "periphery" such as is mine) against Modernity itself. Now one attributes to *ratio* all culpable causality (as objective "understanding," which is set through disintegration) from Nietzsche to Heidegger, or as with the postmoderns. This culpability will be traced back as far as Socrates (Nietzsche) or even Parmenides himself (Heidegger). In fact, the modern *simplifications*—the dualism of an *ego—alma* without a body, the teleological instrumental reason, the racism of the superiority of one's own culture, and so on—have many similarities with the *simplification* that Greek slavery produced in the second interregional system. The Greek *Weltanschauung* was advantageous to the Modern man; however, not without complicity does the Modern man resuscitate the Greeks, as was done through the German romantics.[75] The subsumptive superseding (*Aufhebung*) of Modernity will mean the critical consideration of *all* these simplifying reductions produced since its origin—and not only a few ones, as Habermas imagines. The most important of said reductions, next to the one of the solipsistic subjectivity (i.e., without community), is the negation of the corporeality of said subjectivity, to which are related the critiques of Modernity by Marx, Nietzsche, Freud, Foucault, and Levinas, as well as the ethics of liberation, as we will see throughout the length of this work.

Because of all of this, the concept that one has of Modernity determines, as is evident, the pretension to its realization, as in Habermas, or the type of critiques one may formulate against it, such as that of the postmoderns. In general, every debate between rationalists and postmoderns does not overcome the Eurocentric horizon. The crisis of Modernity (already noted, as we have remarked frequently, by Nietzsche and Heidegger) refers to internal aspects of Europe. The "peripheral world" would appear to be a passive spectator of a thematic that does not touch it, because it is "barbarian," "premodern," or it may simply still be in need of being "modernized." In other words, the Eurocentric view reflects on the problem of the crisis of Modernity solely with the European–North American moments (or even now Japanese), but it minimizes the periphery. To break through this "reductivist fallacy" is not easy. We will attempt to "indicate" the path toward its surmounting.

If Modernity begins at the end of the fifteenth century, with a Renaissance premodern process and if, from there, a transition is made to the properly Modern in Spain, then Amerindia forms part of "Modernity" since the moment of the conquest and colonization (the mestizo world in Latin America is the only one that has as much age as Modernity),[76] since it was the first "barbarian" that Modernity needed in its definition. If Modernity enters into crisis at the end of the twentieth century, after five centuries of development, it is not a matter only of the moments detected by Weber and Habermas, or by Lyotard or Welsch,[77] but we will have to add the very ones of a "planetary" description of the phenomenon of Modernity.

To conclude, if we situate ourselves, instead, within the planetary horizon, one can distinguish at least the following positions in the face of the formulated problematic. In the first place, the "substantialist"—developmentalist[78] (quasi-metaphysical) position on the one hand conceptualizes Modernity as an *exclusively European* phenomenon that had *expanded from the seventeenth century on* throughout all the "backward" cultures (i.e., the Eurocentric position in the "center," or the modernizing in the "periphery"). Modernity is therefore a phenomenon that must be concluded. Some of the ones who assume this first position (e.g., Habermas and Apel), defenders of reason, do so critically, since they think that European superiority is not material, but formal, thanks to a new structure of critical questions.[79] However, the conservative "nihilist" position negates Modernity's positive qualities (of a Nietzsche or Heidegger, for instance) and thus proposes practically an annihilation without exit. The postmoderns take this second position in their frontal attack to "reason" *as such,* with differences in the case of Levinas,[80] although, paradoxically, they also defend parts of the first position from the perspective of a developmentalist Eurocentrism.[81] The postmodern philosophers are admirers of postmodern art, of the *Media.* Although they affirm theoretically *difference,* they do not reflect on the origins of these systems that are fruit of a rationalization proper to the "management" of the European "centrality" in the "world-system," before which they are profoundly uncritical. Because of this position, they do not have possibilities of attempting to contribute valid alternatives (cultural, economic, political, etc.) for the peripheral nations, for the peoples, or for the great majorities who are dominated by the center and/or the periphery.

In the second place, we defend another position, from out of the periphery, one that considers the process of Modernity as the already indicated rational "management" of the "world-system." This position intends to recuperate the redeemable of Modernity and to negate the domination and exclusion in the "world-system." It is then a project of liberation of a periphery negated from the very beginning of Modernity. The problem is not the mere superseding of instrumental reason (as it is for Habermas) or the reason of *terror* of the postmoderns; instead, it is the question of the coming of the "world-system" itself, such as it has developed until today for the last five hundred years. The problem is exhaustion of a civilizing system that has come to its end.[82] What the liberation of diverse types of oppressed and/or excluded populations presupposes is the overcoming of *cynical-managerial reason* (planetary administrative) of capitalism (as an economic system), of liberalism (as a political system), of Eurocentrism (as an ideology), of machismo (in erotics), of the reign of the white race (in racism), of the destruction of nature (in ecology), and so on. It is in this sense that the ethics of liberation defines itself as trans-Modern (since the postmoderns are still Eurocentric). The end of the present stage of civilization shows itself some limits of the "system of 500 years"—as Noam Chomsky[83] calls it.

These limits are, in first place, the ecological destruction of the planet. From the very moment of its inception, Modernity has constituted nature as an "exploitable" object, with the increase in the rate of profit of capital[84] as its goal: "For the first time, nature becomes purely an object for humankind, purely a matter of utility; ceases to be recognized as a power for itself."[85]

Once the earth is seen constituted as an "exploitable object" in favor of *quantum* (of capital) that can defeat all limits, all boundaries, thereby manifesting the "great civilizing influence of capital," it now reaches finally its unsurmountable limit, where itself is its own limit, the impassable barrier for ethical-human progress, and we have arrived at this moment:

> The universality towards which it irresistibly strives encounters barriers in its own nature, which will, at a certain state of its development, allow it to be recognized as

being itself the greatest barrier to this tendency, and hence will drive towards its own suspension.[86]

Given that nature is for Modernity only a medium of production, it runs out its fate of being consumed and destroyed; in addition, it accumulates geometrically upon the Earth its debris, until it jeopardizes the reproduction or survival of life itself. Life is the absolute condition of capital; its destruction destroys capital. We have now arrived at this state of affairs. The "system of 500 years" (Modernity or Capitalism) confronts its first absolute limit: the death of life in its totality through the indiscriminate use of an anti-ecological technology constituted progressively through the sole criterion of the *quantitative* "management" of the "world-system" in Modernity: the increase in the rate of profit. But capital cannot limit itself. There thus comes about the utmost danger for humanity.

The second limit of Modernity is the destruction of humanity itself. "Living labor" is the other essential mediation of capital as such; the human subject is the only one that can "create" new value (i.e., surplus value, profit). Capital that defeats all barriers requires incrementally more absolute time of work: When it cannot supersede this limit, then it augments productivity through technology; but said increase decreases the importance of human labor. It is thus that there is *superfluous humanity* (i.e., displaced humanity). The unemployed do not earn a salary or any money, but money is the only mediation in the market through which one can acquire commodities to satisfy needs. In any event, work that is not employable by capital therefore increases (i.e., there is an increase in unemployment). It is thus the proportion of needing subjects who are not solvent, clients, consumers, or buyers—as much in the periphery as in the center.[87] It is poverty, poverty as the absolute limit of capital. Today we know how misery grows in the entire planet. It is a matter of a "law of Modernity":

> Accumulation of wealth at one pole is, therefore, at the same time accumulation of misery, the torment of labour, slavery, ignorance, brutalization and moral degradation at the opposite pole.[88]

The modern "world-system" cannot overcome this essential contradiction. The ethics of liberation reflects philosophically from out of this planetary horizon of the "world-system"; from out of this double limit configures a terminal crisis of a civilizing process: the ecological destruction of the planet and the extinguishing in misery and hunger of the great majority of humanity. Before these two co-implicating phenomena of such planetary magnitude intersect, the project of many philosophical schools would seem naive, even ridiculous, irresponsible, irrelevant, cynical, and even complicit (as much in the center, but even worse yet in the periphery, in Latin America, Africa, and

Asia); yet these schools are closed in their "ivory towers" of sterile Eurocentric academicism. Referring to the opulent countries of late capitalism, Marcuse had already written in 1968:

> why do we need liberation from such a society if it is capable—perhaps in the distant future, but apparently capable—of conquering poverty to a greater degree than ever before, or of reducing the toil of labour and the time of labour, and of raising the standard of living? If the price for all goods delivered, the price for this comfortable servitude, for all these achievements, is exacted from people far away from the metropolis and far way from its affluence? If the affluent society itself hardly notices what it is doing, how it is spreading terror and enslavement, how it is fighting liberation in all corners of the globe?[89]

The third limit of Modernity is the impossibility of the subsumption of the populations, economies, nations, and cultures that it has been attacking since its origin and since it has excluded from its horizon and thus cornered into poverty. This is the whole theme of the exclusion of African, Asian, Latin American Alterity and their indomitable will to survive. The globalizing "world-system" reaches a limit where the exteriority of the Alterity of the Other, the locus of "resistance," and from whose analectical affirmation there departs the process of the negation of negation of liberation. That is, liberation is launched from the Alterity of the Other, whose negation ("no" to oppression) rejects the negation of oppression (exploitation)—a formulation based on Marxian dialectics.

NOTES

*A version of this essay was first published in *Latin America and Postmodernity: A Contemporary Reader*, ed. Pedro Lange-Churión and Eduardo Mendicta (Amherst, NY: Humanity Books, 2001). All rights reserved. Printed with permission.

1. As a "substance" that is invented in Europe and that subsequently "expands" throughout the entire world. This is a metaphysical-substantialist and "diffusionist" thesis. It contains a "reductionist fallacy."

2. The English translation does not translate the expression Weber uses, "*Auf dem Boden*," which means "*within* its regional horizon." We want to establish that when we say *in Europe*, what we really mean is the development in Modernity of Europe as the "center" of a "global system," and not as an *independent* system, as if it were "only-from-within itself" and as the fruit of a solely *internal* development, as Eurocentrism pretends.

3. This "we" is precisely the Eurocentric Europeans.

4. Max Weber, *The Protestant Ethic and the Spirit of Capitalism*, trans. Talcott Parsons (New York: Charles Scribner's Sons, 1958), 13 (emphasis added). Later on Weber asks: "Why did not the scientific, the artistic, the political, or the economic development there [China, and India] enter upon that path of *rationalization* which is peculiar to the Occident?" (Weber, *The Protestant Ethic*, 25). In order to argue this, Weber juxtaposes the Babylonians, who did not mathematize astronomy, with the Greeks, who did (but Weber does not know that the Greeks learned it from the Egyptians). He also argues that science emerged in the West, and not in India or China; but he forgets to mention the Muslim world, from which the Latin West learned

Aristotelian "experiential," empirical exactitude (such as the Oxford Franciscians or Marcilios de Padua, etc.). Every Hellenistic, or Eurocentric argument, such as Weber's, can be falsified if we take 1492 as the ultimate date of comparison between the supposed superiority of the West and other cultures.

5. G. W. F. Hegel, *The Philosophy of History*, trans. J. Sibree (New York: Dover Publications, 1956), 341.

6. Following Hegel (*The Philosophy of History*), Jürgen Habermas, *Der philosophische Diskurs der Moderne* (Frankfurt: Suhrkamp, 1988), 27.

7. The "world-system," or the planetary system of the fourth stage of the same interregional system of the Asiatic-African-Mediterranean continent, but now (correcting Frank's conceptualization) factially "planetary." See A. G. Frank. "A Theoretical Introduction to 5,000 Years of World System History," Review (Fernand Braudel Center) 13, no. 2 (1990), 155–248. On the "world-system" problematic, see Janet Abu-Lughod, *Before European Hegemony: The World System A.D. 1250–1350* (New York: Oxford University Press, 1989); Rober Brenner, "Das Weltsystem. Theoretische und Historische Perspektiven," in *Perspektiven des Weltsystems* (Frankfurt: Campus Verlag, 1983); Marshall Hodgson, *The Venture of Islam*, vols. 1–3 (Chicago: University of Chicago Press, 1974); Paul Kennedy, *The Rise and Fall of the Great Power* (New York: Random House, 1987); George Modelski, *Long Cycles in World Politics* (London: Macmillan Press, 1987); L. S. Stavarianos, *The World to 1500: A Global History* (Englewood Cliffs, NJ: Prentice Hall, 1970); William Thompson, *Global War: Historical-Structural Approaches to World Politics* (Columbia: University of South Carolina Press, 1989); Charles Tilly, *Big Structures, Large Processes, Huge Comparisons* (New York: Russell Sage Foundation, 1984); Immanuel Wallerstein, *The Politics of the World-Economy* (Cambridge: Cambridge University Press, 1984) and *The Modern World-System*, vol. 1 (1974) to vol. 3 (1989) (New York: Academic Press, 1974).

8. On this point, as I already mentioned, I am not in agreement with Frank on calling the prior moments of the system "world-system"; I call them "interregional systems."

9. Wallerstein, *The Modern World-System*, vol. 1, chap. 6.

10. Wallerstein, *The Modern World-System*, vol. 2, chaps. 4–5.

11. Wallerstein, *The Modern World-System*, vol. 3, chap. 3.

12. See Owen Lattimore, *Inner Asian Frontiers of China* (Boston: Beacon Press, 1962); Morris Rosabi, *China among Equals: The Middle Kingdom and Its Neighbors, 10th–14th Centuries* (Berkeley: University of California Press, 1982). For a description of the situation of the world in 1400, see Eric Wolf, *Europe and the People without History* (Berkeley: University of California Press, 1982), 24 ff.

13. I have been to Masamba, and I saw in the museum of this city, which is a port of Kenya, Chinese porcelain, as well as luxurious watches and other objects of similar origin.

14. There are other reasons for this nonexternal expansion: the existence of "space" in the neighboring territories of the empire, which took all its power in order to "conquer the south" through the cultivation of rice and its defense against the barbarian "North." See Wallerstein, *The Modern World-System*, vol. 1, 80 ff., which has many good arguments against Weber's Eurocentrism.

15. For example, Joseph Needham, "Commentary on Lynn White *What Accelerated Technological Change in the Western Middle Ages?*" in *Scientific Change*, ed. A. C. Crombie (New York: Basic Books, 1963), 117–53; and "The Chinese Contribution to the Development of the Mariner's Compass" and "The Chinese Contributions to Vessel Control" in *Scientia* 96, no. 98 (1961), abril, 123–28; mayo, 163–68. See all of these with respect to the control of ships, which the Chinese had already dominated since the first century AD. The Chinese use of the compass, paper, gunpowder, and other discoveries is well known.

16. Perhaps the only disadvantages were the Portuguese caravel (invented in 1441), used to navigate the Atlantic (it was not needed in the Indian Ocean), and the cannon. This last one, although spectacular, never had any real effect in Asia outside naval wars until the nineteenth century.

17. The first bureaucracy (as the Weberian high stage of political rationalization) is the stilted mandarin structure of political exercise. The mandarin are not nobles, nor warriors, nor

aristocratic or commercial plutocracy; they are *strictly* a bureaucratic elite whose exams are *exclusively* based in the dominion of culture and the laws of the Chinese empire.

18. William de Bary indicates that the individualism of Wang Yang-ming, in the fifteenth century, which expressed the ideology of the bureaucratic class, was as advanced as that of the Renaissance. Th. de William Bary, *Self and Society in Ming Thought* (New York: Columbia University Press, 1970).

19. Through many examples, Thomas Kuhn (*The Structure of Scientific Revolutions*, Chicago: University of Chicago Press, 1962) situates the modern scientific revolution—that is, the fruit of the expression of the new paradigm—practically with Newton (seventeenth century). He does not study with care the impact that events such as the discovery of America, the roundness of the earth (empirically proved since 1520), and so on, could have had on the science and the "scientific community" of the sixteenth century, after the structuration of the first "world-system."

20. Needham, "Commentary on Lynn White," 139.

21. Pierre Chaunu, *Seville et l'Atlantique (1504–1650)*, vol. 1 (1955) to vol. 8 (1959) (Paris: Sevpen, 1955), vol. 8, part 1, 50.

22. A. R. Hall places the scientific revolution beginning with the 1500s. See A. R. Hall, *The Scientific Revolution* (London: Longman, 1983).

23. *Factically,* Colón will be the first Modern, but not *existentially* since his *interpretation of the world* remained always that of a Renaissance Genoese: a member of a peripheral Italy of the third "interregional system." See Paolo Emilio Taviani, *Cristoforo Colombo: La genesi della scoperta* (Novara, Italy: Instituto Geografico de Agostini, 1982); Edmundo O'Gorman, *La invencion de América* (Mexico: FCE, 1957).

24. I. Zunzunegi, "Los origenes de las misiones en las Islas Canarias," *Revista Española de Teologia*, 1 (1941), 364–70.

25. Russia was not yet integrated as "periphery" in the third stage of the interregional system, nor was it in the modern "world-system," until the eighteenth century with Peter the Great and the founding of St. Petersburg on the Baltic.

26. Portugal, already in 1095, has the rank of empire. In Algarve, 1249, the re-conquest concludes with this empire. Enrique the Navigator (1394–1460), as patron, gathers the sciences of cartography and astronomy, and the techniques of navigation and construction of ships, which originated in the Muslim world (since he had contact with the Morrocans) and the Italian Renaissance (via Genoa).

27. Wallerstein, *The Modern World-System*, vol. 1, 49–50.

28. See K. N. Chaudhuri, *Trade and Civilisation in the Indian Ocean: An Economic History from the Rise of Islam to 1750* (Cambridge: Cambridge University Press, 1985).

29. My argument would seem to be the same as Blaut's (*The Debate on Colonialism, Eurocentrism and History*, Trenton, NJ: Africa World Press, 1992), 28 ff., but in fact, it is different. It is not that Spain was "geographically" closer to Amerindia. No. It is not a question of distances. It is that and much more. It matters that Spain had to go through Amerindia, not only because it was closer which in fact took place, especially with respect to Asiatic cultures—although this was not the case with the Turkish Muslim empire that had arrived at Morroco—but because this was the demanded path to the "center" of the "system," a question that is not dealt with by Blaut. Furthermore, it is just the same difference from that of Andre Gunder Frank (Blaut, *The Debate on Colonialism*, 65–80), because for him, the year 1492 marks only a secondary internal change of the same "world-system." However, if it is understood that the "interregional system," in its stage prior to 1492, is the "same" system but not yet as a "world" system, then 1492 assumes a greater importance than Frank grants it. Even if the system is *the same*, there exists a qualitative jump, which, under other aspects, is the original capitalism proper, to which Frank denies importance because of his prior denial of relevance to concepts such as "value" and "surplus value"; therefore, he attributes "capital" to the "wealth" (i.e., use-value, with a virtual possibility of transforming itself into exchange-value, but not capital) accumulated in the first through third stages of the interregional system. This is a grave theoretical question.

30. Enrique Dussel, *1492: El encubrimiento del Otro. Haria el origen del mito de la modernida* (Madrid: Nueva Utopia, 1993).

31. See Dussel, *1492: El encubrimiento del Otro*, appendix 4, where the map of the fourth Asiatic peninsula is reproduced (after the Arabian, Indian, and Malacan), certainly product of Genoese navigations, where South America is a peninsula attached to the south of China. This explains why the Genoese Colón would hold the opinion that Asia would not be so far from Europe (i.e., South America equals the fourth peninsula of China).

32. This is what I called, philosophically, the "invention" of Amerindia seen as India, in all of its details. Colón, existentially, neither "discovered" nor reached Amerindia. He "invented" something that was nonexistent: India in the place of Amerindia, which prevented him from "discovering" what he had before his own eyes. See Dussel, *1492: El encubrimiento del Otro*, chapter 2.

33. This is the meaning of the title of chapter 2 of my already cited work: "From the *Invention* to the *Discovery* of America."

34. See Samir Amin, *L'accumulation à l'echelle Mondiale* (Paris: Anthropos, 1970). However, this work does not develop the "world-system" hypothesis. It would appear as though the colonial world were a *rear or subsequent* and *outside* space to European medieval capitalism, which is transformed "in" Europe as modern. My hypothesis is more radical: the fact of the discovery of Amerindia, of its integration as "periphery," is a *simultaneous* and *co-constitutive* fact of the restructuration of Europe *from within* as "center" of the only new "world-system"—that is, only now and *not before*, capitalism (first mercantile and later industrial).

35. We have spoken of "Amerindia" and not of America, because it is a question, during the entire sixteenth century, of a continent inhabited by "Indians." It is wrongly called because of the mirage that the "interregional system" of the third stage still produced in the still being born "world-system." They were called Indians because of India, "center" of the interregional system that was beginning to fade. Anglo-Saxon North America will be born slowly in the seventeenth century, but it will be an event "internal" to a growing Modernity in Amerindia. This is the *originating* "periphery" of Modernity, constitutive of its first definition. It is the "other face" of the very same phenomenon of Modernity.

36. Unified by the marriage of the Catholic king and queen in 1474, followed immediately by the Inquisition (first ideological apparatus of the State for the creation of consensus), with a bureaucracy, whose functioning is attested to in the archives of the Indies (Sevilla), where everything was declared, contracted, certified, and archived; with a grammar of the Spanish language (the first of national languages in Europe) written by Nebrija, in whose prologue he warns the Catholic kings of the importance for the empire of having *only one language;* Cisneros's edition of the Complutensian polyglot Bible (in seven languages), which was superior to Erasmus's because of its scientific care, the number of its languages, and the quality of the imprint, begun in 1502 and published in 1522; with military power that allows it to reclaim Granada in 1492; with the economic wealth of the Jews, Andalucian Muslims, Christians of the re-conquest, and the Catalans with their colonies in the Mediterranean, and the Genoese; with the artisans from the antique caliphate of Cordoba . . . and so on. Spain is far from being in the fifteenth century the semiperipheral country that it would become in the second part of the seventeenth century—the only picture of Spain which the Europe of the center remembers, as Hegel and Habermas do, for example.

37. The struggle between France and the Spain of Carlos V, which exhausted both monarchies and resulted in the economic collapse of 1557, was played out above all in Italy. Carlos V possessed about three-fourths of the Peninsula. In this way, Spain transferred through Italy to its own soil the links with the "system." This was one of the reasons for all the wars with France: the wealth and centuries of experience were essential for whoever intended to exercise new hegemony in the "system," especially if it were to be the first "planetary" hegemony.

38. This event produced an unprecedented increase in prices in Europe, which was convergent with an inflation of 1,000 percent during the sixteenth century. Externally, this would liquidate the wealth accumulated in the Turkish-Muslim world, and even transform India and China internally. Furthermore, the arrival of Amerindian gold produced a complete continental hecatomb of Bantu Africa because of the collapse of the kingdoms of the sub-Saharan savannah (Ghana, Togo, Dahomey, Nigeria, etc.), which exported gold to the Mediterranean. In order to survive, these kingdoms increased the selling of slaves to the new European powers of the Atlantic, with American slavery produced. See Pierre Bertaux, *Africa: Desde la prehistoria*

hasta los Estados actuales, especially "La trata de esclavos," pp. 133–41 (México, DF: Siglo Veintiuno, 1972); V. M. Godinho, "Creation et dynamisme economique du monde atlantique (1420–1670)," *Annales ESC* 5, no. 1 (enero-marzo, 1950), 10–30; Pierre Chaunu, *Seville et l'Atlantique (1504–1650)*, vol. 1 (1955) to vol. 8 (1959) (Paris: Sevpen, 1955, vol. 8, chapter 1, 57); F. Braudel, "Monnaies et civilisation: de l'or du Soudan à l'argent d'Amerique." *Annales* 1, no. 1, pp. 9–22. The whole ancient third "interregional system" is absorbed slowly by the modern "world-system."

39. All of the subsequent hegemonic power would remain until the present on their shores: Spain, Holland, England (and France partly) until 1945; and the United States in the present. Thanks to Japan, China, and California, the Pacific appears for the first time as a counterweight. This is perhaps a novelty of the twenty-first century.

40. Wallerstein, *The Modern World-System*, vol. 1, 45.

41. This is the entrance to the mine.

42. This text has for the last thirty years warned me against the phenomenon of the fetishism of gold, "money," and "capital." See Dussel, "General," in *Historia General de la Iglesia en America Latina*, vol. 1, 1–724 (Salamanca, Spain: Sigueme, 1983).

43. *Archivo General de Indias* (Sevilla), Charcas 313.

44. Wallerstein, "From Seville to Amsterdam: The Failure of Empire," in *The Modern World-System*, vol. 1, 165 ff.

45. It should be remembered that Spinoza (Espinosa), who lived in Amsterdam (1632–1677), descended from an Ashkenazi family from the Muslim world of Granada, was expelled from Spain, and then was exiled in the Spanish colony of Flanders.

46. See Wallerstein, *The Modern World-System*, vol. 1, 214.

47. See Wallerstein, "Dutch Hegemony in the World-Economy," chapter 2 in *The Modern World-System*, vol. 2. Wallerstein writes: "It follows that there is probably only a short moment in time when a given core power can manifest *simultaneously* productive, commercial and financial superiority *over all other core powers*. This momentary summit is what we call hegemony. In the case of Holland, or the United Providences, that moment was probably between 1625–1675" (*The Modern World-System*, 39). Not only Descartes, but also Spinoza, as we already indicated, is in the philosophical presence of Amsterdam, world "center" of the system—and why not? The self-consciousness of humanity *in* its *"center"* is not the same as a mere *European* self-consciousness.

48. See Wallerstein, *The Modern World-System*, vol. 2, chapter 6. After this date, British hegemony will be uninterrupted, except in the Napoleonic period, until 1945, when it is lost to the United States.

49. See Pierre Chaunu, *Conquete et exploitation des nouveaux mondes (XVIe. siecle)* (Paris: PUF, 1969), 119–76.

50. Europe had approximately fifty-six million inhabitants in 1500, and eighty-two million in 1600. See Cardoso, *Histaria económica de America Latina*, ed. Ciro F. S. Cardoso-Hector Brignoli, vols. 1 and 2 (Barcelona: Critica, 1979), vol. 1, 114.

51. Wallerstein, *The Modern World-System*, vol. 1, 103.

52. See S. Amin, *El desarrollo desigual. Ensayo sobre las formaciones sociales del capitalismo periferico* (Barcelona: Fontanella, 1974), 309 ff.

53. Amin, *El desarrollo desigual*, 312.

54. The colonial process ends for the most part at the beginning of the nineteenth century.

55. The colonial process of these formations ends, for the most part, after the so-called World War II (1945), given that the North American superpower requires neither military occupation, nor political-bureaucratic domination (proper only to the old European powers, such as France and England), but rather the management of the dominion of economic-financial dependence in its transnational stage.

56. "Muslim" means here the most "cultured" and civilized of the fifteenth century.

57. I think that, exactly, to *manage* the new "world-system" according to old practices had to fail because it operated with a variable that made it unmanageable. Modernity *had begun*, but it had not given itself the new way to "manage" the system.

58. Later on, it will also have to "manage" the system of the English island. Both nations had very exiguous territories, with little population in the beginning, without any other capacity

118 *Enrique Dussel*

than their creative "bourgeois attitude" before its existence. Because of their weakness, they had to perform a great reform of "management" of the planetary metropolitan enterprise.

59. The technical "factibility" will become a criterion of truth, of possibility, of existence; Vico's "verum *et factum* conventuntur."

60. Spain, and also Portugal with Brazil, undertook as a state (World-Empire; with military, bureacratic, and ecclesiastical resources) the conquest, evangelization, and colonization of Amerindia. Holland, instead, founded the Dutch East India Company (1602), and later that of "West India." These "companies" (as well as the subsequent British and Danish) are capitalist "enterprises," secularized and private, which function according the "rationalization" of mercantilism (and later of industrial capitalism). This indicates the different rational "management" of the Iberian companies and the different management of the "second Modernity" ("world-system" not managed by a "world-empire").

61. In every system, complexity is accompanied by a process of "selection" of elements that allow, in the face of the increase in such complexity, for the conservation of the "unity" of the system with respect to its surroundings. This necessity of selection-simplification is always a "risk." See Niklas Luhmann, *Soziale Systeme: Grundriß einer allgemeinen Theorie* (Frankfurt: Suhrkamp, 1988), 47 ff.

62. See Dussel, "Critique of the Myth of Modernity," chapter 5 in *1492: El encubrimiento del Otro*. During the sixteenth century, there were three theoretical positions before the fact of the constitution of the "world-system": (1) that of Gines de Sepulveda, the *modern* renaissance and humanist scholar, who rereads Aristotle and demonstrates the natural slavery of the Amerindian, and thus concludes on the legitimacy of the conquest; (2) that of the Franciscans, such as Mendieta, who attempts a utopian Amerindian Christianity (a "republic of Indians" under the hegemony of Catholic religion), proper to the third Christian-Muslim interregional system; and (3) Bartolome de las Casas's position (*Obras escogidas de Fray Bartolome de Ins Casas*, vol. 1 [1957] to vol. 5 [1958] [Madrid: Biblioteca de Autores Espanoles, 1957]), *the beginning of a critical "counter-discourse" on the interior of Modernity*, which in his work of 1536, a century before *Le Discours de la Methode*, he entitles *De unico modo* ("The Only Way") and shows that "argumentation" is the rational means through which to attract the Amerindian to the new civilization. Habermas, as we will see later on, speaks of "counter-discourse" and suggests that said counter-discourse is only two centuries old (beginning with Kant). Liberation Philosophy suggests, instead, that this counter-discourse begins in the sixteenth century (in 1511, in Santo Domingo with Anton de Montesinos!), decidedly with Bartolome de las Casas in 1514 (see Dussel, "General," vol. 1, chapter 1, 17–27).

63. Bartolome de las Casas, *The Devastation of the Indies: A Brief Account*, trans. Herma Briffault (Baltimore and London: Johns Hopkins University Press, 1992), 31. I have placed this text at the beginning of volume 1 of my work *Para una etica dc la liberación latinoamericana* (Dussel, *Para una destrucción de la historin de la eticn* [Mendoza, Argentina: Ser y Tiempo, 1973]), since it synthesizes the general hypothesis of the ethics of liberation.

64. Frequently, in the contemporary histories of philosophy and, of course, of ethics, a "jump" is made from the Greeks (from Plato and Aristotle) to Descartes (1596–1650), who takes up residence in Amsterdam in 1629 and writes *La Discours de La Methode*, as we indicated earlier (*Oeuvres et Lettres de Descartes*, La Pleiade Series [Paris: Gallimard, 1953]). In other words, there is a jump from Greece to Amsterdam. In the interim, twenty-one centuries have gone by without any other content of importance. Studies are begun with Bacon (1561–1626), Kepler (1571–1630), Galileo (1571–1630), and Newton (1643–1727). Campanella writes *Civitas Solis* in 1602. Everything would seem to be situated at the beginning of the seventeenth century, the moment I have called the second moment of Modernity.

65. See Werner Sombart, *Der moderne Kapitalismus* (Leipzig, Germany: Duncker, 1902) and *Der Bourgeois* (Mtinchen: Duncker, 1920).

66. See Ernst Troeltsch, *Die Soziallehre der christlichen Kirchen und Gruppe 1* (Tubingen, Germany: Mohr, 1923).

67. See Habermas, *Der philosophische*, vols. 1–2. Habermas insists on the Weberian discovery of "rationalization," but he forgets to ask after its cause. I believe that my hypothesis goes deeper and farther back: Weberian rationalization (accepted by Habermas, Apel, Lyotard, etc.) is the apparently necessary mediation of a deforming simplification (by instrumental reason) of

practical reality, in order to transform it into something "manageable," governable, given the complexity of the immense "world-system." It is not only the internal "manageability" of Europe, but also, and above all, *planetary* (center-periphery) "management." Habermas's attempt to sublimate instrumental reason into communicative reason is not sufficient because the moments of his diagnosis on the *origin itself of the process of rationalization* are not sufficient.

68. The postmoderns, as Eurocentrists, concur, more or less, with the Weberian diagnosis of Modernity. Rather, they underscore certain rationalizing aspects or mediums (means of communication, etc.) of Modernity, some of which they reject wrathfully as metaphysical dogmatisms, but others they accept as inevitable phenomena and frequently as positive transformations.

69. René Descartes, "Discourse on the Method," vol. 1, part IV, in *The Philosophical Works of Descartes* (Cambridge, UK: Cambridge University Press, 1985), 127.

70. See Dussel, *El dualismo en la antropologia de la Cristiandad* (Buenos Aires: Editorial Guadalupe, 1974) (at the end) and *Metodo para una Filosofia de la Liberación* (Salamanca, Spain: Sigueme, 1974), chapter 2, part 4. Contemporary theories of the functions of the brain put in question definitively this dualistic mechanism.

71. Immanuel Kant, *Träume eines Geistersehers* (1766), A36; in Kant, *Kant Werke,* vols. 1–10 (Darmstadt, Germany: Wissenschaftliche Buchgesellschaft, 1968), vol. 2, 940.

72. Stillman Drake, *Discoveries and Opinions of Galileo* (New York: Doubleday, Anchor Books, 1957), 237–38.

73. See Dussel, *Par la destruccion.*

74. Martin Heidegger, *What Is a Thing?*, trans. W. B. Barton et al. (Chicago: Henry Regnery Company, 1967), 73.

75. See Martin Bernal, *Black Athena, Black Athena: The Afroasiatic Roots of Classical Civilization*, vol. 1 (New Brunswick, NJ: Rutgers University Press, 1989), chapter 5, 224ss.

76. Amerindia and Europe have a premodern history, just as Africa and Asia do. Only the hybrid world, the syncretic culture, the Latin American *mestiza* race that was born in the fifteenth century (the child of Malinche and Hernan Cortes can be considered as its symbol; see Octavio Paz, *El Laberinto de la soledad* [Mexico: Cuadernos Americanos, 1950]) has five hundred years.

77. See, among others: Jean-Francois Lyotard, *La condition postmoderne* (Paris: Minuit, 1979); Richard Rorty, *Philosophy and the Mirror of Nature* (Princeton, NJ: Princeton University Press, 1979); Jacques Derrida, *De La Grammatologie* (Paris: Minuit, 1967), and *L'Ecriture et la Différence* (Paris: Seuil, 1967); Odo Marquard, *Abschied vom Prinzipiellen* (Stuttgart: Reclam, 1981); Gianni Vattimo, *La fine della Modernità* (Milan: Garzanti, 1985); Wolfgang Welsch, *Unseres postmoderne Moderne* (Berlin: Akademie v., 1993).

78. This Spanish word (*desarrollismo*), which does not exist in other languages, points to the "fallacy" that pretends the same "development" (the word *Entwicklung* has a strictly Hegelian philosophical origin) for the "center" as for the "periphery," not taking note that the "periphery" is not *backward* (see Hinkelammert, *Dialectica del desarrollo desigual* and *Critica a la razon utopica*). In other words, it is not a temporal *prius* that awaits a development similar to that of Europe or the United States (like the child /adult) but that instead it is the asymmetrical position of the dominated, the *simultaneous* position of the exploited (like the free lord/slave). The "immature" (child) could follow the path of the "mature" (adult) and get to "develop" herself, while the "exploited" (slave) no matter how much she works will never be "free" (lord), because her own dominated subjectivity includes her "relationship" with the dominator. The "modernizers" of the "periphery" are developmentalists because they do not realize that the "relationship" of planetary domination has to be overcome as prerequisite for *"national* development." Globalization has not extinguished, not by the least, the "national" question.

79. See Habermas, *Theorie des kommunikativen Handelns*, vols. 1 and 2 (Frankfurt: Suhrkamp, 1981), t.l, I, 2, from sec. [B] to sec. [D], and especially the debate with P. Winch and A. MacIntyre.

80. We will see that Levinas, "father of French postmodernism" (from Derrida on), neither is postmodern, nor negates reason. Instead, he is a critic of the *totalization* of reason (instrumental, strategic, cynical, ontological, etc.). Liberation Philosophy, since the end of the 1960s, studied Levinas because of his radical *critique* of domination. In the preface to my work,

Philosophy of Liberation (Maryknoll, NY: Orbis, 1985), I indicated that the philosophy of liberation is a "postmodern" philosophy, one that departed from the "second Heidegger," but also from the critique of "*totalized* reason" carried out by Marcuse and Levinas. It would seem as though we were "postmoderns" *avant la lettre*. In fact, however, we were critics of ontology and Modernity from (*desde*) the periphery, which meant (and which still *means*) something entirely different, as we intend to explain.

81. Up to now, the postmoderns remain Eurocentric. The dialogue with "different" cultures is, for now, an unfulfilled promise. They think that mass culture, the *media* (television, movies, etc.) will affect peripheral urban cultures to the extent that they will annihilate their "differences," in such a way that what Vattimo sees in Torino, or Lyotard in Paris, will be shortly the same in New Delhi and Nairobi; they do not take the time to analyze the *hard* irreducibility of the hybrid cultural horizon that receives those information impacts. Such a horizon is not *absolutely* an exteriority, but it is one that will not be during centuries a univocal interiority to the globalized system.

82. See Fredrick Jameson's work, *Postmodernism or the Cultural Logic of Late Capitalism* (Durham, NC: Duke University Press, 1991), on the "cultural logic of late capitalism as postmodernism."

83. Noam Chomsky, *Year 501: The Conquest Continues* (Boston: South End Press, 1993).

84. In Stalinist real socialism, the criterion was the "increase in the rate of production"—measured, in any event, by an approximate market value of commodities. It is a question of the same time of fetishism. See Hinkelammert, "Marco categorial del pensamiento sovietico," chapter 4, in *Critiea a la razon utópica* (San Jose de Costa Rica: CEI, 1984), 123 ff.

85. Karl Marx, *Grundrisse*, trans. Martin Nicolaus (New York: Penguin Books, 1973), 410.

86. Marx, *Grundrisse*, 410.

87. Pure necessity without money is no market; it is only misery, growing and unavoidable misery.

88. Marx, *Das Kapital*, vol. 1 (1867), 799. Here we must remember once more that the *Human Development Report*, Development Programme, United Nations (New York: Oxford University Press, 1992) already demonstrated in an incontrovertible manner that the richer 20 percent of the planet consumes today (as never before in global history) 82.7 percent of goods (incomes) of the planet, while the remaining 80 percent of humanity only consumes 17.3 percent of said goods. Such concentration is the product of the "world-system" we have been delineating.

89. Hebert Marcuse, "Liberation from the Affluent Society" in *To Free a Generation: The Dialectics of Liberation*, ed. David Cooper (New York: Collier Books, 1967), 181.

Chapter Six

The Singularity of Peripheral Social Inequality

Jessé Souza

The modernization theories that have accompanied the American effort at political reorganization of the "free world" since World War II have lost, for good reasons, the undisputed prestige that they enjoyed until the mid 1960s. Nevertheless, their basic presumption that perceives the relationship between the center and the periphery in the World System as an antinomic opposition between traditional and premodern countries and regions and modern countries and regions continues to be alive in new and hybrid clothes. This is evidence that the surpassal of a theoretical paradigm, even when it is obviously inadequate and insufficient, cannot be "decreed." A theoretical transformation demands the explicit construction of an alternative paradigm that can explain the central issues of the old paradigm in a more convincing form, considering the failures and silences of the previous model.

This is the challenge that I would like to face in this chapter. I would like to try to demonstrate how the naturalization of social inequality and the consequent production of "under citizens" as a mass phenomena in peripheral countries of recent modernization such as Brazil can be more suitably perceived as a consequence, not of a supposed premodern and personalist inheritance, but precisely the contrary, as the result of the large scale modernization process which has gradually been implanted in these societies as a result of worldwide capitalist expansion. In this sense, my argument implies that the social inequality of peripheral societies such as Brazil and its naturalization in daily life is modern, given that it is linked to the effectiveness of modern values and institutions since their very successful importation "from the outside in." Thus, contrary to being "personalist" the process has been effective exactly because of the "impersonality" typical of modern values and institutions. This is what makes this process so opaque and difficult to perceive in daily life.

The importance of a change of paradigm in this field has more than just theoretical repercussions. The current chronic absence of bright opportunities for the future in peripheral countries such as Brazil is related to the obsolescence of the old political projects that were based on the traditional analyses criticized above. The tendency to believe in a "fetishism of the economy" (as if economic growth on its own could resolve problems such as exclusionary inequality and marginalization[1]), the habit of establishing regional cleavages between modern and traditional portions of a country, and even the populist crusade against corruption, are legitimated by this same stew of ideas. They serve as ideological cosmetics that hide the theoretical and political articulation of the specific class conflicts in the periphery. This is the thesis that I intend to defend in this chapter.

The theoretical difficulty in advancing constructive hypotheses in this field demands the articulation of two subsequent steps: 1) building the articulation between the value configuration subjacent to Western rationalism and its institutional anchoring, or that is, reconstituting a social-cultural version of the Marxist theme of "the spontaneous ideology of capitalism"; 2) reflecting upon its application specifically in the context of "peripheral modernity." For the development of the first theme I would like to elaborate on an "insight" not completely developed by Max Weber in the realm of his comparative sociology of religions. I will combine this insight with concepts from two of the most promising critical approaches in sociology in the second half of the past century: the critical theory of recognition, whose principal exponent is Canadian philosopher Charles Taylor, and the sociology of Pierre Bourdieu.

In my view, these two approaches present interesting complementarities that also can be used, to great advantage, for an analysis of peripheral modernity.

As we know, Weber was primarily interested in his monumental sociology of great world religions, in pursuing a comparative analysis of Western rationalism with the great Eastern religions in order to clarify why a new type of Society, which we call modern Western capitalism, arose only in the West and imposed structural transformations on all spheres of social life. Since the "revolution of consciousnesses" of aesthetic Protestantism was perceived as a particularly important moment in the explanation of this singular development in the West, neo-Weberian comparative sociology was marked by the search for "substitutes for the Protestant ethic" to identify both processes of modernization with chances of success, as well as those destined for failure.

One presumption implicit in this analytical strategy was the fact that it maintained not only the premises of "essentialist culturalism," that is a conception where culture is perceived as homogeneous, totalizing, and undifferentiated, but also the stage notion of the sociological tradition of modernization to the degree in which it assumes that non-Western societies either repeat the steps of central Western societies through similitudes of the Protestant revolution—the case of Japan is the most eloquent in this context[2]—or they are condemned to premodernism. Only the repetition of the contingent process of Western "spontaneous modernization" could guarantee a passport to modern economic, political and cultural relations. A good portion of culturalist and institutionalist sociology that is written both about Latin America as well as about Latin Americans, was and is still explicitly or implicitly marked by this presumption.

For Max Weber himself, nevertheless, it appears clear that the explanation of the "spontaneous rise" of Western rationalism in Europe and North America would differ fundamentally from the explanation of the ulterior development of the value and institutional structure of this rationalism as a consequence of the expansion of Western society for the entire planet. Fundamentally, this expansion would take place through the exportation to the periphery of the world system of the fundamental institutions of Western rationalism as "ready-made artifacts" (*fertigen Gebildes als Artefakt*)[3]: the capitalist market with its technical and material range and the centralized rational State with its monopoly on violence and disciplinary power.

The difficulty in discussing this theme is related to the necessarily naturalized conception that we have of social efficiency of the market and State. The generations that are born under the aegis of the disciplinary practices already consolidated in these institutions, the implicit opaque and contingent value hierarchy that runs through it in a nontransparent manner, assumes the naturalized form of a self-evident reality that needs no justification. To respond to the empiric imperatives of the State and the market comes to be as obvious as breathing or walking. We do not know any other way of being since early childhood. Since then we are all made and continually remodeled and perfected to attend these imperatives. It is this reality that allows and confers credibility to the scientific concepts that are unfamiliar with the contingent normative logic of these "sub-systems." It assumes the form of any other natural limitation of existence, such as the laws of gravity, for example, against which we can do nothing.[4]

To advance in the direction of an alternative concept about the logic implicit to the operation of these institutions, therefore, it is necessary to reconstruct what I would like to call, with Karl Marx, the "spontaneous ideology of capitalism." I call it "ideology" since I believe that both the market and the State are composed of value hierarchies that are implicit and opaque to the everyday consciousness, the naturalization of which disguise them as "neutral" and "meritocratic" and is responsible for the legitimation of the social order that these institutions help to maintain. Access to this "spontaneous ideology" is essential for us to be able to perceive the importance of symbolic and cultural access to an understanding of the social production of inequality and under-citizenry, without appealing to the "culturalist essentialism" typical of the approaches that articulate personalism, familialism, and patrimonialism, which disregard the articulation between values and their necessary institutional anchoring, the only link that can explain in what way values influence the effective behavior of agents.

For this desideratum, the contributions of the classics of sociology are precarious. Karl Marx, who invented the theme of "spontaneous ideology" as a specific mark of social domination under capitalism, left us "only" a description of the discontinuity between the production and circulation of commodities. This discontinuity causes the commodity of labor force to "appear" to the consciousness of those involved as if it is effectively sold for its fair value. In this way, the exploration of labor is not transparent. Marx lacks, however, an explicit articulation of the "value hierarchy" that is realized in the action of the market. The Weberian perspective also begins trapped in categories of "philosophy of consciousness," which forces him to find in the subject actor the source of all meaning and morality.[5] Thus, Weber is also incapable of perceiving, in its complete scope, the extension of the value, moral, and symbolic horizon present in these institutional configurations exported from the center to the periphery as "ready made artifacts," according to his formulation.

It is precisely by clarifying this basic aspect of the explanation of the implicit value hierarchy that opaquely runs through the institutional effectiveness of the market and state that I would like to incorporate the reflections of Charles Taylor about the sources of the modern "self."[6] I am not interested here in Taylor's use of his investigations in the context of the debate about multiculturalism or that between liberals and communitarians. I am interested in his comunitarian starting point as a hermeneutic of social space based on his criticism of the "naturalism" that runs through both scientific practice as well as daily life. This perspective can be used to articulate precisely the value configuration implicit to Western rationalism that envisions, as we will see, a specific type of social hierarchy and also a singular notion of social recognition based on it. His criticism of the tendentially reified concept of the State and market as systemic magnitudes, as we see in Jürgen Habermas, for example, appears to me correct and of decisive importance for a more suitable understanding of the process of expansion of Western rationalism from the center to the periphery, which takes place through the exportation of these institutions as ready artifacts in the Weberian sense of the term. The negation of the contingent symbolic and cultural character of these institutional materializations, which perceives them as realities guided according to criteria of formal effectiveness, would be equivalent to reduplicating, in a conceptual dimension, the effect of "naturalism" in daily life.

Essential to Taylor's scheme, and what carries it, in this case, far beyond the Weberian reflection, is that he is able to reconstruct the subjacent and opaque value hierarchy that is materialized in these two central institutions of the modern world, which unreflectedly and unconsciously command our daily dispositions and behavior. What makes the Taylorian reflection of interest to the social sciences, in my view, is that his reconstruction of the "history of ideas" is not an end in itself. Its strategy is to understand the genesis or archaeology of the concepts of good and of how they evolve and acquire social effectiveness. This point is crucial. Taylor is not interested in a mere history of ideas, but how and why they are able to take the hearts and minds of common people. For this reason his undertaking is sociologically relevant. Therefore, in the first place he is interested in the effectiveness of ideas—not their content. The content is only important to the degree that it explains the reasons for their collective acceptance.

Plato is a central figure in this context. He is the systematizer of the fundamental idea for the moral concept of the West, which is the idea that the Self is seen as threatened by desire (which is insatiable) and therefore must be subordinated and ruled by reason. Christianism adopted the Platonic perspective of the dominance of reason over the passions to the degree in which sanctity and the specific "way to [Christian] salvation" is expressed in the terms of Platonic purity. Meanwhile, St. Augustine, by appropriating the Platonic tradition, engendered a radical novelty that would be essential to the specificity of the West: the notion of interiority. It was this link with the religiously motivated need that became the language of irresistible interiority. The link between the dominant ideas of the West and their effectiveness is perceived—in an obvious correspondence with Max Weber—as a process internal to Western religious rationalization. In this way, the ideally articulated concepts of good are linked to specific "ideal interests" based on the "religious" prize of salvation. This explains St. Augustine's paradigmatic place in the Taylorian scheme.

The process of interiorization initiated by Augustine was radicalized by Descartes. Since Descartes there has been a fundamental change in the terms and form in which virtue is conceived.[7] This change is radical given that it inverted the notion of virtue and of good that ruled until then. The former ethics of honor was reinterpreted in terms of the Cartesian ideal of rational control. Rationality was also no longer seen as substantive and came to be procedural. Rationality came to mean thinking according to certain canons. It is this new moral subject that Taylor calls the "Punctual Self." It would be Locke who systematized the new ideal of independence and self-responsibility, interpreted as something free of custom and local authority, transforming the "punctual self" at the basis of a systematic political theory.

The "self" is punctual given that it is unattached to particular contexts and therefore remodelable by means of methodic and disciplined action. For this new manner of seeing the subject, developed a philosophy, a science, an administration, and organizational techniques destined to assure its control and discipline. The notion of the unattached self, by being rooted in social and institutional practices, is naturalized. These ideas, germinated for centuries, of calculating and instrumental reason and of will as self-responsibility, which added up lead to Taylor's central concept of the punctual self, were not able to dominate the practical life of people until the great revolution of the Protestant Reformation. Here is another obvious point in common with Max Weber. For the two thinkers, the Reformation was the midwife of both the cultural and moral singularity of the West. The Protestant revolution realized in practice, in the space of common sense and of daily life, the new notion of Western virtue. For this reason, for Taylor, to the notion of the punctual self must be added the idea of "affirmation of ordinary life" for an understanding of the moral configuration that dominates us today.

The theme of the affirmation of ordinary life is in opposition to the Platonic or Aristotelian concepts that exalted the contemplative life in opposition to the practical life. The revolution Taylor speaks of is that which redefined the social hierarchy to the point that the practical spheres of work and family, precisely those spheres in which everyone, without exception, participates, now come to define the place of the superior and most important activities. At the same time, there is a lack of respect for the earlier contemplative and aristocratic activities. The sacralization of work, especially of manual and simple labor, of Lutheran origin and later generically Protestant, illustrates the historic transformation of large proportions for the entire redefinition of the social hierarchy that is our common thread in this text.

Taylor perceived that the social bases for a revolution of such consequences are due to the religious motivation of the reformative spirit. Upon rejecting the idea of the mediated sacred, Protestants also rejected the entire social hierarchy linked to it. This is the decisive point here. Since the gradations of greater or lower sacredness of certain functions is the basis of the (religious) hierarchy of traditional societies, to devalue the hierarchy based on this order is to withdraw the foundations of the social hierarchy as a whole, both in the religious sphere in the strict sense as well as in the other spheres under its influence. In this way, space was opened for a new and revolutionary (given its equalizing and egalitarian potential) notion of social hierarchy that came to be based on the Taylorian "punctual self," or that is a contingent and historically specific concept of the human being, presided by the notion of calculability, prospective reasoning, self control, and productive labor as the implicit foundations both of its self-esteem as well as of its social recognition.

The social supports of this new concept of the world, for Taylor, are the bourgeois classes of England, the United States, and France. They were later disseminated by the subordinated classes of these countries and later in other countries with important and singular deviations.[8] The concept of labor within this context will not emphasize what is done but how labor is conducted (God loves adverbs). The social link suitable to interpersonal relations will be of the contractual type (and by extension constitutional liberal democracy the suitable type of government). In political language this new world vision will be consecrated under a form of subjective rights and in accord with the egalitarian tendency, universally defined. Taylor will call the set of ideas that are articulated in this context the principle of "dignity." Dignity will therefore designate the possibility of equality made effective, for example, in the potentially universal individual rights. Instead of premodern "honor" that presupposes distinction and privilege, dignity presupposes a universal recognition among equals.[9]

In this context, we are less interested in the Taylorian tension between a homogenizing disciplinary reason and an expressive singularizing reason, such as the existential and political conflict par excellence of late modernity,[10] and more in the repercussions of its discussion about the principles that regulate our attribution of respect and deference, or that is, the attribution of "social recognition" as a basis of the modern notion of legal and political citizenship. The location and explanation of these principles can help us to identify the operating mechanisms, in an opaque and implicit form, in the social distinction between distinct classes and social groups in certain societies. It can help us to identify the "symbolic operators" that allow each one of us in daily life to establish a hierarchy and classify people as more or less worthy of our appreciation or our disdain.

Thus, contrary to the hierarchizing criteria of Hindu civilization, for example, where the principle of ritual purity classified and declassified the distinct social castes,[11] in the West, the implicit basis of social recognition came to be the sharing of a certain psychosocial structure. It is this psychosocial structure that is the basis of the consolidation of rational-formal systems such as the market and the State, and later the principal product of the combined efficiency in these institutions. It is the generalization of these same preconditions that makes possible speaking of "citizenship" or that is, a set of rights and responsibilities in the context of the nation-state shared by all in a presumption of effective equality. Taylor's considerations about "dignity" as a basis for individual self-esteem and social recognition therefore relate to the relationship between the sharing of a contingent emotional and moral economy and the possibility of social recognition for individuals and groups: For the rule of equality to be socially effective, the perception of equality in the realm of daily life must be effectively internalized.

Nevertheless, at the level of the abstraction of reflection developed by Taylor, it is not clear in what way this new hierarchy that comes to be implemented by the market and the States becomes effective as a basis for social classification and of differential value between individuals and social classes. Thus, to advance even one more step in our effort at concretization of analysis, I would like to use the studies of Pierre Bourdieu in order to suitably conceptualize the basic issue that allows thinking of social recognition, objectively produced and institutionally implemented, as the very nucleus of the condition that allows establishing social distinctions based on opaque social signs that are perceptible to everyone in a pre-reflexive manner.

The union of the perspectives of Taylor and Bourdieu appears to me to be interesting from various aspects. They appear to be complementary in the sense that they develop aspects that overcome important deficiencies in each other. It may be said that Taylor lacks a contemporary theory of class struggle. This is to the degree in which he speaks of the point of view of the North American or European intellectual in the late twentieth century, when the central societies are supposedly pacified internally of the more virulent class conflicts, and entering a new phase of rearticulation of their political struggles.[12] Bourdieu, however, presents a sophisticated analysis of the singularly opaque and refracted form that the ideological domination, hiding its class character, assumes in late modernity. I believe that Bourdieu's perspective allows us to go beyond a concept of recognition that assumes, at least tendentially, as effective reality the ideology of equality prevalent in central Western societies. As I hope to demonstrate, this starting point appears to me to be essential, even if important modifications in its theoretical instrumental are needed, also for an analysis of peripheral modernity.

At the same time, on the other hand, the genealogy of the implicit hierarchy that commands our daily life, developed superbly by Taylor, allows precisely clarifying the Achilles' heel of Bourdieu's entire argument. After all, by concentrating solely on the instrumental factor in the dispute for relative power between the classes in struggle for scarce resources, he does not perceive that this same struggle takes place in an intersubjectively produced context, which maintains its contingence and with this the need for its critical perfection, but removes, at the same time, the arbitrary fact of the mere imposition of power of the strongest. The theory of recognition can, in this sense, explain the generative mechanism of the intersubjectively shared "minimum normative consensus." It is this mechanism that contextualizes and filters the relative chances of the legitimate monopoly over the distribution of scarce resources by the various social classes in dispute in a given society, a mechanism that is made secondary and not properly conceptualized by Bourdieu. Despite his unilateralness, however, Bourdieu's contribution to an understanding of the ideological form specific to late modernity, whether central or peripheral, appears to me to be essential.

Taylor, himself, in his text, "To follow a rule,"[13] offers an interesting view of the approximation between the two perspectives that we intend to conjugate here. Taylor, in reality, approximates Bourdieu and Wittgenstein considering a fundamental aspect of his own theory: the notion of "articulation." Taylor affirms that, "if Wittgenstein has helped us to break the philosophical thrall of intellectualism, Bourdieu has begun to explore how social science could be remade, once freed from its distorting grip."[14] Here the common enemy is the rationalist and intellectual trend, dominant in both philosophy and the social sciences. While the intellectual tradition in these two fields of knowledge tends to perceive the understanding of social rule, for example, as a process that is consumed at the level of representation and thinking, abstracting its corporal and contextual component, both Wittgenstein and Bourdieu emphasize the element of "practice." To obey a rule is in the first place a learned practice and not knowledge. The "practice" can be "articulated." That is, it can make explicit reasons and explanations for its "being this way and not any other" when challenged to do so, but, in most cases, this unarticulated background remains implicit, silently commanding our practical activity and encompassing much more than the borders of our conscious representations.

For Taylor, the fact that it is non-articulated practice that commands our daily life, establishes the need to articulate the hierarchy of hidden and opaque values that preside over our behavior. For this reason he names and reconstructs the sources of our notion of self. For Bourdieu, however, the same fact makes urgent a "psychoanalysis of social space." What for most of the sociological tradition is an "internalization of values" which tendentially evokes a more rationalist reading that emphasizes the most conscious and reflected aspect of normative and value-reproduction in society, for Bourdieu the emphasis is, to the contrary, on the pre-reflexive, automatic, emotive, spontaneous, conditioning, or one that is "inscribed in the body" of our actions, dispositions, and choices.

In this context, the basic notion that I would like to use for my own purposes in the context of this selective appropriation is that of *habitus*. *Habitus*, contrary to the rationalist and intellectualizing tradition, allows emphasizing the entire set of cultural and institutional dispositions that are inscribed in the body and that are expressed in the body language of each one of us, transforming, in a matter of speaking, cultural and institutional value choices into flesh and bone. While for Marx the "spontaneous ideology" of capitalism was the fetishism of the merchandise that hid, under the mask of market equality, unequal production relations, for Bourdieu it would be the set of dispositions linked to a peculiar life style that conforms to this *habitus* stratified by social classes, and that invisibly and subliminally legitimates the differential access to material resources and scarce ideas, the spontaneous ideology of late capitalism.

In his classic text about "distinction,"[15] Bourdieu explores the hypothesis, using as an empirical universe contemporary French society, that "taste" is the field par excellence of "social negation" by revealing it as an innate quality, and not one that is socially produced. The primary process of naturalized introjection of this legitimizing criteria of inequalities takes place from the cultural, familial, and educational inheritance on all their levels. What Bourdieu has in mind is the formation of a habitus of class, perceived as a non-intentional learning of dispositions, inclinations, and evaluative schemes that allows its possessor to perceive and classify, in a pre-reflexive dimension, opaque signs of cultural legitimacy. Since social distinction based on taste is not limited to the artifacts of cultural legitimacy, but includes all the dimensions of human life that imply some choice—such as clothing, food, forms of leisure, consumption options, etc.—taste functions as the prime sense of distinction, allowing the separation and joining of people and consequently, the forging of solidarities or constitution of group divisions in a universal (everything is taste!) and invisible form.

In the best pages of *Distinction*, Bourdieu is able to demonstrate, with rich use of the interesting empirical material, that even our choices that are considered the most personal and recondite, from the preference for a car, composer, or writer to the choice of a sexual partner, are, in reality, fruits of the invisible threads that link interests of class or fractions of class, or even relative positions in each field of social practices such as the opposition between the recently arrived challengers and those already established by seniority. These invisible threads interlink and cement both affinities and sympathies, constituting the objectively defined solidarity networks or, on the other hand, forge antipathies soldered by prejudice.

This beautiful idea of *habitus* operating as invisible threads that link people by solidarity and identification and that separate them by prejudice, which is equivalent to a notion of coordination of social actions perceived as unconscious and ciphered, nevertheless limits the richness of a fundamental idea for Taylor: the notion of "articulation" that allows thinking of a "transfer" between the reflective and the non-reflective. After all, if there is something that can be articulated it is because there is something that goes beyond pure unreflective *habitus*. For this reason, the absence of this dimension in Bourdieu's reflection means that the counterposition in relation to the "great illusion" of the social game is only reactively possible, without the questioning of rules as such. This reactive position stems from Bourdieu's concept, thought of in opposition to subjectivism[16] which reduces social space to a space of conjunctural interactions, of which an entire aesthetic and moral (the two terms must always go together) of class are countered objectively to a rival and contrary one, but never in relation to a shared level of common rules.[17]

This is the space where the contradictions of Bourdieu's analysis are more easily seen. The reasoning of the instrumental logic that reduces all social determinations to the category of power is seen here in all its fragility. At the limit it becomes incomprehensible that some social strategies and some "bluffs" work out and others do not. To get away from the absolute arbitrariness in this dimension of analysis it becomes necessary to request "something" beyond the simple "illusion" of the social game. As Axel Honneth points out, the competition between the various social groups only has meaning if we assume the existence of conflicting interpretations about a common field of rules that are recognized in a "trans-classist" manner.[18] It is because of the lack of this dimension that it is not clear why a given leading class would supposedly "choose" certain objectives and not others. In the same way it also does not explain why changes take place in the "command" of the social process, such as, for example, the substitution of a premodern aristocracy by the bourgeoisie at the dawn of modernity.

For both authors that we are discussing, modern society is unique precisely because it produces a configuration, formed by the illusions of immediate and daily meaning, that Taylor denominates "naturalism" and Bourdieu "doxa," which produce a "specific unknowing" by the actors of their own living conditions. For both, only a hermeneutic, genetic, and reconstructive perspective could reestablish the effective, even if opaque and non-transparent, preconditions of social life in a society of this type. Nevertheless, the concrete challenge here is to systematically articulate the unilateralities of each one of the perspectives studied in order to make them operational in the sense of allowing the perception of how morality and power connect in a peculiar way in the modern world and very particularly in the peripheral context.

Perhaps the factor that best expresses the deficiencies of Bourdieu's theory and exposes the need to link it to an objective theory of morality such as Taylor's, is the radical contextualism of his analysis of the French working class. This analysis prevents perceiving collective processes of moral learning that go far beyond class barriers. This can be observed in Bourdieu's analysis about the French case, where the ultimate patamar of his analysis, as the negative fundament of all social distinction, is the situation of "need" of the working class. What reveals the contingent historic character and space-temporality context of this "need" is that it refers to the distinction of consumption habits within a dimension of social pacification typical of the Welfare State. What is seen as "need" in this context, compared to peripheral societies such as the Brazilian one, acquires a sense of historic and contingent consolidation of political struggles and multiple social and moral learning of effective and fundamental importance, which pass unperceived as such by Bourdieu.

Thus I would like to propose an internal subdivision of the category of *habitus* in such a way as to confer it a more detailed historic character, that is nonexistent in Bourdieu's analysis, and to add, therefore a genetic and diachronic dimension to the theme of constitution of *habitus*. Thus instead of speaking only of *"habitus"* generically, applying it to specific situations of class in a synchronic context, as Bourdieu does, I think it is richer and more interesting for my purposes to speak of a "Plurality of *habitus*." If *habitus* represents the incorporation by subjects of evaluative schemes and dispositions of behavior based on a structural social-economic situation then fundamental changes in the economic–social structure should consequently imply important qualitative changes in the type of *habitus* for all the social classes involved in some way in these changes.

This was certainly the case of the passage of traditional societies to modern societies in the West. The bourgeoisie, as the first ruling class in history that worked, soon broke with the dual morality typical of traditional societies that was based on the code of honor and constructed, at least to an appreciable and significant degree, a homogenization of a human type based on the generalization of its own emotional economy—the command of reason over the emotions, prospective calculation, self-responsibility, etc.—to the dominated classes. This process took place in all central Western societies in the most varied manners. In all the societies that were able to homogenize a trans-classist human type, this was a desideratum sought in a conscious and decided form and not left to a supposed automatic action of economic progress. Thus, this gigantic homogenizing historic process that was later deepened by the social and political conquests of the initiative of the very working class—which certainly did not equalize all classes in all spheres of life, but, certainly generalized and expanded fundamental dimensions of equality in civil, political, and social dimensions as examined by Marshall in his celebrated text—can be perceived as a gigantic process of moral and political learning of profound consequences.

It is precisely this historic process of collective learning that is not adequately conceptualized by Bourdieu in his study of French society. It represents what I would like to call "primary *habitus*" in such a way as to call attention to the evaluative schemes and dispositions of behavior that are objectively internalized and "incorporated" in the Bourdieuian sense of the term, that allows the sharing of a notion of "dignity" in the Taylorian sense. It is this "dignity," effectively shared by all classes that are able to homogenize the emotional economy of all their members to a significant degree, that appears to me to be the profound foundation of infra- and ultra-legal social recognition. It in turn allows social effectiveness of the rule of law and equality, and therefore, the modern notion of citizenship. It is this dimension of shared "dignity," in the nonlegal sense of "considering the other" and that Taylor calls attitudinal respect,[19] that must be disseminated in an effective form in society so that we can say that, in this concrete society, we have the legal dimension of citizenship and equality guaranteed by law. It is worth repeating once again: For there to be legal effectiveness of the rule of equality, the perception of equality in the realm of daily life must be effectively internalized.

It is this dimension that therefore demands the effective trans-classist value consensus as a condition for its existence, which is not perceived as such by Bourdieu. It is this absence that allows thinking of relations between the dominant and dominated classes as specular, reactive relations, as zero sum. The radical contextuality of his argument prevents perceiving the importance of historic conquests of this type of society, such as the French, that are made obvious by comparison with peripheral societies, such as Brazil's, where this consensus does not exist. Therefore by calling the generalization of the social, economic, and political preconditions of the useful subject "dignified" and citizen, in the Taylorian sense of intersubjectivity recognized as such, of "primary *habitus*" I do so to differentiate it analytically from two other also fundamental realities: "precarious *habitus*" and what I would like to call "secondary *habitus*."

The "precarious *habitus*" would be the limit below that of "primary *habitus*": that is, it would be that type of personality and of dispositions of behavior that do not meet the objective demands for an individual or a social group to be considered productive and useful in a society of a modern and competitive type, and to be able to enjoy social recognition with all its dramatic, existential, and political consequences. For some authors, even affluent societies, such as the German, already present some segments of the poor and workers who live from social security precisely with these traces of a "precarious *habitus*,"[20] to the degree to which what we are calling the "primary *habitus*" tends to be redefined according to the new suitable levels of recent transformations of globalized society and of the new importance of knowledge. Nevertheless, as we will see, this definition only earns the status of a permanent mass phenomenon in peripheral societies such as Brazil.

What we are calling "secondary *habitus*" is related to the limit above of the "primary *habitus*": that is, it is related to a source of social recognition and respect that *presupposes* in the strong sense of the term, the generalization of primary *habitus* to broad layers of the population of a given society. In this sense, the secondary *habitus* is already part of the social homogenization of the fundaments operative in the determination of primary *habitus* and in turn institutes classificatory criteria of social distinction based on what Bourdieu calls "taste." But the precise conceptual determination of this triadic differentiation of the notion of *habitus* must be coupled to the Taylorian discussion of the moral sources institutionally anchored in the modern world, whether at the center or in the periphery, for its proper problematization. Since the category of "primary *habitus*" is the most basic, since it is from that category that its lower and upper limits can be understood, we should explain its determination a bit. After all, people are not equally favored with the same social recognition by their "dignity as rational agent." This dimension is not as "shallow" as the simple political dimension of subjective "universalizable" and interchangeable rights suggest. The juridic dimension of legal protection is only one of the dimensions—although it is fundamental and very important—of this process of recognition.

If it is the useful, productive, and disciplined work that appears to be behind the "objective evaluation of relative value" of each one in this dimension, then the potential masking of inequalities behind the notion of "dignity" of the rational agent, should be manifest more easily in this dimension. Reinhard Kreckel calls "ideology of performance"[21] the attempt to elaborate a single principle, beyond mere economic property, based on which is constituted the most important form of legitimation of inequality in the contemporary world. The idea subjacent to this argument is that it must have a "consensual background" (*Hintergrundkonsens*), of the differential value of human beings, in such a way that there can be—even if subliminally produced—a legitimation of inequality. Without this, the violent and unjust character of social inequality would manifest itself in a clear form to the naked eye.

To do so, the ideology of performance is based on the "meritocratic triad" that involves qualification, position, and salary. Of these, qualification, reflecting the extraordinary importance of knowledge in the development of capitalism, is the first and most important point that conditions the other two. The ideology of performance is an "ideology" to the degree in which it not only stimulates and rewards the capacity for objective performance, but legitimates permanent differential access to life chances and the appropriation of scarce goods.[22] Only the combination of the triad of ideology of performance makes the individual a complete and effective "signalizer" of the "complete citizen" (*Vollbürger*). The triad also becomes understandable because only through the category of "work" is it possible to assure identity, self-esteem, and social recognition. In this sense, differential performance at work must refer to an individual and can only be conquered by the individual. Only when these preconditions are given can the individual completely obtain personal and social identity. This explains why a housewife, for example, comes to have objectively "derived" social status, or that is, her importance and social recognition depend on belonging to a family or to a "husband." In this sense she becomes dependent on ascriptive criteria since in the meritocratic context of the "ideology of performance" she has no autonomous value.[23] The attribution of social respect to the social roles of producer and citizen come to be mediated by the real abstraction produced by the market and the State to individuals thought of as "support for distinction" that establish their relative value. Kreckel's explanation about the preconditions for the objective recognition of roles of producer and citizen is important to the degree in which it is fundamental not only to refer to the world of the market and distribution of scarce goods as composed of values, as Nancy Fraser does, for example,[24] but is necessary to explain "what values" they are.

After all, it will be the legitimating power that Kreckel calls "ideology of performance" that will determine for the social subjects and groups excluded, because of the absence of the minimal conditions for successful competition, in this dimension, objectively, its social non-recognition and its absence of self-esteem. The "ideology of performance" would thus function as a type of sub-political legitimation encrusted in daily life, reflecting the effectiveness of functional principles anchored in opaque and nontransparent institutions such as the market and the State. It is nontransparent given that the daily consciousness "appears" as if it were the effect of universal and neutral principals that are open to meritocratic competition. I think that this idea helps to concretely confer that which Taylor calls the "moral source" based on the notion of the "punctual self," although his ideological power and ability to produce distinction is not explicitly conceptualized by this author.

Based on the definition and the constitution of an ideology of performance as a legitimizing mechanism of the roles of producer and citizen, which are equivalent in the reconstruction that I am proposing, to the content of "primary *habitus*," it is possible to better understand their lower limit or "precarious *habitus*." Thus, if primary *habitus* implies a set of psychosocial predispositions reflected in the sphere of personality, the presence of the emotional economy and of cognitive preconditions for a performance suitable to attend the demands (variable in time and space) of the role of the producer, with direct reflection on the role of the citizen, under modern capitalist conditions, the absence of these preconditions, in some significant measure, implies the constitution of a *habitus* marked by precariousness.

In this sense, "precarious *habitus*" can refer both to the more traditional sectors of the working class of the developed and affluent countries such as Germany, as Uwe Bittlingmayer indicates in his study,[25] incapable of attending the new demands for continuous formation and flexibility of the so-called society of knowledge (*Wissensgesellschaft*), which now demands active accommodation to the new economic imperatives, as well as the secular rural and urban Brazilian "underclass." In these two cases, the formation of an entire segment of the unadapted, a marginal phenomenon in societies such as the German, and a phenomenon of masses in a peripheral society such as the Brazilian, is the result of the broadening of the definition that we are calling "primary *habitus*." In the German case the disparity between "primary *habitus*" and "precarious *habitus*" is caused by the growing demands for flexibility, which demands an emotional economy of a peculiar type.

In the Brazilian case, the abyss was created at the threshold of the nineteenth century, with the re-Europeanization of the country and its intensification since 1930 with the beginning of the process of modernization on a large scale. In this case, the dividing line came to be traced between the "Europeanized" sectors—the sectors that were able to adapt to the new productive and social demands of Europeanization that took place, also among us, by the importation as "ready-made artifacts" in the Weberian sense, of European institutions and therefore, of an entire vision of the world subjacent to them—and the "precarious" and "non-Europeanized" sectors that tend, because of their abandonment, to a growing and permanent marginalization.

It is important to note that with the designation of "European" I am not referring to the concrete entity "Europe," much less to a phenotype or physical type, but to the place and historic source of the culturally determined concept of the human being that would be crystallized in the empirical action of institutions such as the competitive market and the rational centralized State, since Europe, literally dominated the world in all of its nooks and crannies, including Latin America. The "European" and "European-ness," once again to avoid misunderstanding, perceived as the empirical reference of a particular hierarchy of values that can—as in nineteenth-century Rio de Janeiro, personified by a "mulatto"—be transformed into a dividing line that separates citizen (primary *habitus*) from "under citizen" (precarious *habitus*). It is the attribute of "European-ness" in the precise sense that we are using this term here, that will divide into socially classifieds and declassifieds, individuals, and even entire social classes, in exogenously modernized peripheral societies such as Brazil's.

Since the basic principle of the trans-classist consensus is, as we see, the principle of performance and discipline (the moral source of Taylor's punctual self), it comes to be the generalized acceptance and internalization of this principle that causes the non-adaptation and the marginalization of these sectors to be perceived, both by society as well as by its victims, as a "personal weakness." It is also the universal centrality of the principle of performance, with its consequent pre-reflexive incorporation, that causes the reaction of the unadapted to take place in a field of forces that is articulated precisely in relation to the theme of performance: positively by the recognition of untouchability of its intrinsic value, despite the very position of precariousness, and negatively, by the construction of a reactive wounded lifestyle, that is, openly criminal or marginal.[26]

Meanwhile, the upper limit of primary *habitus* is related to the fact that the differential performance in the sphere of production must be associated with a particular "stylization of life" in order to produce social distinctions. In this sense, what we are calling "secondary *habitus*" would be precisely what Bourdieu had in mind with his study about the "subtle distinctions" that he analyzed in his *Distinctions*. It is in this dimension that "taste" comes to be a type of invisible currency, transforming both the pure economic capital as well as, and especially, cultural capital, "disguised as differential performance," based on the illusion of "innate talent" in a set of social signs of legitimate distinction based on the typical effects of the context of opacity in relation to their conditions of possibility.

But it is also necessary to add the objective dimension of morality, which in the final instance allows the entire process of fabrication of social distinctions that, as we saw, is ignored by Bourdieu. Thus the concept of secondary *habitus*[27] must also be linked, as we did with the concept of primary and precarious *habitus,* to the moral context, even if it is opaque and naturalized, that provides its effectiveness. If we perceive the "ideology of performance" as a corollary for the "dignity of the rational being" of the Taylorian punctual self and as the implicit and naturalized moral basis of the two other forms of *habitus* that we distinguish, I believe that secondary *habitus* can be understood in its specificity, above all, from the Taylorian notion of expressivity and authenticity.

The romantic ideal of expressivity and authenticity is interpreted by Taylor in *The Sources of the Self* as an alternative moral source to the "punctual self," and the principle of performance that commands it, to the degree in which it implies in the narrative reconstruction of a singular identity for which there are no pre-established models. Thus, if the "punctual self" is constituted by criteria that imply universalization and homogenization, in the same way as the categories of producer and citizen that concretely realize it, the "subject" of expressivism is marked by the search for singularity and originality, given that what should be "expressed" in "expressivism" is precisely the affective and sentimental horizon very special to each one. It is in this ideal—that is formed later as a reaction to the rationalizing and disciplinary demands of the institutionally anchored "punctual self"—in which resides the danger of transforming itself into its counterpart in current conditions. The motto of the diagnostic of the epoch elaborated by Taylor in his *The Ethics of Authenticity* is precisely the growing threat of trivialization of this ideal, from its dialogical content of self-invention in favor of a self-referred perspective symbolized in what the author calls the "quick fix."[28]

The theme of "taste" as the basis for social distinction based on what we are calling secondary *habitus*, includes both the horizon of "substantive individualization," based on the ideal of original, dialogical, and narratively constituted identity, as the process of superficial individuation based on the "quick fix." Bourdieu does not perceive the difference between the two forms, given that, for him, by force of his categorical choices, as we saw, the strategy of distinction is always utilitarian and instrumental. For my purposes, however, this difference is essential. After all, the recovery of the objectified dimension, elaborated by Taylor, is what explains, in the final analysis, the appeal and the social effectiveness even of the mass and *pastiche* version of this possibility for individuation.

The personification of "taste" by Bordieu serves, above all, precisely as the definition of "distinct personality," a personality that appears as a result of innate qualities and as expression of harmony and beauty and reconciliation of reason and sensibility, the definition of the perfect and finished individual.[29] The struggles between the various fractions of the dominant class take place precisely through the determination of the socially hegemonic version of what is a distinct and superior personality. The working class—which by definition does not participate in these struggles—is a mere negative of the idea of personality, nearly "non-persons" as Bourdieu's speculation about the reduction of workers to a pure physical force tends to see.[30] In this dimension of "secondary *habitus*" there does not appear to exist any difference in form between the modern societies of the center and the periphery. In this dimension of production of inequalities, contrary to what the "ideology of inequality of opportunities" proclaims in the advanced countries, the two types of society are at the same level.

The basic distinction between these two types of "modern" society appears to me to be located in the absence—in the peripheral societies—of a generalization of the "primary *habitus*" or that is, of the component responsible for the effective universalization of the category of useful producer and citizen in advanced societies. In all the societies that were able to "transclassistly" homogenize this fundamental quality, this was an objective sought as political, moral, and religious reform of great proportions and not left to the task of "economic progress." The "Great Awakening" of the eighteenth and nineteenth centuries in the United States were able to take to the frontier and to the slavocrat South the same moral seeds and religious fervor of the original thirteen colonies.[31] The English Poor Laws can also be understood as an authoritarian form of forcing those not adapted to the Industrial Revolution to adopt the psychosocial requisites of the new society that was created. Also in France, we have similar experience, as the classic book of Eugen Weber *Peasants into Frenchmen* exemplarily shows. The book's title already denotes the process of social transformation of homogenization that is the presumption of social effectiveness of the notion of citizenry.[32]

A concrete example can help to clarify what I have in mind when I seek to emphasize the importance of this factor to a suitable perception of the specificities of central and peripheral modernities. In this way, if I am correct, it would be the effective existence of a basic and transclassist consensus, represented by the generalization of the social preconditions that allows effective sharing in advanced societies of what I am calling primary *habitus*, which guarantees the social efficacy of Law. For example, if a middle-class German or French person kills a lower-class compatriot in an automobile accident, it is highly probable that the driver would be effectively punished under the law. However, if a middle-class Brazilian hits a poor Brazilian, the chances are low that the law would be effectively applied in this case—very low. This does not mean that people in the latter case are not interested in any way with what happened. A police procedure would usually be opened and follow its bureaucratic course. But the result, in the large majority of cases, would be a simple acquittal or a punishment suitable for a minor infraction, as if a chicken or a dog had been hit.

It is the infra- and ultra-juridic dimension of social respect, a socially shared objective dimension, in which the value of the Brazilian *non-Europeanized* poor—or that is one who does not share the emotional economy of the punctual self that is the contingent cultural creation of Europe and North America—is comparable to that of a domestic animal, which objectively characterizes his status as subhuman. In peripheral countries such as Brazil, there is an entire class of excluded and declassified people, given that they do not participate in the basic value context—what Taylor calls "dignity" of the rational agent. This is the condition needed to have a possibility for effective sharing, by all, of the idea of equality in this dimension that is essential for the constitution of a *habitus*, which, by way of incorporating the plastic, adaptive, and disciplinary characteristics that are basic for the exercise of productive functions in the context of modern capitalism, we can call "primary *habitus*."

Allow me to try to specify even more this central idea of my argument in this chapter. I speak of primary "*habitus*" given that it effectively concerns a *habitus* in the sense that this notion acquires in Bourdieu. It is the objectively shared evaluative schemes—even if they are opaque and nearly always nonreflected and unconscious—that guide our action and our effective behavior in the world. It is only this type of consensus—as if corporal, pre-reflexive and naturalized—that can allow, beyond the legal dimension, a type of implicit accord that suggests, as in the example of the auto accident in Brazil, that some people and classes be above the law and others below it. It is as if there exists an invisible network that links the policeman that open the investigation to the judge that decrees the final sentence, running through lawyers, witnesses, prosecutors, journalists, and others, who, through an implicit and never verbalized agreement, wind up acquitting the driver. What links all of these individual intentionalities in a subliminal manner and that leads to an implicit accord among them is the objective and institutionally anchored reality of the nonhuman value of the victim. It is precisely the differential value between humans that is realized in an unarticulated form in all our institutional and social practices.

This is not a question of intentions. No Europeanized Brazilian of the middle class would confess, in sane consciousness, that he considers his compatriots of the low, non-Europeanized classes to be "sub-people." Many of the Europeanized middle class vote in leftist parties and participate in campaigns against hunger and similar movements. The dimension here is objective, subliminal, implicit, and nontransparent. It is also implicit in the sense that it does not need to be linguistically mediated or symbolically articulated. It implies, like the idea of *habitus* in Bourdieu, a complete vision of the world and a moral hierarchy that is based, and is revealed, as a social sign, in an imperceptible form that apparently has little importance; like respectful inclination and the unconscious social inferiority when meeting a superior; by the tone of voice more than by what is said, etc. What exists here are mute and subliminal social accords and consensus. But it is exactly for this reason that they are more effective. It is these accords that articulate—as if with invisible threads—solidarities and deep and invisible prejudices. It is this type of accord, to use the example of the crash victim, that would allow all those involved in the legal process—without any conscious agreement and even against the explicit expectations of many of these people—to declare their middle-class compatriot innocent.

Because of his radical contextualism that implies an a-historic component, Bourdieu does not realize the existence of a transclassist component that creates—in societies such as the French—an intersubjective and transclassist accord that effectively punishes one guilty for hitting a low class French person. This is because this person is effectively in the sub-political and subliminal dimension "one of the people" and "a full citizen" and not only physical and muscular strength or mere animal power. It is the effective existence of this component, nevertheless, that explains the fact that in French society, in a fundamental dimension, independently of belonging to class, all of them are citizens. This fact does not imply, on the other hand, that there are other dimensions of the question of inequality that are also manifest in a veiled and non-transparent form, as is also demonstrated by Bourdieu in his analysis of French society. But the theme of taste, by separating people by links of sympathy and aversion, can and should be analytically distinct from the question of fundamental dignity of legal and social citizenship, which I associate here with what I call primary *habitus*.

The distinction by taste, so magnificently reconstructed by Bourdieu, presupposes in the French case a level of effective equality both in the realm of sharing of fundamental rights, as well as in the realm of the attitudinal respect of which Taylor speaks—in the sense that all are perceived as "useful" members even if they are unequal in other dimensions. In other words, the dimension that we call "primary *habitus*" is added to another dimension that also presupposes the existence of implicit evaluative schemes and a shared unconscious. That is, a dimension that corresponds to a specific *habitus* in Bourdieu's sense, as exemplarily demonstrated by this author from his choices of taste, which we are denominating "secondary *habitus*."

These two dimensions obviously interpenetrate each other in various ways. Nevertheless, we can and should separate them analytically to the degree in which they obey the distinct logic of functioning. As Taylor would say, the moral sources are distinct in each case. In the case of primary *habitus* what is at stake is the effective dissemination of the notion of dignity of the rational agent, which makes the agent productive and a full citizen. In advanced societies this dissemination is effective and the cases of precarious *habitus* are marginal phenomena. In peripheral societies such as Brazil's, precarious *habitus*—which implies the existence of invisible and objective networks that qualify the precarious individuals and social groups as sub-producers and sub-citizens, and this, under the form of unquestionable social evidence, both for the privileged as well as for the victims themselves of precariousness—is a mass phenomenon and justifies my thesis that what substantially differentiates these two types of societies is the social production of a "structural underclass" in peripheral societies.

This circumstance does not eliminate the fact that, in the two types of society, there is a struggle for distinction based on what I call secondary *habitus*, which has to do with the selective appropriation of scarce goods and resources and constitutes crystallized contexts and tendentially permanent contexts of inequality. But the effective consolidation, to a significant degree, of the social preconditions that allow the generalization of a primary *habitus* in the central societies, restricts sub-citizenry as a mass phenomenon to peripheral societies, marking their specificity as modern societies and calling attention to the specific class conflict of the periphery.

The effort of this multiple construction of *habitus* serves to go beyond subjectivist conceptions of reality that reduce them to face-to-face interactions. The auto accident described above, for example, would be "explained" by the personalist hybrid paradigm[33] based on the social capital found in the "personal relations" of the middle-class driver, who would wind up unpunished. This is a typical example of the subjectivist mistake of interpreting complex and dynamic peripheral societies, like the Brazilian, as if the structural social role were played by premodern principles such as social capital in personal relations. In this field, there is no difference between central or peripheral countries. Personal relations are important in the definition of individual careers and chances for social ascension, both in one case as in the other. In the two types of society, however, the economic and cultural capitals are structuring, which the social capital of personal relations is not.

If my analysis is correct, this interpretive scheme would allow explaining both the subjacent value and normative hierarchy, even if in a subliminal and non-transparent form, by the functioning of the market and the State, as the peculiar form through which these opaque signs acquire *social visibility* even if in a pre-reflexive mode. This type of approach would also allow discussing the specificity of peripheral societies such as the Brazilian, allowing to conceptualize both their singular inequalities as well as their complexity and undeniable dynamic elements, without appealing to culturalist essentialisms or personalist explanations—such as "hybrid" approaches, which are required to defend the existence of a premodern nucleus in these societies in order to conceptualize their social ills. The anachronism of this type of explanation, which never theoretically confronts the central issue of explaining in what way the "hybrid" principles are articulated, appears to me to be evident.[34]

Nevertheless, State and market are not the only fundamental realities of these modern societies whether central or peripheral. The public sphere is, as Habermas demonstrated,[35] a *third fundamental institution of modernity*, destined precisely to develop the reflexive criticism and the possibilities of collective learning. Nevertheless, as Habermas himself indicated, an effective public sphere presupposes, among other things, a rationalized "lifeworld," or that is, in the context of the vocabulary that I am using in this text, an effective generalization of "primary *habitus*" in its virtualities of public and political behavior. This implies that in *our specific Brazilian case*, the public sphere would be as internally segmented, as are the State and the market. This aspect goes against certain excessively optimistic analyses about the virtues of this fundamental institution in peripheral societies.

Nevertheless, modern societies, once again, whether central or peripheral, also develop "social imaginaries" that are more or less explicit and reflected, beyond the subliminal effectiveness of the typical institutional apparatus that we call the "spontaneous ideology of capitalism." To an important degree, it is these imaginaries that allow the production of particular collective and individual identities to each specific cultural or national context.[36] In the case of the social imaginary peculiar to Brazilian society, this process only reaches its most definitive and long-lasting version with the consolidation of a Nation Building experience based on the "corporative" and modernizing state of the 1930s. In this sense, the dimension of explicit ideology only corroborates and justifies the implicit dimension of "spontaneous ideology," constituting the specific conditions of a Brazilian "social imaginary." Gilberto Freyre, who was, if not the initiator, given that long before him this symbolic construction was already being constituted, certainly was the great formulator of the "definitive version" of this explicit ideology that became the "State doctrine" taught in schools and disseminated in the most diverse forms of state and private propaganda since 1930.

According to Freyre, the Brazilian singularity comes to be the propensity for cultural encounter, for the synthesis of differences, for unity in multiplicity. It is for this reason that Brazilians are unique and special in the world. They should, therefore, be proud and not ashamed of being "mestizo." Physical types function as reference of social equality and a peculiar type of "democracy" that is Brazilian alone. A major affinity with the "corporative" doctrine that became dominant as a substitution for the previous liberalism since 1930, is difficult to imagine. It is now part of Brazilian identity, both individual as well as collective. All Brazilians "like" to see ourselves in this form. The ideology acquires an emotional aspect that is insensitive to rational considerations. It casts anger and hate on those who question this truth that is so pleasant to native ears. The influence of this idea on the way that Brazil sees itself and is perceived is impressive.

Based on the influence of Freyre, this concept has a history of glory. By means of the concept of "plasticity" imported directly from Freyre, it comes to be central in Sérgio Buarque de Holanda's entire argument of the *cordial man*. This notion is central to Buarque's conception of personalism and patrimonialism, in which it represents the value and institutional singularity of Brazilian social formation. In this way, Buarque was transformed into the creator of the dominant self-interpretation of Brazilians in the twentieth century. For my interests here, it is worth re-raising the idea of the *cordial man*, which reproduces the essentialization and indifferentiation characteristic of the idea of hybridism and of cultural singularity such as a substantialized unity. The *cordial man* is defined as the Brazilian of all classes, a specific form of being human, who has a tendency that is both intersubjective, in the notion of personalism, as well as an institutional dimension, in the notion of patrimonialism.

For my purposes, however, what is essential is that this explicit ideology is articulated with the implicit component of the "spontaneous ideology" of the imported institutional and operative practices also in peripheral modernity, constructing an extraordinary context for obscuration. This has unfortunate consequences both for theoretical reflection and practical politics concerning the causes of inequality, especially for the victims of this process.[37] This appears to me to be the central point of the issue of *naturalization* of inequality, as abysmal as it is, in Brazil as well as in other peripheral societies.

NOTES

1. The fact that a country like Brazil has been the country with largest economic growth in the world from the 1930s to the 1980s, without the rates of inequality, marginalization, and under-citizenship being radically altered, should be a more than evident indication of the mistake of this presumption. This, nevertheless, did not take place and does not take place today.

2. About this theme see the classic work of Robert Bellah, *The Tokugawa Religion: The Values of Pre-Industrial Japan* (Glencoe, IL: Free Press, 1985), and the collection of Shmuel Eisenstadt, *The Protestant Ethic and Modernization: A Comparative View* (New York: Basic Books, 1968).

3. Max Weber, *Die Wirtschaftsethik der Weltreligionen, Hinduismus und Buddhismus* (Tübingen, Germany: J. C. B. Mohr, 1998), 251.

4. I do not admire critical theories, such as the Habermasian, which admit this type of construction in its interior, perceives social conflicts, preferentially, only at the "front" between system and "lifeworld" and no longer within the systemic realities. See the criticism of Joahannes Berger, "Die Versprachlichung des Sakralen und die Entsprachlichung der Ökonomie" in Hans Joas and Axel Honneth, eds., Kommunikatives Handelns: Beiträge zu Jürgen Habermas, Theorie des kommunikativen handelns (Frankfurt: Suhrkamp, 1986).

5. The same occurs with the merely descriptive notion of "charisma." Since there is no presumption of unarticulated "collective meanings" which are responsible for leading, articulating, and providing their own direction, the connection of the leader with his followers becomes "mysterious" and comes to depend on the supposition of the existence, by part of the masses, on extra-quotidian or magical attributes of the personality of the leader.

6. Charles Taylor, *Sources of the Self: The Making of the Modern Identity* (Cambridge: Harvard Press, 1989).

7. Taylor (1989), 159–76.

8. Taylor (1989), 289–90.

9. Charles Taylor, "The Politics of Recognition," in *Multiculturalism* by Amy Gutmann et al. (Princeton: Princeton University Press, 1994).

10. This aspect was developed in a polemical and stimulating manner, serving as the background for a grammar of contemporary political struggles, based on the poles of distribution and recognition in Nancy Fraser, *Justice Interruptus* (New York: Routledge, 1997). For the problematic aspects between the individual and collective dimensions of the theme of recognition, see Seyla Benhabib, *Kulturelle Vielfalt und Demokratische Gleichheit* (Frankfurt: Fisher, 1999), 39–46.

11. Weber (1998), 1–97.

12. For a criticism of Taylor's and Fraser's positions, see Axel Honneth, "Recognition or Distribution?" pp. 52–53 in *Theory, Culture and Society*, vol. 18, issues 2 and 3, 2001.

13. Charles Taylor, "To Follow a Rule," in *Bourdieu: Critical Perspectives*, ed. Craig Calhoun, Edward LiPuma, and Moishe Postone (Chicago: University of Chicago Press, 1993).

14. Taylor (1993), 59.

15. Pierre Bourdieu, *Distinction: A Social Critique of the Judgment of Taste* (Cambridge: Harvard University Press, 1984).

16. Pierre Bourdieu, *The Logic of Practice* (Palo Alto, CA: Stanford University Press, 1990), 42–51.

17. Bourdieu (1984), 244.

18. Axel Honneth, *Die zerrissene Welt des Sozialen* (Frankfurt: Suhrkamp, 1990), 178–79.

19. Taylor, *Sources of the Self: The Making of the Modern Identity*, 15.

20. Uwe Bittlingmayer, "Transformation der Notwendigkeit: prekarisierte *habitus*formen als Kehrseite der 'Wissensgesellschaft,'" pp. 225–54 in *Theorie als Kampf? Zur politischen Soziologie Pierre Bourdieus*, ed. Rolf Eickelpasch et al. (Opladen: Leske und Budrich, 2002).

21. Reinhard Kreckel, *Politische Soziologie der sozialen Ungleichheit* (Frankfurt: Campus, 1992).

22. Kreckel, *Politische Soziologie der sozialen Ungleichheit*, 98.

23. Kreckel, *Politische Soziologie der sozialen Ungleichheit*, 100.

24. Nancy Fraser, "From Redistribution to Recognition?" in *Justice Interruptus* (New York: Routledge, 1997).

25. Bittlingmayer, "Transformation der Notwendigkeit," 233.

26. Florestan, *A integração do negro na sociedade de classes* (São Paulo: ed. Ática, 1978), 94.

27. Axel Honneth, in his interesting criticism of Bourdieu, tends to completely reject the concept of *habitus*, given the instrumental and utilitarian component that it inhabits. By doing so, however, Honneth runs the risk of "throwing out the baby with the bath water," when it appears to me to be important precisely to reconnect the concept of *habitus* with a moral instance that illuminates the individual and collective dimensions, in addition to the instrumental given that is non-renounceable, the theme of moral learning. See Honneth, "Die zerissene Welt der symbolischen Formen: zum kultursoziologischen Werke Pierre Bourdieus," in *Die zerissene Welt des Sozialen* (Frankfurt: Suhrkamp, 1990), 171.

28. Charles Taylor, *The Ethics of Authenticity* (Cambridge: Harvard University Press, 1991), 35.

29. Bourdieu, *Distinction*, 11.

30. Bourdieu, *Distinction*, 384.

31. Robert Bellah, *The Broken Covenant* (Chicago: University of Chicago Press, 1975).

32. Eugen Weber, *Peasants into Frenchmen: The Modernization of Rural France* (Palo Alto, CA: Stanford University Press, 1976).

33. In the version, for example, of Roberto DaMatta, *Carnavais, malandros e heróis* (Rio de Janeiro: Zahar, 1978).

34. About this issue see my book, *A modernização Seletiva: Uma Reinterpretação do Dilema Brasileiro* (Brasília, DF: Editora UnB, 2000), especially 183–204.

35. Jurgen Habermas, *Die Strukturwandel der Öffentlichkeit* (Frankfurt: Suhrkamp, 1975).

36. Charles Taylor, *Modern Social Imaginaries* (Durham, NC: Duke University Press, 2004).

37. It also explains the fact that the insurrectional potential of the lower class from the entire nineteenth century until today is reduced to local and passing rebellions, riots, and pre-political violence in which the conscious articulation of its objectives never occurs.

Chapter Seven

After Colonialism: The Impossibility of Self-Determination

Pratap Bhanu Mehta

I. INTRODUCTION

This chapter is a *tour d' horizon* of the difficulties facing an anti-imperial politics. It is more a series of reflections than a single focused argument. It tries to recover a sense of what an anti-colonial politics was supposed to be about, the conception of political order on which such a politics rested. I argue that claims of such a political order proved to be untenable for a variety of reasons. First and foremost, the claim of founding a political order that was *representative* turned out to be an impossible aspiration in many ways. Second, the claim of such a political order to embody the *identity* of peoples in a way that allowed societies to overcome the estrangements of colonialism also proved to be fraught with difficulty. In fact, representation and identity turn out to be in tension with one another. This casts doubt on the proposition that a political order can be articulated or created entirely through representative forms. These considerations apply to states other than postcolonial states as well. Third, I argue that much of what passes as anti-imperial politics in our contemporary era faces two related difficulties: It finds it difficult to articulate itself in political forms, and it is not straightforwardly able to answer the question of why certain forms of politics and not others signify anti-imperial politics.

II. Empire and Existence

An imperial order epitomizes a constitution of being—reaching through all the realms of being from the material to the transcendental. Imperial orders can structure political possibilities, fix the terms of economic exchange, produce hierarchies of knowledge, and redraw the boundaries between the sacred and the profane. They have the capacity to re-inscribe religion into the sign of the primitive; they reorder a sense of time and history and produce new forms of subjectivity. Imperial orders bring with them a conception of existence and order that attempts to incarnate itself in the visible dominion of the earth. The most audacious empires have constructed the world as an expanse of territory that can be the object of dominion. In practice territorial reach of most empires, impressive as it is, has been limited. Alexander's armies refused to go farther, possibly because they cared less than Alexander about how much more of the world there was left to conquer; the multiplicity of imperial creations has often precluded a monopoly of global control for each of them. The acceptance of the territorial limits to the expansion of empire has not precluded imperial powers from claiming paramount legitimacy for their own projects. Empires may be territorially bounded, but they have claimed the world as their own. It was important for even rival emperors who acquiesced in each other's existence, to think of themselves as the center of the world. An empire was more than simply dominion over territory and people; it was an exercise (literally) in creating a world and controlling its meaning. It was not necessary for creating a world that the whole world is territorially within it. The territories outside the realm of empire were *de jure* within it, whatever the *de facto* limitations on the exercise of power. During the Cold War, the vocabulary of "three worlds" was an unwitting tribute to the idea that empires are about world making. It happened to be the case that there were two different and competing orders of existence, each of which thought its expansion into areas not engulfed by it was inevitable. Each acted as a check on the other's *de facto* territorial claims, but each insisted on its own *de jure* authority ("The world is ours to save").

In the case of empire, the world is a construction internal to the ideology of empire. The *de facto* claims of territories and people that actually constitute the world are irrelevant for questioning the authority of imperial claims. For this reason, empire is impervious to the facts of the matter. These facts are practical obstacles rather than normative claims. An empire would not be an empire if it did not construct and believe in its own normative authority.

Perhaps the most resonantly arresting description of the claims of empires remains Plutarch's account of Alexander. Plutarch argues (or seems to) that the king is greater than the philosopher because he practices all that the philosopher only thinks and dreams about. Plutarch gives an account of the much admired *Politeia* of Zeno, the founder of the Stoics. For Plutarch, Zeno's central claim was that men should not live as separate peoples and polises but should form one polity with a common life and order. But what Zeno merely speculated, Alexander put into action: for Zeno's reason (*logos*), Alexander supplied the deed (*ergon*). Alexander did not give the Hellenes or the Barbarians any special privileges, but was convinced that he was sent by the gods to be "the general harmonizer and reconciler of All." When he brought them together not by reason, he forced them by arms. He even mixed their lives and character, their marriages and their customs. He exhorted them to think of *his oikumene* as *their* fatherland, *his* army *their* citadel. He did away with what we might call ethnic distinctions—the distinction between the Hellenic and the barbaric was no longer going to be marked by customs and clothes. Rather what is excellent (*arête*) should be recognized as Hellenic and what is full of iniquity as barbaric. It was Alexander's plan to gain harmony and peace and community between one and the other.

This description is replete with classical imperial themes. Empires conjoin reason and arms, claiming both normative authority and the force of power. Their normative authority rests upon redefining excellence and reconstituting ways of life in accordance with it. Empires come with a moral mission. Whatever the motives that give rise to empire (profit, plunder, power, restlessness, and sheer ambition) and whatever the means adopted to secure it, these means and the motives do not exhaust the *meaning* of "Empire" which resides in the world it seeks to create, or in its own eyes ends up creating. Empires can be formally inclusive—one need only recognize the excellences they bring to be part of them. Yet they are hierarchical and rest on a rule of difference. The imperial authority has special status: they demand a special kind of recognition and identification. As Plutarch implied, the world was not a given; it was not a material fact, a datum of existence; it was rather something to be made, and something to be shaped in accordance with a particular order of being. Empires abolish the outside, not in a literal territorial sense, but in the sense that the outside always comes absorbed within its own order. The place of other civilizations is already marked: they can be anything from "vacant lands" to "barbarians" waiting to be civilized; they may even have excellences of their own, but those excellences have normative standing at the mercy and behest of the imperial order itself.

Empires need not, of course, exercise total control or assert complete sovereignty. Premodern empires were probably more interested in a symbolic reconstitution of the world in which their own hierarchical preeminence could be recognized (hence lots of emperors of the world could exist simultaneously!). They had less ambition, means, and capacity to envisage a systematic transformation of the terrain over which the life of the colonized was lived. Modern empires have had vastly greater ambitions, in part because a feature of modern states is that they acquire sovereignty over greater areas of life. But even modern empires can vary in the extent to which they usurp sovereign authority from different social groups in the societies over which they exercise power. They can allow a variety of intermediate authorities to flourish within their ambit over some domains of life. They can grant the customs and personal laws of the peoples over whom they preside, indeed even strengthen them. There have been several different forms of "indirect rule" where new indigenous sovereignties over particular areas of social life were created and strengthened with the aid of colonial power. But these modalities of indirect rule are now placed within an overall imperial framework.

Of course, empires come in a variety of shapes and forms, with enormous differences in their sense of mission, their technologies of rule, and political tactics. Empires can be conservative in their demands and purely expedient. But the power of European empires that were enduring comes to be directed upon the society over which they exercise sovereignty. As Eric Stokes classically put it in the case of the British Empire, colonial power moved from being interested in tribute extraction to a power that came to be directed upon Indian society itself. In the memorable words of one nineteenth-century writer, Empire was now to be put on the "surer foundation" of a "dominion over the wants of the universe."[1] Empire was to entail the slow transformation of the terms on which these societies had existed. It was going to create a new world.

It is important to see Empire as creating a new existential order to be able to see what anti-imperial politics might be about, and why the resonance of that politics outlasts the formal existence of what were the empires that invaded. The parameters of anti-colonial politics are, to a certain degree, set by the world an empire creates. What would an anti-imperial politics entail? What would it mean to be against, or dismantle, the world that Empire created? And what would such a politics mean after at least formal decolonization has taken place?

It is a striking fact that anti-colonial politics takes, as its starting point, the thought that Empire is something to be resented. It is an unwelcome and disliked form of regime. But, one might wonder why this animosity toward Empire exists? On a standard narrative of anti-colonial politics, Empire comes to be seen as exploitative, as a drain on material resources, skewing the terms of trade, causing dislocations in the economy, and representing a net transfer of wealth to the metropole. Empires are an ultimate usurpation of authority. Anti-colonial politics seeks to expose the gap between the ruler and the ruled by contesting the authority of the empire. Empiricism also rests on what Partha Chaterjee calls a "rule of difference."[2] By this imperative, the colonized are, across a variety of ideological positions, represented as inferior and sometimes (in more radical occurrences) even considered to be an "Other." Thus, this "rule of difference" comes to be resented. While the precise axis along which the "rule of difference" is constructed varies (even within empires), the experience of subordination remains a palpable fact from which anti-colonial politics draws so much of its intensity. By its very logic, Empire requires a deferral of recognition: if you don't recognize the merit that Empire preaches or are considered incapable of it, you are unworthy; if you do recognize the empire's excellence and use the colonizers' vocabulary, you are a usurper. If you don't use the language of liberty and democracy, you are not worthy of any corporate rights; if you do use these words, you risk impugning the very hierarchy on which Empire is founded.

The colonized might be using the language they are taught, but they use it without judgment. Natives were often likely to be educated beyond their intelligence. Witness Alfred Lyall, complaining about Indians, remarks: "Education acts upon the frame of an antique society as a powerful dissolvent, heating weak brains, stimulating rash ambitions and raising inordinate expectations."[3] Or, if by any chance natives used the language well, they earned the compliment that they were well educated by their colonial masters. At the end of a list of Anglo-Saxon prejudices of which he could think, Nehru wrote: "Is it any wonder that their vision grows dim when they look toward us, and that we should irritate them when we talk of democracy and liberty? These words were not coined for our use." This was the paradox in which all imperial power was caught: it wanted to remake the world but could never quite own up to the fact that the task was ever going to be finished.

But on the reverse side, the "native" had his own in-between: to assert a difference from the normative hierarchies that imperial powers created was to confirm the very thing the colonizer thought about you. But to assimilate to those demands and fashion yourself in accordance with them was to grant him the ultimate victory. The estrangement that colonialism produced was not so much a substantive estrangement—Am I estranged from my tradition?—but an almost existential one. Nothing the colonial subject did could be seen to be authentically his own.

It is of course the case that the domination of colonial power was far from complete. Modes of being, forms of protest, articulation of alternative imaginaries, were always slipping colonial control; even the instruments colonial powers bequeathed were unauthorized. "Sly Civility, a mimicry that was the same but not quite," to use Homi Bhabha's evocative phrase, was a form of hybridity that disrupted colonial domination. It may provide a moment of agency.[4] But the difficulty was that, while there were a lot of aspects to "native" society that evaded colonial control, it is not clear that a solitary anti-colonial will emerge. Exactly what were the terms of struggle that were articulated, and whether they can even be represented, is a contentious issue.[5] But it is doubtful that any social imaginary that existed could have effectively displaced colonial power. It would have been more probable for it to have existed as a politics that worked within its interstices.[6] Even the forms of cunningness and subversion that Bhabha refers to had to take their bearings from the terms set for them. Rather than opening up culture or displacing fixed identifications, mimicry can be seen as exactly the existential estrangement that colonialism entailed: the need for permanent dissimulation. It is true, as Hegel's reading of Rameu reminds us, that dissimulation is a form of agency. There is nothing like getting back at authority by making it unsure of exactly what you are up to—by mimicking it. And anxiety can be self-fulfilling: "What are these natives *really* up to?" becomes a more difficult question to answer. No protestation, either way, will lay to rest the anxiety about the natives' *real* capacities. The following analogy is a good example of the confusion that can arise when observing one's behavior: When Groucho Marx, as Rufus T. Firefly in *Duck Soup*, addresses the court, he explains "Chicolini here may talk like an idiot, and look like an idiot, but don't let that fool you. He really is an idiot." What protestation will ease our anxiety about whether he is really an idiot to rest? So it is with natives.[7]

But this is exactly what caused people like Gandhi to worry about colonialism. The demands of colonial authority necessitated the natives to dissimulate (flattery being the prime example and for Gandhi the principal source of self-abasement). He might have shared Du Bois' harrowing conclusion (rendered in the context of blacks in the South who needed to be politic and sly in order to protect and advance themselves): "The price of Culture is a Lie."[8] Whatever else it might have been, mimicry or sly subversion was not a release from the bondage of spirit that colonialism represented.

By the very operations of its power, colonial rule of difference produces a series of identifications that become almost inescapable for its colonial subjects. It is assumed that They are who they are, their status is what it is, and their rights are what they are, because of their belonging to a particular collectivity. Consciously or unconsciously, colonialism operates by imposing a collectivity onto individuals; the status of the individual is defined by the history that is given to them, by the new hierarchies of being in which they are placed. Any sense of personal identity that natives might have had is caught in the process of this identification. Perhaps it is by creating a sense of "we-ness" that Empires bequeath the most formidable tools to resist it. In this sense "Orientalism" was not so much an issue about the authoritative status of knowledge about others that was produced, or the alliance between knowledge and power. It was rather the ideological process by which agents are rendered expressions of their histories and cultures. Individuals become expressions of their culture; culture possesses persons, rather than being subsumed by them.

An anti-imperial politics analytically accepts this identification of individual and collectivity that is imposed by colonial power, but reverses its significance. Anti-imperial nationalism begins by accepting the premise that, "I am as I am because of who we are." This process of identification is not automatic or unthinking. In some cases it is a product of an acute and growing self-consciousness that can be the source of turning a critical light on one's own history, and coming to a greater self-awareness of how one came to be whom he or she is. The forms of knowledge and the political response this self-awareness produces can vary enormously. It can lead to an unthinking "nativism" as much as it can to an overcoming of tradition; it can lead to a demand for exorcising the colonizer as much as it can lead to a creative synthesis. It can prompt all kinds of political actions; but in the final analysis, it is a politics that has to rest upon the thought that there can be no individual liberation unless there is some kind of emancipation of the collectivity with which you have identified.

The site of this collective emancipation is then called into question. What would be the locus of self-esteem? At first approximation (to simplify), it is the desire to be part of some kind of collective enterprise that can perform the following functions: it should be an enterprise that, at the very least, is committed to the interests of natives, not those of the alien powers. At a very prosaic level, it involves the idea that the political order serves a society's basic interests and needs and protects it from exploitation. One of the central creations of anti-colonial politics was a political order that the people could, in some sense, call their own—an order that represented them. Empire was a usurpation because, whatever its normative goals, it was not duly authorized. Anti-colonial politics was a means for the colonized to regain possession of themselves. It was a way, above all, to overcome what might be called the discrepancy between reality and representation that characterizes Empire. Within empiricism, the political aspirations of subjects could not be given proper and full articulation. Their social reality and their identities could not be fully recognized, and they could not be considered cocreators of this order that acted upon them.

But most importantly anti-colonial politics aimed to create an agency through which a collective will found a voice and one through which the individuality of a people could be expressed. This collective enterprise needed an autonomous will, a part in history, and a capability to establish its own terms of engagement with the world. It would have to be a historical agent whose *actions* were manifest in secular time and earthly history and were a source of meaning. It would be a society with a mission, perhaps of universal significance—not simply, as Hegel had characterized the history of India, a "dumb deedless expansion." It must reflect a society's specificity and its distinctive characteristics. To put into one phrase: an anti-colonial politics, needed to recognize the struggle it faced in creating a nation.

But it is important to remember that at the height of its creativity, anti-colonial politics was a struggle that took on new forms that were, to borrow Dirlik's phrase, "neither of the West nor of the past." Anti-colonial movements sought to terminate colonialism but not by totally exorcising the colonial past. In its most innovative moments, there was a need for the collective order of society not just to internalize the colonial legacy of victimization and humiliation, but also the opportunities and transformations it produced. In the most sophisticated of anti-colonial thinkers, in India and elsewhere, the nation was conceived in terms of a mediating entity. It was not going to be a particularism that opposed the universalism of the colonial powers; it was an attempt to formulate a more robust and authentic alternative universality of which the nation would be a carrier. It would bring into fruition a new development of the human spirit. In the Indian case, this aspiration was certainly true of Gandhi, as it was of Aurobindo.[9] There has thus surely been a shrinkage of nationalist aspirations considering such aspirations no longer even pretend to be the carrier of an alternative universality. In a sense there has been a reproduction of the Hegelian provenance claim that the West has "Reason" and "Universality," while the Rest have "Culture" and "Particularity." Whatever else anti-colonial nationalism did in the early part of the twentieth century, it tried strenuously to overcome this opposition. To paraphrase Fanon, it tried to reintroduce mankind into the world.

III. THE ELUSIVE QUEST FOR REPRESENTATION

Whether or not anti-colonial politics were a success or whether they provided resources for effectively challenging new forms of imperialism is a topic that is perhaps too imperious to venture on. In this section I just want to highlight some of the shoals on which anti-colonial politics foundered, and argue that these failures set quite stringent limits on alternative futures we might be able to imagine in the aftermath of post-colonial condition. I look at two issues: the first is the difficulty of producing the kind of political formation an anti-colonial politics required; the second is whether the attempts to articulate "difference" through that political formation was a plausible aspiration.

A political order raises the issue of representation in two senses. The political order, on the whole, may represent a collectivity, claiming to be authorized by it and an actor and speaker on its behalf. In this sense, political order claims to represent a people. Indeed, it could be argued that a society comes into existence, acquires an identity, and articulates itself by producing a representative that will act for it. Oftentimes, imperial powers justified their colonization of societies by assuming that they were unable to produce this form of representation. It is not the case that societies that were colonized did not have their own forms of government. But it was central to imperial ideology that these forms of government were not thought to articulate the society itself. That is why the figures of anarchy or despotism were central to colonial construction of the political forms of other societies. Both signified the inability of society to articulate itself through a coherent political form. Both signified the fact that "society" had not fully come into existence (in some proper sense of the term). Their ineptitude was furthermore manifest in the very success of colonial power, which, as Mill argued, was entirely a function of the colonial power's superior capacity for collective action. Thus the colonizers could argue that the societies over which they exercised sovereignty were not entities with already established corporate rights. To them, there was no sense in which the political institutions of native societies represented anybody.

It might be true, however, that native societies had a traditional order, a gamut of customary laws and mores, and that this traditional order might have been legitimate in the sense that it was able to govern the lives of the members of its society. This traditional order, furthermore, might have drawn its legitimacy from various sources: from religion or from its association with that which was customary. It is also possible that these traditional political orders represented something else: perhaps an ordered cosmos, or a hierarchical conception of the Chain of Being. But what these political orders did not represent is the idea of "a people." It was not an order that was a product of historical agents. In fact the people who were in traditional political orders were expressive of something else scripted by religion, custom, or tradition. They could not be the originators of a political order; the purpose of the order was not to represent *the people*. In a strange reversal, individuals either represented or were expressions of the orders they inhabited. Both the political order as it existed, and the people in whatever form they took, were demonstrations of something *else*; the relationship between ruler and ruled was mediated through a different form of representation. In this conception, the question "Is this political order *ours*?" either does not make sense or means something different from the modern idea of what it means for a government to represent its people. In modern times the obvious answer to the question "Who or what does the political order represent?" is "the people."

Colonial constructions of precolonial history and of the colonized societies upon which they operated had great incentive to characterize the institutions of these societies as *pre-political*—a trope that is often applied to societies as diverse as the Amerindians and Indians. To have no "politics" is, on this view, to have no agency. One of the less studied aspects of anti-colonial thought is the way in which many thinkers tried to contest Western notion of the "political" and how it was traditionally being associated with "the state"—a relationship that imperial powers seemed to rest their authority upon. For example, the critique of the state that was produced by Gandhi, or in more elaborate sociological form by writers like Radhakamal Mukherjee, tried to question the claim that India never had a genuine "politics." Radhakamal Mukherjee,[10] in particular, tried to argue that the denial that colonized societies had a genuine politics rested on a series of contestable associations that associated the "political" with a particular form of juridical order backed by force. This legal form of the modern state was then set in opposition to social imaginaries that were considered pre-political, like kinship, caste, family, region, or tribe. Politics was then seen as a negation of these elements, as an exercise of sovereignty over and against them. But this conception of the "political," Mukherjee argued, rested on false premises. "Politics," for him, was rather a process of "negotiation" that went through these various identities rather than against them, producing a tapestry of overlapping relations that could not be subsumed under a single harmonious order. It is, on the contrary, the modern state that is anti-political, first in thinking that an overarching sovereignty is possible, and second, in associating such ultimate sovereignty with the epitome of anti-politics: a monopoly over the means of violence.

Whether or not this is a workable conception of politics is another matter, but a spate of writing produced in countries like India at the turn of the century was devoted to two objectives: First, to contest the meaning of the "political" as a way of arguing that Indians had been *agents*; and second, to imagine, as Gandhi tried to, alternative forms of social relationships other than the ones narrowly understood by the colonizers. And finally, the important thing was to see society as *politically constructed* out of its primary constituent diversity. Society was not simply an external fact or an essence, but a world *created* by active agents who bore it as a condition of their self-realization. The question then remains: whether their particular form of political articulation was capable of *representing* society.

A second problem of representation was whether it could occur *within* a political order. In some ways the two issues are related. In an obvious sense the answer to the question "What does a political order represent?" depends upon an answer to the question "Who finds representation within it?" A political order can claim more justly to represent a people when the diverse constituencies within it are represented, in the sense that the political order gives, or at any rate allows, full expression to their identities, needs, and wants. Such representation allows more constituencies to feel at home in that political order, it enables them to think of the political order as, in some sense, their own. But in principle, the question of the representative relationship between the ruler and the ruled is somewhat independent of the question of what the political order as a whole represents.

The formation of a representative political order is thus turned on a paradox. The most formidable obstacles to creating representative democracy are not contingent on the ill-posed question of democratic values—whether members of a particular society have the values in question, whether or not they can understand and respect supposedly complicated ideas like elections, voting, and free discussion. The greatest challenge to creating political representation ultimately resides in the trustworthiness of societal institutions. Who the political community represents and the ensuing dilemma of how well the structures of representation can be trusted, depends on how burdened institutions are by the requests and desires of various identities. It is a sobering thought that there is possibly not a single transition from imperial rule (or authoritarian rule more generally) that has not involved this identity quagmire. From India to Iraq, from Fiji to Sri Lanka, the structure of the dilemma is uncannily the same.

The introduction of representative government introduces a large question: how should representation be organized? This question becomes more, rather than less, acute under conditions of universal suffrage. If there is a significant minority, with some legitimate vestment in its identity, its fears will be swamped by simple numerical majority rules. Minority groups will therefore seek forms of representation that can protect their interests, or give expression to their identities. But here arises a dilemma: if they are given special representation or protection, there might be a majority backlash. The majority fears the entrenchment and institutionalization of what it thinks are unfair concessions to the minority. Minority vestments in identity turn out to be (at least) in tension with the majority's requirement that the state be its own. Take for instance the case of pre-partition India.

What we think of as Hindu-Muslim politics in India was born squarely in the crucible of representative politics, a fact that has become increasingly under-appreciated. To simplify a complicated story for the purposes of illustration, Syed Ahmed Khan had early on sensed that the gradual introduction of representative government might prove to be a threat to Muslims as it might naturally, numerically, advantage Hindus. Thus began a complex debate over Muslim representation that has never quite been solved. Various proposals were floated: separate electorates, the grouping of Muslim majority provinces, and so forth. But, in retrospect, it is clear that no stable solution to this conundrum was forthcoming. Any "extra" concessions to safeguard minority interests would provoke a backlash from some section of the Hindus. Why give Muslims representation that was not true to their numbers? This was the crux of the critiques of various representative schemes by the right wing of Hindu Mahasabha's and Congress.

A different, more regionally oriented solution was also proposed. This was premised on something like a mutual hostage theory. The interests of Muslims in Hindu-majority provinces would be safe-guarded by the fact that there would be a Hindu minority in Muslim-majority provinces. But the question then arose: what about the Center? If Muslims did not have something close to parity or some veto power at the Center, would not the Center be partial to Hindus? But, again, if some such provisions were made for Muslims, some would protest that a violation of the principle of equality was being made, giving Muslims special status. Why should they get parity at the Center? And so the argument went back and forth. Whatever one may think of the history of Hindu-Muslim relations, almost sixty years of negotiations did not produce a single representative scheme that was internally stable and fair, that did not run the risk of leaning in one direction or the other. Meanwhile the aspiration had been unleashed that the state that succeeded Empire be representative. But who was it to represent? "All Indians" would be an obvious answer. But that answer does not solve the problem: how would the identities that differentiate Indians be represented? Partition was a nonsolution, but a nonsolution to a problem that had proven insoluble. That the dilemma of representation resulted in an empire of long duration, and on the backs of a nationalist movement as liberal and progressive as they come, does not augur well for similar problems elsewhere. Alfred Cobban's pithy formulation that India could neither be united nor divided remains an unassailable account of the postcolonial condition—from Cyprus to India and from Iraq to Sri Lanka.

Come to contemporary Iraq, an uncanny rerun of an analogous dilemma. One can take chapter and verse from Royal Commissions from the 1920s—the Donoughmore Commission for Sri Lanka, for example—and find the same issues at play, in more or less the same terms. To simplify a bit, the dilemma is structurally the same. The Shia majority wanted numerical democracy because it favored them. Too much veto power granted to the Sunnis (and Kurds) provoked cries of discrimination by Sistani (the Shia leader); too little veto power granted to the Sunnis, and their interests in a numerical arithmetic are not protected. This arithmetic is made all the more precarious by the fact that Sunnis might have been targets of resentment. It is true that the added fear was that Shias wanted a more orthodox regime, but even if this was not the case, the dilemma of minority representation would have remained. In short, the structure of this dilemma is the same as the example of India: special provisions made to protect minorities cause the majority to argue the simple notion of one person one vote in their cry of discrimination; go for such a simple rule and the minorities remain unprotected. In response, the Americans also tried the regional route: indirect elections through caucuses. Indeed, the idea of indirect elections was discussed extensively in India as well during the thirties. But then, who calls the shots at the center? Doesn't the Center need to be designed in a way that it remains impartial? But to rely solely on numbers automatically privileges the Sunnis and Kurds. So the dilemma continues: will representative government turn into majoritarianism? And if there are special representative safeguards for minorities, will it not produce a political backlash?

There is a cautionary tale embedded in this discussion. It has proven to be almost impossible to find a solution to the conundrum of representation in societies where groups think of themselves as permanent majorities or permanent minorities and demand that representation protect the vestments of these identities. Consociational democracy and some form of power sharing is one possible solution, but its sorry history in places like Lebanon suggests that it is a fragile one. Furthermore, power sharing arrangements through caucuses, as the Americans once thought, will continually run into the fatal problem of who is going to be the neutral enforcer. Add to this the fact that the Kurds have no real reason to stay in Iraq, and too many groups have acquired a stake in violence there, and you have a problem that is all but paralyzing. Either the Americans will have to be committed to a presence of long duration in Iraq—a commitment that will be politically difficult to sustain—or they risk leaving a country in ruins.

It is perhaps a sobering thought that very few authoritarian regimes or empires have made the transition to representative government without these dilemmas over representation fomenting some kind of violence, often leading to partitions. Perhaps this is a dilemma that would have arisen in any post-Saddam transition in Iraq; it has little to do specifically with the American presence. But the fact that the Bush administration seems to have been so obtusely unaware of this dilemma is yet another reminder of the quintessential fault of that administration: its penchant to try and make history without understanding any of it. The issue of whether countries have democratic values is a misleading way of posing the question. The more appropriate question is: Can there be representative arrangements that allow all parties concerned to feel that those arrangements are, in some sense, their own, and protect the vestments they have in their identities? Unfortunately the only stable answer to this question turns out to be paradoxical. Representative institutions function best when there are no permanent identities to be protected; when the question of identity becomes detached from the question of citizenship. There are many paths to this condition: sheer coercion, gradual evolution, or forced territorial consolidation that makes the question of representation irrelevant by completely fusing identity and citizenship. But none of them has ever been brought about by a straightforward democratic solution.

It could be argued, optimistically, that democratic deliberation or debate itself can produce the terms on which the different constituents of the polity can relate to each other. There is a sense in which democratic incorporation is a possibility. Groups can develop common attachments through the process of democratic debate and struggle (and certainly many democratic mass movements have brought about this result), weaving together different strands of identity by knitting them into a common framework. But this is rarer than one supposes for it goes back to the conundrum that this section started with. The central issue is, evidently: what counts as democracy? It is easy enough to argue that whatever counts as democracy should not be equated with simple majoritarianism. This worry about majoritarianism works at a fairly elementary level. Majoritarianism should not be allowed to override rights. It is an obvious fact that the fetish of numbers that democracy has is often the tool of domination. But beyond this warning, everything else is up for grabs. Can the meaning of democracy be filled out independently of the structures of representation it presupposes? But what does it mean to be represented adequately in any given context? *Who decides when the terms of representation are fair? This is not a question that can be settled through representation itself.* One can appeal to some abstract moral argument to allocate the fair terms of representation. But the range of available options that are plausible in terms of any theory of fairness is vast. In principle, "one person, one vote" sounds as fair as parity between communities, as has been the axis of contestation in India, Iraq, and Sri Lanka. Who is to judge the contest between them? Thus the very project of founding a political order that represents something turns out to be an impossible ideal. Thus the founding oddity that the representative claims of a political order taken as a whole had to be, in the end, presumed rather itself negotiated democratically. Wherever that presumption was seriously contested, the dynamics of representation itself were incapable of yielding a workable formula. Thus the range of messy realities: from unworkable partitions to imposed unities, from ethnic cleansing to forced assimilation, it is important to remember that these dilemmas were not peculiar to postcolonial states; Europe had even messier and bloodier resolutions to the dilemma of representation. The claims of anticolonial politics to reconstitute society through representation itself turns out to have been, at best, only a partial project, and one impossible to realize. It is difficult for a political order to be fully representative and to have an identity.

There is a familiar objection to the stance of anti-colonial politics seeking to constitute a representative community by claiming that anti-colonial politics rested upon a normalized conception of identity. Nationalist politics already privileges a certain conception of a nation. The idea that, through the modalities of a political organization, the colonized would be restored to an identity from which they are alienated, only invites the by now familiar questions: Whose identity are we talking about? Which cultural groups? Which class? Which gender? And so on. The establishment of a political community is by no means sufficient to fashion the practices, institutions, and politics by which the diverse constituents of a political community can call their own or by which the community can express *its* freedom. The claim that a political order represents a people is liable to this internal instability. In order to respond to these demands, nations need a more reflexive conception of identity, constantly incorporating new demands placed upon them. Whether this is a viable conception of political identity, or even of the state, is a subject matter for a different occasion.

Bhikhu Parekh, James Tully, and others have tried to outline an attractive model of an open-ended, reflexive identity that has the capacity for acknowledging and, at the same time, transforming difference. Parekh writes poignantly: "we" cannot incorporate "them" so long as "we" remain "we"; "we" must be loosened up to create a new common space in which "they" can be accommodated and become part of a new reconstituted "we."[11] Analogously, James Tully, in a powerfully argued series of papers, has written about the politics of recognition that, "identity politics is about the freedom of diverse people and peoples to modify the rules of recognition and their political association as they modify themselves."[12] Thus, what is required is not a cultural cleansing, not an emancipation from identity (which would be both morally unattractive and politically odious). Instead, what could emerge is a new cultural form, a product of mutual transformation. These conceptions avoid the odious fantasies of a wholly integrated organic cultural or political unity represented by the state on the one hand and a politics unencumbered by the claims of identity on the other. This is an attractive conception, but there are reasons to be skeptical of it. There is an old adage in philosophy: the fallacy of the possible middle. This is the view that a middle position that is philosophically possible must be politically possible or sociologically feasible as well. In some ways one should wonder whether we are now in the process of doing to identity what liberalism did to religion a long time ago. It can accommodate it, but only to the extent that its claims are so attenuated that the stakes of protecting it are very low. Ernest Gellner's claim that a "genuine cultural pluralism ceases to be viable under modern conditions" is a more realistic description of our predicament than images of a multicultural mosaic entail.[13]

IV. REPRESENTATION, DIFFERENCE, IDENTITY

Genuine cultural pluralism is difficult for a number of reasons. Gellner's worry was largely sociological: the requirements of mobility, the imperatives of efficient administration, and the pressures of building states. All lead to different forms of cultural consolidation. But there are also good normative reasons for why pluralism is difficult that arise out of the demands of modernity.

The claims of national and sub-national cultures are not morally different. There are few arguments for the preservation of the latter that are opposed by the former. If we are committed to a single scale of moral judgment that derives from universal norms, it is a scale that is all encompassing. There is a paradox that afflicts all arguments for accommodative conceptions of political community. These conceptions presume that if the national identity is somehow "thinner," demands less sacrifice from its constituent parts, and is open to continual and even far-reaching negotiation, it will allow for "thicker" sub-national identities or partial alternative sovereignties to flourish. But there is something immoral about an argument that calls for the thinning of certain national identities to allow others to more thickly flourish. Why should the scale not remain all encompassing? If the argument is that no conception of identity should be imposed on others, it is presumably because it is wrong to impose conditions on people that they cannot freely accept; such a moral claim should include everyone—identities—national or otherwise—should have to pass the tribunal of justificatory reasons. It is, however, difficult to imagine—at least if one takes moral individualism seriously—that this demand would be compatible with "thick identities" that are held collectively or given allegiance.

One of the lines of reasoning that lies behind giving different cultural communities their own space (even forums of representation) is that outsiders were the ones to place demands for pluralism in the community but could not be held responsible because of their exterior position. But this is a demand that individuals within any culture or subculture can place upon their culture as well. In short there is no escaping the burdens of justification. The demand that one's power—and application of it—be acceptable to those being governed is one that should apply to everyone in the community—all identities alike—and is a demand that even individuals can make. Allowing the citizenry to have opinions on the nature of governmental power, however, comes with consequences: they will be likely to demand political orders that protect the right to dissent or ones that decrease the normative sovereignty of the claims of culture, or of partial identities over individuals within them.

There will, of course, be acute struggles over who has the right to demand justifications, and over the forums in which these reflexive practices will be institutionalized.[14] But whatever "democratization" of the culture—the demand that its requirements be subject to reflexive justification—it is, in the end, probably incompatible with any thick or demanding notions of cultural identity or at least any that can be collectively articulated. What is the mutual transformation of identities that Parekh's vision entails? In terms of a legal regime, in terms of allocating rights and responsibilities, it will look suspiciously like a liberal regime. In terms of the political identity of the state, Parekh, in the end, has to cast his allegiances with an instrumental conception of the state. The business of political order is not representation; it is to be an instrumental contrivance for procuring certain goods and rights. While this purpose attributed to political order may not necessarily be a bad thing, it is costly. It decisively moves away from the idea that the political order is the form in which the agency of society as a whole is realized and through which its identity is expressed. To put it crudely, there is a tension between the demands of representation and the imperatives of identity. What would it mean for a political order to be most representative while encompassing identities?

Yet, there is another reason for why genuine cultural pluralism is not as viable as we would wish. There is a paradox on behalf of the claim that cultural identities become advanced the moment significant aspects of collective life are no longer under the sway of encompassing identities. As nineteenth-century social theorists taught us, large areas of social life—politics, economics, even aesthetics and consumption, and most of what fills everyday lives—is not governed by the rhythms of culture but by the imperatives internal to the domain of these activities.[15] Culture is not simply an encompassing teleology of everyday life or workday existence. If cultures are valued politically, it is less because of their contents, or because they mark out a different way of life (except at the margins) but because they are markers of identity. Cultural identities, like ethnic identities, can no longer be connected to political participation in the form of distinct cultural practices.[16]

This does not mean that the claims of "identity" in politics are about to disappear. In part, cultural and ethnic identities define structures of vulnerability. Overcoming these vulnerabilities may still require mobilization along lines of group identities. In this sense a lot of identity politics is the means through which the terms of participation in democratic societies can be negotiated. Second, cultural identities, like religious ones, face an enormous challenge. Which areas of social life are they going to be embodied in? The disembedding of identities from everyday life practices exacerbates the identity dilemma rather than solves it. As someone once said of religion, "We put ourselves under God's Yoke the most when we feel His presence the least." The shrinking scope of encompassing identities—religious or cultural—leads to articulation of identities that are more abstract, more willful, and more assertive. One sign of this is the fact that cultural identities and practices are defended less and less in the context of reasoning and deliberation; they are not viewed as being embedded in a structure of reason, but more as expressions or claims of an authentic self. Perhaps a lot of identity politics, especially the politics of religious identities around the world, is as Hume—in what still remains the best essay on the moral psychology of religious and cultural politics—put it: "We compensate for real infidelity by the strongest and most positive assertion of bigotry."[17]

The point of all this is to found the following thought: It would seem that the traditional historical potentialities of cultural differences have been exhausted. This sense of having an identity had kept alive the sense of the historical and political destiny of peoples. The demand of anti-colonial politics was that the political order, in some ways, be expressive of this destiny, this mission and specificity that made the peoples a people. The political order was to be a source of deeds, expressing the people as they existed prior to colonization. The conception of political order on which anti-colonial politics rested, the grounds from which it resented the world that Empire sought to create, has shifted from beneath its feet. The idea of a state having a political *identity* makes little sense. One has to give up claim that political order as a whole is responsible for representing anything. It is an instrumentality for securing certain material goods, for protecting basic rights and for performing important functions that might not otherwise be performed: nothing more and nothing less. Furthermore, while conception of political order is certainly workable, it comes at a price. The price is giving up one of the central claims of anti-colonial politics: that having a political order that belonged to the people meant a privileged space of freedom because it was this space that restored the ex-colonized to their own history. It was thought to be the medium through which that society articulated itself and realized its identity.

This transformation of what has been previously attached to the notion of political order, however, may not be a bad thing. Lowering the stakes of politics is often a good idea for the sake of peace. Such an attenuated conception of political order may also have a powerful moral resonance. The function of political order becomes not "our integration into the universe beyond the locus of our own space and time."[18] Instead, it is to elicit fidelity to the idea of having a constitution that can protect basic rights, give expressions for the demands for justification that arise in modern societies, and provide basic material goods. In short, the new political order allows for a constitutional patriotism of sorts. This is not the occasion to go into the viability and merits of this idea. But I would suspect that such a conception of political order is more compatible with a kind of post-historical existence, a politics attenuated to the management of life itself. It is a politics incompatible with the idea that a political order should have a sense of mission and one that includes the will to resist impositions of power upon it. Which areas of the world will evolve into a new equilibrium of post-historical politics, and which will find the conception of a historical destiny of a people alluring, is an open question. But the irony is that if only one nation has a sense of itself as a people with a historical mission, Empire will win.

V. QUESTIONS FOR AN ANTI-IMPERIAL POLITICS

What is anti-imperialism about? On what grounds, if any, does it stand? In a curious kind of way this question does not turn out to be an easy one to answer. As a first approximation, anti-imperialism seems to be an opposition to certain forms of domination. But, one must ask, *what* forms of domination is it attempting to resist? It is very tempting to associate anti-imperialism with opposition to domination as such, just as it is easy to condemn any asymmetry in power relations between societies as "imperialistic." But such association converts imperialism and anti-imperialism into an almost generalized account of human existence. In a certain sense, we are all ensconced in structures of material exploitation and profit. So long as there are states, power will be distributed unevenly in the international system; so long as societies continue to be objectified and there is a demand for authoritative knowledge, someone will produce "truths" about those whom knowledge seeks to represent, and in doing so exercise power over them. The modes of exploitation will change, the balance of power will shift, and new knowledge will be produced, but domination—economic, political, cultural, and material—will continue. Its origins and forms may shift. Anti-imperialism is on this view, not much an end-point, but a constant struggle, a demand for an ever-vigilant politics that is attentive to the relations that exist between what economies, polities, and subjectivities are constituted. Hence we find the curious phenomenon that decolonization is a condition that is never achieved, but endlessly deferred. The framework of action and domination built by departed European empires has, on this view, not been broken; it has merely acquired a new form and emanates from a new center. The forms of domination that classic empires bequeathed continue to touch everything. There is, thus, a constant stream of calls to decolonize everything—from liberalism to the Hindu Mind, from literature to the United Nations, from the World Trade organization to forms of knowledge produced in universities.

There is much to be said for a politics that resists different forms of domination, explicit or implicit. But the question remains: what is anti-imperialist about protesting domination? What counts as a politics of anti-imperialism? Take for instance, a small example: the ways in which, an anti-imperialist politics has come to be identified with anti-capitalism. It used to be, and continues to be the case in much of the postcolonial world, that anybody who argued for free trade or foreign investment was almost automatically described as an agent of imperialism: after all the bourgeoisie could be nothing if not comprador. There is an equivalent of this rhetoric: the supporters of the World Social Summit can claim the moral high ground of embodying an anti-imperialist politics; anyone who so much as thinks about trade or capital is on the wrong side of the "imperialist–anti-imperialist" divide. The indigenous multinational corporation becomes a sign of abdication to imperialism; the NGO with transnational links, a carrier of anti-imperialist politics. The civil-society activist rather than the entrepreneur becomes a sign of resistance to domination. It has never been clear why this should be the case. There are many reasons to worry about this identification of anti-imperialist politics with a kind of anti-capitalist politics. For one thing, in a pure casual sense, it has never been clear, as Burke put it, "that those who yelp loudest on behalf of the poor do the most to help them." In fact this heady equation of anti-capitalism and anti-imperialism that the left has produced in most postcolonial states has probably done more harm than good. At the very least it has foreclosed so many economic possibilities, that it left those it was supposed to help worse off. "Anti-imperialism" provided so much cover for one disastrous economic policy after the other. It itself was, and continues to be, the stratagem by which many vested interests were legitimized. It would thus be irresponsible not to worry about the consequences that forms of anti-imperial politics have often entailed on the ground. I am putting this point polemically in the hopes of inciting a provocation: How does a particular politics or position come to be considered anti-imperial? The same question can be applied to any designation. Many argue that those in favor of modern state forms were criticized for enacting an imperial politics, simply reproducing what their erstwhile masters bequeathed them; opposing human rights regimes was often designated as anti-imperial, as much as opposing safari suits and khaki shorts. Mimicking (not the sly mimicking) European state forms was considered a sign of being imperially trapped while subverting it with alternative possibilities was a sign of emancipation. Why?

Take another issue of more than academic interest. One of the projects of a postcolonial (and post-Orientalist) politics was to ask the question: "How does the Third World write its own history?"[19] This claim was not meant in an essentialist way or in a way that represented mere negation. Its focus was to recover a radical heterogeneity that had been displaced by master narratives of a Eurocentric History. It sought to recover forms of agency, subjectivity, and modes of sociability that had been ignored, displaced, or subjugated or rendered invisible by colonialism. This enterprise has produced some of the most creative historiography of recent times.[20] But the very question of authority that it raised and the authority of colonial knowledge that it sought to replace has been turned back upon it. Again, to put the matter pointedly: Why is Ranajit Guha an instance of Empire writing back—or, if you prefer Gyan Prakash's formulation, the Third World writing its own history—and not Sita Ram Goel (a Hindu nationalist historian, who also claims to bring to light suppressed histories and alternative forms of subjectivity)? There is a great disjunction between the academic construction of what counts as the Third World writing its own history, and its articulation as a political project in postcolonial societies like India. The point is not to enter into a discussion of the relative merits of different forms of historiography (that is not the issue). The point is that these are rival projects of overcoming colonialism. They stem from different normative commitments, whose authority has to be discursively and politically justified. The project cannot be simply "the Third World writing its own history." The question remains, by what canons and to what ends?

The theoretical point is that anti-imperial politics has run aground on the same reefs toward which it tried to push imperialism. By what authority do imperial powers advance their claims? By what authority does anti-imperialism define its content? Implicit in an anti-imperial politics is an appeal to some idea of emancipation. But then, what counts as emancipation? Who makes this determination?

The vacuity of anti-imperial politics is apparent in Hardt and Negri's celebrated *Empire*. For reasons of space, I cannot go into a full discussion of the book, but I want to make one point relevant to their conception of political society. How is legitimate struggle to be articulated? The image that is invoked in their argument is that of a spontaneous aggregation of a plurality of actions that may not be linked to each other. They take it for granted, in the Marxian tradition, that "representation functions to legitimate sovereign power and also alienates it completely from the multitude of subjects."[21] What are the conditions under which the need for any form of representation can be eliminated? It has to be when, as Rousseau argued, the will of a community coincides with the will of the political order that expresses it completely. This identification makes politics an irrelevant activity. But if societies are internally divided, it is difficult to argue that this community would have been constructed through a political process of sorts. Will it not therefore have to be constructed through a kind of representative arrangement? The representative processes of an actually existing state are far from perfect. But there is a great temptation in contemporary invocations of anti-imperial politics to bypass or set themselves against the representative institutions that exist within postcolonial states, in all their precariousness. To put it unkindly, anti-imperial politics embodied in alluring invocations of transnational solidarity often does not address, and in fact actively seeks to bypass, existing representative institutions. It seems to have forgotten the lesson that the most creative forms of anti-colonial politics at the turn of the century taught us: that there is no escaping the necessity of articulating social demands, and the demands of the society, through a representative order.

This question of authority applies to discursive formations that anti-imperial or postcolonial histories were meant to represent. The project of decolonizing knowledge was to undo Eurocentrism by "rejecting those modes of thinking which configure the third world in such irreducible essences as religiosity, underdevelopment, nationhood, non-Westerners" and was in many ways an admirable feat that has been carried out with a great deal of finesse. But how should one categorize the natives who embrace these representations and makes them their own, who wish to be identified through these groupings and conduct their politics and aspirations around them? In some ways this critique only underestimates the provocative question of authority that Ashis Nandy had already raised. Who is to say that the "Brown sahib" is not Indian? Who is to say that "development," "nationhood," and "the public-private distinction" are Eurocentric concepts, whose displacement is a desideratum of a genuine postcolonial politics? Why could not the appropriation of European history itself be a postcolonial gesture? Why does a politics of emancipation necessarily have to displace them, or be necessarily tied to the project of recovering certain forms of sociability and agency and not others? Could we not say of liberal rights, the state, development, and nationhood what Ashis Nandy said of cricket? "Cricket is an Indian game, it only happens to have been invented in England."

All of which takes us to the central problematic of Empire. Who has authority? In what representative scheme will this authority be redeemed? Will the normative premises and practical implications of a lot of the politics and historiographical projects that claim to be postcolonial be made explicit and subject to the process of validation in the public sphere? In other words, what is the conception of justice from which an anti-colonial project springs? How will the *political form* of these conceptions of justice be articulated? My suspicion—and this is only a suspicion—is that, in the final analysis, modern politics has to operate within the horizons of a post-nationalist liberal order. The only other serious competitor on the horizon is one whose conception of a political order as an embodiment of a historical destiny of a people is too fraught to be contemplated with any degree of equanimity. But that leaves us in the unenviable position of contemplating a world where there is only one political community that conceives of itself as constructing an entire world, while the rest are reduced to a post-historical stupor. Whether this will create the conditions for a more sober politics—a conception of political order that speaks prose rather than being expressed in poetry—or whether it will create conditions for a new *Imperium* to persist; only time will tell. Perhaps this is being a little graceless, but the stern demands of our time require a degree of gracelessness.

NOTES

1. Eric Stokes, *The English Utilitarians and India* (Oxford: Oxford University Press, 1959), 41.
2. Partha Chaterjee, *The Nation and Its Fragments* (Princeton: Princeton University Press, 1993), 15–19.
3. Valentine Chirol, *Indian Unrest* (London: MacMillan, 1910), xiii.
4. Homi Bhabha, *The Location of Culture* (London: Routledge, 1994), 86ff.
5. For this issue see the work of *The Subaltern Studies Collective*.
6. The term social imaginary is from Charles Taylor, *Modern Social Imaginaries* (Durham, NC: Duke University Press, 2004).
7. I owe this reference to Don Herzog.
8. W. E. B. Du Bois, *The Souls of Black Folk*, chapter 10. For a worry that the need to keep up appearances disfigured the colonial masters see George Orwell's *Shooting an Elephant*. "For it is the condition of his rule that shall spend his life in trying to impress the natives and so in every crisis he has got to do what the natives expect of him. He wears a mask and his face grows to fit it. I had got to shoot the elephant."
9. "The attainment of independence for me is the search for truth."
10. Radhakamal Mukherjee, *Democracy of the East* (London: P. S. King, 1923).
11. Bhikhu C. Parekh, *Rethinking Multiculturalism: Cultural Diversity and Political Theory* (Basingstoke, UK: Macmillan, 2000), 204.
12. James Tully, *Strange Multiplicity: Constitutionalism in An Age of Diversity* (Cambridge: Cambridge University Press, 1996).
13. Ernest Gellner, *Nations and Nationalism* (Oxford: Blackwell, 1983), 55.
14. Partha Chaterjee, "Secularism and Toleration," in *A Possible India* (Delhi: Oxford University Press, 1999).

15. I argue this claim more fully in "Cosmopolitanism and the Circle of Reason," *Political Theory*, vol. 28, no. 5 (October 2000), 619–39.
16. Anthony Appiah, *Color Conscious* (Princeton: Princeton University Press, 2000).
17. David Hume, *The Natural History of Religion*, in *David Hume: A Dissertation on the Passions: The Natural History of Religion*, Tom Beauchamp, ed. (Oxford: Oxford University Press, 2009 [1757]).
18. Philip Allot, *The Health of Nations* (Cambridge: Cambridge University Press, 2002), 115.
19. Gyan Prakash, "Writing Post Orientalist Histories of the Third World," *Comparative Studies in Society and History*, 1990.
20. One of the most powerful examples remains Dipesh Chakrabarty, *Provincializing Europe* (Princeton: Princeton University Press, 2000).
21. Michael Hardt and Antonio Negri, *Empire* (Cambridge: Harvard University Press, 2000), 84.

Chapter Eight

Indian Conceptualization of Colonial Rule

Bhikhu Parekh

This chapter explores three possible ways India might have perceived the nature and significance of British colonial rule. First, since India had long been subject to internal and external conquests, Indian leaders might have thought that British rule was basically like those that had preceded it (*or* that it represented a novelty unique unto itself). Secondly, I assess how Indians responded to British rule and thirdly, how they explained it: why in their view, they had fallen prey to yet another foreign conquest, especially at the hands of a trading company based thousands of miles away with no apparent plan to conquer the country. These questions will be addressed in turn, beginning with the initial Indian responses to British rule followed by an analysis of its more institutionalized phase—from the early decades of the nineteenth century onward.

But before attempting to describe Indian conceptions of British rule it is necessary to recognize the varying perceptions that might have existed. Different classes, communities, and regions give different answers to questions regarding the imposition: those expressed by elites were not always shared by millions of ordinary Indians, and responses might have also been sculpted by contexts that changed over time. Peasant leaders sometimes rose against colonial economic oppression, though not always against colonial rule, and articulated their thoughts in a language that was unique to them. India thus spoke in several overlapping as well as conflicting voices. But rather than discussing the perceptions of all Indians or attempting to homogenize or impose an unjust arbitrary pattern on them, this paper concentrates on the elite discourse—with specific focus on dominant trends—to avoid getting caught in its multi-strandedness. The reason for such oversimplification is not to avoid the meticulousness of accounting for minor details but is rather an attempt to best fully understand how British colonialism might have impacted India on the whole.

British conquest of India was slow, stealthy, and not premeditated in its origins. Spearheaded by a commercial company rather than a foreign government and coming to India in pursuit of commercial interests on the express promise of good behavior, the East India Company took full advantage of the erosion of Mughal authority, particularly on the Empire's periphery. As local potentates usurped power and created political and economic instability, the Company used its considerable military and economic power to destabilize, pressurize, or overthrow them; played off one against the other; formed shifting alliances; and provoked popular revolts which it then used to justify intervention and annexation. The Mughal Emperor's denunciation of the Company officials as "naughty and disobedient" subjects who had "usurped different parts of the Royal dominion" by "treachery and deceit" (and with a policy of "divide and grab") was widely shared, but had no impact; within a few decades, the Company had extended its control over almost the whole of India, and claimed to inherit the Emperor's authority.

It eventually became clear that British colonialism was a kind of conquest and rule that the Indians had never experienced before. The earlier conquerors either plundered the country and returned with their loot, or settled down as rulers. The British were different—not in their plunder, which was common to earlier conquerors—nor because they were foreigners of a different race, who refused to settle down as this behavior was also true of many conquerors before; for the Indian leaders, British rule was different because their "home" existed elsewhere and was a place to which they frequently returned for holidays or jobs. It was also where their families were based and children were educated; where they gave their loyalties and affections, brought their loots, and from where they ruled India. The British had turned India into an "appendage" of another country and they ruled it according to *their* interests. For the first time in its history, Indian leaders argued, India had come under "foreign" or "alien rule," understood not as rule by foreigners but rule *from* a foreign land. This conceptualization of British rule became common in the 1760s and persisted until its end.

Indian leaders argued that since the British rule was "alien," it had two important consequences—or led to two disturbing practices. First, British rule was inherently exploitative and detrimental to India economically. The rulers took their wealth abroad that they had acquired either through plunder or through collection of revenue. Indian money was neither spent nor circulated throughout India and British money never entered into the country. The economic relation between Britain and India was therefore wholly one-sided; Indian interests were subordinated to those of the British. As Sayid Ghulam Husain Khan explained at the time, the British practice of "scraping together as much money in this country as they can and carrying it in immense sums to the kingdom of England" had "undermined and ruined" India. Since the British rulers never thought of India as their home, they shared no common interests with its people and had no incentive to "promote their good." But, this behavior was somewhat expected; almost all Indian leaders argued that under colonial leadership, it was inevitable that rulers would pursue British interests irrespective of the damage it did to India—and they recognized that if some good was done to India, it was inadvertent, incidental, or meant to promote the far greater good of Britain.

Secondly, Indian leaders argued that since their new rulers took Britain as their constant point of reference and the source of their political and cultural identity, the British saw themselves as a "different people." They set themselves apart from their subjects, lived separately, had only limited and superficial social contacts with them, and never identified themselves with India or Indian people. As many eighteenth-century Indian leaders explained, the British treated Indians with "disdain" and "aversion," "undervalued," and "distrusted" them, and never employed them in positions of power and influence. They subjected even the Indians of noble lineage to a "variety of affronts and indignities," and "esteemed themselves better than all others put together." Even a pro-British Indian such as Ram Mohun Roy observed in a Petition to the British government:

> The better classes of the natives of India are placed under the sway of the Honourable East India Company in a state of political degradation which is absolutely without a parallel in their former history. For even under the Mohomedan conquerors, such of your petitioners as are Hindoos, were not only capable of filling but actually did fill numerous employments of trust, dignity and emolument, from which under the existing system of the Honourable Company's government, they are absolutely shut out.

Roy and others were concerned not so much with getting jobs for themselves as with the way in which the whole "Hindustnee race" was disfranchised. For them racism was inherent in alien rule, and constituted its permanent and ineliminable limitation.

According to the conceptualization of Indian leaders, the British rule was alien in three respects (which separated it from all of the others that had preceded it): it was a rule by and from another country; was primarily self-interested and hence exploitative; and was manned by foreigners who enjoyed their monopoly on economic and political power. It furthermore was a rule that rested on a racist contempt for its subjects. Indians did not mind the British settling in India as others had done before; indeed, some Indians invited British settlers in the hope that they would bring new methods of cultivation and help to develop India. Some of them also did not mind if the British rulers filled the political vacuum left by the disintegration of the

Mughal Empire and established a measure of economic and political stability. But they were all highly critical of the form of alien rule that was ultimately manifested. Many Indian leaders (and a large number of ordinary Indians) felt deeply alienated from the British power that had engulfed their country, and either wanted this new power radically restructured or driven out. As a Frenchman living as a Muslim among the Mughal noblemen in Bengal put it, the British had "alienated all hearts." Even the British officers conceded that "there was not a native but proved disaffected to the English . . . so that no intelligence could be had from any of them, or if any at all, it was always a *suggested* one."

The British rulers therefore faced a problem: their rule was necessarily alien, and hence open to the kinds of criticism made by Indian leaders. This dilemma meant they either had to end their colonial rule in India—which they had no intention of doing—or find ways of legitimizing it and winning the hearts and minds of their subjects. The more perceptive among the British knew (just as many Indian leaders did) that their rule was inevitably impermanent and fragile; it could never shed its alien character and would therefore have to end one day, and no government policies would ever be able to fully overcome or compensate for the elements of subordination, exploitation, and racism that were inherent in it, nor would they be able to appease the constant small and large grievances that had arisen among the Indian people—for that would require British rule to become less "alien." Against this widely shared assumption of impermanence, the British knew that in order to consolidate their rule in the short term, they needed to restrain the East India Company's excesses, offer the country compensatory benefits, moderate their racism, pay some attention to Indian interests, create new classes of well-disposed Indians, and so on. To their credit, some of the British politicians knew that achieving these measures would also benefit Britain's own political life, which was increasingly becoming corrupted by the habits, practices, and attitudes acquired by the Company's officials in India. The rise of liberalism and evangelicalism in Britain generated the idea of a civilizing mission, which further reinforced the idea that British colonial rule needed to be restructured.

From around the 1780s onward, successive British governments took a series of measures to curb the Company's power—imposing a tighter control on its activities, introducing new systems of justice, recruiting Indian officials at lower levels, sending more public-spirited governors, amending the policy of territorial annexation, establishing indirect rule through native princes, instituting new forms of land settlement, establishing English language schools and colleges, and so on. As these several reforms took effect, and were followed by others, the colonial rule underwent important changes; although alien, it began to become indigenized and started to take on an Indian character. It became less rapacious, adventurist, exclusive, and racist.

It also created large classes of Indians, mainly Hindus, who availed themselves to its economic, educational, and administrative opportunities, took to industry and commerce, found jobs in the civil service, acted as intermediaries between the rulers and their subjects, and were people who became inspired by a new vision of the world that was brought to India by new currents of European thought via British rule.

When social classes that had previously exercised considerable power and influence were marginalized, impoverished, and rendered politically invisible, the middle classes became their visible replacements. As new leaders, they enjoyed an ambivalent relationship with the colonial rulers and their own countrymen: while acting as members of both groups they also managed to maintain a separation from the two—claiming to speak for both and while also disowning some aspects of their own ways of thought and life. This sensitivity to colonial rulers on the one hand and to fellow countrymen on the other, however, allowed them to form a relatively distinct autonomous and culturally bilingual social group with a unique identity that bred concerns of its own. Most of the Indian leaders who negotiated the relations between the colonial rulers and their subjects, reflected on the nature and impact of the raj, and later led the independence movement that came from the ranks of the new middle classes. They could play such an important role because they only partially conformed to Macaulay's ideal of a class that was "Indian in blood and colour, but English in taste, in opinions, in morals, and in intellect." Macaulay's Indians would have been culturally unilingual, and could not by definition act as intercultural interpreters. The new middle classes became *both* Indian and English in their ethics and culture—a dual heritage that enabled them to resolve inevitable tensions in their own unique ways—making them indispensable to both their countrymen and their rulers.

The Indian leaders' responses to the new phase of colonial rule were in some respects similar to and in others quite different from that of their predecessors. Their ranks included both Muslims and Hindus—the latter in an overwhelming majority. Some Muslim leaders welcomed the colonial rule on the grounds that it represented new opportunities for Muslim regeneration, a break with the feudal past, and a possible stimulus to modernizing the Muslim society. Many however remained as indifferent or hostile to the new phase of colonial rule as they were to the earlier one. When Delhi passed under British occupation, Shah Abdul Aziz, a leading Muslim divine of Delhi, issued a *fatwa*, insisting that since "Christians were in complete control" India was a *dar-ul-harb*, and that Muslims had a duty to oppose the colonial government. Following him, several religious leaders too declared that it was wrong to learn English, promote better relations with the British, and to serve them as clerks, servants, and soldiers. For decades, large masses of Muslims remained more or less detached from the newly emerging Indian society; turning themselves inward instead of embracing the transformation that was occurring.

Although Hindu attitudes to the colonial rule were a mixture of welcome, indifference, and hostility, a large body of Hindu leaders thought that a moderated British presence was *good*. They all obviously disliked the harm that was done to India; it had come to their attention that the colonial rule had deindustrialized India, distorted its economic development, subordinated Indian interests to those of Britain, and was in general, exploitative. They were also convinced that British rule was racist, sometimes blatantly and at other times subtly, and was demeaning to Indian people, history, and religion. Some Hindus went so far as to argue that the colonial presence undermined their cultural identity, "denationalized" them, and sought to turn their youth into "carbon copies" of the English.

In spite of these criticisms, many Hindu leaders argued that the colonial rule had improved India on several levels. For one, it gave India internal and external security, an impartial system of justice, and the rule of law. It also created security of property and released entrepreneurial energy. India was given global visibility and an uninhibited access to distant parts of the British Empire; the colonial rule brought modernity to India—especially the scientific spirit of inquiry and the ideas of individual liberty and equality—and led Indians to look critically at their institutions and practices. In so doing, colonial rule "revitalized," "awakened," and "regenerated" the Indian people, and gave them the confidence and opportunity to convey their civilizational message to the rest of the world. Both by their example and as a reaction to their rule, the British also aroused a new feeling of nationalism among Indians—causing them to think of themselves as Indians for the first time and alerting them to the need to overcome caste, religious, regional, ethnic, and other divisions. The rise of national consciousness therefore went hand in hand with the development of civic and public life and the civil society; in addition to the virtues of cooperation, concerted action, self-discipline, and mutual respect that went with them. In short, Hindu leaders thought that the colonial rule had breathed new life into their "dead" society, and marked nothing less than their "rebirth" in a form suited to the new "*yuga*."

In the view of Hindu leaders: political subjection, economic exploitation, and racial humiliation were great harms to society, but inertia, lifelessness, ignorance, blind conformity, lack of intellectual curiosity and self-criticism, and severe social inequalities were also great evils. While colonial rule brought some of these tribulations to India, it also successfully removed others—causing such balance to be seen as a positive force by Hindu leaders. Furthermore, they did not believe that India could have removed these evils by its own efforts; they felt that if India was capable of concocting its own remedies for its political, social, and economic ills, it would have done so already. They also felt that the removal of India's problems prior to British colonization could have only been achieved by the gradual exposure to Europe that colonial rule had introduced. Hindu leaders argued that India needed the shock of humiliation to become aware of its evils and the sense of urgency (instilled by Britain's European example *and* exploitation) that was required to deal with them; many of the virtues involved in successfully transforming a nation could have only been acquired by sitting at the feet of those who were already in possession of them—observing the British in action and following the required discipline under their guidance. Colonial rule was therefore both *tapasya* (a penance) and a process of education and growth, both *siksha* and *diksha*; a nation, like a spiritual aspirant, needs a *guru*. The British were "wise teachers" (Bankim), "good gurus" (Ram Mohun Roy), and Indians should learn to be their "apt pupils" (Ghokhale and Ranade). Despite the degradation that is sometimes associated with deeply depending on others for guidance, Hindu leaders saw nothing wrong with seeking the help of others in matters where the other party might be more skillful—to think otherwise undermines the entire prospect of education.

Extending the Hindu theories of *punarjanma* and *moksha* to the life of the nation, Hindu leaders argued that *moksha* (meaning in this case, liberation from the cycle of foreign conquests and emergence into a state of full freedom and self-determination) could not be attained in one life. A nation had to go through several lives, each building on the qualities or *sankaras* acquired in the preceding ones. As Ranade put it, every invasion in its history had "disciplined" India and "developed its character." The British rule was a necessary stage in India's evolution as it worked to develop the valuable intellectual, civic, and political qualities that it had not yet acquired on its own. If India could take full advantage of Britain's example and undergo the necessary "political training," it was bound to emerge a greater and stronger country. National independence was thought of as a "worthwhile" but not an "absolute goal," and one that should be reserved until the country was ready for it (Gokhale and Motilal Nehru). As the *sanyasins* in Bankim's *Anandamath* were instructed by the mysterious voice, Hindu leaders still had much to learn from the British and should therefore refrain from attempting to overthrow its rule.

This moderately positive attitude to the British rule, however, was not confined to the Hindu and Muslim middle classes. It was also shared by some of the influential leaders of the lower castes, especially the *dalits*, such as Joti Rao Phule, Ramaswamy Naicker, Narayana Guru, and even Ambedkar. They argued that they had long been oppressed, even "enslaved" by the Brahmins, and that they were, in some respects, treated better under the British who did not practice untouchability and did not mind social and religious contacts with the *dalits*. The lower classes also appreciated the modern ideas of human dignity and equality that Britain brought forth to India; ideas used by the *dalits* to overthrow the Brahmanic "tyranny." Once the British introduced representative institutions, Hindu leaders were forced to cultivate the *dalits* and suitably restructure the Hindu society to acknowledge support in numbers rather than according to caste. For many *dalit* leaders, British rule opened up the possibility of their social and political emancipation and was therefore welcomed. Some even thought of it as a "divine gift" and a "just" punishment for the *karma* that the Brahmins must have accumulated during their reign of exploiting other castes.

In light of this discussion of Hindu leaders' assessments of colonial rule, it is easy to see why they thought they had been easily conquered by a trading company. It was common at the time to blame the superior British military power for its strength in capacity and organized action. Most Hindu leaders rejected both ideas. The British, more importantly, conquered India, not as much by their military power, as by creating internal divisions and rifts among the Indians and playing them off against each other (Vivekananda, B. C. Pal, Lala Lajpat Rai, and others). Blaming Britain's superior capacity on its ability to organize efficiently would have also been futile; nothing prevented the Indians from organizing or acting in unity to save themselves—to trust each other, and subordinate their individual interests and egos to the larger cause of self-defense against colonial dominance (Bankin, Gokhale, Gandhi, Jawaharlal Nehru, and many others).

What Hindu leaders perceived to be the reason for British colonial rule was contingent on each person's own character or *sanskaras* and social structure. What were perceived to be the character and structural flaws of each demographic varied according to different leaders, but there was a broad agreement that there were inherent problems embedded in the caste system, egoism, false pride, social inequalities, lack of political and organizational skills, hedonism, misguided otherworldliness, lack of concern for the poor and oppressed, and so on. As Gandhi put it, the British had not taken India; Indians had given it to them, and the apparent British strength was largely an obverse of Indian weakness. Tagore put the same point more eloquently when he said that the English presence was an "external incident, mere *maya*," behind which lay "the truth about ourselves." The *maya* had no power of its own; it both reflected and reproduced India's own weakness. In Tagore's view, one foreign rule would be followed by another, and if all foreign rule ended, it would be followed by the rule of India's "own" foreigners. According to Tagore, this cycle could only be broken if Indians developed their intellectual and moral powers. He explains, "We must win our country not from some foreigner but from our own inertia, our own indifference" (these views were echoed alike by Bankim, Gokhale, Ranade, Tilak, Naoroji, the two Nehrus, and many others).

Hindu leaders were convinced that once they developed the appropriate intellectual and moral qualities and the consciousness of nationhood or of being a "single people" (*ekprajā*), national independence would be easily won, and once gained—never lost. India would demand freedom as the very necessity of its nature: its citizens would not be able to be themselves and express their distinct identity in the absence of nationalism and independence. Indians would furthermore gain appreciation for freedom, and would gain the capacity to safeguard themselves from having to submit to the rule of an outsider in the future. Tilak put it well when he observed, "I said that it was our 'right' to have Home Rule, but that is a historical and a European way of putting it. I go further and say that it is our 'dharma.'" To him as to others, *dharma* meant one's true nature, one's characteristic mode of self-expression and self-activity.

A large body of Hindu leaders therefore either welcomed colonial rule or accepted it as a regrettable historical necessity advancing a distinctly Hindu metaphysic of colonialism that was suspiciously similar to the British justification of colonial rule. Hindu motives were mixed: some were employed by the Raj and had an interest in flattering their masters. Nearly all of them were British-educated, shared British values, and had heavily vested interests in the colonial culture—both emotionally and politically. Some of them had deep doubts about their own (and their countrymen's) capacity to rule themselves. As Nehru once said, as in a prison, under a colonial rule, people tended to exaggerate their weaknesses, undervalue their strengths, and develop low self-esteem. While all this is true, it would be wrong to dismiss Hindu colonial supporters as collaborators or ideologically brainwashed colonial victims. Many of them were genuinely patriotic and resented colonial subjection, but felt convinced that with all its degradations, the British rule had shaken them out of their inertia, released regenerative forces, and helped them build up valuable civic and political institutions. They might have been wrong, but their sincerity is not something that should be called into question.

The Hindu tendencies to build on colonial institutions rather than break with them, to marginalize the traditional India as of little real value, to criticize themselves and accept responsibility for their problems and failures rather than blame the colonial rule, to receive new thoughts and not to turn inward, to resort to a dubious metaphysic to make sense of their world, etc. are just a few examples of how the Hindu conceptualization of colonial rule was ultimately translated into a new form of Indian nationalism. But, why Hindu leaders had such unbridled support for Britain's rule is a complex historical question that goes beyond the scope of this paper. What is important to note is that the Hindu way of thinking (which was also shared by many other Indian leaders as already mentioned) was a powerful strand in nationalist thought and greatly affected how the leaders of independent India would go about reforming Indian culture and society in the future.

Chapter Nine

Resistance to Colonialism: The Latin American Legacy of José Martí[1]

Ofelia Schutte

In a lecture presented to the Latin American Subaltern Studies Group meeting at Rice University in October 1996, the Indian historian Ranajit Guha, founder of the South Asian Subaltern Studies Group, refers to some of the "salient aspects of modernity's intersection with colonialism" (Guha 2001, 41). One of these, which I think characterizes the Latin American condition just as much as the South Asian, is, in Guha's words, the fact that "the colonial experience has outlived decolonization and continues to be related significantly to the concerns of our own time" (Guha 2001, 42). Whether in the colonized or in the colonialist parts of the world, even after political decolonization, the aftereffects of colonialism live on, inherent not only in the realm of politics but in the ordinary daily experiences of the people. This experience to which Guha alludes is specifically marked by history. In different parts of the world, historical specificities distinguish the special characteristics of colonialism's sequels. The interpretation of history itself becomes an arena for the exercise of the will to decolonization—and then by extension, any pedagogical or policy-oriented intellectual exercise, along with other activities particularly in the spheres of culture and politics.

In this chapter, I will highlight the interpretation of history launched in 1891 by José Martí in his political manifesto "Nuestra América." I emphasize ideas and themes in the essay intersecting with our current critical interests regarding postcoloniality and the resistance to colonialism in Latin America. Because most of Latin America achieved independence in the nineteenth century, one historical difference vis-à-vis Asia and Africa is the greater chronological length of our postcolonial period. Nonetheless, readings of a nineteenth-century political thinker such as Martí can help us determine where to draw the line on the nature of postcolonial thought and its appropriate methodologies. The interpretation of history itself becomes highly contested since contemporary interests stand to gain or lose depending on its successful outcome.

One of the guideposts affecting the interpretation of history is the epistemic/methodological framework informing our discursive practices. Most Spanish American colonies attained independence during the nineteenth century, thereby antedating what the West calls "postmodernity."[2] For this reason, the epistemic framework that guided Spanish America's postcolonial criticism has distinct features differentiating it from late twentieth and early twenty-first century postcolonial critique, both in Latin America itself and in other parts of the global South. In particular, arguments for emancipation from colonialism in nineteenth-century Latin America rest on an acceptance of what Lyotard called the "grand narratives" of emancipation—more specifically, narratives based for the most part on a liberal model of progress. What is perhaps less known, and therefore a focus of my discussion, is that despite the fact that hegemonic liberal narratives often tended to be Eurocentric, narratives of progress in Latin America were sufficiently fluid for some to challenge Eurocentrism. Indeed, a constant factor in the postcolonial debates regarding Latin American cultural identity is the degree to which European culture should be appropriated or resisted as the new Latin American nations sought to define their place in world history.

From Lyotard's point of view, such grand narratives are no longer warranted or believable as of the end of the twentieth century. I would grant that a healthy kind of skepticism toward grand narratives is preferable to their wholesale acceptance. Yet, in order to understand the character of postcolonial critique in the global South, whether a century ago or in our own time, it is necessary to set aside the view that postcolonial critical thought must comply with postmodern or poststructuralist epistemic guidelines. Clearly, if we reduce our epistemic framework unnecessarily, we may miss important contributions that for historic or cultural reasons do not fit within the stipulated framework. As a result, the knowledge generated could be misleading or significantly flawed. Recognizing at least the abstract legitimacy of a plurality of narrative styles will enable us to attend to the views from nondominant parts of the world relative to the West. What is important—having in principle acknowledged the plurality of narrative styles—is to engage critically with the ideas and arguments voiced therein in the posture of an open discussion or dialogue.

My twenty-first century "conversation" with the nineteenth-century thought of José Martí takes advantage in part of Edward Said's observation, in his 1994 Afterword to *Orientalism*, that there is a significant distinction between "postcolonial" and "postmodern" thought. In particular, Said observed that postmodernism still tends to be Eurocentric and ahistoric while postcolonial critique counters these two perspectives (Said 1994, 348–49). Moreover, at least some postcolonial critics continue for valid reasons to use the grand narratives of emancipation that seemed useless to Lyotard (1979). Said's distinction allows Latin Americans to embrace postcolonial critique without necessarily having to limit their epistemic standpoints to postmodern tenets. In this case, I think the indispensable targets of postcolonial critique are the economic, political, and cultural conditions of postcoloniality and the discussion of strategies needed to reduce or eliminate the effects of colonialism in the global South. In this regard, both Martí's thought and the discussion concerning Cuba's position in the aftermath of colonialism are of special interest.

I. JOSÉ MARTÍ'S LEGACY OF "NUESTRA AMERICA," OR WHOSE NATION? WHOSE CULTURE?

Cuba is one of the most interesting countries in the Western Hemisphere when it comes to the analysis of colonialism and postcoloniality. Unlike most other "Hispanic-American" nations, which obtained their independence from Spain in the earlier parts of the century, during Martí's lifetime (1853–1895) Cuba was still a colony of Spain. A fervent partisan of Cuba's national independence, Martí lived abroad for most of his adult life, often engaged in projects aimed at liberating his native island from colonialism. Martí lived in New York City during the last period of his short life, from 1880 to 1895 (and prior to departing to fight for Cuba's independence, where he was killed in May 1895 by Spanish troops). It seems that in addition to sharpening his keen political sense and his love for that part of the Americas that he called "our America" (*nuestra América*)—a term to which I will return in a moment—Martí's sojourn in the United States allowed him to conceptualize colonialism as a recurring political system in modern times. He had a double sense of vision as he envisioned Cuba's liberation from colonial status. On the one hand, there was the evident necessary war to be fought against the colonial power, Spain. But, on the other hand, there was the diplomatic struggle to prevent what Martí foresaw as an emerging economic and political colonialism of the government and business interests of the United States toward the Hispanic Caribbean, Mexico, Central, and South America. In the case of Cuba, this meant fighting for Cuba's independence on two separate fronts: one, against Spain's past and current dominance; the other, against the United States' emerging and projected future dominance.

In the case of the Hispanic American republics, the struggle Martí proposed was to resist U.S. economic and political hegemony on political and diplomatic terms. In fact, it seems to me that Martí probably saw the latter goal as a necessary condition for helping to maintain Cuba's independence in the long term. So, while he gave his life for Cuba's actual independence from Spain, he was also preparing the ground for a united Latin America resisting the expansion of U.S. economic and political power over the entire hemisphere.[3] Martí envisioned a united front emerging from Latin America itself, against a second round of colonialism, this time instigated not by Europe but by the United States in a phase of intensive capitalist expansion—what in 1894 Martí called simply "the America that is not ours" (OC 6:35).[4] The name of the collective entity Martí wished to safeguard from U.S. interventionism and expansionism is what he called "nuestra América" (our America)—a term he seems to have used initially during his stay in Guatemala between 1877 and 1879 to designate an anti-colonialist Indo-Hispanic America (OC 7:98; OC 18:131 ff).[5] As the years passed, Martí's notion of "our America" developed further, referring to the indigenous, black, and mestizo populations along with all the peoples whose cultural and political priorities were to the "natural" and creative humanity found in America rather than the norms and values imported or received by force from abroad (Martí [1891] OC 6:17; 2002, 290–91). Such peoples could overcome "the hierarchical constitution of the colonies" ("*la constitución jerárquica de las colonias*") by the "democratic organization of the Republic" ("*la organización democrática de la República*") (Martí [1891], OC 6:19; 2002, 292). He is referring here to the forms and structures of power, which could either promote or undermine good government. But, at the same time, the new republics were frail when compared to the huge economic power of the United States, which he believed was intent on preventing their full development to suit its own expanding economic interests.

In a famous passage dated from November 1889 at a time when the government of the United States had organized the first hemispheric congress of American states, Martí wrote:

> Spanish America knew how to free itself from the tyranny of Spain; and now, after judging the precedents, causes, and factors of the invitation [to the aforementioned congress], it is urgent to state—because it is the truth—that the hour has come for Spanish America to declare its second independence.[6] (Martí [1889] OC 6:46)

What is the "second independence" to be from, if not from another type of colonialism?[7] At the time, the goal of Latin American liberalism was the *political* independence of the new national republics. In the language of Latin American nineteenth-century political liberalism, "independence" or "national independence" meant freedom from colonial rule. But the liberals' interpretation of independence was insufficiently critical of the economic dependence they were establishing with Western powers. Rising above his contemporaries' views of these matters, Martí defended the continent's ethnic diversity while analyzing an emerging pattern of hemispheric *economic* domination for the primary benefit of the interests of the more powerful party which could severely undermine the presumed national independence of the less powerful. Martí's analysis of the economic dependence to which the Hispanic American countries would be subjected is based jointly on a cultural analysis of what he sees as the driving spirit behind the United States' will to dominance: "a people that begins to look at freedom, which is the universal and perennial aspiration of the human being, as its own privilege, and to invoke it [freedom] in order to deprive other peoples of it" (Martí, OC 6:53).[8]

Martí's analysis of cultural politics gained immensely from his unique biographical position as a Cuban exile who had both traveled and lived in Spain and several Latin American countries, as well as eventually settling in New York City in the 1880s and early 1890s.[9] Making the most of a large network of contacts and compatriots throughout the Americas, he paid close attention to political and economic events in Latin America and the United States as he put together his plan to found the Cuban Revolutionary Party. Founded in Key West, Florida, in 1892, the CRP aimed at unifying Cubans and earning favorable world opinion in support of the final stage of Cuba's war of independence against Spanish colonial rule.[10]

Martí was able both to foresee and clarify some of the dangers imminent to the South as the United States increasingly exercised its economic powers over existing Hispanic lands at the end of the nineteenth century.[11] Despite his clearly articulated analysis of the U.S. agenda as it convened the existing Latin American governments for a meeting in Washington in 1889–1890, the political resistance he hoped to see from the Latin American governments invited to Washington was not to take place. Nonetheless, parts of the political strategy that he developed over one hundred years ago to resist the North's cultural hegemony are still relevant today. His perspective is challenging. It involves the commitment to both denounce injustice and struggle against it—a choice not everyone is willing to take. The legacies of colonialism are not easily defeated. Postcolonial political criticism needs to have both a vision and a strategy if it is to succeed. When we focus on resistance to colonialism, it seems that a large component of this resistance must be strategy. Martí's article "Nuestra América" (1891) contains an outline for such a strategy.

II. "NUESTRA AMÉRICA" AS A POLITICAL STRATEGY

Given the fact that Martí had already articulated his view that a "second independence" was needed for the nineteenth-century Hispanic American republics, based on his detection of what I would call a "colonial intentionality" on the part of the U.S. expansionist political and economic interests to use the Latin American countries primarily to suit their own benefit at the latter's expense, the text "Nuestra América" can be looked at as a rhetorical strategy to rally the unified sentiment of his Latin American readers against U.S. hegemony in the region. It is in embracing the vision of "Nuestra América" ("Our America") as different from the America to our North that Martí hoped to rally a movement of resistance to the U.S. economic and political hegemony taking place—or, as in the cases of Cuba and Puerto Rico, imminently positioned to take place—*after* the demise of Spanish colonialism.

Martí begins "Nuestra América" with a call to a battle of ideas based on the "weapons of judgment," which he claims are much more valuable than the actual tactics of war. This confirms the view I proposed earlier regarding his desire for a united front that would bear diplomatic weight against U.S. hegemony in the region. Characterizing a village mentality as one that fails to be concerned about the relationship between the local and the global (I am rephrasing him using current terms) and, in that context, failing to see that "giants in seven-league boots" can step on them, Martí calls for the awakening of any remaining village mentality in America ([1891] 2002, 288).

The obstacles Martí faced for people to rally behind his vision of "nuestra América" rested not only in ignorance and apathy with regard to the need for political change, but in important structural problems that were a part of Latin American history. Martí's essay addresses both the external menace and the internal outlooks that must be changed to resist it. Among the latter, two of the most important were (1) overcoming the hierarchical and authoritarian mentality inherited from the colonial period and (2) embracing the multiracial composition of the continent which he called *"nuestra América mestiza"* ([1891] OC 6:19).[12] I argue that without invoking the terms "colonialism" and "racism" in this essay, Martí was fighting a combination of both.[13] He also constantly battled the Ibero-American upper- and middle-class prejudices against working and humble people, reporting that their gaze was focused on imitating European fashionable trends: "These sons of carpenters who are ashamed that their father was a carpenter! These men born in America who are ashamed of the mother that raised them because she wears an Indian apron" ([1891] 2002, 289). He does not argue that whoever is born in America, or is of indigenous, black, or mestizo origin, or comes from a certain class, is in a cognitively privileged position to understand his or her political situation. In fact, he is fully aware that the masses, just as with the middle class, can only make progress if their consciousnesses are awakened and take on an anti-colonialist stance.

Martí bases the process of liberation from colonialism on the mediating role played by instituting an anti-colonialist republic and, of course, by the consciousness of all those who create and defend it, even giving up their lives if necessary ([1891] 2002, 293). So far this coincides with liberal political sentiments of the time, which took a stand against the conservative ideologies inherited from the colony and which tried to provide a mediating role for incorporating indigenous and mestizo contributions toward a new national project.[14] But Martí also inserted a strong dose of anti-hierarchical "Americanism" with naturalist features into his platform. It is his naturalism that provides the conceptual link between affirming a multiethnic America and overcoming the hierarchical mentality of the colonial period. He claimed that in our America one had "to govern with the soul of the earth and not against or without it" ([1891] 2002, 292).[15] The failure to govern appropriately meant that postcolonial Latin America was tired of having to accommodate between "the discordant and hostile elements it inherited from its perverse, despotic colonizer" and "the imported forms and ideas" ([1891] 2002, 292) that, lacking local reality, have delayed "the logical government" (*el gobierno lógico*) (Martí [1891] OC 6:19).

What does Martí mean by "the logical government"? From what he says in the essay, he seems to mean a government founded on the specific needs of its people, not on imported, so-called universal formulas derived from European models—or for that matter, from models imported from the United States. This position is key to the importance his thought carries for postcolonial critics and movements up to our own time. While Martí invokes Enlightenment notions of reason and freedom, and of "the right of man [human being] to the exercise of his reason" ("*el derecho del hombre al ejercicio de su razón*" [OC 6:19]) in his view the exercise of reason is not necessarily mediated by European values or extraterritorial powers. He refers favorably to "the natural man" or to the "real man": "the natural man . . . knocks down the justice [*justicia*] accumulated in books because it is not administered in accordance with the evident [*patentes*] needs of the country" ([1891] OC 6:18). Further on he invokes an Enlightenment ideal of moderation, appealing to the "serene harmony of Nature" (OC 6:19–20) and the "continent of light," where with the help of a new generation engaged in "critical reading [*lectura crítica*] . . . the real man is being born to America, in these real times" ([1891] 2002, 293).

The real or natural man (or human being) of whom Martí speaks is someone for whom the European concept of racial divisions and the socially hierarchical society built on it do not apply. He places the distinction among races as something that can provoke "futile hatreds" among peoples and instead proclaims that "the justice of nature" reveals "the universal identity of man" or, in today's terms, of the human being ([1891] 2002, 295–96). "The soul," he continues, "equal and eternal, emanates from bodies that are diverse in form and in color. Anyone who promotes and disseminates opposition and hatred among the races is committing a sin against humanity" ([1891] 2002, 296). On this view he claims that "there is no racial hatred, because there are no races" ([1891], 2002, 294). By "race" Martí appears to mean a class of human beings that, on account of their color or related physical characteristics, is thought to be superior or inferior to any other human type. Although the concept post-dates him, Martí appears to think of "race" as a socially constructed category. Specifically, he thought of it as a category that delimits the humanity of the human being. In other words, for Martí, the notion of "race" was always already imbedded within the discourse of racism. In historical terms, he was probably correct but he lacked the critical framework by which to speak of "race" as a socially constructed category. What he did was to claim that in "nature" there was no such thing (this point will be returned to later when the implications of his views for the Cuban revolution of 1895 are discussed).

The "natural man" (or human being) of whom Martí speaks refers to people of every color, all of whom he embraced in his alternative concept of "nuestra América mestiza" ([1891] OC 6:19).[16] He reasoned that racial prejudices were socioculturally constructed and could indeed result in significant injustice toward targeted populations. This is why he warns that there are indeed some acquired characteristics, dispositions, and interests that accumulate over time in various peoples and that, at restless national moments, can trigger in a dominant group what I have called "colonial intentionalities" toward others whose appearance, color, and customs differ from theirs. Such colonial intentionalities are described by Martí as "ideas and habits of expansion, acquisition, vanity, and greed . . . that . . . , in a period of internal disorder or precipitation of a people's cumulative character" could rise to the forefront and threaten the weaker countries, which are represented as "perishable and inferior" by the dominant power ([1891] 2002, 296). Surely he uses diplomatic terms here to point out the potential for U.S. expansionism toward the "isolated" and relatively "weak" Latin American republics. He thinks the problem that he has outlined—in our terms, the nascent conditions for neocolonialism—cannot be averted and that, for the sake of the coming centuries' peace, the facts of the impending problem should be brought to light ([1891] 2002, 296).

Just as Martí enunciated a policy of governing according to the needs of specific peoples in the light of reason and avoiding racial prejudice, he held a view of the type of education that the peoples of "our America" should receive in order to reach maturity in their democratic forms of government. He engaged in a tacit polemic with the Argentine ruler and educator Domingo Sarmiento, who had proposed the binary model of "civilization or barbarism" according to which the civilizing goal of the Hispanic American republics should be the importation of European ideas and the overcoming of the rural (considered backward) ways of life and thinking found in the Argentine pampas (Sarmiento [1845] 1998). Without naming Sarmiento, Martí defended a different model of education and cultural development for the American republics. "The battle is not between civilization and barbarity," he declared, "but between false erudition and nature" ([1891] 2002, 290). Here we see that Martí recognized the binary by which Western colonizing thought places "barbarity" on the side of "nature," raising its own colonizing project to that of a civilizing mission. But he wisely pointed out that this binary is a form of "false erudition" and a false antagonism between culture and nature. Since due to their exclusive reliance on Western models no Hispanic American university curricula analyzed what is "unique to the peoples of America," he asks what kind of education will those aspiring to govern their countries receive ([1891]2002, 291). In a pragmatic but also moral vein, he decried that unless the pursuit of truth included seeking out the truth about your own people—and by this he meant seeking out the subaltern populations that were marginalized from knowledge, culture, and power—it would not be possible to solve the problems that affect the people or the country.

Just as education should place priority on Our American history, the manner of government should derive from the very own "constitution" of the country (*la constitución propia del país*) ([1891] OC 6:17),[17] even if the aim seems to be conceived by Martí as a universal one: to attain a state in which all those who contribute to it, especially through their work, enjoy freedom and prosperity. This is an Enlightenment model, with one major variation. The methods and institutions through which a reasonable government will be achieved are simply autochthonous. While Martí appealed to Enlightenment concepts of "reason" and "liberty," for him, both of these were grounded in the recognition and appreciation of a non-Eurocentric approach to Latin America's sociocultural reality. Over the span of the twentieth century, a significant tradition of Latin American philosophical and political thought has been based on this Martían *nuestra Americanista* ideal, which has functioned as a criterion of freedom from colonialism and neocolonialism in diverse contexts. Perhaps the best known of these is the selective appropriation of Martí's ideas by the Marxist leadership of the Cuban revolution. But many other examples abound, including a strong influence on a sector of twentieth-century Latin American philosophy (Schutte 1993; Cerutti Guldberg 1998) and on the politics of United States, Latino, and Chicano studies since the 1980s (Saldívar 1990; Acosta-Belén 1999).

III. MARTÍ'S OVERTURNING OF EUROCENTRISM

What possible outcomes can Martí's thought yield today for postcolonial theory in the United States? I will explore two sides of this question in this section. First, I juxtapose Martí's position in "Nuestra América" to that of his nineteenth-century contemporary, Sarmiento (1811–1888), in *Facundo*

(1845). *Facundo* is generally considered a paradigm of the Eurocentric nationalist position in nineteenth-century postcolonial Latin America. In this text Sarmiento outlines the dichotomy between "civilization" and "barbarism" in the context of Argentina, which he diagnoses as two societies with opposing values within the same country. I show that Sarmiento's binary opposition between "civilization" and "barbarism" is supported by three other binaries, each of which is overturned by Martí to construct and defend a multicultural non-Eurocentric vision of Latin America. The three attending binaries are those of civilization/nature, the urban/the rural, and Europe/America. For Sarmiento, the first of these terms must conquer the second if there is to be any progress for the Argentine nation. Martí instead proposes a perspective on nature, the rural, and America that, by contrast, places the hopes of civilization and progress on the side of a balanced and critical view of Latin America's relationship with Europe and the United States. In addition, he defends the multiethnic peoples of the Americas, including peasants and people of humble means.

Second, I point out some differences between the reasoning Martí used to advance his *nuestra Americanista* perspective against nineteenth-century Eurocentrism and the reasoning some of us would use today at the start of the twenty-first century. While Martí was successful in overturning Sarmiento's Eurocentric model of national identity and progress, he employed a naturalist discourse currently outdated if we are to advocate comparable non-Eurocentric, multicultural goals for our times.[18] In this respect, the principal difference between Martí's conceptual framework and ours is that he appealed to nature to oppose social prejudice (a social construction) whereas today we take our concept of nature, too, to be largely a product of sociocultural construction. This allows us to make further distinctions that a person of Martí's generation and learning may have missed—for example, with regard to gender. In conclusion, I argue that despite the differences in our conceptual frameworks, the position Martí advocated in "Nuestra América" should be a central element in the historical and political appreciation of the relevance of Latin American political thought for postcolonial theory and studies in our own time.

We may begin to unravel Martí's overturning of Eurocentrism by examining his deconstruction and transmutation of the "civilization versus barbarism" metanarrative that, following Sarmiento's account, ruled much of Latin America's nineteenth-century liberal political thought. Sarmiento associated cultural progress with the "triumph of European civilization, its institutions, and the wealth and liberty that come from it" (Sarmiento, 59). He argued that nineteenth-century Argentina, as emblematic of "new American societies," was caught in an epic struggle "between European civilization and indigenous barbarism, between intelligence and matter" (59). Sarmiento provided a demographic context for this struggle: it is the struggle of the city against the desert (81), of modernity against feudalism. "On the Argentine plains . . . [s]ociety has completely disappeared; all that is left is the feudal family, isolated, enclosed within itself, and with no collective society" (54). Pointing out that when the people are dispersed among vast tracts of land, the basic elements of modern civil society are absent, he argued that under such conditions it was not possible for the police to work or to catch delinquents or for children to receive standardized instruction in schools (54). Sarmiento claimed that the gaucho way of life in the Argentine pampas represented the site of barbarism. Even so, Sarmiento's powerful descriptive prose can be said to foster many inconsistencies. For example, Roberto González Echevarría notes that "in trying to eradicate the gaucho, Sarmiento turned him into a national symbol" (2003, 15).

Sarmiento argued that cities such as Buenos Aires and Córdoba contained "books, ideas, civil spirit, courts, rights, laws, education: all the points of contact and alliance that we have with Europeans" (79). Moreover, he attributed the genealogy of South America's independence from colonialism to "the circulation of European ideas" (79). Such ideas, he claimed, were of no interest in the countryside, so that the revolution of independence that created the new South American republics was the product of urban, European-based thinking, even if the countryside population used the struggle to its own advantage. Two lifestyles within the same country opposed each other: "The man of the city wears European dress, lives a civilized life as we know it everywhere. . . . The man of the country wears other dress, which I will call American, since it is common to all peoples; his way of life is different, his needs, specific and limited" (53). The ideas of progress, laws, access to education, civic organization, and various other institutions found in cities could not be found in the countryside. Sarmiento fails to note the differences both among Europeans and among Americans. Obviously there were both conservative and progressive ideas in nineteenth-century Europe. Moreover, even progressive ideas in Europe did not extend necessarily to women's rights or to non-Europeans in the colonies. Had this not been the case, the Spanish colonies, Haitians, and colonized others around the world would not have had to fight or shed blood for their liberation. Similarly, to reduce all non-European dress to a single label, "American," fails to account for the ethnic and class differences within a very diverse South America. It seems that for Sarmiento "European" became a signifier for progress or, conversely, that he labeled "European" whatever he promoted as "progress," on the assumption that his audience will already have made the same association. In sum, to that which appeared to show the absence of European values or resistance to such values, he assigned the label "barbarism."

When political, economic, and cultural progress is seen as dependent on a nation's association with European ideas and with the replication of European political institutions on American soil, there is little question that the farther removed something or someone may appear from European culture, the less civilized it will seem. Moreover, what is less civilized appears as a possible or actual threat to civilization, so that the metanarrative of civilization versus barbarism can easily be mapped on to the religious narrative of good against evil. Suppression and eradication of barbarism (and, by association, of evil) are legitimated under such narratives. Under the more extreme forms of this ideology, a person's worth is measured only in terms of values associated with a particular ethnicity—namely, the European, or what appears to resemble it.

The reason Martí is able to overturn the terms of Sarmiento's binary is because Martí held a very different concept of moral value. For Martí all human beings are equal by nature insofar as they are human; they distinguish themselves as morally virtuous or deficient according to their *individual* actions, not according to their ethnicity, to which books they have read, or to the region of the country or the world in which they reside. While Martí defends the notions of cultural identity and difference, he rejects their use to claim that individuals or people of one group are superior or inferior to those of another group. "Both Latinos and [Anglo-]Saxons are equally capable of virtues and defects," he wrote in the journal *Patria* in 1894.[19] The virtues and vices characterizing various ethnic or racial groups are socially constructed, if by "social construction" we include people's interaction with the landscape or natural environment, which Martí thought was an important part of a culture. This does not mean that there are no ethnic traits, or that ethnic traits are easily overcome; peer approval, customs, and personal pride for one's own cultural traditions weigh heavily on the repeated performance of ethnic characteristics. Nonetheless, it is possible by critical reading, noble ideals, and work toward humanitarian common goals to overcome narrow-mindedness and prejudice. For Martí, intellectual progress is not based on how well Latin Americans understand European (and later, North American) culture, but on how well they understand their own economic, cultural, and political realities. Actually, since local and regional realities included interactions with these other societies and cultures, what he advocated is the ability to understand both in relationship to each other, with the proviso that the priority should be to understand Latin American reality on non-Eurocentric terms. To do so effectively one must set aside the idea that European or North American ideas and institutions must serve as unconditional models for Latin Americans. Instead, Martí held that to be knowledgeable in our America is to be a creator of values, particularly since these are emerging societies whose models of government are not pre-given. They must be created (and at times even be invented) based on the actual circumstances and needs of the people. "*Governor*, in a new country, means *Creator*" (2002, 290).

The people, in turn, are conceived in an inclusive way: those at the margins of society are not excluded from the representations of national or continental identity. When Martí thought of "nuestra América," he had a different vision of Latin America than the one Sarmiento arrived at in Argentina. Martí had in mind places where he had lived such as Guatemala and Mexico with their vast indigenous populations as well as the Caribbean, with its great ethnic and racial diversity, including its sizable African-descendant population.

Whereas Sarmiento saw two Argentinas (and by extension, two South Americas)—one, European-like, and the other, primitive—Martí reversed his glance toward Europe and saw two Spains—one bent on prolonging its colonial hold over Cuba (which Martí characterized as brutal) and the other, at least potentially sympathizing with the prospect of Cuba's independence from colonialism.[20] In other words, even within Spain and among Spanish descendants Martí noticed and addressed the dialectic between colonialist and anti-colonialist sentiments. This type of differentiation is extremely important because it deflates the rushed and oversimplified stereotypes that so often bitterly fuel religious, ethnic, and racial wars. Martí's approach is not exempt from generalizations (some of which will be addressed below). But his interest in the diversity of the social and natural environments that help to contextualize human character allows for flexibility in the otherwise tight "match" (seen in Sarmiento's *Facundo*) between a person's identity and the "location" from which she or he speaks, or acts.

IV. "RACE" AND "NATURE" IN OUR AMERICA

As mentioned above, Martí advocated complete equality of rights among the races. Illustrating this point in his 1893 article, "My Race," which is devoted to Cuban racial issues, he notes that "no man has any special rights because he belongs to one race or another: "say 'man' and all rights have been stated" (2002, 318). Martí's position stands out for its anti-discriminatory quality, particularly with regard to white-on-black racism. But what can members of discriminated races do to obtain or defend their rights if the prevailing historical understanding of "human" is insufficient to promulgate them? Martí held that, whether used by blacks or whites, it is a form of racism to use race as a marker of superiority or of a "special character" (2002, 319) that would grant some persons or group of persons "differential rights" (*derechos diferenciales*) over others on account of their race. But he made one exception— namely, "the right of the black man to maintain and demonstrate that his color does not deprive him of any of the capacities and rights of the human race" (2002, 319).[21] He called this principle—which could be extended to what we know of today as affirmative action—a "*just* racism" (emphasis added; 2002, 319). Strongly committed to a racial equality platform for all

Cubans, Martí believed that the Cuban revolution's victory over colonialism would redress the problems of racism and slavery that the Spanish colonial regime had imposed on the island.[22] With history's hindsight, we must move beyond Martí on this matter since the outcome of historical events has shown that racism, as an effect of colonialism, has not been eradicated from our Latin American cultures. In fact, Martí's death in 1895 kept him from theorizing on this any further as conditions took a turn against the advent of the free, racially egalitarian republic for which he laid down his life.

Clearly, Martí opposed any notion of biological racial identification as a basis for qualifying a person's moral, civic, or political status. He claims that "blacks, like whites, can be grouped according to their character—timid or brave, self-abnegating or egotistical," and that the principle for uniting in political parties or comparable associations was "an affinity of character," which was "more powerful than an affinity of color" (2002, 319–20). He made these statements in conjunction with the claim that in Cuba there would not be a race war—something that the colonial (racist) Spanish propaganda had voiced would be a threat if the island were to achieve national independence. The anti-colonial Cuban forces had forcefully declared the end of slavery while both blacks and whites fought side by side against Spain in the various phases of the Cuban revolution.[23] Martí and other Cuban revolutionary leaders promoted the concept of full racial equality at the foundation of the Cuban nation but, as some argue, at the cost of limiting the public debate about racial differences in Cuba.

Martí's position in his article "My Race" has been widely contested. For example, Ada Ferrer argues that the leadership of the Cuban revolution was intent on deterring the emergence of an oppositional racial movement in Cuba. She holds that the statements about "racial transcendence" that Martí and other revolutionary political leaders made in the context of late nineteenth-century Cuban nationalism "were not abstract propositions about transcending race." Rather, they were statements about political interests and strategy—the goal being to keep the Cuban nationalist movement united and not subject to racial divisions (Ferrer, 243–44). Ferrer is right in arguing that the view expressed by Martí on the question of race served a strategic purpose in advancing the cause of a unified Cuban nationalism in a particular historical context. Yet I differ from Ferrer in her dismissal of the abstract principle characterizing Martí's position which, I believe, can be shown to be both theoretically coherent and deeply held—and therefore, more than simply instrumental to a political purpose. Martí's position should not be represented so much as "racial transcendence" as, rather, "racial egalitarianism." His view regarding racial equality was, moreover, a consistent philosophical position at the abstract level. For Martí it was also a deeply moral conviction which he firmly believed in as a principle guiding both public and family life.[24] Martí held a straightforwardly egalitarian position, specifically arguing (as egalitarian positions are known to do) for nondiscrimination and inclusiveness of those parts of the population that had historically been oppressed racially.

Ferrer also argues that the Cuban leadership's position on racial transcendence left "little room . . . not only for black political activism but perhaps also for black subjectivity in general" (Ferrer, 229). Here a distinction should be made between Martí, who died in 1895, and the subsequent use of his ideas. As far as Martí's own views are concerned, his egalitarianism does allow for black and other forms of colored subjectivity. What it denies is that individuals have special constitutional rights, or that they are more prone to vice or to virtue, simply on account of their race. As a corollary, it also denies that anyone is more or less of a Cuban on account of his or her race. This is why, if and insofar as the political project was to achieve *Cuban* independence, his vision indeed was of a project that would not be fought on racial terms. In "Nuestra América," Martí's notion of *nuestra América mestiza* was in fact that of a multicolored, multiethnic America where inclusiveness would prevail. Given the historical circumstances of Cuba at the time, he thought that the best way to create inclusiveness was to avoid political activism based on race. He seems to have thought that to insist on racializing political action was to fall into a trap from which it would be difficult to exit—given the type of racial divisiveness that could impact society as a result of such action.

Martí did not take time to distinguish the human right of people to be able to affirm their cultural heritages—a practice that can be distinguished philosophically, but perhaps not always politically, from the racist practice of ascribing biological superiority to a particular race. Nonetheless, from the position that he takes in "Nuestra América," it is clear that he strongly affirms the right of peoples to defend their cultural heritage—so much so that this is the basic premise he defends in "Nuestra América." He does distinguish, however, between affirming one's cultural heritage and the practice of cultural imperialism. In fact he attempts to persuade the reader that articulating and communicating a Latin American *nuestra Americanista* perspective is a strong deterrence to the cultural imperialism of the North. From this angle it does not contradict his views to argue that, given the resiliency of white dominance, it is imperative for blacks, mestizo, and indigenous peoples to defend their cultural heritages in the strongest possible terms. This is why his symbol of a multicolored America, contained in the figure of *nuestra América mestiza*, continues to be so powerful.

Martí's argument about the moral and political insignificance of biological racial differences is reminiscent to some extent of some early second-wave Western feminist arguments from the 1960s and 1970s regarding the irrelevance of biological sexual characteristics in the classification of human beings.[25] At the time, it was common for egalitarian feminists to claim that the sexual difference between male and female should not be considered any more salient than whether someone was tall or short, or whether someone's eyes were blue or green. The rhetorical question was repeated over and over again: why differentiate—is it in order to discriminate? Egalitarian feminists held that it was not possible to think of sexual difference without the hierarchical pattern of male-over-female superiority that a patriarchal and masculinist culture had ingrained in people's minds and habits. Similarly, they held that feminists who insisted in viewing sexual difference in reverse terms, attributing superior moral or ontological value to women, were trapped in the same patriarchal ideology regardless of whether the traits they associated with femaleness were celebrated rather than ridiculed or devalued. Eventually the hypothesis of the social construction of gender and sexuality enabled feminists to speak about sexual and gender differences while at the same time criticizing the ideologies of homophobia and normative heterosexuality that so often inform the representation of sexual and gender differences in our culture.

Martí's insistence that racial difference is a redundant marker in human identity seems to emerge from similar sentiments as those of the egalitarian feminists who asked: why differentiate? Is it to discriminate? Proponents of identity politics highlighting sexual or racial differences will not accept such an egalitarian position because, in their view, the specific difference—not (only) the racism or sexism that produced its meaning, as the egalitarian would have it—is what is being erased. If Martí had had access to the contemporary theory of the social construction of race I believe he could have adapted it to his purposes.[26] Instead, living when he did, he relied on a discourse of naturalism accepted in nineteenth-century narratives of nationalism. He projected his idealist views on nature and then argued that "by nature" all men are equal. In isolation from other considerations, this type of argument is not very persuasive because it is quite possible to appeal to nature in order to argue the contrary point. Have racists not claimed that "by nature" some races are far superior to others? What allows Martí to use "nature" against racism is that he appeals to it in order to undo Eurocentrism in the Americas. He uses "nature" to decolonize the Eurocentric imagination and the symbolic order that sustains it. The ideological links among Eurocentrism, colonialism, and racism against the native American, black, and mestizo populations are typically present in the history of our America. In appealing to nature as a force of freedom against these oppressions, Martí opened a kind of ontological ground on which to rethink and resist the legacies of colonial racist oppression. It was also a way of inducing / persuading *criollos* like him to remove themselves from their class and/or race privileges and try to see themselves on the same plane as others who lacked such social status. Existentially speaking, "nature" could serve as an equalizer in these respects. In other words, Martí appealed to the natural equality of souls whose bodies appear "diverse in form and color" in order to rid himself and other white *independentistas* of their white racial identification in a culture where "white" had signified conqueror, oppressor, and colonizer. He realized precisely that by identifying as equally human as everyone else, whites too could side with the oppressed against colonial power and its subsequent legacies. At the time, many black Cuban leaders joined Martí's racial egalitarian vision. It is this trans-racial bond against oppression that he felt to lie at the very core of the Cuban struggle for independence from colonial rule.

V. MARTÍ'S LEGACY AND THE CRITIQUE OF COLONIAL DISCOURSE

Martí's double legacy—one to Latin America through his concept of *nuestra América* and his stand against hemispheric cultural and economic imperialism; the other, to Cuba, through his concept of a truly independent, self-governed, and racially egalitarian, republic—has traversed the whole of the twentieth century and continues to be relevant today. During this period of over one century conceptual frameworks, literary styles, and political ideologies have come and gone—some for good, while others adapted or readapted in response to changing circumstances. New conceptual frameworks have also emerged such as post-structuralism and postcolonialism. The hemispheric context in which Martí wrote can now no longer be so easily separated from a global context. This means that some of the commonalities and differences between Latin America and other colonized regions in the global South—principally Asia and Africa—also demand our attention. The capitalist globalization of the economy in the last part of the twentieth century and the beginning of the twenty-first have also fueled our hemisphere's South-to-North migration so that we can no longer assert (if it had ever been possible) that "nuestra América" was limited geographically to the Caribbean and Latin America. Indeed, today "nuestra América" has also unleashed its presence within and alongside the borders of the continental United States. Postcolonial theory takes into account such matters and is a logical place for Martí's *nuestra Americanista* perspective to find an intellectual place.

The discussion of Cuba's position in the aftermath of Spanish colonialism was complicated by the Spanish-American War of 1898 and the subsequent U.S. hegemony over the island, particularly until the end of Cuba's "first republic" in 1933. With the 1959 revolution Cuban nationalism gradually fell in the arms of Marxism-Leninism. But, even so, Latin American Marxism was a different kind of creature than the forms Marxism had taken in Europe, the Soviet Union, and Asia.[27] The cultural roots of Cuban Marxist-led nationalism became evident after the dissolution of the Soviet Union, when the nation was forced to adapt to changing political and economic global conditions, but not to the extent that it would comply with the U.S. government's idea of how the country ought to be governed. Martí's view of not importing the structure of government from abroad plus appeals to notions of national sovereignty led Cubans to claim that as an independent republic they had the right to chart their own course and not to capitulate to pressure from the North. The impasse regarding what constitutes colonialism in our own times has not subsided. Critics refer to the Cuban government as a dictatorship, while others contend that, above all, freedom for Cuba means freedom from U.S. imperialism. Regardless of its internal method of government Cuba became a symbol, for many people around the world, of a small island that has continued to defy the world's greatest superpower in the face of considerable economic and political obstacles. Ironically, the United States has contributed significantly to this image by taking unusually harsh measures against its neighbor especially at a time when it trades profusely with communist China and has established diplomatic relations with Vietnam. It makes one wonder whether Cuba's exceptional treatment by the United States is not an instance, among others, of the dreaded new form of economic colonialism that Martí hoped could be averted before it was too late.

Meanwhile, in the United States, recent non-Cuban readings of Martí credit him with opposing colonialism and promoting a diverse, multicultural concept of Our America (with especial relevance to the dialectic of contemporary North/South transnational relations). José Saldívar adapts Martí's ideas to the call for diversifying the canon in American Studies in such a way that the subaltern works of Latinas/os, Native Americans, and American writers of color can find prominent recognition for their cultural productions. In what he called "the dialectics of our America," Saldívar extrapolated Martí's analysis of U.S. political, economic, and cultural hegemony over Latin America to challenge the marginalization of ethnic literatures and criticism from the field of American Studies in the United States. Influenced by Edward Said's critique of Orientalist discourse as well as Roberto Fernández Retamar's Marxist cultural analyses of Latin American and Caribbean resistance to Western colonialism and U.S. imperialism, Saldívar—from the standpoint of Chicano studies—revalidated Martí's notion of *nuestra América* as a useful perspective for reclaiming the missing voices from Our America in the North American literary canon. He likens Martí's role in promoting the notion of *nuestra América*, which serves to ground the legacy of anticolonialist Latin American and Caribbean cultural production, to Emerson's essay, "The American Scholar" (1837), "which established the grounds for a national, popular American literature" (Saldívar 1990, 66).[28] But for Saldívar, what radicalizes Martí's conception of *nuestra América* even further, enabling its implications and repercussions to link up with the late twentieth-century debates on the role of postcolonial intellectuals in U.S.

ethnic and cultural studies, is the materialist reconversion of Martí's notion by the Cuban Marxist postcolonial critic Roberto Fernández Retamar.[29] "Fernández Retamar has produced perhaps the most powerful model of oppositional critical practice in Our America since Martí," wrote Saldívar in 1990 (Saldívar 1990, 73; Fernández Retamar 1989).

From the encounters of radical and progressive writers gathered at the Casa de las Américas Cuban cultural center, directed by Fernández Retamar, Saldívar deduced (correctly, in my view), that there was much that the literature of the Americas (North and South) had in common, but that to appreciate what they had in common one had to apply a genealogy regarding the regimes of power they were resisting. In this regard, José Martí's "Nuestra América"—later enhanced by the Calibanesque rebellion against colonialism embraced by Fernández Retamar and many other postcolonial writers and intellectuals—was the definitive text through which subsequent alliances for or against colonialist regimes of power could be interpreted. The outcome of this analysis is to link together powerful works by writers of color in the United States with the Latin American and Caribbean leftist postcolonial writers, understanding that, despite the wide differences in style or languages of composition, what unites them are their alternative visions for "our America" and their resistance to that "other America" which is not ours—the America complicit with the work of Western colonialism.

For many U.S. Latinos/as in the United States, the social implications of Martí's notion of "nuestra América" are even more powerful than their academic repercussions. In this vein, Martí's anti-colonialist vision of two oppositional Americas, broadly construed and reinterpreted in our own times of global capitalist acceleration impelled by the United States and the transnational migration of people from South to North, is both conscious of internal differentiations among Latin America's exploited groups and especially relevant to the construction of a contemporary oppositional pan-Latina/o or trans-Latino hemispheric consciousness. As the Puerto Rican feminist and Latina scholar Edna Acosta-Belén states: "[Martí's] pan-national affirmation of a multicultural and multiracial *nuestra América* also takes on great contemporary significance as we strive to put an end to European and Anglo-American ethnocentrism by decolonizing and deconstructing the cultural mythologies and received knowledge about subaltern groups perpetuated within the dominant Western tradition" (Acosta-Belén 1999, 86). In fact, Martí's idealization of a voluntary *nuestra Americanista* identity over a century ago now seems immensely helpful as a strategy to guide the construction of the new pan-ethnic "Latina/o" identities imposed on or adopted by immigrants from the Caribbean and Latin America to the United States. One of the advantages of Martí's notion of *nuestra América* noted by Acosta-Belén, in addition to its oppositional anti-colonialist quality, is its transcending of national boundaries, in a way that can ground "reciprocal interactions and bidirectional exchanges" among the U.S. Latina/o and Latin American/Caribbean populations, rather than treat each as a separate entity lodged within national borders (Acosta-Belén 1999, 82–83).

With regard to international relations, Jeffrey Belnap, coeditor of an important recent anthology on Martí, points to the importance of Martí's formulation of *"nuestra América"* for contemporary geopolitics in a transnational hemisphere. Belnap refers to "the incisive lucidity of Martí's most influential piece of newspaper prose, "Our America" (1891), an essay that, after a century, still serves as a necessary touchstone for any analysis of inter-American cultural politics" (Belnap 1998, 192). The same judgment is shared by many Latin Americans. For example, the Argentine-Mexican philosopher Horacio Cerutti Guldberg, writing on the one hundredth anniversary of its publication, stated that Martí's essay "appears to have been written yesterday or, better said, tomorrow" (Cerutti Guldberg 1996, 119). Martí's essay continues to serve critics of colonialism as a guide for the interpretation of hemispheric relations, Latin American culture, and most recently, Latino culture in the United States.

From these forms of recognition it is only a step further, as I have done, to assign Martí an important position in postcolonial studies. In this context, even more diverse interpretations of Martí's thought could come to the fore. The Argentine-U.S. postcolonial theorist Walter Mignolo underlined Martí's relevance to Latin American postcolonial thought by stating that "José Martí was a postcolonial Caribbean intellectual, in today's sense of 'postcolonial'" (Mignolo 2000, 196). Mignolo did not elaborate on his important comment. It is not easy to interpret the impact of Martí's position on a number of issues, such as race or the future of the Cuban nation. It is also not easy, in our current methodologically post-foundationalist academic age, to deal with a poet, a writer, a political leader, and a patriot who achieved the extraordinary stature of José Martí. Latin American postcolonial thought, however, challenges us to insert worldly considerations into our academic theorizing. The very conditions of economic, social, or political oppression have meant that activism and/or political involvement have often taken place side by side with intellectual and literary endeavors. Even today, engaged postcolonial intellectuals keep alive a strong interest in popular social movements or contribute artistically to their societies in ways that link the academy with public life.

To conclude, I have argued that we must expand our concept of postcolonialism in the United States to make room for Latin American thinkers, many of whom, like Martí, wrote outside the parameters of postmodern critique.[30] He is not alone in this role, but his relevance is sufficiently important to warrant major consideration.[31] Moreover, there is a difference between theorizing about Latin American postcoloniality with a focus on South America and the Caribbean, Mexico, and Central America regions (that have historically been much more vulnerable to U.S. intervention); as Mignolo has posited, our "loci of enunciation" will yield different perspectives on "theorizing postcolonial cultural histories" (Mignolo 2000, 180, 182–84). In this vein, the Uruguayan critic Hugo Achúgar reminds us that "one thing is to be postcolonial in English and another in Spanish, Portuguese, Bayano, Quechua, Aymara, Guarani, Papiamento and equivalents" (Achúgar 1998, 278). As Achúgar states, postcolonial thought in Latin America can be modern, postmodern, or non-Western, and includes, as Martí's vision of Our America did, both migrants and non-migrants. As a Cuban-American, I could not possibly begin to understand colonialism in this hemisphere without reading Martí. His thought reveals aspects of our present-day cultural and political realities whose roots go back to conditions in the making for well over a century. Martí's brilliant and passionate thinking continues to enrich our understanding of the many facets of resistance to colonialism, both historically and even today.

NOTES

1. Translations from the Spanish-language works listed in the notes and references are my own. In a few cases I have departed from the wording of texts available in English translations of José Martí. In such cases, I indicate this by referencing only the Spanish-language edition for these passages.

2. In the interpretation of history, the poststructuralist questioning of the transparency of language and of the subject of modern history strongly affect the contemporary critique of colonial discourse within a postmodern context. See Patricia Seed, "Colonial and Post-Colonial Discourse," *Latin American Research Review*, 26, no. 3 (1991), 182–86.

3. Surely Martí did not imagine that—as the twentieth century demonstrated—Cuba would undergo a political revolution that would attempt to resist U.S. hegemony on its own or with the help of an extra-continental power such as the Soviet Union, without the backing of the majority of Hispanic American republics.

4. In the 1891 article "Nuestra América" Martí contrasted the Indo-Hispanic, African-descendant, and creole cultures of "our America" with the Anglo-based cultures of the United States. Roberto Fernández Retamar has called attention to Martí's use elsewhere of the expression "European America" (Roberto Fernández Retamar, *Caliban and Other Essays*, trans. Edward Baker [Minneapolis: University of Minnesota Press, 1989], 21, 24, 27 and passim; Martí, *Obras Completas de José Martí*, [hereafter cited as OC] 25+ volumes [Havana: Editorial Nacional de Cuba, 1963–65], 8:442), a term that Retamar takes as a defining contrast to "nuestra América." Martí referred to "la América Europea" (European America) in an 1884 article describing a graduating ceremony at Vassar. The article contains an interesting statement regarding his support for the advanced education of women (mellowed by his simultaneous endorsement of women's "feminine" traits). See "Una distribución de diplomas en un colegio de los Estados Unidos" in OC 8:440–45.

5. For a discussion of Martí's political formation during this period, see also Fernández Retamar, "Prólogo," in Martí, José, *Política de nuestra América*, edited by José Aricó (Mexico City: Siglo XXI, 1979), 26–28.

6. "De la tiranía de España supo salvarse la América española; y ahora, después de ver con ojos judiciales los antecedentes, causas y factores del convite, urge decir, porque es la verdad, que ha llegado para la América española la hora de declarar su segunda independencia" (OC 6:46).

7. In fact, Martí used the term *colonialismo* to describe the nature of the economic manipulation the United States was engaging in before and during the 1889 hemispheric congress. He refers to "the [economic] battle the United States is preparing to have with the rest of the world" and questions why the United States should wage its [trade] battles against Europe "over the American republics, and try out *in free peoples its system of colonization*?" (emphasis added; OC 6:57). This article was written in New York on November 2, 1889, and published December 20, 1889, in *La Nación*, Buenos Aires.

8. "un pueblo que comienza a mirar como privilegio suyo la libertad, que es aspiración universal y perenne del hombre, y a invocarla para privar a los pueblos de ella" (OC 6:53).

9. For a chronology of Martí's life, see *José Martí: Selected Writings*, ed. and trans. by Esther Allen, Introduction by Roberto González Echevarría (New York: Penguin, [1893] 2002), xxvii–xxxii. For a biographical essay on Martí's life and the historical reception of his work in Cuba and Latin America, see Oscar Martí, "Martí and the Heroic Image," *José Martí's "Nuestra América": From National to Hemispheric Cultural Studies*, ed. Jeffrey Belnap and Raúl Fernández (Durham, NC: Duke University Press, 1998), 317–38.

10. The two earlier stages of the war had been the Ten Years' War or Big War (1868–1878) and the Little War (1879–1880).

11. The earlier part of the nineteenth century had shown the territorial expansion of the United States over previously Hispanic lands in the northern part of the continent. Florida was purchased from Spain in 1819. Texas, California, Arizona, New Mexico, and parts of Colorado, Nevada, and Utah were part of Mexico in the earlier part of the nineteenth century. Texas was part of Mexico until 1835 and California until 1847. The rest were ceded to the United States by the Treaty of Guadalupe Hidalgo that concluded the Mexican-American War in 1848 (see James Dunkerley, "Latin America since Independence," in *The Cambridge Companion to Modern Latin American Culture*, edited by John King [New York: Cambridge University Press, 2004], 29). In 1855 the United States offered to buy Cuba from Spain for one hundred million dollars. Spain was not interested (Martí 2002, xxvii).

12. Various translators have used "our *mestizo* America" to translate this phrase, although for Martí "our America" is gendered female and is described as having the qualities of a nurturing, freedom-loving mother. I am therefore retaining the term *mestiza* in the feminine. It is a *mestiza* America (not a masculinized "mestizo" America) that Martí invokes and theorizes as "ours." A famous speech of his from December 1889, "Madre América" ("Mother America") invokes the continent that nourishes its children to independence from colonialism in feminine, maternal terms. See "Mother America," in *Our America by José Martí: Writings on Latin America and the Cuban Struggle for Independence*, ed. Philip S. Foner (New York: Monthly Review Press, 1977), 69–83.

13. The debate over whether Martí took sufficient steps to fight racism in Cuba will be considered below.

14. For a classic study on nineteenth-century Latin American intellectual liberalism, including its limitations, see Beatriz González Stephan, *La historiografía literaria del liberalismo hispano-americano del siglo XIX* (Havana: Casa de las Américas, 1987).

15. In terms of contemporary global politics, Martí's position in favor of indigenous peoples and peasants, and against the power of foreign corporations over regional and local resources, could be seen as having some interesting affinities with the movement that the Indian environmental activist Vandana Shiva calls "earth democracy."

16. The term *mestizaje* has had multiple meanings and uses in the history of Latin America. It is important to take its meaning in context. It is widely known that the term has been used in racist ways to whiten and erase the presence and contributions of African-descendant and indigenous peoples. However, it has also been used to challenge racism. I take it that Martí invoked the expansive, rather than the reductionist, sense of "mestizaje."

17. The translation by Esther Allen is possibly misleading here by referring to "the country's natural constitution" (Martí 2002, 290). Philosophically speaking, what is "propio" is neither reducible nor equivalent to what is natural, since it can be "propio" (of one's very own, of its very own) in a cultural or historic sense. I also prefer to read the next sentence ("El gobierno no es más que el equilibrio de los elementos naturales del país" [OC 6:17]) as meaning that government is nothing but the balance of the country's natural elements, which

allows for personal judgment and collective action in recognizing and/or facilitating such a balance, rather than Allen's "The government is no more than an equilibrium among the country's natural elements" (Martí 2002, 290). If Martí had meant the latter, he could have used the proposition "entre," meaning "among," but he did not.

18. This point is also shared by Jeffrey Belnap, "Headbands, Hemp Sandals, and Headdresses," *José Martí's "Nuestra América": From National to Hemispheric Cultural Studies*, ed. Jeffrey Belnap and Raúl Fernández (Durham, NC: Duke University Press, 1998), 208. I assume that the reason for this is that today we are more aware that what we call "nature" is also largely a cultural construction.

19. "de virtudes y defectos son capaces por igual latinos y sajones" (OC 28:291).

20. Martí's testimonial article, "Political Prison in Cuba," published in 1871 in Spain, is a telling example of this practice, already well defined for him at the age of eighteen.

21. I do not think that Martí's principle of "just racism" is incompatible with the twentieth-century principles of affirmative action (called "reverse discrimination" by its opponents in the United States) as long as the measures are understood to be temporary and the measures' objectives are as stated. He apparently did not think such measures would be necessary in post-revolutionary nineteenth-century Cuba because the Republic itself would be founded on non-discriminatory principles and during the struggle many black leaders had already taken positions of power and responsibility in the revolutionary movement. The Spanish American War, which interrupted the Cuban patriots' struggle for independence from Spain and imposed U.S. control over the island in 1898, cut short the vision for which Martí gave up his life in 1895. With the United States imposing its own (anti-*nuestra Americanista*) conditions for granting Cuban independence, the difficulties of achieving Martí's racial egalitarianism became fully apparent. For a comprehensive study of the racial question in Cuba, see Alejandro de la Fuente, *A Nation for All: Race, Inequality, and Politics in Twentieth-Century Cuba* (Chapel Hill: University of North Carolina Press, 2001).

22. Spain did not abolish slavery in Cuba until 1886, and did so in the aftermath of the treaty ending the Ten Years' War in 1878 (See Foner, pp. 13–14 and note 14). As a youth Martí witnessed slavery in both the city and the countryside of Cuba. A section of his *Versos sencillos* describes the impact upon witnessing the slave trade and a lynching on a small boy (presumably himself) who "swore / to wash the crime away with his life." "Un niño lo vio: tembló / De pasión por los que gimen: / Y, al pie del muerto, juró / Lavar con su vida el crimen" (2002), 280–81. See also Hebert Pérez, "Martí, Race, and Cuban Identity," *Monthly Review* 55, no. 6, 2003.

23. In "My Race" Martí claimed that the first Cuban constitution of independence (1869) proclaimed by the rebels freed the slaves, but this goal was not actually achieved within rebels' control until December 23, 1870, when the last provisions against slavery were removed (Foner, p. 314). De la Fuente dates the themes of abolition and equality among the rebels as becoming prominent in 1871 (Fuente, 26).

24. To the racist and sexist question, "would you marry your daughter to a Negro?" Martí responded that marriage is "the voluntary union between two beings of diverse sexes" (Martí 1978, 33). If the daughter "that I would like to have," he wrote, fell in love with a black man and her companion of choice was both educated and of high moral character, he would support his daughter's wishes. Martí's words on this subject were published for the first time in 1978 by Cuban scholars working on a new critical edition of his writings. See also Pérez, 2003. I thank John Du Moulin for this reference. Over the years Martí reunited several times with his wife, Carmen Zayas Bazán (with whom he had a son born in Havana in 1878), but ultimately the reconciliations were unsuccessful. He is widely believed to have had a daughter out of wedlock with Carmen Miyares de Mantilla in New York City in 1880. See Martí, 2002, xxix. The Spanish colonial government did not lift the prohibition on interracial marriage until 1881 (Stolcke, 39–41).

25. On the issue of sexual difference Martí was not egalitarian. For the most part he follows the normative notions of gender difference held by his Latin American contemporaries.

26. He could have also considered "social construction" in an expanded sense, including the interaction of individuals and communities with the natural landscape where they travel or reside.

27. One of the most prominent founders of Latin American Marxism was José Carlos Mariátegui (1894–1930). For an analysis of his work, see Ofelia Schutte, *Cultural Identity and Social Liberation in Latin American Thought* (Albany: SUNY Press, 1993), 18–71.

28. A similar point was made by Foner in the Preface to his edition of Martí (1977, 9). Foner attributes the observation about Emerson to Gordon Lewis, but does not provide a reference for it.

29. Retamar published his influential essay, "Calibán," for the first time in *Casa de las Américas*, in 1968 (Havana, September-October 1971).

30. Walter Mignolo proposed the category "postoccidentalism" (in place of "postmodernism" or "postcolonialism") to name the tradition of Latin American thought, but despite its conceptual value, the term has not caught on ("Posoccidentalismo: el argumento desde América Latina," in *Teorías sin Disciplina: Latinoamericanismo, poscolonialidad y globalización en debate*, edited by S. Castro-Gómez and E. Mendieta [Mexico City: University of San Francisco and Miguel Angel Porrúa Editores, 1998], 33). Mignolo credits Roberto Fernández Retamar ("Our America and the West," *Social Text* 15, Fall [1976] 1986) for the term "postoccidental."

31. For additional reading and perspectives beyond Martí, see José Carlos Mariátegui, *Seven Interpretive Essays on Peruvian Reality*, trans. Marjory Urquidi (Austin: University of Texas Press, [1928] 1971); Fernández Retamar 1986, 1989; Schutte 1993; Mignolo, *The Darker Side of the Renaissance* (Ann Arbor: University of Michigan Press, 1995); John Beverley et al., *The Postmodernism Debate in Latin America* (Durham, NC: Duke University Press, 1995); Santiago Castro-Gómez and Eduardo Mendieta, eds., *Teorías sin Disciplina: Latinoamericanismo, poscolonialidad y globalización en debate* (Mexico City: University of San Francisco and Miguel Angel Porrúa Editores, 1998); Sara Castro-Klarén, ed., *Latin American Women's Narrative: Practices and Theoretical Perspectives* (Madrid and Frankfurt: Iberoamericana and Vervuert, 2003); Eduardo Mendieta, *Latin American Philosophy: Currents, Issues, Debates* (Bloomington: Indiana University Press, 2003); Mark Thurner and Andrés Guerrero, eds., *After Spanish Rule: Postcolonial Predicaments of the Americas* (Durham, NC: Duke University Press, 2003).

Chapter Ten

Subaltern History as Political Thought

Dipesh Chakrabarty

I. POLITICS AND HISTORY

In his 1982 essay "The Politics of Historical Interpretation: Discipline and De-Sublimation," Hayden White made a remark that deserves elaboration. Referring to an early nineteenth-century essay by Schiller on the idea of the sublime, White said: "Historical facts are *politically* domesticated precisely insofar as they are effectively removed from displaying the aspect of the sublime that Schiller attributed to them in his essay of 1801."[1] White's statement is cited approvingly in F. R. Ankersmit's paper "Hayden White's Appeal to the Historians," an essay that generally defends White with some passion against his more simple-minded detractors.[2] What did White mean by "political domestication" of historical facts? Ankersmit, respectfully reduces "the politics of interpretation" to the question of subverting the distance and the distinction between objectivity and subjectivity. He cites Simon Schama's brilliant books *Dead Certainties* and *Landscape and Memory* as successful examples of narratives that take up, intentionally or otherwise, White's challenge by deliberately blurring the boundary between fact and fiction. There is much to be gained from Ankersmit's thoughtful defense of White. But I do think that to reduce the meaning of the word "political," in White's expression "political domestication of historical facts," to the question of subject-object distinction is to underestimate the political charge of that expression itself. White himself provides a more expansive reading of his own sentence. He says:

> [B]oth for the Left and the Right . . . [the] aesthetics of the beautiful presides over the process in which historical studies are constituted as an autonomous scholarly discipline. . . . For this tradition, whatever "confusion" is displayed by the historical

record is only a surface phenomenon: a product of lacunae in the documentary sources, of mistakes in ordering the archives, or of previous inattention or scholarly errors. If this confusion is not reducible to the kind of *order* [emphasis added] that a science of laws might impose on it, it can still be dispelled by historians with the proper kind of understanding.[3]

White prefers the vision of history as "sublime"—something innately disorderly and hence constitutionally incomprehensible—to the usual vision of the historian who sees historical process as containing some inner order that historians are supposed to discern. The usual function of the historical explanation is to produce, precisely, an ordered reality. White follows Schiller in thinking of the beautiful as orderly and the sublime as that which resists ordering. "[I]n so far as historical explanations become understandable ... or explainable," writes White, "they can never serve as vision for a visionary politics more concerned to endow social life with meaning than with beauty" (72). This sentence reveals the idea of "politics" that White might have had in mind in speaking of "political domestication" of historical facts. Historical reality has no order in itself. To endow it with meaning is the responsibility of the human (in this case, the historian). When the historian writes as though the ordered reality of historical narratives in something that existed "naturally" in the world—independent of the historian's act of ordering reality—then she or he abnegates our need to take responsibility for putting "meaning" where none existed. If we, as historians, accepted such responsibility as ours, we could have used archives for producing narrative accounts for which we would have been responsible. By doing this, we would have acknowledged both the innate disorderliness of reality and the vision that inspired the "meaning" we sought in it. Instead of owning responsibility for the order, their explanations produce and thus acknowledge historical reality as sublime; historians, White complains, remain on the side of the beautiful by imagining "objective" historical realities whose hidden order can indeed be deciphered. "Endowing social life with meaning" is, for White, an act with existential reverberations. Modern ideologies "impute a meaning to history" but one that only renders history's "manifest confusion comprehensible to either reason, understanding, or aesthetic sensibility." The imputation of a meaning that introduces order into history, "politically domesticates" historical facts; for "to the extent that they [modern ideologies] succeed in doing so [i.e., give history a meaning—author's note], they deprive history of the kind of meaninglessness that alone can goad living human beings to make their lives different for themselves and their children, which is to say, to endow their lives with a meaning for which they alone are fully responsible."[4]

Ankersmit thus produced an interpretation of White's statement that definitely helps to illustrate the problem of what White called "the middle voice," a voice that is neither active (subject) nor passive (object), and one that goes someway toward mitigating the subject-object dichotomy that normally underpins historical prose. This is a concept that Hayden White introduced in a controversial essay on the difficulties of representing the victims' experience of the Nazi Holocaust. Using Barthes' famous essay "To Write: An Intransitive Verb?" White pointed out that "although modern Indo-European languages offer two possibilities for expressing this relationship [the one 'an agent can be represented as bearing toward an action,'—author's note], the active and the passive voices, other languages have offered a third possibility, that expressed, for example, in the ancient Greek 'middle voice.'" Such "modernist" modes of representation, White argues, may allow us to circumvent the problem created by the persistence, in historian's prose, of nineteenth-century realism.[5] Escaping such realism, for White, is a question of escaping the subject-object duality that sometimes constrains the capacity of History or the discipline to represent historical experience.

Ankersmit favours White's idea of the "middle voice" but his exposition runs the risk of taking politics out of the expression "political domestication." The subject-object distinction, in the destruction of which Ankersmit looks for politics, belongs more to the realms of epistemology than to those of politics. White's own interpretation, on the other hand, is admittedly much more expansive than that of Ankersmit's, but it leaves the nature of "politics" somewhat undecided in the expression "political domestication." Both the Left and the Right, he says, seek to privilege the beautiful over the sublime, the idea of order over the confusion of history. He prefers a future in which people act with a sense of the profound meaninglessness or confusion that characterizes history—which would in turn enable them to take responsibility for the future that they choose. White thus envisages particular kinds of historical subjects and agents who are constituted to be capable of taking responsibility for their choices.

The idea that confusion is innate to the historical process is attractive and entirely plausible. White exhibits a great profoundness for the bold proposition that unless historical narratives find a way of embracing or at least acknowledging the confusion that exists in history, historical facts remain, as White says, "politically domesticated." But Ankersmit and White's explanations of what this phrase might mean do not exhaust the meaning of the word "political" in White's expression. People taking responsibility for their decisions in the face of the meaninglessness of the world are too much a figment of a particular Western history. Indian or South Asian history cannot be read into that image. Thus there are two problems with the explanations at hand: Ankersmit reduces the scope of the political to the question of avoiding objectification of reality—a goal worthy in itself but reductive of the meaning of the political. White's own explanation, on the other hand, ends up over-specifying the historical agent/subject to whom he ascribes the capacity to be political (which renders his view of the human subject Western and existential).

And yet something about the expression "political domestication of historical facts," and in White's idea of an innately meaningless historical process, speaks to what happens in the usual narratives of domination and resistance in South Asian history and histories elsewhere. The next section will explore further the possibilities opened by White's insistence, following Schiller, on the sublimity of history—but with the example of the Indian series Subaltern Studies both for reasons of familiarity and also to create a conversation between White's own concerns that circulate scrupulously within the bounds of Western historiography and those that arise from attempts to write histories of subalterns outside of the West.

II. SUBALTERN HISTORY

Subaltern Studies was an instance of politically motivated historiography. It came out of the Marxist tradition of history writing in South Asia (and in South Asian studies generally) and was markedly indebted to Mao and Gramsci in the initial formulations that guided the series. The tradition of history writing on the Left in India was deeply, though unsurprisingly, influenced by English Marxist or socialist historiography; the so-called history from below tradition was pioneered by the likes of Edward Thompson, Eric Hobsbawm, Christopher Hill, George Rudé, and others. Just as Thompson's work on English popular history was predicated on the question "what contributions did the lower orders of society make to the history of English democracy?", historians in the *Subaltern Studies* series began by asking a similar question: "What contributions did the subaltern classes make on their own to the politics of nationalism in India, and hence to Indian democracy as well?"[6] But here the similarity ended. English Marxist narratives of popular histories were molded on developmental time: the peasant died or was superseded to give rise to the worker who, through struggle for rights, one day metamorphosed into the figure of the citizen. The peasant or tribal of the Third World who—as if through a process of telescoping of the centuries—suddenly had the colonial state and its modern bureaucratic and repressive apparatus thrust in his face, was, in this mode of thinking, a "pre-political" person. He or she was someone who did not understand the operative languages, as it were, of modern, governing institutions and who still had to deal with them. In terms of the English "history from below" propositions, it was only over time, undergoing a process of intellectual development, that the subaltern classes could mature into a modern political force. *Subaltern Studies* began by repudiating this developmental idea of "becoming political."

The peasant or the subaltern, it was claimed, was *political* from the very instance they rose up in rebellion against the institutions of the Raj.[7]

The question of in what sense the peasant was meant to be political, however, needs to be set aside. What is more important here is the way the legacies of both imperialism and anti-colonialism speak to each other in this implicit debate on whether the subaltern became political over time (through some kind of pedagogic process) or whether the subaltern was constitutionally political. Developmental time, or the sense of time underlying a stagist view of history, was indeed a legacy of nineteenth-century colonialism in India. This, stated in my book *Provincializing Europe*, was the time of the "not yet." European political thinkers such as Mill (or even Marx) employed this temporal structure in the way they thought of history. Nationalists and anti-colonialists, on the other hand, repudiated this imagination of time in the twentieth century in asking for self-rule to be granted immediately, without delay, now. What replaced the structure of "not yet" in their imagination was the horizon of the "now."[8]

The British argued against giving self-rule to educated Indians in the nineteenth century, by saying that they were not representative of the "people." The answer came from Gandhi who, following his entry into Indian politics during the First World War, made the main nationalist party, the Indian National Congress, into a "mass" organization by enlisting peasants as ordinary, the so-called four-*anna*, who were members with voting rights within the Congress. The "mass base" of the Congress enabled its leaders to claim the status of being "representative" of the nation even if the poor and the non-literate formally did not have a vote under the Raj. The educational gap that separated the peasant from the educated leaders was never considered a problem in this idea of representation. The peasant, it was assumed, was fully capable of making citizenly choices that colonial rule withheld from them. From the very beginning of the 1920s, Gandhi spoke in favor of universal adult franchise in a future, independent India. The peasant would thus be made a citizen overnight—that was the "now" the nationalists demanded—without having to live out the developmental time of formal or informal education. In the constitutional debates that took place in the Constituent Assembly right after independence, the philosopher, and later statesman, Radhakrishnan argued for a republican form of government by claiming that thousands of years of civilization—even if formal education was absent—had already prepared the peasant for such a state.[9]

What underwrote this anti-colonial but populist faith in the modern-political capacity of the masses was another European inheritance, romanticism. It is, of course, true that the middle-class leaders of anti-colonial movements involving peasants and workers never quite abandoned the idea of developmental time. Gandhi's writings and those of other nationalist leaders often express a fear of the lawless mob and see education as a solution to the problem.[10] But this fear was qualified by its opposite, a political faith in the masses. In the 1920s and the 1930s, this romanticism marked Indian nationalism generally—many nationalists who were not Communist, for instance, would express this faith. Francesca Orsini of Cambridge University, who works on Hindi literature, has recently excavated a body of evidence documenting this tendency. To give but one example from her selection, here is Ganesh Shankar Vidyarthi (1890–1931), the editor of the Hindi paper *Pratap*, editorializing on 31 May 1915:

> The much-despised peasants are our true bread-givers [*annadata*], not those who consider themselves special and look down upon the people who must live in toil and poverty as lowly beings.[11]

Or Vidyarthi again on 11 January 1915:

> Now the time has come for our political ideology and our movement not [to] be restricted to the English-educated and to spread among the common people [*smanaya janta*], and for Indian public opinion [*lokmat*] to be not the opinion of those few educated individuals but to mirror the thoughts of all the classes of the country... democratic rule is actually the rule of public opinion.[12]

One should note that this romantic-political faith in the masses was populist as well, in a classical sense. Like Russian populism of the late nineteenth century, this mode of thought not only sought political "goodness" in the peasant but also, by that step, worked to convert so-called backwardness of the peasant into a historical advantage. The peasant, "uncorrupted" by self-tending individualism of the bourgeois and oriented to the needs of his or her community, was imagined as already endowed with the capacity to usher in a modernity different and more communitarian than what was prevalent in the West.[13] An important result of the very restricted nature of franchise under colonial rule and the induction of the peasant and the urban poor into the nationalist movement was that constitutional law-making councils and the street emerged, as it were, as rival and sometimes complementary institutions of Indian democracy. "In the [legislative] Councils and the assemblies," wrote Shrikishna Datt Palival (1895–1968) in an essay in the Hindi monthly *Vishal Bharat* (February 1936), "one meets power and wealth face to face [and] the rulers' rights are kept safe in a temple where [people's] representatives are denied entry, just like untouchables [in a Hindu temple]."[14] The very restrictions put on constitutional politics then meant that the field, the factory, and the street became major arenas for the struggle for independence and self-rule—and it is these arenas that subaltern subjects with their characteristic mode of politics (including practices of public violence) entered into public life.

Mass-politics of Indian nationalism thus shared something in common with the global characteristics of populism: the tendency to see a certain political goodness in the peasant or in the masses; the tendency also to see historical advantage where, by colonial judgment, there was only backwardness. To see "advantage" in "backwardness" was also to challenge the time of stagist ideas about history; it was to twist the time of the colonial "not yet" into the structure of the democratic and anti-colonial "now."

This short history of the romantic-populist origins of Indian democratic thought—though not of Indian democracy as such and the distinction is important—suggests a point fundamental to my exposition. The insistence, in the early volumes of *Subaltern Studies* (first published in 1982) and in Ranajit Guha's *Elementary Aspects of Peasant Insurgency in Colonial India* (1983), that the peasant or the subaltern was always *already* political, not "pre-political" in any developmentalist sense, was thus in some ways a recapitulation of a populist premise often implicit in the anti-colonial mass movements in British India.[15] But there was a difference too: the populism in *Subaltern Studies* was more intense and explicit. There was, first of all, no "fear of the masses" in *Subaltern Studies* analysis. Absent also, and this went against the grain of classically Marxist or Leninist analysis, was any discussion of the need for organization or a party. Guha and his colleagues drew inspiration from Mao (particularly his 1927 report on the peasant movement in the Hunan district) and Gramsci (mainly his *Prison Notebooks*). This was, after all, the seventies: a period of global Maoism that Althusser and others had made respectable, and excerpts from Gramsci's notebooks had come out in 1971. Both Gramsci and Mao were celebrated as a way out of Stalinist or Soviet Marxism after Czechoslovakia of 1968. Many of the historians in *Subaltern Studies* were participants in or sympathizers of the Maoist movement that shook parts of India between 1969 and 1971.[16] Yet, significantly, neither Mao's references to the need for "leadership of the Party" nor Gramsci's strictures against "spontaneity" featured with any degree of prominence in *Elementary Aspects* or *Subaltern Studies*. Guha's focus remained firmly on understanding the nature of the practices that made up peasant insurgency in a period after the coming of colonial rule but before they had been inducted into nationalism. Guha wanted to understand the peasant as a collective author of these insurgencies by doing a structuralist analysis of the space (and time) creating practices of mobilization, communication, and public violence that constituted rebellion (and thus a subaltern domain of politics). There were limitations, from Guha's socialist point of view, to what the peasants did, but these limitations did not call for the mediation of a party. A cult of rebellion marked the early efforts of *Subaltern Studies*, reminiscent of one of Mao's sayings popular during the Cultural Revolution: "to rebel is justified." Indeed, from a global perspective, one might say that *Subaltern Studies* was the last—or the latest—instance of the long history of the romantic-popular search for a non-industrial revolutionary subject that was initiated in, among other places, Russia in the nineteenth century; that fundamentally shaped Maoism in the twentieth century; and that left its imprint on the antinomies and ambiguities of Antonio Gramsci.

The global romantic search for a revolutionary subject outside of the industrialized West is exhausted today. Such a subject by definition could not be the proletariat. Yet it was difficult to define a world-historical subject that would take the place of the proletariat. Would the revolution, as Trotsky said, be an act of substitutionism? Could the peasantry, under the guidance of the party, be the revolutionary class? Would it be the category "subaltern" or Fanon's "the wretched of the earth"? When the young, left-Hegelian Marx thought up the category of the proletariat as the new revolutionary subject of history that would replace the bourgeoisie—this he did before Engels wrote his book on the Manchester working class in 1844—there was a philosophical precision to the name and it seemed to match on to the class of workers born of the industrial revolution. But names like "peasants" (Mao), "subaltern" (Gramsci), "wretched of the earth" (Fanon), and "the party as the subject" (Lenin/Lukacs) have neither philosophical nor sociological precision. It is as if the search for a revolutionary subject that was not-the-proletariat (in the absence of a large working class) was an exercise in a series of displacement of the original term. A telling case in point is Fanon himself. The expression "the wretched of the earth," as Fanon's biographer David Macey has pointed out, alludes to the Communist Internationale, the song, "Debout, les damnés de la terrre / Arise, ye wretched of the earth," where it clearly refers to the proletariat.[17] Yet Fanon uses it to mean a different subject he cannot quite define, but he is clear that, in the colony, it cannot be the proletariat; early in his book he cautions that "Marxist analysis should always be slightly stretched every time we have to do with the colonial problem."[18]

A collective subject with no proper name, a subject who can be named only through a series of displacements of the original European term "the proletariat" is a condition of both failure and of a new beginning. Where is the beginning? First of all, the very imprecision speaks of the inadequacy of Eurocentric thought. The history of this imprecision amounts to the acknowledgment that if we want to understand the nature of popular political practices globally with names of subjects invented in Europe, we can only resort to a series of stand-ins (never mind the fact that the original may have a simulacrum as well). This is because we are working at and on the limits of European political thought even as we admit an affiliation to nineteenth-century European revolutionary romanticism. Recognizing the stand-in nature of categories like "the masses," "the subaltern," or " the peasant" is the first step toward writing histories of democracies that have emerged through the mass-politics of anti-colonial nationalism. There is a mass-subject here.

But it can only be apprehended by consciously working through the limits of European thought. A straightforward search for a revolutionary world-historical subject only leads to stand-ins. Hardt and Negri's "multitude," is, for all the brilliance of their analysis of global capitalism, another such stand-in. But their use of the category "multitude" does register a question and a task of our times: how do we name and write histories of the mass-subject of politics today?[19]

Another failure of *Subaltern Studies* is clear here that serves as yet another beginning. Guha's great insight of peasant insurgency was that it was an act of a collective subject, not of a collection of individuals. As a historian, Guha did not want to psychologize this subject. He did not write either about a Jungian collective unconscious or have recourse to any idea of "mob" or "crowd" or even revolutionary group psychology. In other words, he did not see the collective in the model of an individual or as making up a "one." It came into being conjuncturally; there was no need to conceive of it as something as a transcendent entity continuing from one rebellion to another though, clearly, insurgencies were mediated by memories of other insurgencies. Guha's own creative, though problematic, approach to apprehending this subject lay through marrying French structuralism with a Hegelian idea of a retrospectively read consciousness.[20] I am not sure that the method succeeded. There were many criticisms of the lack of a proper sociology to his method, of the fact that he treated so-called tribals, rich peasants, poor peasants, and the landless on a par. Who exactly was the subaltern? The critics had a field day shooting us down with these questions. But I think there was something salutary in Guha's insistence that the subject of an insurgency was collective and in his refusal to see this collective either additively—as a collection of individuals—or as something having a mind or psychology of its own. In other words, this was not a subject whose history could be written on a biographical model of birth and subsequent growth toward maturity (the model prevalent in labor histories). In other words, even the idea of the subject—an autonomous, sovereign being—had to be "stretched" (in Fanon's sense of the word) in order to be at all pliable in the context of subaltern history.

This negative gesture of Guha's throws a profound challenge to the discipline of history. Historians of collective practices often practice a methodological individualism that aligns the discipline with the practices of the state or the elites. Imagine how inquisitors and the police deal with collective acts they consider threatening or subversive. They pull individuals out of the collective for the purpose of interrogation.[21] The same happens in the court of law. Indeed, attempts on the part of historians such as George Rudé to humanize the revolutionary "crowd" by finding individual "faces" in it, is predicated on a prior individuation by the interrogatory process of the police and the court. This mode of individuation may be easily recognized as something central to the very operation of disciplinary power, as Foucault once said: it individuates in order to control. But this tendency to treat the collective agent as a collection of so many individuals—when we know that the rioting crowd has indeed a collective agency—is also central to a very particular form of political thought: the Hobbesian understanding of state sovereignty. Historians of the subaltern classes uncritically ally themselves with such thinking when they follow the police and the law in dissolving the collective agency of the "crowd" or "the masses" into the story of "so many individuals ("ringleaders" or not).

The political philosopher Etienne Balibar captures well the "fear of the masses" that is built into this individuating procedure. He makes the point in the context of a discussion of the difference between Spinoza's and Hobbes' attitude toward "the masses" that Spinoza called "the multitude." I need to quote Balibar *in extensor*—the relevant and important point comes at the very end of the quote. Balibar writes:

> Hobbes no less than Spinoza, of course, is a theorist haunted by the fear of the masses and their natural tendency to subversion. His entire organization of the state, including the way in which the distinction between the public and the private sphere operates, can be understood as a system of preventive defense against the mass movements that form the basis of civil wars . . . and of revolutions. It is in this context that the *multitudo* becomes in his writings the initial concept in the definition of the contract [*Leviathan*, chs. 17, 18] . . . , in order to constitute the system juridically and establish it ideologically (on equality). *But in Hobbes's writings it is only a question of a point of departure*, which is immediately left behind. Hobbes carefully separates the two elements that Spinoza wants to bring together (thus intimately combining democratism and Machiavellian realism). For Hobbes, the multitude that establishes the contract is not the concept of the mass; it is the concept ("methodologically" individualist, as current Anglo-American sociologists say) of a "people" always already decomposed, reduced in advance (preventively) to the sum of its constituent atoms (people in the state of nature), and capable of entering one by one, through the contract, into the new institutional relationship of civil society.[22]

Thus, historians who follow un-self-consciously the methodological individualism of the police and the law fail to produce what Jacques Rancière who writes exactly on this point calls "forms of knowledge proper to the age of the masses." The very nature of collective agency in popular action escapes their grasp. Instead, their empirical-individualist method silently aligns them with the Hobbesian, part-royalist myth of the sovereignty of the state. For this Hobbesian individualism only "founds an alliance," to continue to cite Rancière, "between the point of view of science and that of the royal palace." Rancière has a name for the kind of empiricism that marks, say, the pioneering researches of Rudé. He calls it "royal-empiricism."[23] The practice does violence to the history of the subject or the nature of agency involved in the performance of collective acts. Historians, however, often follow the methodological leads of their sources. They attempt to reach the collective world of the peasant or the urban poor through documents that have already performed a methodological violence by making individuals speak to acts performed by a collective.

It is this path that Guha refused to take in his analysis of peasant violence. Guha's refusal gives us a beginning as to how we might think about "mass" subjects of democracies such as the Indian one where the street, as already stated, is as much an arena of politics as the parliament is. Riots, public violence, looting, burning, destroying are all practices that are as much a part of democracy in India as are elections, debates, and changing forms of law-making bodies. There are collective subjects of these mass-political acts of public life. If we think, from some normative position, that public violence is a sign of "backwardness" of Indian democracy—a phase that "more mature," Western democracies have already been through—we reinvent the historicist time of the "not yet." At the same time, we cannot any longer afford to romanticize this subject as "revolutionary." The crowd venting its desires and anger on the streets of Calcutta or Bombay is not world-historical in its implications, not at least in the way Hegel or Marx would have used the expression "world-historical." Yet it exists; it is contemporaneous and interactive with other constitutions of subjecthood or agency in Indian democracy. It is also ever-changing: ethnographic accounts of collective violence in South Asia mark significant transformations over time. Indeed, something that was said repeatedly during the recent violence against Muslims in Gujarat was that these riots were different from what India had seen before. Yet the received social-science disciplines do not give us ready-made means with which to write histories of these mass-political subjects. Guha was the first historian who raised this question by his methodological insistence that peasant insurgency needed to be studied as a form of modern politics. His own vision of this modernity was still too tied to the idea of "a comprehensive reversal" of the relationships of domination that made up Indian society—a familiar socialist vision—but now that we know that the mass-subjects of Indian democracy, once nurtured into being by romantic-populist aspects of nationalism, will not necessarily traverse paths already charted in Western political theory, *Subaltern Studies* can be thought of as an initial attempt to create for the modern practices of public and collective violence in India; a long and deep past that also challenges the conventions of the discipline of history. The mass-political subject of democracy has a history; *Subaltern Studies*, one might say, is part of its genealogy.

III. STAYING ON THE CUSP

It is now necessary to return to Hayden White's proposal about the "middle voice" and his point about the sublime nature of historical process and to connect it to genealogies of democracy. The middle voice, as already discussed, was about historians attempting to avoid the subject-object dichotomy that is usual to historical realism. The idea of the sublime, in White, corresponded to the notion that historical processes, because of their innate disorderliness, always retained a degree of incomprehensibility. How do these ideas help in writing subaltern history or in thinking about the problems of writing that subaltern histories pose? The conclusion can only be indicative rather than completely demonstrative, for Hayden White's challenge, as Ankersmit noted, is yet to be taken up by historians. But the work of my colleague, Shahid Amin, in *Subaltern Studies*, shows how subaltern history does indeed provide us with moments that are amenable to White's thoughtful and creative suggestions.

Shahid Amin's acclaimed book *Event, Metaphor, Memory: Chauri Chaura 1922–1992* studies peasant nationalism both under British rule and under the postcolonial government.[24] Amin remains sensitive throughout to the problems of translation—in both literal and metaphorical senses—that peasant speech invites him to the foreground. The English word "volunteer" had metamorphosed, in the speech of these peasant followers of Gandhi, into the somewhat lexically meaningless word "otiyar." Amin begins his discussion by noting the connection between the two words but soon goes on to demonstrate how "otiyar" could not be assimilated into the word "volunteer," and how this was a nugget of local speech and imagination that was best left untranslated. The word "otiyar," Amin shows, was over-determined by too many signs to be available for easy, sociological analysis.[25] In other words, the word *otiyar* was the product of collective social imaginings. The agent of that imagination would have to be a collective. Naujadi; the peasant woman who is the main protagonist of Amin's story, mentions names of individuals who were present at the time of nationalist action—"[Sharfuddin] was there; Nazar Ali was there, Salamat-father-in-law was there; Nageshar my *devar* (husband's younger brother) was there; Rameshar was there."[26] But it is clear that in naming individuals, she is not individuating them, she does not intend to fill out their biographies. Individual names are invoked to mark the presence of a collective agency just as common parlance references "uncle so-and-so" or "aunt so-and-so" simply to mark the points of connection in the collectivity that is kinship. The point, in subaltern history, is precisely not to render these names into the carriers of biographical individuality.

Similarly, when working on factory inspectors' reports on the jute mills of Calcutta in the early part of the twentieth century, complaints were made on the part of the inspectors, often European, that workers would "clamor" as a matter of habit instead of speak, and they would have to instruct the laborers to speak one by one. It was, of course, the clamor that was the speech of a collective agent though in my research then I generally missed the cue as did the inspectors themselves.

These are moments when both the partial incomprehensibility of the historical process and the need to adopt a "middle voice" become visible. Here Amin's instinct for not leaving chunks of peasant prose untranslated was right. This prose was necessarily collective (otherwise it would be a sign of pathology). These untranslatable words made sense in their own context of evolution. The historian, faced with these instances, is caught between the objectifying impulse of the discipline and the hermeneutic desire to go native. Hayden White's call for recognition of the "sublime" nature of the historical process and for the narrative deployment of the "middle voice" shows us a way of staying on the cusp. Indeed, if my argument is right, than it is only by staying on this cusp—that is, by refusing to either objectify or to go native—that we can work toward producing methods for studying the genealogy of the "mass-political" subjects of Indian (and other) democracies.

NOTES

1. Hayden White, "The Politics of Historical Interpretation: Discipline and De-Sublimation," *The Content of the Form: Narrative Discourse and Historical Representation* (Baltimore: Johns Hopkins University Press, 1997), 72.
2. F. R. Ankersmit, "Hayden White's Appeal to Historians," *Historical Representation* (Palo Alto, CA: Stanford University Press, 2001), 256.
3. White, 1997, 70–71.
4. White, 1997, 72.
5. Hayden White, "Historical Employment and the Problem of Truth," *Probing the Limits of Representation: Nazism and the Final Solution*, ed. Saul Friedlander (Cambridge: Harvard University Press, 1992), 48. See also page 52. An angry denunciation of White's position is elaborated in Carlo Ginzburg's essay "Just One Witness" in the same volume, 83–96. Martin Jay's essay ("Of Plots, Witnesses, and Judgments," 97–107) attempts to produce a middle ground between White and Ginzburg if not the "middle voice."
6. See E. P. Thompson, *Whigs and Hunters: The Origin of the Black Act* (New York: Pantheon Books, 1975).
7. I discuss this in some detail in my essay "A Small History of *Subaltern Studies*" chapter 1 in my *Habitations of Modernity: Essays in the Wake of Subaltern Studies* (Chicago: University of Chicago Press, 2002), 1.
8. See the discussion in the Introduction to my book *Provincializing Europe: Postcolonial Thought and Historical Difference* (Princeton, NJ: Princeton University Press, 2000).
9. See Chakrabarty (2000) "Introduction" for details.
10. See Gyanendra Pandey's essay on the topic in Ranajit Guha and Gayatri Chakravorty Spivak, eds., *Selected Subaltern Studies* (New York: Oxford University Press, 1988).
11. Francesca Orsini, "The Hindi Public Sphere and Political Discourse in the Twentieth Century," unpublished paper presented at a conference on "The Sites of the Political in South Asia," Berlin, October 2003.
12. Ibid.

13. For an excellent discussion of this point, see Andrzej Walicki, *The Controversy Over Capitalism: Studies in the Social Philosophy of the Russian Populists* (Notre Dame, IN: University of Notre Dame Press, 1989), chapters 1 and 2, in particular the section "The Privilege of Backwardness."

14. Cited in Orsini, "The Hindi Public Sphere."

15. Ranajit Guha, *Elementary Aspects of Peasant Insurgency in Colonial India* (Delhi: Oxford University Press, 1983), chapter 1.

16. Shahid Amin, "De-Ghettoising the Histories of the non-West," Gyan Prakash, "The Location of Scholarship," and my "Globalization, Democracy, and the Evacuation of History?" in *At Home in Diaspora: South Asian Scholars and the West*, eds. Jackie Assayag and Veronique Benei (Bloomington: Indiana University Press, 2003).

17. David Macey, *Frantz Fanon: A Biography* (New York: Picador, 2000), 177.

18. Frantz Fanon, *The Wretched of the Earth*, trans. Constance Farrington (New York: Grove Press, 1963), 40.

19. Michael Hardt and Antonio Negri, *Empire* (Cambridge: Harvard University Press, 2000), part 4.

20. This may be seen as operating throughout the text of *Elementary Aspects*.

21. Carlo Ginzburg's work is very instructive on this point. See his essay, "The Inquisitor as Anthropologist" in *Clues, Myths, and the Historical Method*, trans. John and Anne C. Tedeschi (Baltimore: Johns Hopkins University Press, 1989), 156–64. See also Carlo Ginzburg, *The Night Battles Witchcraft and Agrarian Cults in the Sixteenth and Seventeenth Centuries*, trans. John and Anne Tedeschi (Baltimore: Johns Hopkins University Press, 1983).

22. Etienne Balibar, "Spinoza, the Anti-Orwell: The Fear of the Masses," in *Masses, Classes, Ideas: Studies on Politics and Philosophy Before and After Marx*, trans. James Swenson (New York: Routledge, 1994), 16. Emphasis added.

23. Jacques Rancière, *The Names of History: On the Poetic of Knowledge*, trans. Hassan Melehy (Minneapolis: University of Minnesota Press, 1994), 21–23.

24. Shahid Amin, *Event, Metaphor, Memory: Chauri Chaura 1922–1992* (Berkeley and New Delhi: University of California Press and Oxford University Press, 1995).

25. Amin says: "In Naujad's mind, chutki [a pinch of grain], bhik [alms], and gerua [ochre] clothes together distinguished the otiyars of Chauri Chaura," 176.

26. Ibid., 175–76.

Chapter Eleven

Double Consciousness and the Democratic Ideal

Emmanuel C. Eze

This chapter situates the *origins* of identity concepts, "double consciousness," "postcolonial ambivalence," and "moderate Muslim," in their historical contexts of modern racial slavery, imperialism, and postcolonialism (Section 1. My historical references are to the history of the British Empire and colonialism in the Americas, India, and Africa[1]). Then I examine the *present* social and political implications of identities characterized by these psychological concepts whose historical origins, I hope, would become clearer (Section 2). Finally, I ask how the identities so characterized may or may not be compatible with key forms of democratic ideas in current liberal social and political theories (Section 3).

I. EMPIRE AND COLONIALISM

In 1615 the British Isles had been an economically unremarkable, politically fractious and strategically second-class entity. Two hundred years later the Great Britain had acquired the largest empire the world had ever seen, encompassing forty-three colonies in five continents. The title of Patrick Colquhoun's *Treatise on the Wealth, Power and Resources of the British Empire in Every Quarter of the Globe* (1814) said it all. They had robbed the Spaniards, copied the Dutch, beaten the French and plundered the Indians. Now they ruled supreme. Was all this done "in a fit of absence of mind"? Plainly not. From the reign of Elizabeth I onwards, there had been a sustained campaign to take over the empires of others. Yet commerce and conquest by themselves would not have sufficed to achieve this, no matter what the strengths of British financial and naval power. *There had also to be colonization.*[2]

Colonialism has led to racism, racial discrimination, xenophobia and related intolerance, and . . . Africans and peoples of African descent, and people of Asian descent and indigenous peoples were victims of colonialism and continue to be victims of its consequences.[3]

In 1789, Gholam Hossein Khan, the Indian author of *Seir Mutaqherin: Or Review of Modern Times*, made some observations about British colonialism in the pages of the same work. The British colonizers of India, he wrote, have "a custom of coming for a number of years, and then going away to pay a visit to their native country." This apparently innocent habit of frequent return to the motherland was, however, coupled with a more troubling phenomenon. To the custom of home leaves, Khan noted, the British joined "that other one of theirs, which every one of those emigrants holds to be of Divine obligation, I mean, that of scrapping together as much money in this country as they can, and carrying it in immense sums to the kingdom of England." The consequences of these two habits, Khan lamented, were seriously threatening the health of Indian economy and the stability of the social fabric. Working together, both habits were "undermining and ruining this country." In the decade he was writing, Khan calculated that no less than nineteen million British pounds were transferred from India to Britain.[4]

Recent research has found evidence to corroborate Khan's claims about the economic and social impact of the British colonial presence in India. In fact, accounts by contemporary historians confirm what Khan feared would come to pass—in terms of the colonial drain on Indian economy, and the resulting "ruin" of the local population. Ferguson, for example, believes that British colonialists did not merely repatriate wealth from India; the colonial enterprise necessitated two other kinds of political and economic underdevelopments that would lead directly to greater hardships for Indians and, combined with frequent famines, to the depopulation of the native inhabitants of the country. In addition to carting money and other resources out of India, the colonialist had to tax Indians in order to raise and maintain a colonial army. Indians, in this sense, had to pay taxes to fund the conquest of their own country—and the sum required in tax was quite substantial.

"In India," writes Ferguson, "the impact of British taxes was even greater [than the cost of repatriated money], for the spiraling cost of the Indian Army was the one item of imperial expenditure the British taxpayer never had to pay." It is also observed that, "Disastrously, the ratcheting up of taxes in Bengal coincided with a huge famine, which killed as many as a third of the population of Bengal—some five million people."[5] Khan, it seems, saw a clear connection not only between "the vast exportation of coin which is carried away every year to the country of England," but also the impact of this capital flight on the Indians left to pay huge taxes from earnings in an economy thus already internationally undermined by capital flight. "The decrease of products in each District," Khan wrote, "added to the innumerable multitudes swept away by famine and mortality go on augmenting the depopulation of the country."[6] The impact of the colonial presence was yet severe because even when the British population spent their money in India, they preferred to spend on goods imported from Britain, leading to further depression of local industries. "As the English are now the rulers and the masters of this country, as well as the only rich men," Khan wryly noted, "to whom can those poor people look up to for offering the productions of their art, so as to benefit by their expenses?"[7]

British colonialism in Nigeria during the 1800s suggests that the Indian experience conformed to a general pattern in the British colonial processes. Frederick Lugard—later Lord Lugard—was one of the architects and practitioners of the British colonization in West and East Africa. In his important work, the *Dual Mandate*, a book which is both a handbook and theoretical justification of colonization, Lugard explained: "Let it be admitted that European brains, capital, and energy have not, and never will be, expended in developing the resources of Africa from motives of pure philanthropy." England, he argued, "is in Africa for the mutual benefit of her own industrial class, and of the native *races* in their progress to a higher plane." In this gap—the racial gap assumed between Africans and the economic interests of Europe, and in an emergent transatlantic capitalism exhibited by the rapid rise in Britain's industrial and material needs—lies what we could call a universal colonial compact. The compact, implicitly or explicitly, says: We will bring to the inferior races the true religion (ours, Christianity), the true culture (ours, Anglicism), and the true civilization (ours, the Western). In return for these goods coming from a "higher" racial plane, however, we will take the land by force; use the colonized as paid or unpaid, forced or voluntary labor; and we will tax them to establish a colonial army, the lower ranks of whom are to be raised from among the colonized, and this army will ensure that none of the natives' chiefs, priests, or kings could successfully reject the colonial contract.

In the Americas, the Caribbean, Africa, and India the racial element in the colonial project was not much different—because the colonialist considered himself a member of a superior race apart. The first major armed anti-colonial revolt in Jamaica, where the ruling class was exclusively white, was racially motivated, and occurred in October of 1865. The seeds of one of the earliest major confrontations between colonial settlers and native Indians, mainly Bengalis, were sown between 1872 and 1883, and had racial overtones. During this period the official policy was that, though both British and Indian magistrates could share the same rank in the civil service structure and had graduated from the same British-based system of training, an Indian judge could try no white settler, on account of the settlers' claim to racial privilege. A typical argument in defense of this policy was that "The education which the government has given them [Indian magistrates] . . . they use chiefly to taunt it in a discontented spirit. . . . And these men . . . now cry out for power to sit in judgment on, and condemn the lion-hearted *race* whose bravery and whose blood have made their country what it is, and raised them to what they are."[8] The origin of the formation of the Indian National Congress, in fact the birth of the Indian nationalism as such, has been traced to the practices of legal racial inequality by the settlers in law and in many other aspects of economic, social, and political life.

It would indeed be impossible to comprehend colonialism or anti-colonialism without the racial factors—the claim by the colonizer that he belongs to a "higher" order of racial moral existence, while the colonized is supposed to be a willing or unwilling subject, at the "lower" end of the same racial order. The traces of elements of this racial morality, assumed by the colonizer as universal, can be found in many colonial practices. For example, the earliest English term for colonization was "plantation" because, according to Sir John Davies, the settlers in the colonial territories thought of themselves, and were regarded by their home governments, as "good corn" in the midst of native "weeds." The colonial territory was thus a realm of contrast: Life versus Death, Good versus Evil, etc., and, in the ensuing conflicts, skin color was often taken as the clearest marker of who belonged to which category. "Plantation," as V. Y. Mudimbe also remarked, suggests a normative space: gardening, cultivation, and settled life—as opposed to the wild.[9] From such a colonial normative perspective, one could better understand the more direct characterization of the intent to colonize such as this: "In theory," Ferguson writes, a plantation would have been "just another word for colonization, the ancient Greek practice of establishing settlements of loyal subjects out on the political margins"; but the reality is otherwise: modern European colonialism understood as plantation "meant what today is known as 'ethnic cleansing.'"[10] The native populations, now considered bad "weeds," are to be cleared away to make room for the settlers, the good "crops" overflowing from a Europe in need of expansion. The implication is that the native territories—India, Africa, the Caribbean, and the Americas—were thought of as virgin, uncultivated, lands waiting—asking—for Europe to colonize it. From this and a similar universe of moral discourse, the concept of *terra nulla* was put into circulation. Popes and Emperors declared stretches of earth they could not have visited as no-man's-land, and granted, by Bulls and Concessions, absolute rights over the lands and the peoples to adventurers, pirates, and speculators.

The fruits reaped by European powers from "plantations" in the Americas, Africa, Asia, and the Pacific were immense. Khan's study of India and the impoverishment of its population was just one example. About Africa, Lugard claimed—in words that anticipated Hannah Arendt's lucid analysis of colonialism as "alliance between mob and capital"—that "when the economic pressure caused by the rapidly increasing population of Europe began to exert inevitable influence, in driving men to seek for new markets and fresh supplies of food and raw material," it was the exploitations of Africa, America, and India that "met the demand for several centuries." Lugard noted that the imperial conquest of the ocean "directly led to the expansion of the peoples of Europe." While Khan calculated the colonial profits by its inverse effect of "ruining" India's economy and the population, Lugard calculated the benefits of colonialism by the speed of growth of the white population in Europe—an index of prosperity that is not surprising when considering that economists like Thomas Malthus were predicting a universal catastrophe to result from global overpopulation and scarcity. Contrary to the Malthusian predictions, Lugard notes that following 1492, when Columbus reached America, and 1494, when Vasco da Gama rounded the African Cape, the relief offered to Europe by the colonial settlements was near miraculous. "In the fifteenth century," he wrote,

> the population of Europe was about 70 million. At the end of the next three centuries it is said to have been 150 million, and additional 10 millions having migrated overseas. But [at] the close of the succeeding century—which witnessed the industrial revolution, and the advent of the steam navigation—it is estimated at nearly 450 millions, with 100 millions additional emigrants. Thus, while the population of Europe only doubled itself in the three centuries prior to 1800, it more than trebled itself in the following century.

Lugard indicates that for Britain alone, the population in 1600 was 4,800,000, in 1800 about 16,000,000, and in 1900 about 42,000,000.[11]

It would seem that Thomas Malthus has indeed been proven wrong, but this would be the case only if we ignored the true meaning of the processes of colonization as a form of "plantation." How many ethnic groups were "cleansed" in order to make room for the colonial European expansion? Lugard's nineteenth-century calculation conforms quite closely with figures advanced by today's historians. In 2003, Ferguson calculated that between the early 1600s and the 1950s, "more than 20 million people left the British Isles to begin new lives across the seas," and "only a minority ever returned."[12] How many of the colonized peoples' resources (material and symbolic) had to be "repatriated"—(as Khan complained in the case of India) or, in an arrangement Lugard euphemistically called mutually beneficial "commerce"— in order to nourish Europe's exploding population and the insatiable capitalist engines of its Industrial Revolution?

Race, Capitalist Slavery, and the Colonial Project

Colonialism as a mode of imperial expansion was part of a larger historical process—it contributed to Europe's self-fashioning into a force of global capitalist modernity. The brutality of this modern economic process is nowhere as evident as in the institution of transatlantic slavery. The antiquities in all societies—from the Athenian through the Ashanti to the Roman—seem to have known slavery in some form: indentured servitude, religious caste systems, or other forms of extreme class division within a society that renders a particular section of population exploitable, with or without rights of citizenship. But scholars of slavery agree that there was something unique and unrepeatable about *modern, transatlantic, and racial* African slavery. For the first time in human history the enslaver did not call the enslaved "dog" or "beast" merely metaphorically. On account of skin color, it was presumed that Africans were a "race unlike any other"—a race whose enslavement, regardless of class or caste, was considered "scientifically" valid. From high theorists of colonization (e.g., Hegel, Hume, etc.) to the direct beneficiaries of the institution (e.g., British Jamaican and American "planters," such as John Long and Samuel Cartwright) modern European intellectuals, on the basis of a strange influence of an Old Testament myth about a Ham cursed by God, believed that they have found a natural and legitimate "article of trade" in the person of the "black" African.

In addition to the economic, religious, and cultural reasons to colonize, dispossess, and "civilize," other nations, it was the theory of racial difference that most served as justification for transatlantic slavery. John Newton, the composer of the perennial religious hymn "Amazing Grace" became a successful slave trader *after* his conversion to evangelical and missionary Christianity, sailing across the Atlantic to import captured Africans for sale throughout the Americas. In a letter of 26 January 1753 to his wife, a letter composed during one of his voyages with his African "cargo," he mused:

> The three greatest blessings of which human nature is capable, are, undoubtedly, religion, liberty, and love. In each of these how highly has God distinguished me! But here are whole nations around me, whose languages are entirely different from each other, yet I believe they all agree in this, that they have no words among them expressive of these engaging ideas: from whence I infer, that the ideas themselves have no place in their minds. And as there is no medium between light and darkness, these poor creatures are not only strangers to the advantages which I enjoy but are plunged in all the contrary evils.[13]

As Newton considered himself to be a "fine" self-whitened, good, loving, and intellectual Christian, the force of arms and enslavement of his blackened, demonized, and chained Africans seemed not only possible but also naturally ordained by Nature and by God Himself.[14]

But the fact that the "nature" of the African became the basis of the arguments for and against slave trade implicitly reflects the success those in power (with vested trade interests) enjoyed in shaping public opinion. The highly charged racist terms backing arguments for slave trade furthermore only added fuel to the fire that was advancing the territorial colonization of the African continent (the Berlin Conference of 1884, at which competing European empires carved up Africa among themselves or their commercial proxies, is an example of the righteousness that surrounded this colonial process). The slave trade therefore indirectly influenced and powerfully fueled colonization. Because of the arguments of the slave traders, Europe's empires and colonialists were able to present themselves and their "plantation" projects as the best legitimate alternative to slave trade. They were colonizing Africa, the imperialists argued, not for reasons of conquest but rather to develop more legitimate commerce. In fact, the intellectual architects of colonization like Livingstone and Lugard found it easier to argue that they were in Africa for the mutual benefit of the colonizer (the higher race) and the colonized (the lower race) precisely *because* of the extreme phenomenon of transatlantic slave trade: it was assumed that, because of race and the difference race ought to make, the colonization of Africa by Europe must be an enterprise whose "benefit . . . can be made reciprocal." But the extent to which this reciprocity was realized is called into question when observing that while the economy of England and the rest of Europe grew, that of India, Africa, and the First American peoples declined or, in many cases, entirely collapsed; while Europeans multiplied and settled America, Africa, and the Pacific, the indigenous populations of these places were catastrophically declining and, in some cases, entirely wiped out—they were ethnically and genetically cleansed by famine, disease, arms, the cultural forces of evangelism or the racist practices of "white" cultures.

The processes of empire—slavery, colonization, and racial supremacy—were thus an outcome of gradual processes, but processes whose intents and points of acceleration could be easily marked. In the 1680s, writers were able to distinguish between England and, quite narrowly, the "the British Empire in America." As late as 1743, it had still been possible to speak, with clear geographical delimitations in mind, of "the British Empire, taking together as one body, viz. Great Britain, Ireland, the Plantations and Fishery in America, besides its Possessions in the East Indies and Africa." But by 1762, it became possible to think, indistinctly, as Sir George Macartney had, about "this vast empire on which the sun never sets and whose bounds nature has not yet ascertained."[15]

The consequences of these modern colonial processes spread across the globe, and as the 2001 Durban Declaration makes clear, are still very much with us.[16] Furthermore, the hypocritical nature of the "reasons" given for imperialism and colonization are obvious—even to those who produced them. An early "hero" of African colonization, David Livingstone, on 14 May 1858 (a short while before his departure for a second time as missionary and explorer to Africa, and having just delivered a rousing lecture to students at Cambridge University urging the graduates to join him in the endeavor[17]), wrote in a letter to a confidant:

> I take a practical mining geologist from the School of Mines to tell us of the Mineral Resources of the country [Richard Thorton], then an economic botanist [Dr. John Kirk] to give a full report on the vegetable productions—fibrous, gummy and medicinal substances together with the dye stuffs—everything which may be useful in commerce. An artist [Thomas Baines] to give the scenery, a naval officer [Commander Norman Bedingfeld] to tell of the capacity of the river communications, and a moral agent to lay the foundation for knowing the aim [his brother Charles, a Congressional minister]. All this machinery has for its ostensible object the development of African trade and the promotion of civilization but what I have to tell to none but such as you in whom I have full confidence is that I hope it may result in an English colony in the healthy highlands of Central Africa.[18]

Most highlands of Central Africa, including the head of the Zambezi River surveyed by Livingstone and his team, proved, in fact, unsuitable for any successful planting of an English colony. But the intent was clear, and failure to achieve the intention in this case could be characterized as an exception rather than the rule.

II. THE POSTCOLONIAL PRESENT: THE EMPIRE STRIKES BACK

Some historians pretend to be at a loss when asked about the forces that led to the demise of the slave trade and, eventually, the colonialism which justified itself in part by claiming to be a "legitimate" and morally worthy alternative to slave trading. Others accurately point out the failures of the earliest colonial projects to convert Africans to the Christian religion. From daily diaries of missionaries, colonial anthropological studies, and anti-colonial writings, evidence suggests fierce cultural resistance on behalf of natives to all forms of conquest and colonization. The complaints Livingstone confided to his diaries during his first mission to Africa were typical. After seven years of preaching the Gospel in Southern Africa, and after having learned the Bakwena language, Livingstone appears to have made only one convert—and a backsliding one at that. The neophyte, Chief Sechele, according to Livingstone's complaints, goes straight from the church back into his hut "to drink beer." Maintaining his evangelical optimism, however, Livingstone thought: "A minister who has not seen as much pioneer service as I have done would have been shocked to have seen so little effect produced by an earnest discourse concerning the future Judgment." But situations rapidly deteriorated. The chief soon enough completely lapsed, beyond beer drinking, to polygamy.

In *Things Fall Apart,* a novel in which the dominant theme is the British colonial penetration of Eastern Nigeria, Chinua Achebe conveys a story about a dialogue between Christian evangelists and their potential converts.

> When they had all gathered, the white man began to speak to them. He spoke through an interpreter who was an Ibo man, though his dialect was different. . . . Many people laughed at his dialect and the way he used words strangely. Instead of saying "myself" he always said "my buttocks." . . . And he told them about this new God, the Creator of all the world and all the men and women. . . .
> At this point an old man said he had a question . . .
> "If we leave our gods and follow your god . . . who will protect us from the anger of our neglected gods and ancestors?"
> "Your gods are not alive and cannot do you any harm," replied the white man. "They are pieces of wood and stone."
> When this was interpreted to the men of Mbanta, they broke into derisive laughter.
>
> [T]he interpreter spoke about the Son of God whose name was Jesu Kristi. Okonkwo, who only stayed in the hope that it might come to chasing the men out of the village or whipping them, now said:
> "You told us with your own mouth that there was only one god. Now you talk about his son. He must have a wife, then." The crowd agreed.
> "I did not say He had a wife," said the interpreter, somewhat lamely.
> "Your buttocks said he had a son," said the joker. "So he must have a wife and all of them must have buttocks."
> The missionary ignored him and went on to talk about the Holy Trinity. At the end of it Okonkwo was fully convinced that the man was mad. He shrugged his shoulders and went away to tap his afternoon palm-wine.[19]

The interaction between evangelical Christians and native Africans is therefore depicted rather playfully in *Things Fall Apart.* But other postcolonial African writers have imagined more graphic responses coming from targeted population who have suffered from the irrationality and violence of colonial evangelization.

By all accounts, Africa remained unconvertible to Christianity until well into the late 19th century. This is a fact difficult for many to imagine, given the number of Christians in Africa today (for example, there are currently more Anglican Christians in Nigeria than in England itself). But modern colonial Christianity got its foothold in Africa only *after* Europeans had shifted the strategies of colonization from "commerce"—both legitimate and illegitimate—to military conquest. Once the larger political economy has been forcefully reoriented into a global framework that dislocated the Indian or African economies in favor of the British, it was easy for the natives to grasp how they could achieve economic and social upward mobility: to participate in "Progress" one had to be educated in the colonial systems. But without exception, the colonial formal education systems were founded or staffed by missionaries or agents of colonial governments, and Baptism into the proper Christian faith was a strict requirement for admission.[20]

The earliest documented anti-colonial revolt in India—a mutiny of Sikh and Muslim soldiers against their British officers—was a result of rumors about the colonial interests of the British to convert Sikhs and Muslims to Christianity. When rumors circulated that the British officers had deliberately oiled bullets issued to the army with fat from cows and pigs, Sikhs and Muslims in the military considered this proof that the British wanted not only commerce and government, money and power, but also to suppress Indian religions and cultural traditions. When the soldiers refused to accept the bullets so believed to have been contaminated by unholy grease, and faced with court-marshal, they struck out, massacring a good number of the British officers and their dependents. The reprisal was swift and gruesome. But the point is noteworthy: the first shot fired in anti-colonial resistance in India was not in defense of land or state but of religion and culture. After the mayhem, the official colonial policy changed. Colonial administrators were henceforth instructed to avoid "interfering" with Indian religion and traditions, and missionaries to India were required to have a license from the Colonial Secretary's office, with strict restrictions on open evangelization.

What led to the demise of the transatlantic African slave trade was equally complex. While some historians believe that there was "an astonishing volte face" in moral sensibility in England (a moral switch, it is said, "flicked in the British psychic"), others recognize that the power of such moral flicker was less than the full story. "What was going on to turn Britain from the world's leading enslaver to the world's leading emancipator"[21] included a widespread evangelical religious awakening: the missionary movement was a powerful political lobby in Parliament which truly believed that colonization should be designated to the spread of Christianity, Commerce, and Civilization, not inhuman practices of trade to fellow humans, no matter the skin color. The Gospel makes no distinction between Jew and Gentile—categorizing all brothers as equal in the Lord. Evangelical Quakers, Methodists, and Unitarians therefore constituted a formidable abolitionist movement. Their movement, headquartered at the Holy Trinity Church in Clapham, London, tirelessly organized campaigns across the country, gathering millions of signatures on numerous anti–slave trade petitions to the Parliament. A medal designed by the Unitarian Josiah Wedgewood, depicting a black man in chains, with surrounding letters "I am not a Man and a Brother?" became one of the most potent symbols of anti-slavery ever invented.

But there were other forces operating to the advantage of the abolitionists, namely, the business motive. Prominent British economists, most of them secularist liberals, had warned that, on strictly economic terms, slavery was uncompetitive and, in the long run, less profitable than trade in free labor. Adam Smith, for example, was one of those who advanced what must have seemed to be the counterintuitive but scientific argument that free trade in free labor "comes cheaper in the end" than forced, uncompensated, slave labor. Other Enlightenment thinkers, who also saw that the path to progress in industry was through mechanization of processes of production, regarded slavery as a backward-looking economic institution. Although they were by no means opposed to slave trade or slavery on the grounds of human rights as one might have expected, and despite the facts that some of them specifically harbored anti-black sentiments, most Enlightenment thinkers (including those who were personally or professionally invested in the institution of slavery) saw slavery as a form of labor that was woefully inefficient not only because it relied on the manual but also because it relied on the coercion of the unwilling. This acknowledgement came in large part due to enlightened thinkers' understanding of science and technology and belief in the economic and social progress such advancements promised Europe. Both Adam Smith and Adam Ferguson believed that Britain could dominate its economic relations with what was a revolutionary United States if it relied on science and technology to modernize its home industries *and* made moves to discontinue the supply of African slaves being shipped to American plantations. Such a strategy would position Britain not just as the dominant economic power in Europe—e.g., vis-à-vis France and Holland, both of whose international transactions and colonial economies were also heavily dependent on slave trade and slave labor—but also throughout the world. To lead the modern world, the enlightened economists and investors argued, industries had to be mechanized at home; trade in humans needed to be replaced by the more legitimate trade in raw materials (palm oil, cocoa, coffee, gold, etc.) that would work to feed an industrial revolution; England would then reap the benefits of both economic prosperity and moral prestige, at home and abroad, that would come from abolishing the primitive practice of slave trading.

A curious combination of forces thus led the British Parliament to ban the slave trade in 1807 (slavery itself was banned throughout British territories in 1833). The Navy used to police the seas in enforcing the ban, against all countries. The Navy also played a major role in facilitating the return of freed slaves to a West African settlement, Freetown, in Liberia. As predicted by the economists, at the close of the eighteenth century, Britain had pulled "ahead of her rivals as a pioneer of new [industrial] technology." Its scientists and engineers were in the vanguard of a revolution that transformed the global economy through modernization. The Industrial Revolution was thus born in Britain, and it changed the world economy. Henceforth the largest flow of goods from Africa to Britain was no longer Africans themselves but raw industrial materials. In the wake of Britain's new economy, the rest of Europe and the American colonies were increasingly forced to recognize the primitive nature of slave labor, and to undertake massive re-tooling of their local economies if they were to remain internationally competitive in an increasingly mechanized, industrial, modern economy. Even some African monarchs, a few of whom had profited handsomely from slave trade, could see the writing on the wall—one of them, King Gezo, expressed his confusion: "The slave trade has been the ruling principle of my people. It is the source of their glory and wealth. Their songs celebrate their victories and the mother lulls the child to sleep with notes of triumph over an enemy reduced to slavery. Can I, by signing . . . a treaty, change the sentiments of a whole people?"[22]

The successes of the campaign against slave trade and of nineteenth-century Liberia convinced both abolitionists and anti-colonialists that freedom for slaves, and national independence for the colonized, were within reach. By the mid-twentieth century, anti-colonial agitation intensified across the British empire: from South Asia to North, East, West, and Central Africa decolonization was the trend in most European colonies that had a non-white majority. With the exception of South Africa and Zimbabwe, almost all of Africa was under majority rule by the end of the 1960s. Since then we have even witnessed what some—especially those determined to block it—have called "reverse colonization." Since the 1950s, it is estimated that more than a million people from all over Britain's former Empire have come as immigrants to Britain. The trend, though less pronounced, is the same in other post-imperial European countries. The empire, it seems, is "fighting back," and the new fight is generating wide sets of new issues: xenophobia, racism, and harsh immigration laws that sometimes prevent even genuine asylum seekers from gaining a foothold at the metropolitan centers of nations some of which are still, ironically, nostalgic for past imperial grandeur.[23]

III. RACE, NATION, AND AMBIVALENCE IN POSTCOLONIAL SUBJECTIVITY

W. E. B. Du Bois's doctoral dissertation was entitled "The Suppression of the African Slave-Trade to the United States of America, 1638 to 1870."[24] This scholarly work may be characterized as among the earliest academic attempts in the United States to establish reliable knowledge of the sources and nature of the Negro's existence in the country's "plantations." At the nation's independence from Britain, with the Declaration that "all men are created equal," it is curious that neither the First Americans nor the Africans were positively included in the Declaration. Opponents of the American Independence movement duly noted the irony, and relished it.[25] Du Bois's study was thus important because it not only studied this peculiar negative process of integration of Africa into the modern world but also the racism that informed the reasons produced to justify the trade and institution of slavery in the United States. Du Bois's statistics about slave trade, like others about the expansions of British empire in Africa and India, explain the economics of the institution of slave plantations in the United States, the racial consequences in terms of social and political depravations of African Americans, and the enduring frictions these conditions created between African Americans and the majority white population. Du Bois's observations about global and specific modalities of the racialized conditions are most famous, whether they come in lapidaries like *The problem of the twentieth century is the problem of the color line*, or in meticulous analysis of the post-Emancipation African American's existential identity crises in a self-whitened United States. If we keep in mind that the political economy rooted in plantation slavery remained intact within the United States after its independence declaration as well as after the abolition of slavery, it is not surprising that the arguments of slave traders and slave holders—arguments that contested the humanity of Africans—remained a default opinion in white attempts to later justify institutions of racial segregation and inequality that existed amid what was supposed to be a population of equal coexistence according to the words written in the Declaration of Independence.

By Du Bois's account, the history of the modernized African in the national union of the United States was, for too long and like that of the Native American, a history of an original, willful, exclusion—an exclusion based, in the case of the African American, upon capitalist economic depredation in the South, political opportunism in both the North and the South, and morally questionable ideologies of racialism. In Du Bois's work we learn that legal racial segregation in the United States was the earliest example of the *apartheid* that "white" colonialists throughout the European empires eventually adopted to keep majority "black" or "colored" populations in economic, political, and social bondage. In the beginning paragraphs of the first chapter of *The Souls of Black Folks*, for example, Du Bois observed:

> They approach me in a half-hesitant sort of way, eye me curiously or compassionately, and then, instead of saying directly, How does it feel to be a problem? They say, I know an excellent colored man in my town; or, I fought at Mechanicsville; or, Do not these Southern outrages make your blood boil? At these I smile, or am interested, or reduce the boiling to a simmer, as the occasion may require. To the real question, How does it feel to be a problem? I answer seldom a word.[26]

But Du Bois provides that word (or the African American response to the racial insinuations of white people) in *The Souls*, from his own biography and also from a historical sociology of the African American people.

Many commentators like to call Du Bois a "Race Man," but often forget to make clear that, like anti-imperialists and anti-colonialists anywhere (e.g., Gandhi, Césaire, Fanon, Senghor, or King), Du Bois was playing a racial hand that the architects of empire, colonialism, slavery, and white supremacy had dealt by developing the very *idea* of race. "Race," as theorists from Todorov to Mills remind us—and as we saw in Section 1, in the writings of British colonialists—was entirely a modern European idea; an invention driven by minority settler populations of European descent who needed terms in which their own claims to colonizer superiority (and thus the inferiority of the colonized) could be represented—either as a Divine ordinance or as a Natural fact. Du Bois, in *The Souls*, was clearly caught in the pseudometaphysics of history generated by white thinkers and worked to cement what should have been considered an established racial disorder. "After the Egyptian and Indian, the Greek and the Roman, the Teuton and the Mongolian," he ventured, "the Negro is a sort of seventh son, born with a veil, and gifted with second-sight." But none of the subsequent arguments of *The Souls* or his other writings (like "Conservation of Races," where he offered biological as well as historical arguments to justify the cosmic missions of each supposedly racial type) were able to convince a reader who did not already believe in the existence of races (as one might believe in a religion), that non-racialized modern processes could exist amid the ever racialization of human populations. Why, for example, should seven races exist when five, eight, twelve, twenty, or any other number of plausible divisions can just as easily be conceived?

The strength of *The Souls*, instead, lies elsewhere. In describing the African American as "second-sighted," Du Bois was providing an existential and psychological description that is instructive in understanding the psychological legacies of economic, political, and social policies of slavery and then racial segregation, in the colonial and postcolonial United States as in elsewhere. The racially blackened slave or the freed Negro in the whitened nation-spaces of the Americas, Du Bois recorded, comes to racial awareness of the self "through the revelation of the other world." This revelation, he explained,

> is a peculiar sensation, this double-consciousness, this sense of always looking at one's self through the eyes of others, of measuring one's soul by the tape of a world that looks on in amused contempt and pity. One ever feels his two-ness,—an American, a Negro; two souls, two thoughts, two unreconciled strivings; two warring ideals in one dark body, whose dogged strength alone keeps it from being torn asunder.[27]

Clearly, it is in the interface of the original pseudoscientific claim (about racial groups) and the ancillary claim (about the racial othering of the Negro) that there emerges, for Du Bois and in the idea "race," the possibility of a narrative of History as a Racial Cosmic Event; an event within which the African American is expected to define an appropriate subjectivity—a subjectivity we could, accordingly, refer to as a Racial Self.

IV. THE RACIAL SELF AS A REVOLUTIONARY POSTCOLONIAL SUBJECT

This last point—including the general criticism of Du Bois's philosophy of race—merits elaboration. Unlike previous criticism of Du Bois on this account, e.g., by Anthony Appiah (or, more accurately, how Appiah's earlier work on these issues might have held itself open to criticism), there are more careful distinctions to be made. Biology and anthropology reveal that there is no scientific truth that can factually explain the concept of "race." But, as mentioned in earlier discussion of the methods of imperialism, colonialism, and African slavery, racialism was founded on, and has successfully anchored itself in, modern societies and in history. It is worthwhile to recognize, as a judgment of the Supreme Court of United States recently has done in the process of mediating the claims and counter-claims about race-inflected policies of affirmative action in university admissions, that the histories of racialism in the United States as elsewhere, and their consequences in terms of access to higher education and other forms of economic and social class mobility, may be overcome within the twenty-first century.[28] This would work to further discredit arguments for racism that have perpetuated the behavior of empires such as Britain's in the past.

But is it not necessary to question the premise to Du Bois's criticism and ask what could be meant by discovering a "true" self-consciousness? If Du Bois's main complaint had been that the African American could not look at himself or herself unless through the eyes of self-whitened others, how else, we should ask, does anyone get to know oneself if not through the eyes of others? The truth, of course, was that Du Bois sought to theoretically articulate a psychology of the racialized black self—a blackness presumed by racists to be both physical and moral, but in truth born in the contexts of extreme inequality in economic, political, and social relations. The power of race in the colonial or slave-capitalist contexts is one that Du Bois—unlike Lugard who duplicitously dreamed about an imagined "uplift" of the "inferior" races by their very subjection—radically problematized and unrelentingly critiqued. Du Bois was troubled, not by the co-constitution of the races into an American nation; but rather (from the point of the view of those Frantz Fanon called the "wretched of the earth") by the racist terms of the national compact.

Du Bois saw the economic profits and the moral debauchery of both plantation slavery and colonialism as deforming a "historical self"—not only that of the slave or of the colonized but also that of the master and of the colonizer. Institutions of slavery and colonialism (establishments and processes that perpetuated racist legacies) he argued, could not yield acknowledgment of true self or national consciousness, not just to the slave or to the emancipated black but also to the white American who, in the context of the national Declaration of Independence, required such national consciousness. Instead, both the racialized self of the individual and of the nation are left with a "strange sensation" of "two-ness." The African does not wish to be whitened, nor does the American wish merely to be Africanized.[29] As far as Du Bois was concerned, one must forge a Higher Self: at once African and American. This ideal, Du Bois believed, was achievable. And as far as he could see, only one thing stood in the way, and so this was the key issue: Was the Negro a citizen or not? If yes, why was it that the Negro is "cursed and spat upon by his fellows," or "the doors of Opportunity closed roughly in his face?"

Background information about the terminology Du Bois uses to describe the problems of self and national integration may be helpful here. It is well established that Du Bois's earliest uses of the concept of "double consciousness" derived from a context of medical and moral pathology. The documentary evidence for this starts from his "Strivings of the Negro," an essay first published in the *Atlantic* magazine in 1897 but reproduced as the first chapter of the *Souls* in a slightly modified title, "Of Our Spiritual Strivings." In the decade in which the magazine essay was published, as in fact throughout much of the nineteenth century in the United States, "double consciousness" was a term found only in medical journals. It originally referred to what was regarded by the medical establishment of the time as a "Negro Disease" or *Drapetomania*. According to the physician Samuel Adolphus Cartwright who discovered the illness as an epidemic among African-American slave populations in the southern parts of the United States, drapetomania was a mental illness defined by "an irrestrainable propensity to run away."[30] The slaves who ran away were not thus motivated by a love of liberty, but rather patients whose weakness of mind for liberty was to be medically—in fact, surgically—cured. Gradually, however, drapetomania seeped into general psychological and moral literature. Double consciousness was loosely extended from stricter medical contexts and poetically deployed to describe numerous afflictions suggesting incapacity for absolute self-dedication not just to an institution (e.g., the economy of slavery) but also to many other questionable regimes of social and political control that were in place during the nineteenth century.

In his uses of "double consciousness" Du Bois, certainly, was aware of its history. He intended to communicate the pain of self-redemption and the moral tragedy of the psychology of a self so divided from within. But he was lucid enough to attribute these painful and moral conditions not to any natural disposition in the black slave in the Americas or in the colonized on the African continent. They were the institutions of slavery and colonization, Du Bois argued, that produced the psychological and moral—and in the United States during his lifetime, increasingly, national—split personality that afflicted both individual and country. Redemption lay in the moral and heroic pursuit of a Higher Self, just as the Negro does, a pursuit that can begin for the nation only when the injustices of slavery, colonization, and ideologies of racial supremacy and their legacies have been recognized and dismantled.

The central problem of double consciousness, for Du Bois, therefore became a kind of historical suffering with a metaphysical relevance to quest for liberty and national integrity. The Negro, rather than being a mere victim, becomes a revolutionary subject—a person with a "second sight," a sight that alone could see or bear witness to the truth of a hidden meaning of History. The Negro in America or in the colonial contexts acquired for Du Bois a historical *mission* not just in the Americas or Africa but also to the rest of the world. This mission, first, was to discover and make explicit the gift to the world that only the second-sighted could bring—the gift itself being fruits of wisdom from suffering, survival, and hope. Like the Indians, the Mongolians, the Teutons, etc., the Negro is called in his and her suffering by History to deliver the race's specific racial genius; it is through the struggle in racial double-consciousness that the Negro achieves an original, universal compact with Providence. The famous Creed prefacing Du Bois's *Dark Water* captures these sentiments:

> I believe in God, who made of one blood all the nations that each on earth dwell.... I believe in the Negro Race: in the beauty of its genius, the sweetness of its soul, and the strength in that meekness which shall inherit this turbulent earth ... I believe in Service—the humble, reverent service, from the blackenings of boots to the whitening of souls; for the Work is Heaven, Idleness Hell, and Wage is the "Well done!" of the Master, who summoned all of them that labor and are heavy laden.... I believe in the Prince of Peace. I believe that War is Murder ... I believe in the Training of Children, black even as white.... Finally I believe in patience, ... patience with God![31]

Some metaphors from Hegel might allow one to see that Du Bois dialectically came to a trans-racial answer to the racial (or racist) questions that modern European colonialism and slavery in the United States had posed. Like Senghor in Africa, Du Bois nursed the idea that in the cauldron of African colonialism and American slavery lay the seeds of emergence of a truly universal liberation of the self—of the colonizer as of the colonized—from Nature. It was therefore in the pursuit of moral greatness for all races that Du Bois, as Senghor thought, lay the conditions of freedom and integrity for the colonized, as well as for the colonizing cultures and civilization.

V. POSTCOLONIAL AMBIVALENCE, DOUBLE CONSCIOUSNESS, AND THE DEMOCRATIC IDEAL

In theory, there is a more nuanced—more, radical—stand than Du Bois assumed on the questions of race, nation, and the self. For purposes of contrast, Du Bois's solution to the problems of double consciousness can be called *heroic and romantic*. This designation is apt because Du Bois's discourse on the quest for an African American self is transcendentalist, with religious echoes. In this regard Du Boisian psychology is Platonistic and Cartesian. For this tradition, a divided soul calls for heroic ("whose dogged strength alone keeps it from being torn asunder"), mythical ("I believe in God"; "I believe the Negro Race"; etc.), and ambivalently, ambiguously ("patience, . . . patience with God") historical transcendent acts of reconciliation. But, first, it is equally obvious that for Du Bois: history, even of race and ethnicity, remained a requirement for any such talk of self or social transcendence and reconciliation. Second, the meta-language of such struggle of the soul will no longer be the exclusive domain of medicine or psychology, or even of pedestrian social morality and abstract, literary, tragedy. The "soul," for Du Bois, became also material of a quest for a historical racial authenticity and social justice. The quest for Unity of Self is, in this regard, in parallel to the larger quest for a historical, universal, Union of the Races.

The various theoretical strengths of this heroic and romantic stand are obvious, and one more can also be highlighted. Du Bois, operating from a social scientific framework, watered down the concept of self usually entirely dependent on religion, and submitted the theological notion, as well as Cartwright's most extravagantly ideological medical schema, to a severe historical test. For example, in "W. E. B. Du Bois and the Idea of 'Double Consciousness,'" Dickson D. Bruce, Jr. points out that Emerson employed the term "double consciousness" to describe the struggle of being pulled back and forth between the realm of the divine and the rigors of daily existence. For Emerson, therefore, "The worst feature of this double consciousness is that the two lives, of the understanding and of the soul, which he leads, really show very little relation to one another: one prevails now, all buzz and din; the other prevails then, all infinitude and paradise, and, with the progress of life, the two discover no greater disposition to reconcile themselves."[32] Terri Hume Oliver also notes that Du Bois—a careful reader of Goethe—could have had in mind Faust's: "Two souls, alas! Reside within my breast / And each withdraws from, and repels, its brother."[33] But Du Bois's use of the concept of the double consciousness in *The Souls* is thoroughly sociological. It is therefore remarkably different from these religious poetic transcendentalist traditions.

In the particular case of the African-American's conditions of subjection, we should understand, Du Bois wanted one to see that the same conditions beckoned both to the oppressed and oppressor, though in different ways, to a certain greatness of self and of soul. It was therefore in the pursuit of the spirit of race-historical transcendence that Du Bois would offer, in response to the question "What does the Negro want?"; that the African American wants only to take his or her place among others as "a co-worker in the kingdom of culture, to escape both death and isolation, to husband and use his best powers and latent genius." It was also an insight into the forces that lead to thwarting of this universal desire—by slavery, colonialism, or anti-black racial prejudices—that Du Bois hoped readers of *The Souls* would come to appreciate.

But there is another equally modern, scientific tradition of psychological and political understanding of integrity of self that Du Bois, clearly, sidestepped. I will call this the *Humean* option. In contrast to the traditions of the psychology of self in religion or in the romantic poetic transcendentalism, Hume's contentions about self-identity in the *Treatise of Human Nature* are important to consider. In this writing, Hume argued that the "experimental method" (i.e., empirical method, which he introduced into moral reasoning), a method Du Bois himself would prefer in his more ethnographic studies (e.g., in *The Philadelphia Negro* series, where Du Bois practiced urban social history, and descriptive statistics), could not yield any science or metaphysics of the self. For Hume the idea of self-identity gives no reliable picture of an authentic unitary "substance" called self, around which a notion of a metaphysical authenticity or integrity—racial or otherwise—could be scientifically legitimated. With this historical capacity for self-identification, but with nothing metaphysically or psychologically eternally subsisting this identification, a Humean could not talk of a "divided" self, individual, racial, or national, except materially, sociologically, or historically. Du Bois, can be seen to have been modern in his ethnography and sociology of African and Negro histories, but less so in his racial theological psychology of the black soul. His lamentations about the anguish and the evil of double consciousness—an anguish and social evil theorized as locatable as well as redeemable in the Afromodern experience—suggest this interpretation. For what could the science of this anguish and its moral judgment communicate, beyond the historically specific environment within which colonialism and white American cultures distorted the lives of the African slaves, and the slaves' quests for freedom as African Americans? Once *The Souls* had succeeded in displacing the concept of double consciousness—from its ideological framing, in the medical and psychological literature as drapetomania, to its meanings as historical practices of freedom against non-natural oppression—Du Bois, it seems, had no desire to sidestep the consequences of the pseudometaphysical characterization of the Black—or the White—racial self. Paradoxically, it is likely that this pseudometaphysics of race, enabled Du Bois, without any contradictions, to compose *The Souls* as a sociology of freedom.

But what are the implications of this racial sociology of freedom to contemporary social democratic theories? What would be a democratic racial or postcolonial subjectivity? Is there a democratic legacy in the racial idea of double consciousness or postcolonial theories of ambivalence? These questions arise when one considers if the historical salience—if not the very idea—of "race" or the "colonial" could have substantially exhausted itself in the virtues of acts of freedom inherent to the modern, postmodern, and postcolonial re-inventions of identities—a process that Du Bois himself, in theory and in practice (e.g., the Niagara Movement in the United States, the self-exile to independent Ghana, etc.) anticipated. These questions can maybe be addressed indirectly.

In the essay "What is a Muslim?" written in the early 1990s, Akeel Bilgrami develops a model of introspection that sheds some light on examples of conflicts of identities. But, in a polemic against the Clash of Civilizations thesis, he also isolated a specific example of conflicts of identities: "There is," he writes, "widespread today a more interesting conflict *within* the hearts of moderate Muslims . . . a conflict made the more excruciating because it is not always explicitly acknowledged by them." This conflict, he goes on to explain, "requires a careful scrutiny . . . of what the specific demands and consequences of one's particular [identities] are in specific historical or personal circumstances."[34] In parallel to the *hyphenated* African-American, what is a *moderate* Muslim's religious identity in a capitalist, secular, liberal, democracy? Like Du Bois's critical challenge to medical accounts of black double-consciousness, accounts that located this consciousness as an illness in the Negro's natural or moral character, Bilgrami wants us to understand that no scientific or philosophical warrant grants, *a priori*, to capitalist secular liberalism a status of neutrality in these contexts. Even from a liberal perspective, it should be recognized that there is no rational value in framing these or similar identity conflicts as race versus democracy, or the religious (Muslim) versus the secular (Liberal); neither race-blindness, secularism, nor liberalism could automatically confer the right to describe the issue of double consciousness, the ambivalence of postcolonial subjectivity, or the conflict within the moderate Muslim as a conflict between "moral truth and falsity." Putting it bluntly, and using the moderate Muslim as an example, "liberal and secular values," Bilgrami remarks, "have no purely philosophical justification that puts them outside the arena of essentially contested substantive moral and political values."[35]

Are we left then with conflicts of values or identities *fundamentally* held? I would argue that one can hold a substantive identity fundamentally without becoming a fundamentalist. To say that an identity or a belief is "fundamental" to a person's identity means only that the person's sense of integrity, or violation of this sense of integrity, is connected to the system of beliefs that underwrites the identity. But nothing here suggests that there is only one such belief system that a person could subscribe to, nor that all the possible fundamental identities underwritten by the system of beliefs are automatically compatible. Even where a set of identities is consistent, it could still be the case that one holds different members of the set as a fundamental commitment at different times, and for different reasons. In fact, the moderate Muslim might entertain the idea that one could identify oneself as a Muslim in this place for this length of time, and as something else somewhere else for another length of time. It is as if one could "grade" commitments to an identity or identities according to "thick" or "thin": the thicker suggesting proximity to the core of what one considers one's "self" at any time, and the farther away from this core one's identity becomes more negotiable and therefore "thinner." But even this idea of "core"—as earlier suggested—leaves no impression in the moderate's interior conflict or introspection that any core is more "essential" or more abiding than the supposedly peripheral or "inessential." Such "inessential" commitments may, in situational clusters or serially, surprise by revealing themselves, at their own times and in their circumstances, as equally core and thick. The idea of a "fundamental" commitment, for the moderate is, in short, more formal than substantive.

In a choice illustration of this core argument, Bilgrami tells a story that bears repeating. The existential, social, and (I would like to believe) political attitude to self, faith, race, and nation that this example highlights conforms closely to the psychological model of identity that, earlier, I characterized as Humean.

> I once shared a flat with a close friend, who was an appallingly successful drug dealer. He had made far more money than I thought was decent, and was money made on the steady destruction of people's lives, some of whom were talented, even brilliant, in the university. One day, while he was out, the police arrived at the door. They said that they did not have sufficient evidence to produce a warrant and search the place, but they were morally certain that he was guilty, and all they needed was for his roommate to express the slightest suspicion. That would give them enough to legally search his premises. I had long quarreled intensely with my friend about his cynical profiteering from drugs and had come to find him utterly reprehensible in this respect. But faced with the question from the police, I found myself turning them away.[36]

It would be an error to read this dilemma as the familiar "If I had to choose between my country and my friend, may God help me to choose my friend." Our conclusion would be different if, for example, instead of the police, the story had said that our protagonist had been confronted by a delegation from the *Ulamma*. The better analogy might be to another story that we could use to illustrate Du Bois's revised concept of double consciousness: an African

American professor of philosophy at a New York University remarked that he was very concerned about terrorism in a cosmic way but, on a daily basis, on account of a cross between his gender and his skin color, he believed he *should*, by objective analysis of potential harm to his person, be more concerned about the police.[37]

If these opinions reflect the sentiments of significant segments of racial, religious, or postcolonial minority populations (the "second-sighted," in Du Bois terms) in the United States, the questions implicit in these opinions, and which we should address, bearing classical social and political theories in mind, are obvious. One of these questions would be: What is the function of trust—trust in fellow citizens, in civil institutions and their public spaces of shared life—for the functioning of a democracy? Is it possible that racial double consciousness and postcolonial or postfundamentalist religious liberal ambivalence, even as we celebrate their unarguably social revolutionary potential in modernity and postmodernity, retains some of these revolutionary characteristics as claims for diversity, but that it is also a claim fueled by deformations in the social body? I prefer this sociological reading of the question to Du Bois's pseudometaphysical or theological arguments for racial or any other forms of difference. Likewise, this question clearly does not permit a return to any longing for a pre-Weberian enchanted sense of community. The issue is not whether individuals or communities that form nations could become racially fundamentally, religiously fundamentally, or markedly fundamentally committed. Plainly, they do. But it would be useful to interrogate in what sense such fundamental "identities," even in their most lucid forms, may be responses to what, following the example of continental philosophers, one might characterize as a different, and differed order of lack in the subject. Such a lack—the contours of which fundamental commitments to race, religion, "the market," or political nationalism might themselves be merely the existential figures—demands, it seems, more careful historical analyses, and patience, than the usual rhetoric of the liberal Right or the liberal Left is willing or capable to exercise.

NOTES

1. I have therefore liberally relied on the most recent comprehensive study of the phenomena, namely, Niall Ferguson, *Empire: How Britain Made the Modern World* (London: Penguin, 2003).

2. Ferguson (2003), 51–52.

3. Durban Declaration of the World Conference against Racism, Racial Discrimination, Xenophobia, and Related Intolerance, 2001.

4. Seid Hossein Khan, *The Seir Mutaqherin: or Review of Modern Times: Being an History of India, From the Year 118 to the Year 1194* (Calcutta: Cambray and Co., [1789] 1903).

5. Ferguson (2003), 47–48.

6. Many historians are convinced that British economic policies—notably *laissez faire* and the faith that "market forces" will correct for the impact of the 1877 famine—contributed to the neglect that led to many more deaths than would have been necessary under appropriate government intervention measures. Some historians have compared the British colonial policy in this famine to the Nazi uses of hunger against the Jews in Germany. But others disagree, noting as difference the fact that while it was wrong for any government to rely on market forces to stave off a major farming, the actions of the British colonial government, unlike Hitler's, was not murderous in intent if in fact.

7. Khan (1789).

8. J. J. J. Keswick, Calcutta business tycoon, in Ferguson (2003), 200.

9. V. Y. Mudimbe, *The Idea of Africa* (Bloomington: Indiana University Press, 1994).

10. Ferguson (2003), 56.

11. Frederick Lugard, *The Dual Mandate in Tropical Africa* (London: Frank Cass & Co., 1965), 3, note 1.

12. Ferguson (2003), 53.

13. John Newton, in Ferguson (2003), 79.

14. Against those who would excuse slavery on grounds that the African was less human than any other or yet to be "civilized," David Livingstone, who had the advantage of having lived in Africa (though as an unsuccessful evangelist; he discovered that Africans were not interested to replace their own religious myths with those of the Christian church), was quick to draw on this experience for his defense of the dignity of the African. In Africa, rather than in chains at sea or enslaved in the plantations of the New World, Africans, Livingstone wrote, are "wiser than their white neighbors." In contrast to those who write about Africa without ever having lived among them, Livingstone offers that for all the years he spent on the continent, he "never entertained any suspicions of foul play while among pure Negroes and was with one or two exceptions always treated politely, indeed so thoroughly civil were the more central tribes [that] . . . a missionary of ordinary prudence and tact would certainly secure respect." Because of these experiences he not only refused to believe he wrote in any attribution of "incapacity of the African in either mind or heart," but also claimed: "In reference to the status of the Africans among the nations of the earth, we have seen nothing to justify the notion that they are of a different 'breed' or 'species' from the most civilized." Livingstone, in Ferguson (2003), 129.

15. George Macartney, in Ferguson (2003), 35.

16. The Biafra genocide of the 1960s in modern Nigeria and the on-going civil strife in the Igbo regions of that country, as well as today's ethnic cleansing of so-called black Africans in the Darfur region of Sudan, could be said to have been set in motion by the British colonial states which engineered the political geographies of both modern Nigeria and modern Sudan. At national independence, the reins of state in both countries were unequally yielded—in continuation of the colonial policy of Indirect Rule, a policy first formulated by Lugard—to powerful feudal Islamist elements in each country.

17. "The sort of men who are wanted for missionaries," Livingstone exhorted, "are such as I see before me. I beg you to direct your attention to Africa; . . . I go back to Africa to try to make an open path for commerce and Christianity; do you carry out the work which I have begun. I LEAVE IT TO YOU." Livingstone, in Ferguson (2003), 155.

18. Livingstone, in Ferguson (2003), 156.

19. Achebe, *Things Fall Apart* (New York: Anchor Books, 1994), 144–46, passim.

20. As recently as the early 1960s, my parents could not get me admitted to a Catholic school until I changed my name, through a Baptismal ritual, from Chukwudi ("God with us") to Emmanuel (also "God with us"!). The first, because of its Igbo sound, was considered by the officiating priests and nuns, who were also the school's admission officers, as too close to my great-grandparents' "pagan" background (my parents themselves, as my grandparents, had converted to Christianity, though all continued to speak the Igbo language instead of colonial English or the Catholic ritual language of Latin).

21. Ferguson writes: "This was an astonishing volte face . . . After the British first came to Sierra Leone in 1562 it did not take long to become slave traders. In the subsequent two and a half centuries . . . more than three million Africans were shipped into bondage in British ships [alone]. But then toward the end of the eighteenth century, something changed dramatically; it

was almost as if a switch was flicked in the British psyche. Suddenly they started shipping slaves back to West Africa and setting them free." Ferguson (2003), 115–16.

22. Kezo, in Ferguson (2003), 115.

23. Whether we read about these new problems in the memoirs of Mahatma Gandhi, the psychoanalytic racial theories of Frantz Fanon, or in the hearty poems of Wole Soyinka, such as his 1962 "Telephone Conversation," generations of writers from the outposts of Europe's self-exhausted empires commemorate experiences of postcolonial racism that greet the postcolonized "native" in the metropolitan centers of Old Europe. Today, when it is not open discrimination in accommodation, it may be corporate pay structures that pay the postcolonial immigrant 30 percent less for equal work. Whether up from plantation slavery in the Americas, or up from the underbelly of the extremities of ex-British and ex-European colonies, racism and xenophobia on global scales, as the Durban Declaration maintained, remain among the most severe consequences of the modern imperial expansions of Europe and its colonization of other peoples.

24. W. E. B. Du Bois, "The Suppression of the African Slave-Trade to the United States of America, 1638–1870," Doctoral Thesis, Harvard University, 1895 (published 1896).

25. Samuel Johnson remarked, in *Taxation No Tyranny*, "How is it that the loudest YELPS for liberty come from the drivers of Negroes?" (London: T. Cadell, 1775).

26. Du Bois, *The Souls of Black Folks* (New York: Bantam, 1989), 1–2.

27. Du Bois (1989), 3.

28. The Supreme Court of the United States, *Gratz et al. v. Bollinger et al.*, no. 02615, decided 23 June 2003. Whether the Court's optimism is realistic or not, it provides nevertheless a right prism through which to think about the problem of race and racialism in the coming centuries. Unlike the distinctions that may obtain in non-human species, or across species, racial identities, the Court implicitly acknowledged, may not be thought of as natural kinds, but instead as social and historical divisions.

29. "The history of the American Negro," Du Bois wrote, "is the history of this strife—this longing to attain self-conscious manhood, to merge his double self into a better and truer self. In this merging he wishes neither of the older selves to be lost. He would not Africanize America, for America has too much to teach the world and Africa. He would not bleach his Negro soul in a flood of white Americanism, for he knows that Negro blood has a message for the world. He simply wishes to make it possible for a man to be both a Negro and an American," Du Bois (1989), 3.

30. Available records indicate that, in addition to being a medical officer in the Confederate army, Cartwright was also "a professor of diseases of the Negro," in the Medical Faculty of the University of Louisiana. His "cure" for drapetomania was simple: amputation of the toes—surely, to prevent the slave's run for freedom. Extended studies of Cartwright's medical work may be found in Alexander Thomas and Samuel Sillen, *Racism and Psychiatry* (New York: Carol Publishing Group, 1974) and J. D. Guillory, "The Pro-Slavery Arguments of Dr. Samuel A. Cartwright," *Louisiana History* 9 (1968): 209–27.

31. Du Bois, "Preface," *Dark Water: Voices from within the Veil* (New York: Harcourt Brace, 1920).

32. Ralph Waldo Emerson, "Transcendentalist," 1843; in *The Emerson Reader* (New York: Library of America, 1983).

33. Terri Hume Oliver, "'Double Consciousness' in *Souls*," Introduction to *The Souls of Black Folks* by W. E. B. Du Bios (New York: W. W. Norton, 1999).

34. Akeel Bilgrami, "What is a Muslim? Fundamental Commitment and Cultural Identity," *Critical Inquiry*, Summer (1992), 824–25.

35. Bilgrami (1992), 827.

36. Bilgrami (1992), 827.

37. This conversation occurred a few days after Ahmadu Diallo, a West African immigrant, was "mistakenly" shot forty-one times by two New York Police officers.

Chapter Twelve

Colonialism and the State of Exception[1]

Margaret Kohn

> No philosophy, no analysis, no aphorism, be it ever so profound, can compare in intensity and richness of meaning with a properly narrated story.
>
> —Hannah Arendt

The Hola concentration camp was located in a remote and desolate area of Kenya. In 1959, the seventh year of the State of Emergency, it was divided into two sections. There was an "open camp," for former members of the Mau Mau movement who were willing to cooperate with British officials but still too dangerous to return home. The "closed camp" contained about five hundred of the most hard-core prisoners who had endured years of detention, torture, hunger, and brutality without confessing their oaths to support the Mau Mau movement. The British press and the House of Commons had begun to show some interest in the fate of the massive numbers of Kenyan detainees, and a motion to authorize an independent inquiry into the conditions in the camps had recently failed by a vote of 288 to 232. The local British officials decided that they had to dismantle the camps quickly, but first they had to break the last of the detainees, even if this meant systematically employing torture.

On March 3, 1959, Hola's Camp Commandant, G. M. Sullivan, decided to implement the Cowan Plan, which was a systematic application of methods that had been used haphazardly throughout the Emergency. The plan was based on the concept of "dilution," a tactic that had been successful in other camps. Hard-core inmates were broken up into small groups, surrounded by British officials and African guards, and beaten until they agreed to confess their oaths and comply with all commands. Given the prisoners' commitment not to violate their oath of secrecy, this amounted to an order to beat them to death. And that is exactly what happened. According to one survivor of the Hola Massacre, the guards selected around one hundred detainees and brought them to a work site, where they were ordered to dig an irrigation trench.[2] Hundreds of armed African guards had been called in to execute the plan. When the detainees refused to begin work, claiming they couldn't possibly complete the task in the time allotted, Sullivan blew a whistle and the guards began beating them with clubs, sticks, and shovels. After a second whistle, the officers counted six dead bodies. Sullivan blew a whistle again and the massacre continued until there were ten dead and dozens more severely injured.

The camp officials tried to cover up the massacre, claiming that the ten men died after accidentally drinking tainted water, but overwhelming evidence contradicted this account. An investigation ensued, and Senior Resident Magistrate W. H. Goudie concluded, "In each case death was found to have been caused by shock and hemorrhage *due to multiple bruising caused by violence.*"[3] Despite the undeniable evidence of excessive force, Goudie found that no criminal wrongdoing had occurred. He concluded that it was impossible to decide which blows were legitimate attempts to force detainees to work and which were excessively punitive. In any case, the actions were carried out under the directive of the Cowan Plan and the judge felt that it was not the responsibility of the judiciary to evaluate questions of colonial policy.

Although the massacre at the Hola Camp attained some notoriety in the British press, it was by no means a unique instance of violence against Mau Mau detainees. In her book *Imperial Reckoning: The Untold Story of Britain's Gulag in Kenya*, Caroline Elkins documents widespread patterns of rape, torture, and murder. She estimates that 1.5 million Kikuyu were detained during the State of Emergency (1952–1959), either in concentration camps or in villages that were surrounded by trenches and barbed wire to cut off any contact between Mau Mau guerrillas and their supporters. British officials put the number of Kikuyu dead at 11,000, but Elkins uses demographic data to support other estimates that the number of casualties is closer to 100,000.[4]

Ironically, the State of Emergency that was implemented in order to secure British rule may have accelerated decolonization. Although the Emergency achieved the goal of crushing the Mau Mau, it also made colonial government more costly, both economically and politically. Moreover, it undermined the popular myths that European control over Africa brought legality, civilization, and economic development to indigenous peoples. From one perspective, some might see this episode in colonial history as evidence that it is ultimately impossible to defeat a popular movement for national liberation. But this optimistic assessment overlooks the long-term political consequences of the State of Emergency. The State of Emergency was an intensification of existing modes of colonial governance that destroyed the remnants of indigenous sources of authority and order and replaced them with unmitigated coercion. This essay focuses on the work of two African intellectuals, Ngugi wa Thiong'o and Achille Mbembe. Both have suggested that the State of Emergency reveals the inner logic of "colonial rationality." Furthermore, they both draw attention to the way that this logic continues to structure postcolonial states and undermine popular government. Their work advances current debates in political theory by deepening our understanding of the political effects of the state of exception. Moreover, their approach to the concept of the state of exception, with its attentiveness to the lawlessness at the heart of legality itself, illuminates the problem of founding a new state out of the violent vestiges of the old order.

THE STATE OF EXCEPTION

In the past decade there has been renewed interest in the related concepts of martial law, emergency powers, and the state of exception. The state of exception exists when the response to crisis involves granting prerogative to the military or the executive and curtailing the rights of citizens and their representatives.[5] In the field of political theory, this interest has focused on the controversial work of Carl Schmitt and Giorgio Agamben. Agamben published a timely book entitled *State of Exception* that concluded that the state of exception (or martial law) is a space devoid of law. He argued that it is not the logical consequence of the state's right to self-defense, nor is it a straightforward attempt to reestablish the juridical order by violating the letter of the law.[6] For Agamben, martial law and other exceptional measures reveal the Janus face of sovereignty: the power to declare the state of exception is the same power that invests individuals with rights.

Until recently, most of the scholarly research on the state of exception had focused on the paradigmatic case of Weimar Germany and the influential writing of Carl Schmitt.[7] The age of empire, however, forced an earlier generation of political and legal theorists to confront the conceptual difficulties that emerge when the law provides for its own suspension.[8] In the nineteenth century, the frequent and bloody use of martial law to quell uprisings in the colonies was the occasion for extended public and scholarly debates about the nature and limits of the law.[9] Surprisingly few contemporary political theorists have considered the significance of emergency measures in consolidating colonial rule and structuring postcolonial governance.[10]

Two notable exceptions are Achille Mbembe and Ngugi wa Thiong'o. Ngugi is a novelist and critic who lived through the State of Emergency as a youth in rural Kenya. Two of his best-known novels, *A Grain of Wheat* and *Weep Not Child,* are extended reflections on the moral and political ramifications of the Emergency.[11] His treatment of the topic, however, differs from the existing literature. Most of the debates about the state of exception—for example the famous dispute between William Carlyle and John Stuart Mill about martial law in Jamaica—take the legitimacy of colonialism for granted.[12] The subject of disagreement is confined to the necessity, effectiveness, and negative consequences of extralegal measures. Ngugi approaches the topic from the opposite perspective and forces the reader to ask what the emergency tells us about the legitimacy of colonialism itself. The most interesting aspect of his work, however, is his penetrating and complex analysis of the colonial approach to law and exception and the way that it structured the postcolonial state. Ngugi's literary depiction of postcolonial Kenya is similar to Mbembe's theoretical concept of *commandement,* the distinctive form of governmentality in colonial and postcolonial regimes. Drawing on the work of Mbembe and Ngugi, this essay tries to understand the way that the colonial polity's distinctive approach to law and exception contributed to the authoritarian character of many postcolonial African states.[13]

NGUGI'S EMERGENCY STORIES

Ngugi enriches our theoretical understanding of the state of exception by depicting the social and political consequences of the State of Emergency that the British declared in colonial Kenya from 1952–1959. Ngugi came of age during the State of Emergency and his writing is particularly attentive to the micropolitical effects of the tactics employed during the Emergency (torture, screening, arbitrary arrest and incarceration for extended periods, forced labor, and mass confinement in villages surrounded by barbed wire).[14] In his novels, he captured the way that these tactics undermined the capacity for resistance and weakened alternative (e.g., noncolonial) sources of order.

Ngugi's analysis of the state of exception is also distinctive because of his concern with the legitimacy of the *state* rather than the legitimacy of the *exception.* He has no interest in asking whether exceptional measures are appropriate means of safeguarding the sovereignty of the state, since this question is posed from the perspective of the colonizer. Instead, he looks at the issue from the opposite perspective and asks how the Emergency undermines a politics of resistance and weakens alternative (e.g., noncolonial) sources of order. Not only is Ngugi's anti-colonial perspective distinctive, but his style is original too. Ngugi's critique of colonial legality is developed in a series of literary works that describe the political and psychological consequences of the Emergency.

Weep Not, Child is Ngugi's first and most autobiographical novel.[15] It is set in the late 1940s and 1950s and traces the story of a family of landless peasants during the Emergency. The novel explores the way that violence and repression destroy the fabric of the community. The story is told from the point of view of the youngest son, Njoroge, the only member of the family who has the opportunity to go to school. The British colonial government is depicted through the figure of Mr. Howlands, the white farmer who owns land taken from Njoroge's father, Ngotho. Mr. Howlands is both a settler and the local administrator. As the violence escalates, Howlands serves as police officer, law-maker, and executioner. The power of the British government is also exercised through the figure of Jacobo, the loyalist Kikuyu chief.

The conflict over the ownership of land is a source of anguish that motivates the characters in the novel. Ngotho feels an intense connection to his ancestral land and works diligently for Mr. Howland in order to protect his *shamba*, the land which he feels is part of himself. Mr. Howlands initially sees Ngotho as a dedicated and grateful employee. When the Kenyan nationalist movement calls a strike to protest terrible labor conditions, Mr. Howlands warns his employees that anyone who participates will be fired. This strike is the event that sets off a chain of violence that tears apart the ties between fathers and sons, husbands and wives, as well as the more precarious bonds that link white and black in the system of forced colonial labor.[16] The first act of violence is domestic. Ngotho slaps his wife when she begs him not to take part in the strike and risk losing his job. This scene of domestic conflict draws attention to the way that the looming Emergency undermined the traditional sources of order within the Kikuyu community and even within the family itself.

When Jacobo, the loyalist Chief, addresses a crowd of workers in order to convince them not to strike, Ngotho rises from the audience to confront him. The audience surges forward and then the police attack the crowd, shooting and beating the unarmed workers, including Ngotho. Although Ngotho survives, he is fired from his job and his family is forced to leave their huts, which are located on land owned by Jacobo. Under the pressure of poverty and dislocation, Ngotho's family falls apart. One son goes to join the Mau Mau fighters in the forest and another goes to Nairobi to find work. After Ngotho is arrested in connection with a Mau Mau attack on Jacobo's home, he is brutally tortured and dies from his injuries. Despite Njoroge's academic success at Siriana, a prestigious missionary-run preparatory school, he is not immune from the reach of the Emergency and is himself detained and tortured. The novel ends on a pessimistic note; Njoroge is forced to leave school to support his mother because his brothers are in prison awaiting execution.

What does this novel tell us about the Emergency? The most prominent theme is the way that the Emergency undermined the unity of the Kikuyu people. The white minority's economic and political control over the vast

African population would have been difficult without allies, which meant that there had to be some segment of the African population that benefited from white rule. In order to effectively implement a regime of coercion, the British government simultaneously had to organize consent. At first the colonial state relied on cultural assimilation carried out by institutions such as the church and school system. These institutions were supposed to breed a new generation of English-speaking subjects who were deeply committed to the colonial order. This technique of cultural assimilation, however, proved to be more difficult than expected. Although many Kenyans converted to Christianity, the influence of European missionaries was permanently weakened during the Circumcision Controversy of the 1920s. The Protestant missionaries opposed the practice of female circumcision, which was the most important life-cycle ritual in traditional Kikuyu culture. When the missionaries decided to forbid their converts from participating in this rite-of-passage, masses of African Christians left the European dominated institutions to establish their own independent churches and schools. This issue inspired the first large-scale political mobilization. In an effort to stamp out the practice of female circumcision, the missionaries pressured local Native Councils to enact a ban. Opponents of the ban formed the Kikuyu Central Association (KCA), which was committed to resisting the "civilizing mission" of the colonial state.[17] Much to the surprise of the British government, many of the Africans who were educated in the missionary schools and churches became the leaders of this nascent movement for self-government. This meant that the colonial government had to seek new allies.

In *Weep Not, Child*, Ngugi depicts a system of local government organized around "chiefs" whose authority came from the colonial state rather than the local community. In the precolonial period, the Kikuyu did not have a system of chiefs but instead relied on a more informal process of consultation. In many parts of Africa, the chieftaincy was a colonial institution that was set up to facilitate colonial administration.[18] The British established a system known as indirect rule, which relied on chiefs who were supposed to administer customary law. As Mahmood Mamdani has shown in *Citizen and Subject*, this "customary law" was a hybrid invented by the colonizer and had several important benefits for the colonial state. First, indirect rule was a matter of expediency. The colonial bureaucracies typically had only a handful of experienced white officials to govern extremely vast territories; therefore they needed to delegate administrative tasks. Second, the system created a group of Africans whose personal power was dependent upon colonial authority. Third, it used a nascent theory of multiculturalism to rationalize the treatment of Africans as second-class citizens. The colonial administration prescribed customary law as a concession to the indigenous people's desire to be judged by their own traditions and practices. But it also provided a rationale for a dual system of justice that treated whites as citizens and

Africans as subjects. The concept of "customary law" reinforced Africans' exclusion from equal treatment under the law, because it provided none of the legal protections guaranteed to white settlers but all of the obligations including onerous taxes and forced labor. Even where "customary law" was employed, the colonial administrators still had the final power to overturn the decisions of native courts or to enforce compliance with national rules. According to Mamdani, customary law, as invented by the colonizer, was never concerned with the problem of limiting state power, only enforcing it.[19] In a similar vein, Martin Chanock argues that the invention of customary law provided a screen that obfuscated the far-reaching institutional changes brought about by colonialism.[20]

The customary law created as an instrument of indirect rule incorporated elements of traditional practices, but these were distorted by the vastly changed power dynamics of colonialism. For example, in the precolonial polity, when a village elder adjudicated a dispute, he did so with the knowledge that his authority depended on widespread legitimacy. This informal accountability provided a check on abuse and despotism. Under the new system of indirect rule, however, the "chief" was backed by the coercive power of the colonial state and had little need to build consensus or respect shared norms. Mamdani describes this system as "decentralized despotism."[21] This is exactly what Ngugi depicts in his novels. In *Weep Not, Child* Chief Jacobo is responsible for carrying out Mr. Howlands' orders and ensuring the compliance of other villagers. In return for his support of the regime, Jacobo had amassed a significant amount of land, which was the main source of both wealth and prestige in Kikuyu society.[22] Since land was extremely scarce, he used his lands to ensure that any resistance was crushed. When Ngotho challenged Jacobo, he and his family had to leave their huts, which were built on Jacobo's land. Ngotho could not appeal his exile by turning to public opinion, because Jacobo's authority came from Mr. Howlands.

The political structure of indirect rule also directly contributed to the colonial project of extracting resources. It played an important role in the economic transformation of Kenya, a process which accelerated during the Emergency.[23] The new chiefs were involved in the distribution of communal lands. In the colonial period, the Kikuyu were confined to reservations that did not contain enough agricultural land to feed the population, therefore decisions about how to allocate this land had enormous consequences. Those without land had to go to work on white farms and accept any wages to survive. During the Emergency, the land of Mau Mau detainees was frequently given to Loyalists and Home Guards. This process of concentration contributed to the transformation of Kenya from subsistence peasant agriculture to more commercial agriculture. The Emergency helped create a class of black landowners and landless laborers. This process, which had already begun under early phases of colonialism, intensified during the Emergency, because over one million people were relocated and forced into fortified villages or camps. Ngugi paints a picture of the Emergency as a radicalization of practices that had their roots in the structure of the "normal" colonial state.

Weep Not, Child articulates a critique of colonial legality and the system of indirect rule. It indicts both the white and black faces of the colonial state. The most explicit statement of this critique comes in a scene where Njoroge's family is gathered in his mother's hut and they hear the news that Jomo Kenyatta, the political leader of the nationalist movement, has been convicted of supporting the Mau Mau. Njoroge's mother laments:

> The white man makes a law or a rule. Through that rule or law or what you may call it, he takes away the land and then imposes many laws on the people concerning that land and many other things, all without people agreeing first as in the old days of the tribe. Now a man rises and opposes that law which made right the taking away of the land. Now that man is taken by the same people who made the laws against which that man was fighting. He is tried under those alien rules. Now tell me who is that man who can win even if the angels of God were his lawyers."[24]

This statement is an indictment of the Emergency, which made it a capital crime to take an oath of solidarity, to possess a weapon, to criticize the government, or to give material aid to the fighters in the forest. It is a critique of the farce of a trial that was the basis of Jomo Kenyatta's imprisonment.[25] But more importantly, it is an astute observation that the Emergency is not a temporary aberration but instead reflects the true nature of colonial legality. As we will see below, Ngugi develops this argument in his theoretical writings, notably his prison memoir *Detained*.

Ngugi's third novel, *A Grain of Wheat*, also explores the psychological and political consequences of the Emergency. This time, however, the story is set on the eve of Kenyan Independence and Ngugi draws attention to the political challenges faced by the postcolonial state. Like *Weep Not, Child*, it shows how the Emergency undermined precolonial social and political practices without providing viable alternatives. *A Grain of Wheat* describes the life of one village as it prepares for the Uhuru (independence) celebrations; the story unfolds through a series of flashbacks that depict life before the Emergency. The novel explores the choices made by a group of characters, whose political commitments to land and freedom are complicated by their desires for recognition, love, and safety. Gikonyo is a Mau Mau supporter who confesses his oath in order to win his release from the concentration camp and return home to his beloved Mumbi. Karanja is the loyalist chief who betrays his oath and denounces his friends in order to avoid deportation. Mugo is a traitor who is mistaken for a hero.

In *A Grain of Wheat*, Ngugi uses the character of the District Officer, Mr. Thompson, to expose structural character of colonial violence. Unlike Mr.

Howlands, who is portrayed in a purely negative light, the white District Officer in *A Grain of Wheat* is a more complex character. The first scene with Thompson (which takes place immediately before Kenyan independence) makes it clear that he has all of the arrogance and ignorance that characterize race relations under colonialism. He treats Karanja as his personal messenger, ignores him, and then berates him for knocking too loudly.[26] But a flashback makes it clear that Thompson's decision to enter the colonial service was not motivated by greed or ambition. Instead, it was inspired by a very Kiplingesque desire to spread the benefits of British civilization.[27] Thompson was moved by a casual meeting with two African students in London. These Africans were Anglicized in dress and speech. They were knowledgeable about literature and history and enthusiastic about the "British Mission in the World." Thompson recalled, "I was convinced that the growth of the British Empire was the development of a great moral idea: . . . it must surely lead to the creation of one British nation, embracing peoples of all colours and creeds, based on the just proposition that all men were created equal."[28] Thompson was inspired by the idea of the civilizing mission: Britain would bring the rule of law, science, technology, economic progress, and humanistic culture to savage peoples. After a period of tutelage, the newly civilized savages would exercise self-government and share equally in the benefits of prosperity and culture. Ngugi is not simply mocking Thompson's profound misunderstanding of colonial practice. By crediting Thompson with genuinely idealist motives, Ngugi foregrounds the political and structural character of colonialism. If all of the settlers and bureaucrats were depicted as ignorant, brutal, and selfish, then it would be tempting to see colonialism as an individual psychopathology. The existence of well-meaning administrators such as Thompson, however, is a stronger indictment of colonialism because it shows that the structure itself, rather than the character of the agents, is responsible for the violence of colonialism. In the novel, excerpts from Thompson's diaries reveal how he assimilated the racist categories of the colony and became more violent in response to attacks by the Mau Mau. The Thompson who was eventually responsible for the deaths of eleven prisoners during the Emergency (an obvious reference to the actual Hola massacre) is shown to be the inevitable product of colonial institutions.

A Grain of Wheat, like Ngugi's earlier novels and stories, focuses on the Emergency as a primal trauma that destroyed the precarious sources of solidarity and resistance under colonialism. The novel captures the way that the community, like the Kenyan nation, was torn apart by the divide-and-conquer strategy employed by the British during the Emergency. For the first time he also considers how this experience poses problems for the postcolonial order. The novel depicts the complex relations between a group of villagers during December 1963, the moment of transition from colonial to postcolonial rule. But Ngugi makes it clear that the highly orchestrated rituals celebrating national independence mask unresolved conflicts between resistance fighters, loyalists, fellow-travelers, the remnants of the white power structure, and a range of individuals deeply scared by memories of what they did to ensure their own survival. Some critics read the ending of the novel—Mugo's public admission of guilt and the tentative reconciliation between Gikonyo and Mumbi (who bore an illegitimate child while her husband Gikonyo was in detention)—as a sign of optimism about the possibility of truth and reconciliation.[29] I reach a very different conclusion and see *A Grain of Wheat* as one of Ngugi's most pessimistic works. It no longer reflects his early faith in education as a path toward individual development. Nor does it encourage a populist belief in collective regeneration through anti-imperialist and anti-capitalist struggle, a theme that became prominent in later works such as *Petals of Blood*. Instead, it depicts a community torn apart by the social forces of colonial modernity and the violent legacy of colonial repression, a community with no institutional or ideological basis for reconciliation. The ending offers at most a vague hope that the personal connection between individuals and the birth of a new generation may heal the open wounds.

Despite its obvious achievements as a depiction of the psychology of betrayal and its consequences for communal coherence, *A Grain of Wheat* is still very much a conventional novel. It describes complex and realistic characters that undergo personal transformation. Although political events drive the plot, the characters are motivated by interpersonal relations and emotions such as love, pride, and shame. Ngugi's more explicitly political work has been much more controversial. Some critics have dismissed his political novels and plays as didactic because they foreground explicit political argument and de-emphasize realistic and/or psychologically complex characterizations.[30] *The Trial of Dedan Kimathi* (coauthored with Micere Githae Mugo) is probably the most openly didactic of Ngugi's literary works. It is a play that aims to teach the Kenyan people about the history of colonialism, resistance, and the violent repression of that history at the hands of the British.[31] It is not a psychological exploration of resistance and betrayal but rather a Brechtian staging of events and actions that expose the absurdity of the legalism used to justify the violent defense of British colonial rule. Like Brecht's epic theater, Ngugi and Micere's script uses generic labels such as "woman," "boy," and "girl" to describe some of the characters. These labels turn the characters into representative figures and draw attention to the structural rather than individual causes of their actions. Although Dedan Kimathi is a historical figure who was executed for his role in the Mau Mau movement, the play is not a dramatization of the actual trial but rather a highly stylized attack on the British ideology of the rule of law and its role in mystifying the basis of British authority.

The play begins with a set of mimed scenes depicting African history: a black king with a white slave trader; a slave auction; a ruthless black plantation overseer whipping slaves. The final scene in this prelude links together the past and present; it is a depiction of the "screening" process used during the Emergency, which consisted of a hooded collaborator identifying fellow villagers as supporters of the Mau Mau. This vivid reminder of the rule of law during the Emergency, which was based on anonymous denunciation and detention without charge or conviction, set the stage for the action of the trial.

The courtroom drama opens with a scene that casually exposes the bases of colonial society: the color line and the monopoly on violence. In the courtroom, whites and blacks sit on opposite sides talking among themselves. When a black clerk orders the spectators to be quiet, it is not entirely clear whether he is only addressing the blacks. A white settler shouts "how dare you" and the other whites pull their guns.[32] The settler is outraged because a black official has unwittingly challenged the rigid hierarchy of colonial society. It is also significant that a number of spectators immediately pull their weapons, because Dedan Kimathi is charged with possession of a firearm, which is a capital offense for blacks under the Emergency Laws.

The scene is staged in a way that draws attention to the absurdity of the ritual legalism of the trial. For example, Kimathi does not initially respond when the judge asks for his plea, so the judge threatens to put him in prison for contempt of court. This threat of a prison sentence for contempt, however, is ridiculous, since Kimathi's execution is a foregone conclusion and a dead man cannot be punished for contempt. Again the judge asks, "Guilty or not guilty?"[33] In his response, Kimathi puts the colonial state on trial. He does this by challenging the question itself. He asks, "By what right dare you, a colonial judge, sit in judgment over me?" What follows is a debate over the legitimacy of the court itself. In response, the judge takes a patronizing tone, suggesting, "Perhaps you don't understand. Maybe your long stay in the Forest has . . . I mean . . . we are here to deal fairly with you, to see that justice is done."

During his courtroom appearance, Kimathi makes an economic, a democratic, and a cultural argument against the legitimacy of the colonial courts. He does not take the position that the Emergency Laws are a violation of the rule of law because he assumes that, far from being exceptional, they reflect the core logic of the colonial order. Instead, he tries to expose the way that the violence of the Emergency, which the settlers perceive as an aberration and blame on the Mau Mau, is a necessary product of the violence of colonialism. His first argument against the legitimacy of the trial is based on the undemocratic character of the laws. He insists, "I will not plead to a law in which we had no part in the making."[34] The judge responds, "Law is law. The role of law is the basis of every civilized community." The judge defends what legal theorists call a realist view of law. The law is what those in charge say it is and its legitimacy does not depend on any preexisting moral principle. Its legitimacy is based on a tautology; it is legitimate, because it creates law and order, which is necessary for civilization. Kimathi challenges this view and insists that law is not the same as force because law is based on consent. The colonial rule of law is an oxymoron because colonialism is a political order based on force not consent. Furthermore, it is premised on unequal rather than equal treatment of two groups of people, natives and settlers.[35]

Kimathi also exposes the economic basis of the colonial legal order. Whereas the judge insists that there is a single universal law, Kimathi responds that the ostensible universality of the law simply disguises the fact that in reality there are two laws, one for the poor and hungry and the other for the man of property.[36] The judge counters, "I am not talking about the laws of Nyandarua jungle." In response, Kimathi deftly reverses the terms of the binary that equates settlers with civilization and Africans with barbarity. He asks, "The jungle of colonialism? Or exploitation? For it is there that you'll find creatures of prey feeding on the blood and bodies of those who toil." Kimathi elaborates on the ways that the law has been used to enforce compulsory labor, a mystified form of slavery. Native Kenyans were forced into wage labor by the British state, which charged taxes equivalent to two months' wages and imprisoned anyone unable to pay. The judge responds, "There's no liberty without law and order" to which Kimathi replies, "There is no law and order without liberty." In this concise exchange, the play summarizes a long and complex debate about the nature of law. Kimathi's democratic-socialist critique of the "rule of law" has been developed in more detail in works such as Franz Neumann's *The Rule of Law* and E. P Thompson's *Whigs and Hunters: The Origin of the Black Act*. The play captures the essence of this argument about the class character of the law while also foregrounding the distinctive colonial dimension of the issue.

The play makes it clear that the coercive side of the law is necessary when individuals and groups have the courage to resist the hegemonic forms of order established through religion, greed, need, and habitual deference. The real, inner trial of Dedan Kimathi is not the drama that unfolds in the courtroom in front of the colonial judge. Instead, Kimathi's trial takes place after he is returned to his cell. It takes the form of three temptations that appear to him in prison during a break in the courtroom drama. The first temptation comes from a settler named Shaw Henderson who encourages Kimathi to confess and collaborate in exchange for his life. To underscore the point about the illusory nature of legal objectivity and neutrality in the colonial state, Henderson is played by the same actor as the judge, and Kimathi draws attention to this, stating "you cannot deceive me, even in your many disguises."[37] Henderson illustrates another face of colonialism. This time he does not make any pretense of legality or neutrality. He explains that his motive for sparing Kimathi's life is purely prudential. He admits, "Look, between the two of us, we don't need to pretend. Nations live by self-interest. You challenged our interests: we had to defend them. It is to our mutual interest and for your own good that we end this ugly war."[38] But Kimathi does not share Henderson's assessment of his own interest. Kimathi's primary interest is communal regeneration not his own survival. He views interest in a collective rather than an individualistic sense, therefore he concludes that his interest lies in inspiring others to continue the fight against slavery and exploitation.

The second and third delegations are important because they draw attention to the temptations offered by collaboration with the neocolonial state rather than the colonial order. This time, Dedan Kimathi is asked to give up armed resistance and collaborate with the powers behind the colonial state rather than with the state itself. The temptation is greater because now exploitation has a black face. The second delegation is made up of a multiracial group of businessmen, who try to entice Kimathi with the lure of material wealth. The white banker emphasizes the opportunities for black elites to profit in the coming postcolonial polity, while the black businessman nods his head in silent agreement. The third delegation is made up of three blacks; an African businessman, a politician, and a priest. They also urge Kimathi to confess, describing the earthly and spiritual benefits of collaboration. Ngugi and Micere make it clear that they see a connection between collaborating with colonialism and collaborating with Kenyatta's neocolonial regime.

The *Trial of Dedan Kimathi* makes the connection between colonial and postcolonial (il)legality explicit. This is a motif that extends through Ngugi's work. He depicts the Kenyan State of Emergency not as an exception but rather as the truth of the colonial order, an order and a law based on coercion not consent. Nevertheless, the Emergency had distinctive characteristics that he exposes in detail. The intensification of violence undermined communal solidarity by starkly opposing individual self-interest and communal good. It tore apart the existing social order and left a polity made up of opportunists, survivors, and resisters—a very fragile basis for the postcolonial order. From Ngugi's perspective, this was by no means an unintended consequence of the Emergency. The British realized that decolonization was inevitable, therefore the Emergency was not really an attempt to prevent Kenyan independence. It was a struggle to plant the roots of the neocolonial order. It did so by destroying its most resolute adversaries, undermining the sources of unity, and ensuring that collaborators would have privileged access to the economic bases of power.

RULE AND EXCEPTION IN THE POSTCOLONIAL POLITY

The demystification of "law and order" is an underappreciated theme that runs throughout Ngugi's novels and plays. Ngugi's most pointed analysis of the politics of law and exception, however, is found in *Detained*, his prison memoir. The memoir does not describe his experience as a youth during the Emergency but rather his imprisonment by the postcolonial Kenyan government.[39] The connection between the colonial and postcolonial legal system is a central theme in *Detained*. The first scene of the book highlights this connection. A prison warder asks, "professor . . . why are you not in bed . . . What are you doing?" Ngugi answers, "I am writing to Jomo Kenyatta in his capacity as an ex-detainee."[40] The warder replies that the cases are different because Kenyatta's was a "colonial affair." But Ngugi insists that his own imprisonment is a neocolonial affair and ruefully concludes that Kenyatta learned how to jail Kenyans from the British.

The central argument in *Detained* is the claim that there is a causal link between the colonial culture of fear and the repressive tactics of the independent Kenyan state. In order to make this argument, Ngugi has to refute the view that the Emergency was an exceptional period with little in common with either the pre-Emergency British state or the postcolonial government. He provides evidence that the brutal measures employed during the Emergency were not exceptional but rather intensifications of existing practices. Ngugi challenges the view that the Mau Mau uprising and the counterinsurgency strategies of the British were an aberration in an otherwise successful civilizing mission. He argues that the legal order, with its adaptable flexible institutions of direct and indirect rule, was always guaranteed by the extralegal violence because it was the only way to achieve compliance with an unjust social order.

In *Detained*, Ngugi provides several examples of what he calls the "culture of legalized brutality" in the period before the Emergency. In March 1907, Colonel Grogan and four white associates flogged several Kenyans for carrying a rickshaw too high. Even though the black victims had to be hospitalized, Grogan and his men were given a sentence of a week and they were allowed to serve this sentence at home while entertaining guests.[41] In 1919, two British peers beat a Kenyan to death and burned his body. They were found guilty of "a simple hurt" and fined 2,000 shillings. One subsequently became an official charged with dispensing justice to the "natives." Ngugi lists a number of similar examples and concludes:

> Thus all these eruptions of brutality between the introduction of colonial culture in 1895 and its flowering with blood in the 1950s were not aberrations of an otherwise humane Christian culture. No. They were its very essence, its law, its logic, and the

Kenyan settler with his sjambok, his dog, his horse, his rickshaw, his sword, his bullet, was the true embodiment of British imperialism.[42]

According to Ngugi, the post-independence ruling class had been socialized in this understanding of law as a means of domination rather than a limit on the power of government. Moreover, they also inherited a set of detention laws, rules, and practices that reinforced this view.[43] Ngugi cites the Native Courts Regulations of 1897, which provided for the preventative detention of any Kenyan likely to commit an offense as well as anyone critical of the government. Any Kenyan deemed to be dangerous to the colonial order could be arrested without trial. The Vagrancy Regulations of 1898 made it possible to detain Africans moving about without employment or means of subsistence. The Native Pass Regulations gave the colonial governor the power to control the movement of Kenyans and the Preservation of Order by Night Regulations of 1901 set up the legal framework for declaring curfews.[44] Detention was widely used not only to prevent any type of political resistance but also to create a large mass of people who could legally be exploited for slave labor. Nor were these restrictions a peculiarity of the British government in Kenya. The Natal Code of Native Law of 1891 (South Africa) was even more draconian, providing that colonial administrators had "absolute power" to supply labor for public works and to move any tribe or portion thereof to any part of the colony.[45]

Many of these provisions were incorporated in the post-independence legal system. Although the notorious Emergency Powers Order of 1939, which provided the legal basis for the State of Emergency in the 1950s, lapsed, some of its key components were incorporated into the Preservation of Public Security Act. According to Ngugi, the repudiation of "emergency" was semantic not substantive. Given the strong negative associations with the term "emergency," the new Kenyan government chose to justify these provisions in terms of "public security." Nevertheless, many of the illiberal and anti-democratic measures implemented during the Emergency—including detention without trial, executive discretion, and the absence of civil and political liberties—were enshrined in law. Thus for Ngugi, the legacy of the colonial legal system was an authoritarian mode of governance that was adopted with little modification by the postcolonial African elites.

In *Detained* Ngugi also considers the political logic of extralegal detention. He makes two interesting points. First, he reflects on the ritualistic aspects of extralegal detention. Although detainees are hidden from view in unidentified prisons with little access to the legal system, there is nevertheless a visible theatrics of power. The audience for this political theater is the populace, which must be taught to fear the state. As an example, Ngugi notes that he was arrested at his home during the middle of the night. The police arrived in two Land Rovers, one of which had a flashing red and blue light on its roof, as if publicizing the arrest to the community. He was chained and guarded by policemen with machine guns. The armed members of the special services who searched his home were backed up by additional police with long-range rifles. This theatrical show of force was hardly necessary to arrest an intellectual who had no history of violence and would have willingly responded to a summons to appear at the police station. The ritual of fear continued at the gates of the prison; the entire area surrounding the prison was put under curfew so that no one would be able to identify the arriving prisoners. Far from disguising the repressive actions, a rigid curfew at midday actually drew attention to the arrival of new political prisoners. According to Ngugi, the goal is to inculcate a culture of silence and fear that makes the people feel weak and powerless before the state.[46] The world of the detainee is hidden to augment inscrutability, but his disappearance is also publicized in order to increase general insecurity. The detainee is hidden insofar as his relatives do not know where he is incarcerated and he himself does not know the nature of his crime or the length of his sentence; at the same time, the goal is to make sure that the population recognizes its vulnerability. Through inscrutability and dramatic violence, the state comes to seem like a "malevolent, supernatural force."[47]

Ngugi also points out that the symbolic use of detention and torture is an economic way of exercising power. Intellectual and cultural figures are threatening to the government when they have a connection to a mass movement. It is the mobilization of the people, not the ideas of intellectuals, that the government fears. But it is impossible to arrest an entire community, so the government identifies a few individuals, labels them as power hungry agitators and punishes them. Ngugi explains,

> Ideally the authorities would like to put the whole community of struggling millions behind barbed-wire, as the British colonial authorities once tried to do with Kenyan people. But this would mean incarcerating labour, the true source of national wealth: what would then be left to loot?[48]

Although Ngugi does not use the language of law and exception, this remark explains why something like the State of Emergency was an exception, albeit one that revealed the logic of the law itself. During normal times, a mode of governmentality that fosters fear, self-interest, and passivity ensures compliance; when hegemony breaks down, then the "exceptional" side of law and order—the use of force rather than fear—is necessary.

Ngugi's work makes a number of contributions to the literature on the state of exception. Most notable is his narrative rendering of the micropolitics of life under Emergency Law. Reading his novels made me think of Hannah Arendt's claim that, "No philosophy, no analysis, no aphorism, be it ever so profound, can compare in intensity and richness of meaning with a properly narrated story." His most recent novel *Wizard of the Crow*, is a particularly searing and satirical indictment of postcolonial African dictatorship. With its seven hundred pages, multiple story lines, and layers of allegory, magical realism, and absurdist humor, it is a novel that defies any simple summary. Rather than trying to do so, I turn to the work of Achille Mbembe, political theorist who develops a similar critique of postcolonial governmentality.

COMMANDEMENT IN THE POSTCOLONY

Achille Mbembe is a contemporary historian and political theorist. Born in Cameroon and educated at the Sorbonne, he is the author of three books on colonial and postcolonial Africa. His most recent study *On the Postcolony* defies disciplinary norms by employing a poetic style that combines history, literary analysis, empirical political science, philosophy, and psychoanalysis.[49] Mbembe argues that the political science literature on Africa is based on reductionist assumptions. Furthermore, the dominant concepts such as democracy and civil society emerge out of European historical experience and hide more than they illuminate. According to Mbembe, the more theoretically oriented discipline of postcolonial studies, however, is not much better because it focuses too much on discourse and representation and fails to interrogate the relationship between cultural practices and their material or economic dimensions. *On the Postcolony* provides alternative mode of analysis that exposes the continuity between specific practices of colonial rationality and their spectral reappearance in postcolonial Africa.

According to Mbembe, colonial sovereignty rested on a specific imaginary of the state, which he calls *commandement*. The main feature of *commandement* was a distinctive combination of law and lawlessness. The essential lawlessness of colonial rule was rooted in the act of founding itself: violent conquest. This meant that colonial rule based its legitimacy on force rather than on consent, mutual benefit, or tradition. It also maintained its authority through a system of coercion supplemented by arbitrary rule.

The story of the foundation of the colonial polity through conquest bares little resemblance to the liberal myth of the social contract. According to social contract theory, rational individuals voluntarily recognize the need to cede some of their natural liberty in order to create a sovereign authority capable of protecting their rights. Even in the more pessimistic Hobbesian version of this story, the sovereign creates a climate of predictability that makes it possible for each individual to pursue his interests.[50] The founding of the colonial state begins very differently. One society uses its military superiority to conquer another in order to exploit the native people and resources for the colonizers' benefit. It defines its own practices, economic organization, religion, and system of government as "civilization." It calls the culture and practices of the conquered society "barbarous." From this point of view of "civilization," barbarians will benefit from adopting the values and way of life of the conqueror, but due to their irrationality and incapacity, they will not choose it. The underlying premise is the logic of *commandement*: the assumption that the native peoples are not capable of consent and therefore must be compelled.

Even after the end of armed resistance to conquest, the colonial polity was still structured on the model of warfare rather than consent and civil society. Native peoples were frequently governed by martial law or an equally draconian native code while European colonists were granted representative institutions and civil liberties.[51] Mbembe concludes that in both theory and practice, the colonial polity was the exact opposite of the liberal polity.[52] In the colonial state, there was no room for debate or discussion, no system of checks and balances, and no institutions designed to limit the governments' power over the native people.

Despite its authoritarian character, the colonial project was frequently justified as a civilizing mission that brought the rule of law to peoples governed by brutal despots. How is this possible? Part of the answer has to do with the dual nature of the concept of *Recht*, a German term that is translated as right or law. Right can refer both to the sovereign's right to command and the individual's right to protection from the power of the state. According to liberal theory, these two dimensions are related. The right of sovereignty is a consequence of the individual's natural right to freedom. Mbembe notes that the opposite is true in the colonial context; the supreme right of the colonial state, e.g., its monopoly on violence, is simultaneously the supreme denial of right.[53] Law was defined as the set of practices necessary to maintain an order controlled by and legible for the European colonists. This law was both the means and the end of colonialism.

The *régime d'exception* was rationalized as a way to bring about discipline and obedience, which were considered necessary preconditions for the rule of law.[54] According to the logic of colonialism, the rule of law had to be suspended in order to bring about the type of social order that made law possible. This argument is a radicalization of the position held by John Stuart Mill. Mill insisted that representative institutions were only possible when a people achieved a degree of civilization (e.g., economic development and complex social organization). In order to achieve this level of economic and social development, a people must become accustomed to obedience and discipline, which usually required a period of despotic government. According to Mill, despotism could foster democracy and force could facilitate freedom. But Mill himself did not go so far as to conclude that a *régime d'exception* could bring about the rule of law. In fact, he insisted on just the opposite view.[55] Mill argued passionately and unsuccessfully that a colonial government that failed to adhere to the rule of law would not build civilization abroad and would undermine law at home. Despotism might be necessary to advance civilization, but it must be carefully limited by law in order to ensure that it did not become tyrannical, selfish, and arbitrary. A tyrannical government would not advance the capacities and interests of the subject people.

Despite (or perhaps because of) Mill's career as a bureaucrat in the British East India Company, he misunderstood the logic of colonial government. He believed that colonialism could be founded on the rule of law and failed to recognize that the colonial state was inevitably based on *commandement*. According to Mbembe, one of the defining characteristics of *commandement* was "the lack of distinction between ruling and civilizing."[56] Since obedience was taken to advance civilization, obedience became both an end and means. Performing rituals of obedience became part of the theatrics of colonial power and any reluctance to play the assigned role was met with severe punishment. From the perspective of the colonizers, this punishment, no matter how disproportionate and brutal, advanced civilization and therefore could not really be contrary to law or morality. The colonists' demand for ritualistic obedience also had material benefits. The underlying motive for colonialism was still economic; it was a way to provide resources for the metropole and privileged economic opportunities for the European population. In order to reap these benefits, the colonists had to compel the native population either by extracting natural resources from mines or growing cash crops on plantations for export. In the colonial imaginary, however, this system of forced labor was not figured as exploitation because labor was a means to inculcate the virtues of self-restraint, perseverance, and productivity.

In *On the Postcolony*, Mbembe identifies *commandement* as the distinctive practice of colonial sovereignty. Yet he also recognizes that there are a number of similarities between colonial and feudal sovereignty. Mbembe notes, "One characteristic of *commandement* in the colonies was the confusion between the public and the private; agents of the *commandement* could, at any moment, usurp the law and, in the name of the state, exercise it for purely personal ends."[57] This is very similar to feudalism, which also granted juridical power to patriarchs and elided the lines between personal service and political obligation. In fact, the early phases of colonialism were often organized on feudal principles. From the Spanish *encomienda* to the British East India Company, European sovereigns regularly granted private individuals or companies the right to raise taxes and armies, fight wars, compel labor, and settle disputes in the colonies.

Is *commandement* simply another way of describing the patriarchal government of the ancient régime? Not really. There are also a number of differences between the *ancien régime* and the colonial polity. Although both are based on a strong distinction between ruler and subject, in most colonial polities this was marked by racial and cultural difference. Unlike feudal society, colonial society lacked a shared language, religion, and history; therefore there were no shared norms to help limit the despotic exercise of power. Even in places where the indigenous people gradually adopted the colonizers' language or religion, the colonizers were deeply attached to a social order based on their own superiority (and the economic benefits attached to a caste society) and the racial distinctions proved very stable. A second important difference between the ancient regime and the colonial polity has to do with state capacity. Feudal lords may have exercised juridical power over their subjects, but they could not necessarily count on a very strong state to help them exercise domination. By the zenith of colonialism in the late nineteenth century, European powers wielded a very sophisticated state apparatus that ensured control over their empire.

According to Mbembe, *commandement* was a "*régime d'exception*," in other words, a polity that was not governed by the common law. The term *régime d'exception,* however, does not imply that the despotic character of colonial government was the exception rather than the rule. Perhaps a better term would be the English concept of martial law, which captures the way that the departure from the common law or civil code could itself become codified. The colonial *régime d'exception* diverged from liberal norms in at least two different ways. First, as indicated above, colonialism was often structured by royal charters creating private governments with elaborate privileges and immunities. King Leopold's privately owned "Congo Free State" is the most notorious example.[58] Second, even in colonies that were directly governed by European states there was no sense that a single law applied equally to all people residing in the same territory. Most colonies had a differential system of law distinguishing the rights and duties required of Europeans and natives. In some cases different legal status attached directly to persons (citizens versus subjects). In other cases, the law classified natives as members of national, tribal, or religious groups and disputes between members of the same group were governed by customary law. Of course, disputes between settlers and natives were still decided by colonial courts composed exclusively of settlers. Some colonies relied on territorial distinctions, providing for accountable government in European areas and martial law in native areas.[59] These territorial distinctions were often reinforced by a system of pass controls and legal segregation to ensure that natives could not live in European areas.

CONCLUSION

In his literary works, Ngugi explored the psychological and micropolitical transformation wrought by the Emergency. In his prison memoir *Detained*, he concluded that the techniques of colonial governmentality were still employed by the postcolonial state. *Commandement* is "an imaginary of the state" that inflates the right of the sovereign to command while disavowing the political and civil rights of the common people. It was a state of exception that made the rule of colonialism possible. The measures employed during the Kenyan Emergency—mass detention, torture, the relocation of entire villages, confiscation of land—these were extreme manifestations of colonial violence and, as Ngugi, demonstrates, they were effective at undermining the solidarity of peasant communities. Yet this demystified violence was a threat always lurking just below the surface of colonial normalcy. The European minority felt its power to be precarious and therefore a sense of looming crisis was endemic. The only way to reassure the colonizers was to demand a highly ritualized theatrics of submission. Obedience was both a means and an end, a way to ensure the profitability of colonialism and to civilize colonial subjects. Once obedience was equated with civilization, demanding total obedience became a moral imperative.

For Mbembe, the concept of *commandement*, however, is not simply a reformulation of familiar criticisms of colonialism. He is concerned with the way in which *commandement*—with its distinctive political logic and supporting practices—came to structure the postcolonial polity. Mbembe challenges the conventional wisdom that the postcolonial potentate (the figure that political scientists often call the patrimonial leader) is the atavistic resurgence of precolonial tribal authority. He tries to demonstrate the underlying continuity between the colonial and postcolonial forms of governmentality. He identifies "the étatisation of society, the socialization and state power, and the privatization of public prerogatives" as the three key dimensions of "postcolonial African authoritarianism."[60] Each of these hybrid formations has roots in the fundamental confusion between public and private that was characteristic of the neo-feudal structure of colonial governance. Similarly, many postcolonial regimes have also used force against their own citizens, violated individuals' civil rights, and adopted repressive "emergency measures." In other words they have jealously protected their patrimony, government by *commandement*.

NOTES

1. An earlier version of this paper was presented at the 2007 Association for Political Theory Conference. I greatly benefited from the comments of my fellow panelists. I would especially like to thank my collaborator Keally McBride, who introduced me to Ngugi. A version of this chapter appears in Margaret Kohn and Keally McBride, *Political Theories of Decolonization* (Oxford University Press, 2011). All rights reserved. Used by permission of the publisher.

2. The issue of forced labor was controversial because the detainees argued that they had not been convicted of any crime and therefore could not be punished by hard labor. They claimed that they were equivalent to prisoners of war under the Geneva Convention and could not be forced to work. See Josiah Mwangi Kariuki, *Mau Mau Detainee: The Account by a Kenyan African of His Experiences in Detention Camps, 1953–1960* (Nairobi: Oxford University Press, 1975).

3. Caroline Elkins, *Imperial Reckoning: The Untold Story of Britain's Gulag in Kenya* (New York: Henry Holt, 2005), 347.

4. Elkins (2005), 429.

5. Clement Fatovic, Paper presented at the American Political Science Association Meeting, August 2006.

6. Giorgio Agamben, *State of Exception*, trans. Kevin Attell (Chicago and London: University of Chicago Press, 2005).

7. Giorgio Agamben, *Homo Sacer: Sovereign Power and Bare Life*, trans. Daniel Heller-Roazen (Palo Alto, CA: Stanford University Press, 1995); William E. Scheuerman, *Between Norm and Exception: The Frankfurt School and the Rule of Law* (Cambridge, MA: MIT Press, 1997); Ellen Kennedy, *Constitutional Failure: Carl Schmitt in Weimar* (Durham, NC: Duke University Press, 2004).

8. Nasser Hussain, *The Jurisprudence of Emergency* (Ann Arbor: University of Michigan Press, 2003).

9. Rande Kostal, *A Jurisprudence of Power: Victorian Empire and the Rule of Law* (Oxford: Oxford University Press, 2005).

10. There are several exceptions, including Hussain, *The Jurisprudence of Emergency* and Kostal, *A Jurisprudence of Power*.

11. For a general discussion of the political theory that emerges in Ngugi's writing, see M. S. C. Okolo, *African Literature as Political Philosophy* (Dakar: CODESRIA Books, 2007).

12. See Margaret Kohn and Daniel O'Neill, "A Tale of Two Indias: Burke and Mill on Racism and Slavery in the West Indies and America," *Political Theory* (34): 2006.

13. Ngugi's analysis of postcolonial Kenya bares a striking resemblance to Mbembe's. In *Petals of Blood* he advances the view that independence has done little more than put a black mask on the face of neocolonial exploitation. Although African elites now run the government and have a share of economic privilege, the basic political structure of *commandement* and the economic system of imperial capitalism remain unchanged. But Ngugi's analysis of the colonial *régime d'exception* has distinctive elements that are worth considering in some detail.

14. In this paper I use the term Emergency to refer to the period of Kenyan history (1952–1960) when the country was governed by special laws adopted to combat the Mau Mau. These laws included measures that made it a capital crime for natives to take an oath of solidarity, to possess a weapon, to criticize the government or to give material aid to the fighters in the forest. The Emergency also refers to practices such as torture, screening, arbitrary arrest and incarceration for extended periods, forced labor, and mass confinement in villages surrounded by barbed wire. These practices were widely used and reflected the colonial government's view that it was fighting a civil war and therefore the rule of law did not apply.

15. *Weep Not, Child* was Ngugi's first published novel (London: Heinemann 1964). His second novel, *The River Between*, was written first (London: Heinemann, 1965).

16. The colonial state implemented a series of measures to ensure that peasant cultivators were forced into the wage-economy where they would have to work for low wages on white farms. First, the government established reserves limiting the areas where Kikuyu could live.

Those who couldn't gain access to the limited supply of land were forced into wage labor. Second, the government enacted a hut tax that amounted to the equivalent of two months of African wages. To ensure the docility of labor, they also implemented a pass system and anyone outside of the reserves without a valid labor contract could be fined or imprisoned. See Bruce Berman, *Control and Crisis in Colonial Kenya: The Dialectic of Domination* (London: Currey, 1990).

17. Lynn M. Thomas, *Politics of the Womb: Women, Reproduction, and the State in Kenya* (Berkeley: University of California Press, 2003).

18. See E. Adriaan et al., eds., *Sovereignty, Legitimacy, and Power in West African Societies: Perspectives from Legal Anthropology* (Hamburg: Lit Verlag, 1998).

19. Mahmood Mamdani, *Citizen and Subject: Contemporary Africa and the Legacy of Late Colonialism* (London: James Currey, 1996).

20. Martin Chanock, *Law, Custom, and Social Order: The Colonial Experience in Malawi and Zambia* (Cambridge: Cambridge University Press, 1985).

21. Mamdani (1996), 37–61.

22. Jomo Kenyatta, *Facing Mount Kenya: The Tribal Life of the Gikuyu* (Nairobi: Heinemann, 1978).

23. Bruce Berman, *Control and Crisis in Colonial Kenya: The Dialectic of Domination* (London: James Currey, 1990), 368.

24. James Ngugi, *Weep Not, Child* (London and Ibdan: Heinemann 1967), 84–85.

25. The scholarly consensus is that Kenyatta was not a supporter of the Mau Mau. There is also evidence that the Judge (Ransley Thacker) was bribed to ensure a conviction despite the paucity of evidence. See John Lonsdale, "Kenyatta's Trials: Breaking and Making an African Nationalist," in *The Moral World of the Law*, ed. Peter Cross (Cambridge, Cambridge University Press, 2000), 196–239.

26. Ngugi wa Thiong'o, *A Grain of Wheat* (revised edition) (Oxford and Johannesburg: Heinemann, 1986), 34. Although these page numbers are from the revised edition (because it is more widely accessible), my reading is based on the original edition.

27. Edward Said, *Culture and Imperialism* (New York: Vintage, 1994).

28. Ngugi wa Thiong'o (1986), 53.

29. For example, Patrick Williams concludes that "uncertainties notwithstanding, the general implications of the points in the preceding paragraphs seem reasonably clear: the nation (the people) can be relied upon to work things out for themselves." Ngugi wa Thiong'o (1986), 76. For a similar view, see Jan Mohamed, *Manichean Aesthetics: The Politics of Literature in Colonial Africa* (Amherst: University of Massachusetts Press, 1983).

30. See, for example, C. B. Robson, *Ngugi wa Thiong'o* (London: Macmillan, 1979).

31. David Cook and Michael Okenimpke, *Ngugi wa Thiong'o: An Exploration of His Writings* (Oxford: James Currey, 1997), 172.

32. Ngugi wa Thiong'o and Micere Githae Mugo, *The Trial of Dedan Kimathi* (London and Nairobi: Heinemann, 1977), 23.

33. Ngugi and Micere (1977), 25.

34. Ngugi and Micere (1977), 25.

35. To translate Kimathi's argument into the language of European legal theory, his position is a radicalization of the well-known position of Dicey who advanced a political understanding of the rule of law (e.g., parliamentary supremacy) and challenged the German concept of *rechtstaat*, a formal notion that rulers are bound by the laws that they make. For an excellent discussion of this issue, see Franz Neumann, *The Rule of Law: Political Theory and the Legal System in Modern Society* (Heidelberg and Dover: Berg, 1986); Judith N. Shklar, "Political Theory and the Rule of Law," in Hutcheson and Monahan, eds., *The Rule of Law: Ideal or Ideology* (Toronto: Carswell, 1987); H. L. A. Hart, *The Concept of Law* (Oxford: Oxford University Press, 1994).

36. Ngugi and Micere (1977), 25–26.

37. Ngugi and Micere (1977), 32.

38. Ngugi and Micere (1977), 34.

39. In *Detained* Ngugi explains that the motive for his arrest was not the critical views contained in his English language novels but rather his involvement in the Kamiriithu Commu-

nity Education and Cultural Centre. Together with the villagers, he wrote and produced a play that told the story of Kenyan history from the perspective of peasants and workers. When government officials heard about this project, they withdrew the permit for public performance, raised the cultural center to the ground, and arrested Ngugi.

40. Ngugi wa Thiong'o, *Detained: A Writer's Prison Diary* (Nairobi and London: Heinemann, 1981), 4.

41. Ngugi (1981), 32–33.

42. Ngugi (1981), 40.

43. Yash P. Ghai and P. McAuslan, *Public Law and Political Change in Kenya: A Study of the Legal Framework of Government from Colonial Times to the Present* (New York and Nairobi: Oxford University Press, 1970).

44. These examples are cited in Ngugi (1981), 44–45.

45. Mamdani (1996), 63–64.

46. Ngugi (1981), 19.

47. Ngugi (1981), 19.

48. Ngugi (1981), 13.

49. Achille Mbembe, *On the Postcolony* (Berkeley: University of California Press, 2001).

50. For an interesting, thoughtful analysis and critique of social theory, see Carole Pateman, *The Sexual Contract* (Cambridge: Polity Press, 1988). See also Charles Mills, *The Racial Contract* (Ithaca, NY: Cornell University Press, 1997).

51. See for example, Alexis de Tocqueville, *Writings on Empire and Slavery*, ed. Jennifer Pitts (Baltimore: Johns Hopkins University Press, 1999).

52. Mbembe (2001), 25.

53. Mbembe (2001), 25.

54. See, for example, W. F. Finlason, *The history of the Jamaica Case founded upon official or authentic documents, and containing an account of the debates in Parliament and the Criminal Prosecutions arising out of the case* (London: Chapman and Hall, 1868).

55. Mill was the most outspoken critic in Parliament of the use of martial law in the colonies. He also took a very vocal and controversial role criticizing the government for failing to prosecute John Edward Eyre, the colonial governor of Jamaica, for atrocities committed against blacks during a state of emergency. See Kostal, 2006.

56. Mbembe (2001), 31.

57. Mbembe (2001), 28.

58. See Adam Hochschild, *King Leopold's Ghost: A Story of Greed, Terror, and Heroism in Colonial Africa* (New York: Houghton Mifflin, 1998).

59. Alexis de Tocqueville, "Essay on Algeria," in *Writings on Empire and Slavery*, ed. Jennifer Pitts (Baltimore: Johns Hopkins University Press, 1999).

60. Mbembe (2001), 46.

Index

Aboriginal nations, 53
Achebe, Chinua, 227
Achugar, Hugo, 200
Acosta-Belén, Edna, 199
Adair, James, 25
Africa, xi, xii, xv, xvi, 84, 98, 101, 102, 107, 112, 181, 192, 197, 219, 221, 222, 223, 224, 225, 226, 227, 229, 230, 231, 233, 234, 235, 237, 243, 244, 245, 247, 248, 253, 254, 257, 259, 263
Africa, Eastern, 100, 221
African Americans, 230, 231, 232, 233, 234, 236, 237, 238, 239
African slavery, 223, 230, 233
Agamben, Giorgio, 245
Alaska, 100, 101
Alexander the Great, 147, 148
Alfred, Taiaiake, 72
Algeria, 87
Algonquians, 64, 69
Althusser, Louis, 211
America, xiii, xv, 10, 24, 25, 26, 59, 158, 159, 182, 183, 184, 185, 186, 187, 188, 189, 190, 191, 193, 195, 196, 198, 219, 222, 223, 225, 229, 233, 237
America, Hispanic, 105, 183, 185, 188
America, native, 63, 196, 198, 227, 231
American Revolution, xii
Americas, xi, xii, 35, 53, 54, 58, 63, 64, 183, 185, 189, 192, 196, 199, 221, 222, 224, 232, 234, 235

Amerindia, 9, 24, 25, 28, 35, 98, 99, 100, 102, 105, 107, 110, 155
Amin, Shahid, 216, 217
Amsterdam, 102, 104, 106
Anglo-America, xii, xiv, xvi, 214
Anglo-Saxon, 151, 192
Ankersmit, F. R., 205, 206, 207, 216
Appiah, Anthony, 233
Arendt, Hannah, xii, 89, 222, 258
Argentina, 188, 189, 190, 192, 193, 200
Ashanti, 223
Aristotle, 126
Asia, xi, xv, xvi, 37, 84, 98, 100, 102, 104, 105, 107, 112, 181, 197, 207, 208, 215, 219, 222
Athens, 223
Atlantic Ocean, 98, 99, 101, 102, 104
Augsburg, 102
Augustine, St., 125
Aurobindo, 153
Austria, 102
Aziz, Shah Abdul, 175

Baghdad, 99, 102
Baines, Thomas, 226
Bakwena language, 226
Balibar, Etienne, 214
Bedinfeld, Commander Norman, 226
Belnap, Jeffrey, 200
Bengal, 220, 221
Bentham, Jeremy, 39

Berlin Conference of 1884, 224
Berry, Christopher, 24
Bhabha, Homi, 151
Bilgrami, Akeel, 238, 239
Bittlingmayer, Uwe, 135
Bohemia, 102
Bolivia, 104
Bombay, 215
Bourdieu, Pierre, 122, 127, 128, 129, 130, 131, 132, 133, 136, 137, 139, 140
Brazil, 98, 105, 121, 122, 133, 136, 138, 139, 140, 141, 142, 143
Brecht, Bertolt, 252
Britain, 7, 11, 37, 39, 40, 41, 59, 61, 142, 150, 171, 172, 173, 174, 176, 177, 178, 179, 209, 211, 216, 219, 220, 221, 223, 225, 227, 228, 229, 230, 243, 244, 246, 247, 248, 251, 252, 254, 255, 256, 257, 258; colonialism, xvi, 171, 172, 176, 178, 179, 220, 221, 223, 227, 231; Parliament, 11, 229, 243
British East India Company, 172, 173, 174, 261
Bruce Jr., Dickson D., 236
Buarque de Holanda, Sérgio, 143
Buenos Aires, 191
Burke, Edmund, 4, 165
Bush, George W., 159

Calcutta, 215, 216
California, 100
Calvinism, 109
Cambridge University, 209, 225
Canada, 84
capitalism, 112, 121, 122, 123, 124, 129, 134, 135, 139, 142, 165, 197, 212, 223, 231, 233, 238, 251
Caribbean, 6, 98, 102, 105, 183, 192, 197, 198, 199, 200, 221, 222
Carlos V, 102, 105
Carlyle, William, 245
Cartwright, Samuel Adolphus, 223, 234, 236
de las Casas, Bartolome, 107
Catalonia, 102
Cayugas, 63
Central America, 200
Chakrabarty, Dipesh, xv, 209
Chanock, Martin, 248

Chaplin, Joyce, 63
Charles II, 57, 58
Charlevoix, 30
Chaterjee, Partha, 150
Chaunu, Pierre, 101
Chin, Wang, 100
China, xi, 38, 39, 98, 100, 101, 102, 105, 197
Chomsky, Noam, 111
Christianity, 5, 8, 107, 125, 175, 221, 224, 226, 227, 228, 247, 256
Circumcision Controversy, Kenyan, 248
Cobban, Alfred, 157
Cocke, Captain Lasse, 60, 69, 70
Cold War, 14, 147
Colón. *See* Columbus, Christopher
Colonial Secretary's office, 228
Colquhoun, Patrick, 219
Columbus, Christopher, xi, 101, 102, 222
commandement, 259, 261, 262, 263
commercium, 4, 14
Committee of Trade and Plantations, 58
Communism, 209, 212
communitarianism, 124, 210
"Congo Free State," 262
conservatism, 186, 191
contractarianism, xii
Córdoba, 191
Covenant Chain confederation, 64
Cowan Plan, 243, 244
Cree, 91
Crusades, 101
Cuba, 105, 182, 183, 185, 187, 189, 193, 194, 195, 196, 197, 198, 200
Cultural Revolution, 211
customary law, 155, 248, 249
Cyprus, 157
Czechoslovakia, 211

Darnton, Robert, 4, 9
Davies, Sir John, 222
Declaration of Independence, 230, 233
Delaware, 54, 56, 57, 56, 59, 60, 63, 64, 65, 66, 69
Delhi, 175
democracy, 142, 150, 151, 156, 158, 159, 162, 163, 208, 210, 211, 212, 214, 215, 216, 217, 236, 238, 240, 253, 254, 257, 260

Derrida, Jacques, 70
Descartes, René, 102, 104, 108, 125, 236
despotism, 154, 260, 262
Diderot, Denis, xiv, 2, 4, 5, 6, 7, 8, 9, 10, 11, 12, 13, 14, 15, 16
Dirlik, Arif, 153
Domingo de Santa Tomas, 104
Donoughmore Commission, 158
double consciousness, 219, 232, 234, 235, 236, 237, 238, 239
doux commerce, 16
Du Bois, W. E. B., 152, 230, 231, 232, 233, 234, 235, 236, 237, 238, 239, 240
Dunbar, James, 21, 23, 28, 33, 35, 36, 37, 42
Durban Declaration, 225

East Indies, xi, 32, 225
Echevarría, Roberto González, 190
egalitarianism, 126, 195, 196, 197
Egypt, 102, 231
Elkins, Caroline, 244
Emerson, Ralph Waldo, 198, 236
Empire, 147, 149, 150, 152, 153, 157, 163, 164, 166, 168, 172
Engels, Friedrich, 212
England, 11, 40, 56, 58, 59, 60, 61, 63, 64, 68, 71, 98, 104, 126, 167, 172, 174, 175, 176, 178, 208, 210, 220, 224, 225, 226, 227, 228, 262; colonialism, 53, 54, 55, 56, 58, 61, 63, 65, 71, 174; Poor Laws, 138
Enlightenment, xii, xiii, 2, 4, 5, 8, 12, 14, 15, 16, 21, 98, 187, 189, 228
Eurocentricism, 97, 98, 102, 106, 110, 111, 112, 166, 167, 182, 189, 190, 192, 196, 199, 212
Europe, xi, xii, xiii, xiv, xv, xvi, 1, 2, 3, 4, 5, 6, 7, 8, 9, 10, 11, 13, 15, 16, 21, 28, 32, 33, 35, 36, 37, 39, 40, 41, 42, 53, 54, 56, 59, 60, 61, 64, 65, 87, 91, 92, 97, 98, 99, 100, 101, 102, 104, 105, 106, 107, 109, 110, 123, 135, 136, 139, 159, 164, 165, 174, 176, 178, 182, 183, 186, 187, 188, 189, 190, 191, 192, 193, 197, 199, 206, 209, 212, 216, 221, 222, 223, 224, 228, 230, 231, 244, 261, 262, 263
Europe, Anglo-Germanic, 106

Europe, Eastern, 98, 105
European colonialism and settlement, xi, xiii, xii, xiv, xvi, 53, 54, 56, 58, 59, 61, 63, 64, 196, 222, 235, 260

Fanon, Franz, xvi, 153, 212, 213, 231, 233
feminism, 195, 196, 199
Ferguson, Adam, 23, 28, 220, 222, 223, 228
Fernández Retamar, Roberto, 198, 199
Ferrer, Ada, 194, 195
feudalism, 190, 261
Fiji, 156
Finland, 57, 59, 60, 63, 64, 66
First Legislative Assembly of Pennsylvania, 60
First Nations, 91
Five Nations, 64, 65
Flanders, 98, 102, 104, 106
Florida, 185
Foucault, Michel, 66, 108, 109, 213
France, 4, 5, 8, 10, 11, 61, 63, 64, 66, 87, 98, 104, 126, 138, 140, 173, 213, 219, 228
Fraser, Nancy, 134
Free Society of Traders, 57
French Revolution, xii, 98
Freud, Sigmund, 109
Freyre, Gilberto, 142, 143

Galileo, Galilei, 108
Gandhi, Mohandas, xvi, 152, 153, 155, 156, 178, 209, 216, 231
Gellner, Ernest, 160, 161
Genoa, 98, 101, 102
Germany, 97, 109, 98, 133, 135, 245
Ghana, 238
Ghulam, Sayid, 172
Gibbon, Edward, 12
globalization, 2, 3, 5, 13, 14, 15, 16, 133, 197
Glorious Revolution, xii
Goel, Sita Ram, 166
Goethe, Johann, 236
Goudie, W. H., 244
Gramsci, Antonio, 208, 211, 212
Great Awakening, 138
Great Britain, 7, 219, 225. *See also* England; Scotland

Greece, 22, 102, 109, 231
Grogan, Colonel, 256
Grotius, Hugo, xii, xiii, 2
Guarani, 201
Guatemala, 183, 192
Guha, Ranajit, 166, 181, 211, 213, 215
Guldberg, Horacio Cerutti, 200
Guru, Narayana, 177, 213

Habermas, Jürgen, 102, 106, 107, 109, 110, 111, 124, 142
habitus, 131, 132, 133
Haiti, 191
Hammer, Heinrich, 102
Hardt, Michael, and Antonio Negri, 18n15, 166, 212
Haudenosaunee, 54
Hegel, Georg Wilhelm Friedrich, 97, 151, 153, 212, 213, 215, 223, 235
Heidegger, 108, 109, 110
Herder, Johann Gottfried, 4
Hill, Christopher, 208
Hinduism, 127, 157, 164, 166, 173, 174, 175, 176, 177, 178, 179, 209, 210
Hirschman, Albert, 16, 18n18
Ho, Cheng, 100
Hobbes, Thomas, xii, 213, 214, 259
Hobsbawm, Eric, 208
Hola concentration camp, 243, 244, 250
Holland. *See* Netherlands
Holme, Thomas, 57
Holocaust, xiv, 206
Home, Henry, Lord Kames, 21, 22, 23, 37, 43n6
Home Rule, 179
Honneth, Axel, 130
Hume, David, 163, 223, 237, 239
Hungary, 102
Hupacasath, 72
Hurons, 64, 65
Hussein, Saddam, 159

Iberian peoples, 102
Imperialism, 2, 147, 148, 150, 152, 154, 156, 164, 165, 166, 167, 195, 197, 198, 209, 219, 223, 224, 231, 233, 251, 256
India, xi, xvi, 7, 23, 27, 28, 37, 38, 39, 41, 54, 59, 60, 61, 69, 94, 96, 98, 100, 101, 102, 105, 150, 153, 155, 156, 157, 158, 159, 167, 171, 172, 173, 174, 175, 176, 177, 178, 179, 186, 207, 208, 209, 210, 211, 215, 217, 219, 220, 221, 222, 223, 224, 227, 228, 230, 231, 235
Imperium, 168
Indian Constituent Assembly, 209
Indian National Congress, 209, 221
Indies trading companies, 2, 6, 11
Indigenous, 81, 82, 84, 91, 92, 149, 165, 190, 244, 248, 261
Industrial Revolution, xii, 138, 223, 229
Innu, 91
International Monetary Fund, 14
"Interregional System," 98, 100, 101, 102, 105
Iraq, 156, 157, 158, 159
Ireland, 225
Iroquois, 53, 54, 56, 59, 61, 63, 64, 65, 66, 69
Islam, xi, 102
Italy, 98, 102
ius gentium, 1, 3
ius cosmopoliticum, 3

Jamaica, 221, 223, 245
James, C. L. R., xvi, 21, 23, 27, 37, 42
Japan, 122
Jennings, Francis, 56, 64
Jones, William, 38
Jordan, Terry, 59
Judaism, 8, 228
Jung, Carl, 213

Kames, Lord. *See* Homes, Henry, Lord Kames
Kanienkeha, 91
Kanien'kehaka, 91
Kant, Immanuel, 2, 3, 4, 108
Kaups, Matti, 59
Kenya, 243, 245, 246
Kenyatta, Jomo, 250, 255, 256
Khan, Gholam Hossein, 220, 222, 223
Khan, Husain, 172
Khan, Syed Ahmed, 157
Kikuyu, 244, 247, 248, 249
Kimathi, Dedan, 252, 253, 254, 255
Kirk, Dr. John, 226
Kreckel, Reinhard, 134, 135
Kuhn, Thomas, 100, 107

Kupperman, Karen, 59
Kurds, 158

Labat, Jean Baptiste, 25
Late Woodland Owasco, 65
Latin America, xi, xvi, 110, 112, 122, 136, 181, 182, 183, 184, 185, 186, 188, 189, 190, 192, 193, 195, 197, 198, 199, 200
law, rule of, 87, 132, 176, 250, 253, 260
Lebanon, 158
Lenin, 197, 211, 212
Lenman, Bruce, 28
Lenape, Lenni, 54, 55
Leopold, King of Belgium, 262
Lepanto, 104
Leroy Little Bear, 91
Levinas, 109, 110
liberalism, 124, 126, 142, 157, 160, 162, 164, 167, 174, 182, 184, 186, 190, 228, 238, 240, 257, 259, 260, 262
Liberia, 229, 230
Lisbon, 102
Livingstone, David, 224, 225, 226
Locke, John, xii, 25, 125
Logan, James, 69, 70
Long, John, 223
Loyalists, 249
Lugard, Lord Frederick, 221, 222, 223, 224, 233
Lyall, Alfred, 151
Lyotard, Francois, 110, 182

Macartney, Sir George, 225
Macaulay, Thomas, 175
Macey, David, 212
Machiavelli, Niccolo, 214
Mahicans, 64
majoritarianism, 159
Malthus, Thomas, 222, 223
Mamdani, Mahmood, 248, 249
Marcuse, Herbert, 112
Mariategui, Jose Carlos, xvi
Mao Tse-Tung, 208, 211, 212
Martí, José, xvi, 181, 182, 183; "My Race," 194; "Nuesta America," 181, 183, 185, 186, 188, 189, 190, 192, 195, 197, 198, 199, 200; Patria, 192
Marx, Groucho, 151

Marx, Karl, xiv, 105, 109, 113, 122, 123, 124, 129, 166, 189, 197, 198, 208, 209, 211, 212, 215
Maryland, 58, 59, 60, 63, 66
Mau Mau, 243, 244, 249, 250, 252, 253, 256
Mbanta, 227
Mbembe, Achille, xvi, 244, 245, 258, 259, 260, 261, 262, 263
Mediterranean, 98, 101, 102, 104, 105
Memmi, Albert, 84, 85, 87
Merrell, James, 56, 63, 69
Mesopotamia, 102
Methodists, 228
Mexico, 98, 104, 183, 192, 200
Micere, Githae Mugo, 252, 255
Mignolo, Walter, 200
Mill, James, 37, 38, 39, 40
Mill, John Stuart, 21, 22, 23, 27, 31, 37, 39, 40, 41, 42, 154, 209, 231, 245, 260, 261; "Civilization," 39, 40, 41; "A Few Thoughts on Non-Intervention," 39, 41, 42; *On Liberty, Considerations on Representative Government*, 39, 41
Minisinks, 63
modernity, xi, xii, xiii, xiv, xv, 97, 122, 127
Mohawk, 64, 91
Mongol Empire, xi
Mongolian, 231, 235
Mudimbe, V. Y., 222
Mughal Empire, xi, 172, 173
Mukherjee, Radhakamal, 155
multiculturalism, 124
Muslim society, 101, 102, 105, 157, 173, 175, 177, 215, 219, 228, 238

Nandy, Ashis, 167
Naoroji, 178
Natal Code of Native Law of 1891, 257
Native Courts Regulations of 1897, 257
Native Pass Regulations, 257
native peoples, 151, 152, 153, 155, 260, 262
naturalism, 124, 125, 131, 143, 196
Naujadi, 216
Nazi, 206
Needham, Joseph, 100
Negri, Antonio. *See* Hardt, Michael

Nehru, Jawaharlal, 178
Nehru, Motilal, 151, 177, 178, 179
Netherlands, 8, 10, 11, 57, 59, 61, 63, 64, 65, 66, 98, 104, 106, 219, 228
Neumann, Franz, 254
New Sweden Settlement, 57, 59
Newton, John, 224
New World, 9, 10, 11
New York, 58, 63, 64, 65, 183, 185
New Zealand, 84
Ngugi wa Thiong'o, 252, 255, 256, 257, 258, 263; *Detained*, 250, 256, 257, 263; *A Grain of Wheat*, 245, 250, 251, 252; *Petals of Blood*, 251; *The Trial of Dedan Kimathi* (Micere Githae Mugo), 252, 255; *Weep Not, Child*, 245, 247, 248, 249, 250; *Wizard of the Crow*, 258
Nietzsche, Friedrich, 108, 109, 110
Nigeria, 221, 227
North America, xvi, 54, 84, 98, 110, 123, 139, 192, 198, 199

Old Testament, 223
Oliver, Terri Hume, 236
Oneidas, 63
Onkwehonwe, 79, 80
Onondagas, 63
orientalism, 152, 166, 198
Orsini, Francesca, 209
Ottoman Empire, xi, 98, 99
L'Ouverture, Toussaint, 4

Pacific Ocean, 98, 101, 222
Palival, Shrikishna Datt, 210
Panama, 105
Parekh, Bhiku, 160, 162
Parmenides, 109
patrimonialism, 143
Penn, William, 54, 55, 56
Pennsylvania, xvi, 54, 55, 56, 57, 59, 60, 61, 63, 64
periphery, 61, 97, 98, 121, 122
personalism, 141, 143
Peru, 98, 104
Plato, 125, 236
pluralism, 161, 162
Plutarch, 148, 149
Pocock, J. G. A., 12, 17n2
populism, 210, 211, 215, 251

Port Alberni, 72
Portugal, 10, 98, 100, 101, 102, 105, 200
postcolonialism, postcolonial condition, postcolonial studies, xv, xvi, xvii, 157, 165, 166, 168, 181, 182, 219, 226, 238, 245, 251, 255, 256
Potosí, 104
Prakash, Gyan, 166
Preservation of Order by Night Regulations of 1901, 257
Privy Council, The, 61
Protestantism, 122, 125, 126, 247
Public Security Act, 257
Puerto Rico, 185, 199
Pufendorf, Samuel, xii
Puritanism, 109

Quechua, 200
Qutb, Sayyid, xvi

racial self, 232, 233, 237
racism, 174, 176, 187, 193, 194, 196, 197, 219, 222, 223, 224, 230, 233, 237, 240, 250
Radhakrishnan, 209
Raj, 208, 209
Rameu, 151
Ranade, 176, 177, 178
Rancière, Jacques, 214
Raus, Virgina, 102
Rawls, John, xii, xiii
Raynal, Abbé, 4, 5, 14, 15, 16, 34, 37
realism, 214
Recht, 260
Reformation, 98, 125
Renaissance, 98, 100, 101, 102, 105, 106
republicanism, 209
Richter, Daniel, 56, 63, 64, 65
Robertson, William, 21, 22, 23, 24, 25, 26, 27, 28, 29, 34, 35, 37; *The Histoire philosophique et politique des établissements et du commerce des Européens dans les deux Indes*, 4, 5, 6, 8, 9, 10, 11, 12, 15
Romanticism, 209, 210, 211, 212, 215, 236
Rome, 22, 102, 223, 231
Rousseau, Jean-Jacques, xii, 34, 35, 166
Roy, Ram Mohun, 173, 176
Royal Commissions, 158

Index

Rudé, George, 208, 213, 214
Russia, xi, 98, 101, 210, 211

Said, Edward, xv, 182, 198
Saldivar, José, 198, 199
Sarmiento, Domingo, 188, 189, 190, 191, 192, 193
Schama, Simon, 205
Schmitt, Carl, 245
Scientific Revolution, xii, 100, 101
Scotland, 23, 24, 37, 39, 40; Scottish Enlightenment, 22, 23, 24, 33, 39
Sechele, Chief, 226
Senecas, 63
Senghor, Leopold, xvi, 231, 235
Seville, 102, 104, 107
Shackamaxon, 56
Shia, 158
Sicily, 102
Siconese, 59
Sikhism, 228
Sinus Magnus, 102
Sistani, 158
Smith, Adam, 4, 21, 22, 23, 228; *Lectures on Jurisprudence*, 29; *Theory of Moral Sentiments*, 29, 32, 35
social contract theory, xii, xiii, 259
socialism, 211, 215, 254
Society of Traders, 66
Socrates, 109
Sombart, Werner, 106, 107
South Africa, 257
South America, 28, 191, 193, 199, 200
Soviet Union, 197
Spain, xi, 9, 10, 98, 100, 102, 104, 105, 107, 110, 182, 183, 184, 185, 191, 193, 194, 197, 200, 219, 261
Spanish-American War of 1989, 197
Spanish colonialism, 106, 185, 193, 197
Spanish settlements, 61
Spinoza, 104, 214
Spivak, Gayatri, xv
Sri Lanka, 100, 156, 157, 158, 159
Stalin, Joseph, 211
State of Emergency, Kenyan, 243, 244
state of nature, xii
Stoicism, 148
Stokes, Eric, 150
Subaltern Studies, 208, 211, 213, 215

subjectivism, 130
Sugrue, Thomas, 56, 64, 68
Sullivan, G. M., 243
Sunnis, 158
Supreme Court of United States, 233
Surinam, 7
Susquehannocks, 54, 55, 56, 57, 59, 60, 61, 63, 64, 65, 66, 68, 69, 71
Swanendale, 59
Swedish Delaware, 65

Tagore, Rabindranath, 178
Tartar states, xi
Taylor, Charles, 122, 124, 125
teleology, 162
Teuton, 231, 235
Thompson, E. P., 208, 254
Thorton, Richard, 226
Tilly, Charles, 62
Todorov, Tzevtan, xiv, 231
Tomlins, Christopher, 58
Troeltsch, Ernst, 107
Trotsky, Leon, 212
Tucker, Josiah, 35
Tully, James, 53, 54, 55, 66, 67, 71, 160
Turkey, 101, 104
tyranny, 260

Uhuru independence celebrations, 250
Unitarianism, 228
United East India Company, 2
United Nations, 164
United States, 84, 97, 105, 126, 138, 183, 184, 185, 228, 230, 231
Uruguay, 200
utilitarianism, 39, 137

Vagrancy Regulations of 1898, 257
Vasco de Gama, 101, 222
Vatican Index, 4
Venezuela, 105
Venice, 101, 104
Vespucci, Americo, 102
Vidyarthi, Ganesha Shankar, 209, 210
Vietnam, 197
Virginia settlements, 65
Vishal Bharat, 210
de Vitoria, Francisco, 2

Wallerstein, Immanuel, 104, 105
wars of religion, xii
Wasáse, 79, 86, 87, 93
Weber, Eugen, 138
Weber, Max, xi, xii, 97, 100, 106, 107, 109, 110, 122, 123, 124, 125, 135, 240
Wedgewood, Josiah, 228
Welfare State, 131
West, Benjamin, 56
Western societies, 97, 100, 122, 123, 124, 132, 155, 182, 183, 184, 188, 195, 198, 199, 207, 208, 210, 212, 215, 221
West Indies, 32
White, Hayden, 205, 206, 207, 208, 216, 217
white supremacy, 231
Williams, Robert, 53, 54, 55, 64, 71
Wittgenstein, Ludwig, 128
World Social Summit, 165
"World-System," 98, 121
World Trade Organization, 14, 164
World War I, 209
World War II, 121

Young, Iris Marion, 53, 54, 55, 66, 67, 71

Zacateca, 104
Zea, Leopoldo, xvi
Zeno, 148
Zimbabwe, 230

About the Contributors

Jacob T. Levy is Tomlinson Professor of Political Theory at McGill University. He is the author of *The Multiculturalism of Fear* (2000) and of articles including "Indigenous Self-Government" in *Nomos*; "Not So *Novus* an *Ordo*: Constitutionalism Without Social Contracts," in *Political Theory*; "Federalism, Liberalism, and the Separation of Loyalties," in *The American Political Science Review*; and "Beyond Publius: Montesquieu, Liberal Republicanism, and the Small-Republic Thesis," in *History of Political Thought*.

Iris Marion Young was, at the time of her death, professor of political science at the University of Chicago, and had earlier been professor of public and international affairs at the University of Pittsburgh. She was the author of dozens of books including *Justice and the Politics of Difference*; *Throwing Like a Girl and Other Essays in Feminist Philosophy and Social Theory*; *Intersecting Voices: Dilemmas of Gender, Political Philosophy and Policy*; *Inclusion and Democracy*; *On Female Body Experience*; and *Global Challenges*. She was widely recognized as one of the leading political philosophers and feminist theorists of her generation; her work and contributions have been recognized by the establishment of an endowed Iris Marion Young/Susan Moller Okin Prize for the best article in feminist theory, by the American Political Science Association; an endowed named award and lecture series in civic engagement at the University of Pittsburgh; an endowed named lecture series in gender studies at the University of Chicago; a special issue of *Hypatia*, the leading English-speaking journal of feminist theory and philosophy; and the collection of essays *Dancing with Iris*, edited by Ann Ferguson and Mechthild Nagel. Her final book, *Responsibility for Justice*, has recently been published by Oxford University Press.

Taiaiake Alfred is professor of human and social development and director of Indigenous Governance Programs at the University of Victoria, Canada. He is author of *Peace, Power and Righteousness: An Indigenous Manifesto* (Oxford), and *Heeding the Voices of Our Ancestors: Kahnawake Mohawk Politics and the Rise of Native Nationalism* (Oxford).

Dipesh Chakrabarty is professor of history and South Asian languages and civilizations at the University of Chicago. He is author of *Habitations of Modernity: Essays in the Wake of Subaltern Studies* (Chicago), *Provincializing Europe: Postcolonial Thought and Historical Difference* (Princeton), and *Rethinking Working-Class History: Bengal, 1890–1940* (Princeton). He is a founding member of the Subaltern Studies Editorial Collective and is coeditor of the journal, *Critical Inquiry*.

Enrique Dussel is professor in ethics at the Universidad Autonoma Metropolitana and the Universidad Nacional Autonoma de Mexico. He has been visiting professor at Frankfurt University, Notre Dame University, California State University, Union Theological Seminary, Loyola University, Vanderbilt University, Duke University, and Harvard University. He is author of more than fifty books in several languages, including *Philosophy of Liberation* (Orbis Books), *The Invention of the Americas* (Continuum), and *The Underside of Modernity: Apel, Ricoeur, Taylor and Rorty* (Humanities).

Emmanuel C. Eze was at the time of his death associate professor of philosophy at De Paul University. He was the author of *Achieving Our Humanity: The Idea of the Postracial Future* (Routledge) and editor of three anthologies of African philosophy.

Vicki Hsueh is associate professor of political science at Western Washington University. She has published articles on the Constitution of Carolina and the question of colonial knowledge in the *Journal of the History of Ideas and Postcolonial Studies*.

Margaret Kohn is associate professor of political science at the University of Toronto. She is the author of *Radical Space: Building the House of the People* and *Brave New Neighborhoods: The Privatization of Public Space*.

Pratap Bhanu Mehta is president of the Center for Policy Research in New Delhi, a member of the Global Faculty of the New York University Law School, and a leading Indian public intellectual. He has been a professor at Harvard University and Jawaharlal Nehru University. He is author of *Facing Democracy* (Penguin). He has published articles on Indian political thought,

Max Weber and Hindu ethics, constitutionalism, ethics and international affairs, and democratic theory.

Bhikhu Parekh is a Centennial Professor at London School of Economics. He was for many years professor of political theory at the University of Hull, UK. He has been a visiting professor at Harvard University, University of Pennsylvania, and McGill University. He is the author or editor of more than twenty books, including *Gandhi's Political Philosophy* (Notre Dame), *Hannah Arendt and the Search for a New Political Philosophy* (Humanities Press), and *Contemporary Political Thinkers* (Johns Hopkins University). He has been a member of the British House of Lords since 2000.

Jennifer Pitts is associate professor of political science at the University of Chicago. She is the editor and translator of *Alexis de Toqueville: Writings on Empire and Slavery* (Johns Hopkins University) and the author of *The Turn to Empire* (Princeton).

Ofelia Schutte is professor of philosophy at the University of South Florida. She is author of *Cultural Identity and Social Liberation in Latin American Thought* (State University of New York Press) and *Beyond Nihilism: Nietzsche without Masks* (University of Chicago Press). She has authored more than fifty articles and book chapters on Latin American philosophy, feminist philosophy, and Nietzsche's thought.

Jessé Souza is professor of social sciences (*ciencias sociais*) at the Universidade Estadual Norte Fluminensa in Brazil. He is the author of *A Modernizacao Seletiva: Uma reinterpretacao do dilemma brasileiro* and *A Construção Social de Subcidadania*.